Emily Brand is an author, historian [...] social history and romantic relations [...] century. She has written for *The* [...] *Times* and *Washington Post*, and pre [...] history and classic literature for the [...] *of the House of Byron* was selected for BBC Radio 4's *Book of the Week* and the *Sunday Times*'s 'Best Summer Reads' 2020, and was shortlisted for the Elma Dangerfield Prize.

Praise for The Fall of the House of Byron

'Thoroughly researched and juicily readable . . . As a crisp and seductive tour through the history of a family who never knew when to say no – to a drink, a bet, or a sexual invitation – this is a treat' *Daily Telegraph*

'In this luscious slice of popular history, Emily Brand knits together all the naughtiest Byrons of the Georgian period into a glittering family tapestry . . . [She] is particularly good at describing the outrageous excess of aristocratic life . . . Brand has done an excellent job of placing the sexploits of the Byron family into the context of a broader social and political history . . . Beneath the shimmering surface, this feels like a fable for our times' *Mail on Sunday*

'Compellingly plotted and Emily Brand renders a deeply imagined world . . . [Her] work is often sumptuous, global in scope, and insightful in understanding its brutal, passionate characters' *Irish Times*

'Pacey, well observed and written with gusto' *Literary Review*

'Ravishing . . . delectable' *Sunday Times*

'Gloriously entertaining . . . [the book has] a novelistic depth, which is added to by rich topographical descriptions and a packed historical backdrop' *The Spectator*

'A rollick through the poet's ancestry . . . [and] the Byron family's astonishing, hilarious, morally abhorrent lust for life' *New Statesman*

'A lightness of touch belies the enormous amount of research that has clearly gone into every page . . . a superb family biography'
BBC History Magazine

'An engaging and intelligent account . . . This will justly be regarded as the definitive work about the wider Byron family' *The Critic*

'Stranger than fiction, as dark as any gothic drama, the story of the Byron family has cried out for a modern telling. Emily Brand's utterly gripping account of the Byrons' gilded decline into tragedy and scandal is a triumph of detective work and literary skill'
Amanda Foreman

'Brand's meticulous research brings to life the colourful characters of the Georgian era's most notorious families with all the verve and skill of the era's finest novelists . . . A powdered and pomaded, sordid and silk-swathed adventure' Hallie Rubenhold

'Brand is a great historian, equal to the huge challenge of telling the story of history's most turbulent and colourful lives' Dan Snow

'Brand has succeeded in painting a hauntingly beautiful portrait of the Byron dynasty. Theirs is a story of sex and scandal, but also of the fragility of life, the unyielding passion of the human heart, and the oppressive weight of the past. From the first to the last, the ghosts of the Byrons call out to us through Brand's evocative prose. Magnificent'
Rebecca Rideal

'*The Fall of the House of Byron* is a mesmerising tale of sex, obsession, madness, invention, and reinvention. The women take the spotlight in this poignant and exquisitely researched page-turner. A provocative rethinking of a famous family. A tour de force'
Charlotte Gordon

'Combining new research with a pacey narrative, Emily Brand introduces the glamorous and flawed Byron dynasty – William, the "Wicked Lord", pleasure-seeking Isabella, and "Foul-Weather Jack" – a family inheritance to match the wildest imaginings of their most notorious descendant. A riveting read!' Kathryn Sutherland

The Fall of the House of Byron

Scandal and Seduction in Georgian England

EMILY BRAND

CREDE BYRON

JOHN MURRAY

First published in Great Britain in 2020 by John Murray (Publishers)
An Hachette UK company

This paperback edition published in 2021

1

A CIP catalogue record for this title is available from the British Library

Paperback ISBN 978-1-473-66432-6
eBook ISBN 978-1-473-66431-9

Typeset in Bembo by Palimpsest Book Production Limited, Falkirk, Stirlingshire

Printed and bound in Great Britain by Clays Ltd, Elcograf S.p.A.

John Murray policy is to use papers that are natural, renewable
and recyclable products and made from wood grown in sustainable
forests. The logging and manufacturing processes are expected to
conform to the environmental regulations of the country of origin.

John Murray (Publishers)
Carmelite House
50 Victoria Embankment
London EC4Y 0DZ

www.johnmurraypress.co.uk

Contents

Author's Note

On Spellings and Dates

Original spellings have been retained in contemporary source material and mistakes and inconsistencies marked by [*sic*], unless otherwise stated. In 1752 Britain transitioned from the Julian to the Gregorian Calendar, leading to a 'loss' of eleven days. I have not adjusted for this, leaving all dates as they were written in contemporary sources.

On Newstead Abbey and Source Material

The structural exterior of the building that now stands is relatively similar to that the young poet first saw and toured in 1798, apart from the lack of the stone staircase entrance, which was demolished in the nineteenth century. The interior, however, was significantly altered during the residence of the poet's successors. As well as drawing from contemporary inventories, visitor descriptions and sale catalogues, my reconstructions for the tour in the Introduction owe a great debt to the work of Rosalys Coope and Pete Smith.

While some imaginative colour is necessarily given to the Introduction – largely, in the exact order in which the rooms were toured – the rest of the narrative is drawn from historical source material. A thought is not attributed to a protagonist unless that thought was expressed in their own letters, memoirs or similar; the weather is not described unless specified in their own accounts or those of local newspapers. Matters of both space and ease of reading do not allow for a note unless a direct quotation is used, but further details of sources consulted can be found in the Notes and Bibliography.

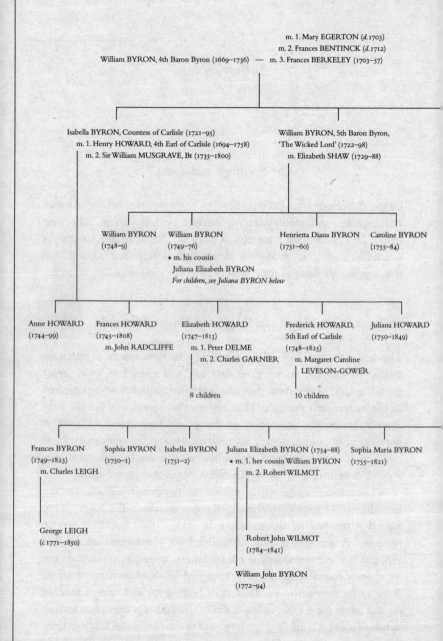

m. 1. Mary EGERTON (d.1703)
m. 2. Frances BENTINCK (d.1712)
William BYRON, 4th Baron Byron (1669–1736) — m. 3. Frances BERKELEY (1703–57)

Isabella BYRON, Countess of Carlisle (1721–95)
m. 1. Henry HOWARD, 4th Earl of Carlisle (1694–1758)
m. 2. Sir William MUSGRAVE, Bt (1735–1800)

William BYRON, 5th Baron Byron,
'The Wicked Lord' (1722–98)
m. Elizabeth SHAW (1729–88)

William BYRON
(1748–9)

William BYRON
(1749–76)
★ m. his cousin
Juliana Elizabeth BYRON
For children, see Juliana BYRON below

Henrietta Diana BYRON
(1751–60)

Caroline BYRON
(1755–84)

Anne HOWARD
(1744–99)

Frances HOWARD
(1745–1808)
m. John RADCLIFFE

Elizabeth HOWARD
(1747–1813)
m. 1. Peter DELME
m. 2. Charles GARNIER

8 children

Frederick HOWARD,
5th Earl of Carlisle
(1748–1825)
m. Margaret Caroline
LEVESON-GOWER

10 children

Juliana HOWARD
(1750–1849)

Frances BYRON
(1749–1823)
m. Charles LEIGH

Sophia BYRON
(1750–1)

Isabella BYRON
(1751–2)

Juliana Elizabeth BYRON (1754–88)
★ m. 1. her cousin William BYRON
m. 2. Robert WILMOT

Sophia Maria BYRON
(1755–1821)

George LEIGH
(c.1771–1850)

Robert John WILMOT
(1784–1841)

William John BYRON
(1772–94)

The House of Byron

Vice Admiral John BYRON,
'Foul-Weather Jack'
(1723–86)
  m. Sophia TREVANION
    (1730–90)

Richard BYRON
(1724–1811)
  m. Mary FARMER
    (1749–1827)

3 children:
Richard BYRON (1769–1837)
John BYRON (1770–1805)
Henry BYRON (1775–1821)

Charles BYRON
(1726–31)

George BYRON
(1730–89)
  m. Frances LEVETT
    (1736–1822)

7 children:
Isabella BYRON (1755–1834)
William BYRON (1756)
George BYRON (1756)
John BYRON (1758–1824)
Frederick George BYRON (1764–92)
Frances Elizabeth BYRON (1768)
Francis BYRON (1777–96)

John BYRON, 'Mad Jack'
(1757–91)
  m. 1. Amelia OSBORNE
    (née DARCY)
    m. 2. Catherine GORDON

    George Gordon BYRON,
    6th Baron Byron (the poet)
    (1788–1824)

3 children:
Sophia Georgina BYRON
Unnamed Boy
Augusta BYRON
  (1783–1851)

George Anson BYRON
(1758–93)
  m. Charlotte Henrietta
    DALLAS

4 children:
Isabella Sophia Georgiana BYRON
Juliana Maria BYRON
George Anson BYRON,
  7th Baron Byron
John James BYRON

Charlotte BYRON
(1760–1)

Augusta Barbara Charlotte
BYRON (1762–1824)
  m. Christopher PARKER

6 children:
Peter PARKER
Margaret Antoinetta PARKER
John Edmund George PARKER
Julia Maria PARKER
Augusta Georgiana PARKER
Charles Christopher PARKER

Introduction: The Shattered Window

Newstead! what saddening change of scene is thine!
Thy yawning arch betokens slow decay!
The last and youngest of a noble line
Now holds thy mouldering turrets in his sway.

Elegy on Newstead Abbey

Late Summer, 1798

Joe Murray is a bearish but sentimental steward in his early sixties with a tendency to start bellowing bawdy songs when he has had a drink. He has been a fixture of the Byron estate for over forty years, and shows little sign of slowing (though nowadays he does, admittedly, bulge slightly around the middle). As a young man he worked aboard the late lord's private fleet of replica warships, keeping them 'seaworthy' – though of course they never left the lake – and occasionally dodging live cannon shot for the entertainment of well-to-do visitors. When he was eventually brought in to the household, he jovially held court in the servants' hall and earned as much popularity below stairs as above – even if his hunting ditties were not always appreciated by those possessed of more delicate ears.

He has seen the halls filled with antique masterpieces and scientific curiosities, and the grounds teeming with visitors dressed in royal livery. He has watched his lordship's family grow – poor little Caroline was newly born when he took the position – and fall slowly, tragically apart. He has enjoyed the comforts of serving a noble house, finding pleasant employment in managing the household, dashing off correspondence on behalf of his 'dear late Lord', and indulging in his pipe and a glass of port by the fire.[1] Those days now seem a cacophony of noise: chattering chambermaids, the bells sending them scurrying; the Molyneux children back to gawp at the boats; that howling wolf pup. His own dear wife, Anne, joined him at the Abbey in her final years, as their children and grandchildren embarked on their own paths. A melancholy peace has settled now he is the only one left.

The last twenty years have seen the Abbey stripped of its treasures and the crowds of his lordship's laughing guests reduced to frowning lawyers and the occasional fawning niece or nephew. Even the family line itself has dwindled and died, thanks to the ravages of fever and the fatal precision of a cannon fired in distant Calvi.

Day after day his lordship dined alone, clinging desperately to the memory of past magnificence. *Joe!* he called. *Joe, put the claret on the table!* But the old man always left the bottle untouched. This last spring he had rasped out his final hours as the lonely estate hummed with the plaintive song of crickets. (The villagers, so easily swept up in tales about the old recluse at the Abbey, whispered that he had cultivated a swarm inside the house and allowed them to 'race' over his body, in some twisted remembrance of his old sporting glories.) He had died in his bed, after a long struggle, in the middle of the night. (When he took his final breath, the gossips declared, the crumbling ruin momentarily trembled to life as hundreds – thousands? – of mournful insects abandoned its halls forever.)

Joe takes up his pipe and wonders what the day will bring. He continues to take great pride in both his own appearance and that of his 'poor Old Newstead', and has patched each up as best he can in some small defiance of the unforgiving ravages of time.[2] He sweeps through the house until satisfied that everything is in order, breaking the stillness with the dull sound of footsteps on stone. Past empty walls and through corridors hanging with damp. In places the roof hasn't survived and rainwater weeps down grimy bedchamber walls, but he has done his best. He checks the neatness of his pale grey hair – those bushy eyebrows to match – and straightens his waistcoat and jacket. The only living remnant of a once bustling household, he is preparing to welcome the new little lord for the first time.

A coach rattles into the courtyard, winds around a curious-looking fountain and comes to a stop before a sweeping stone staircase. The journey from Aberdeen to Nottinghamshire has taken days and the three travellers stretch their limbs as they step out to survey the building looming over them.

The marriage of styles is – unusual. A pale stone mansion clings to the mouldering ruin of a priory, forcing ancient arches into an awkward alliance with its more modern, stately elegance. Tall windows stretch up the front of the house and glint as they catch the late summer sun, but it is the ruined facade of the original priory wall, to the left, that draws the eye. Of its three old Gothic arches, that on the left has been bricked over, that on the right filled in with a rudely rectangular window and the one in the centre – its glittering stained glass long since destroyed – stares blindly onto an overgrown lawn, and the gawping visitors. Weeds creep along the stone and dangle listlessly into the empty space. If the newcomers squint they might see, high up in a niche, the Virgin Mary and Child gazing serenely out to the west – over a rippling expanse of clear lake, a pair of miniature forts defending their banks against a forgotten enemy and a miniature castle perched on a distant hill.

The weariness of the party is forgotten in the excitement of seeing the estate at last. Catherine, a harried widow of thirty-three, is finally reaping some reward for her emotionally draining and financially disastrous marriage. Once a hopeful and bookish Scottish heiress, she had been seduced amid the soft candlelight of a Bath ballroom and left heartbroken when her husband had departed for – and promptly died in – revolutionary France. (The experience has embittered her both against her husband's family and against 'love, desperate love, the worst of maladies in my opinion'.)[3] She has since raised their only son in her own country and in increasingly pinched circumstances. The prospect of her precious George being lord of all this is an immense relief. At her side the nursemaid May Gray stares in wonder at this picturesque retreat, so far removed from anything she has known in the noisy, grubby throng of Aberdeen.

And finally the boy himself, with curly brown hair and bitten-down nails – a bad habit his mother hates – already feeling the exhilarating weight of an inheritance that was never meant to fall to him. At just ten years old he has taken up the title and estates of his grandfather's elder brother, a distant and entirely disinterested relative he never knew.

At first he was overwhelmed – bursting into tears when his name was called out in school with its new prefix, *Dominus* – but he seems to have settled into the idea. Until now immersed in the Highlands heritage of his mother and a virtual stranger to his paternal family, today George Gordon Byron is introduced for the first time to what he will call 'the melancholy mansion of my fathers': Newstead Abbey. [4]

As the coachman settles the horses they are met by Catherine's solicitor, John Hanson, a businesslike but welcoming man with beetling eyebrows and a shock of white in his sideburns. He has travelled up from London with his wife to help manage the Byron affairs (they are, he will later tactfully note, 'in confusion'), and is pleased to put faces to the names of clients who have kept him occupied in recent months. [5] Both mother and son are inclined to plumpness and speak with a Scottish drawl. They appear fond of each other. Perhaps buoyed by the new company or making up for the boredom of his long journey, George speaks with a confident swagger that persuades Hanson he is 'a fine sharp Boy', if a little spoiled. [6] When asked what he misses most about Scotland, George pipes up that his only regrets are being obliged to leave the wild Highland scenery and a little girl named Mary.

The prospect of uncovering Newstead's murky past – which far precedes the arrival of his ancestors – presents an exciting adventure for a boy already fascinated by the parade of history. Its origins are bathed in violence. The priory itself was established in the eleventh century by Henry II, as part of his atonement for the murder of the archbishop Thomas Becket. During the sixteenth century the dissolution of the monasteries saw its treasures cast into the pond by monks hoping to save them from the marauding king's men; during the civil wars of the seventeenth century it was reportedly ransacked by the Parliamentarian troops who mobilised against the king and his supporters. And, since then? It is clear that George is eager to explore, and Hanson obliges by guiding them up the stone stairs – which the boy negotiates with a pronounced limp – and through a heavy door. The tour begins, and Newstead's ghosts begin to gather around them.

They step first into the Grand Hall, a spacious medieval chamber used by the monks as a dining room. Light streams in through the tall windows overlooking the courtyard on their left. Adorning the upper panes is the Byron family crest – a shield set beneath a mirror-gazing mermaid and flanked by two chestnut horses. (The iconography is fitting for a family with proud nautical associations and a less commendable passion for horse racing; the motto *Crede Byron* – 'Trust in Byron' – has perhaps lost some integrity in recent years.) A vaulted ceiling arches over them, the exposed wooden beams supporting four long chains and four corresponding old lamps collecting dust. Apart from the smell of the hay – which has been stuffed in bundles up against the walls and scattered itself out across the floor – there is little else to take in. They do not miss the exquisite statues that once filled the niches in the walls, the sombre hunting trophies or the grand old paintings of roaring lions and American eagles, all long since lost.

Having crossed the hall – perhaps peering out at the lake on the way – they enter a small drawing room papered in dull green, where the only real point of interest is an intricate wooden carving above the fireplace. The colours are peeling, but it is easy to make out the prominent Byron heraldry surrounded by curious figures, some pale and some dark-skinned, men bearing spears and women in richly embroidered caps.

Descending a few steps, the group poke their heads into a second, high-ceilinged drawing room in faded red, before returning to the Grand Hall and the galleries running from it. The faint shuffling of hooves can be heard somewhere below, but Hanson is already striding ahead.

Before them lies a warren of small rooms in various states of dilapidation, but carrying some lingering fragments of their previous inhabitants. A spiral staircase leads up to a chamber, once part of the old prior's lodgings, boasting little furnishing apart from a chimney-piece fashioned from the tombstone of an unwitting fourteenth-century resident. With the names of the dead literally inscribed on the bones of the building, it is unsurprising that this wing seems to bristle with something otherworldly. George thrills in it. (In the years to come, 'Old Joe' Murray's tales of the sinister robed monk haunting these rooms will delight the young lord, who is perhaps already earmarking this as his own bedchamber.)

The elevated view from here affords a better perspective over the Upper Lake, with its abandoned battlements and forts settled into a lazy slumber. Where crows once scattered in alarm at the blasts of cannons and delighted applause, their descendants caw at one another in peace. Weeds stretch out in murky waters where only a generation ago a doomed young man had laughingly received toasts to his future, surrounded by family and friends.

Carefully winding back down to the first floor, the party ambles around what was once the most admired stretch of the house – four long galleries, snaking around the cloister quadrangle at the heart of the building. Two hundred years ago they had echoed with the benevolent ramblings of George's ancestor Margaret as she descended into insanity, and the despair of her devoted husband John. (This couple, George's five times great-grandparents, had reportedly died on the same day – as if, a neighbour wrote, 'some strange sympathy in love or nature, tied up their lives in one'.)[7] More recently, the galleries were filled with books, Renaissance masterpieces and tempestuous Dutch seascapes, inspiring a generation of siblings to seek out adventures of their own. Now, the library is gone and the bareness of the walls merely highlights an accumulation of dirt and dust. A glance at the quadrangle outside offers nothing but a dried-up pool and weeds marking their dominion across the courtyard and up the cloister walls.

The next suite of rooms – formerly the bedchambers and dressing rooms running along the cloisters – fell from use many years ago and are unlikely to impress. Perhaps it is here that the boy could, if he searched, find the names and birthdays of his grandfather's generation – Isabella, William, John, Richard, Charles – where they had been painstakingly etched onto a windowpane with a diamond seven decades ago. One bedchamber, at least, clings to the vestiges of its former loveliness: the ceiling is dominated by an oval painting of a cloudy sky bordered with coats of arms commemorating the first two marriages of George's great-grandfather William, 4th Lord Byron. (William evidently did not anticipate any further romantic entanglement as his third spouse Frances – George's own great-grandmother – was not afforded any space.) The cheerful cherubs and preening mermaids give no hint of his two young brides' unhappy fates. The other rooms are uninhabitable, with parts of the roof so decayed that the afternoon sun glares down on the damp, rotting wallpaper.

When they reach the largest room in the house – the Great Dining

Hall, now 'deserted and forlorn' – George and his mother gaze around at its promise of grandeur.[8] On one side of this long, panelled chamber sits a splendid black and white marble chimneypiece; on the other, a row of tall sash windows overlooks the south gardens. Grotesque faces grin from buttresses stretching down either side of the wall. Above them hangs a laced plasterwork ceiling old enough to have witnessed the family's grief when, a century and a half earlier, a band of seven Byron brothers went to war for their king and only one returned. In happier times, the flickering fire gave a warm glow to the faces of dancing servants, of gentlemen making toasts and of George's own grandfather John as a curious, wriggling infant.

Continuing the tour, the party comes abruptly to the bedchamber of the late owner: William, 5th Lord Byron. It's not exactly what one might expect for the private quarters of an English aristocrat – his handsome chintz fabrics and mahogany furniture long since sold – but one item on the wall is bound to catch the eye of a ten-year-old boy. There, as if in pride of place, hangs a dull but ominous sword with a knotted hilt. Is this the weapon his predecessor had plunged into the belly of a childhood friend, forever cleaving the Byron name with whispers of *murder*? George concludes so.

They wander through the rest of the south-east wing – breakfast parlour, study, drawing room – but it is the view out to the east that captures the eye: a sculpted rectangular pond, a swathe of parkland cloaked in bilberries and a dark wooded grove where (superstitious locals whisper) the old lord's *devils* lurk. The landscape is otherwise oddly barren of trees but not entirely devoid of feature – ramshackle fencing winds through miles of farmland, stretching out to several small villages, a quarry and an old mill.

Out of sight, his new tenants press on with their daily routines: preparing for the harvest season, struggling with the day's washing, enjoying a pot of ale in the Red Lion or writing the next Sunday sermon. The extent of the inheritance is irresistible to Catherine – who had been a woman of fortune before she laid eyes on Jack Byron – and perhaps barely fathomable to a young boy raised in a modest apartment. Until war had claimed the life of a distant cousin four years ago, he had been set to inherit nothing but his father's debts. Catherine had learned of their sudden change in fortunes through hearsay, her husband's family apparently not feeling obliged to honour her with a letter. It is still sinking in.

The stone passages, servants' quarters and storage rooms in the damp, lower levels of the house are all that remain to be explored. A whitewashed cloister walk stretches beneath the picture galleries, leading to an atmospheric medieval chapterhouse that served generations of Byrons as a private chapel. Any sense of reverence is quickly dispelled by the gentle lowing of cattle and a distinctly rural stench drifting over from the west side of the building. Hanson explains that the hall undercroft is used to house some of the Newstead herd. On the walls of the large but cheerless kitchen some former employee has daubed the warning WASTE NOT – WANT NOT in large letters, and the apartments around it are, in the words of one later visitor, 'reduced to a heap of rubbish'.[9]

A turn around Newstead is a journey in itself – in later years, during his residence here, George will joke that it is half a mile from his writing desk to his bedchamber. The Abbey hasn't been subjected to such scrutiny since the Great Sale, when flocks of eager collectors and nosy neighbours toured the house, clutching their auction catalogues, and picked off its valuables like crows. It was the nail in the coffin for Newstead – since then most visitors have merely grieved at the sight of such a place crumbling into dust.

But Hanson is surprised to discover that his clients are far from put off by its rude appearance. In fact, he is hard pressed to dissuade the mother and son from moving themselves in immediately – they are enchanted.

The party stay on at the Abbey for the next three weeks to assess the extent of disrepair and discuss how to handle the financial challenges it presents. Despite her solicitor's tactful pessimism, Catherine's eagerness to begin restorations is undimmed. She consults her stepdaughter Augusta Byron – George's elder half-sister – and insists that 'whatever money [is] judg'd necessary should be laid out upon it'.[10] Hanson, who has been hoping to wrap up the business as expediently as possible, politely masks his disappointment.

A dismayed George is packed off to stay with a pair of old women in nearby Nottingham, one of whom is his great-aunt Frances, who boasts the tenuous family connection of being the old lord's brother's wife. (For her kindness this elderly Mrs Byron, one of the few members of the family to give Catherine the time of day, will soon be immortalised in one of George's very first poems as 'As curst an old lady as ever was seen'.)[11] Until he turns twenty-one, the Abbey will be let to a tenant.

Though she has often regaled George with stories of the 'cut-throat ancestors' on his Scottish side, Catherine struggles to discuss his father's family without descending into insults – only at displays of insolence and ungratefulness does she acknowledge his inheritance as 'a true Byrrone' ('which', he comments archly to his half-sister, 'is the worst epithet she can invent').[12] Before they came to England news of the family had trickled in from his reticent aunt Mrs Leigh, in letters bordered with black in mourning for her parents, her siblings, her aunts and uncles. Suddenly thrust into acquaintance with his father's three surviving sisters, a clique of velvet-clad cousins, and the affable Old Joe Murray – later described as 'a walking & living Legend of Newstead' – George begins to discover just how Byronic he truly is.[13]

The man George will grow to be is known to history for many things: his love affairs, his taste for the flamboyant, his lust for adventure and – above all – his poetry. But by the time he takes that first tour of Newstead his family name is already steeped in tragedy, romance and adventure. Since falling into Byron hands in 1540, the Abbey has played host to the boisterous theatrical troupe of its first owner, the 'Great Beard' of its second and the broken heart of its third. It saw the family elevated to the peerage in reward for their services on the battlefield and (if diarist Samuel Pepys is to be believed) those of 'that whore my Lady Byron' in Charles II's bedroom.[14] It saw successive generations ignore warnings that debts were eating into their estates 'like a moth in your garment', and one lord was even tricked by his own children into signing away control of the estates while inebriated.[15] The Byron men had already acquired a reputation for military stamina and sexual prowess. In 1677 George's twice times great-grandfather had been flattered in verse with the question, 'Is't not enough the Byrons all excell, As much in loving, as in fighting well?' – a century later his grandfather was cheekily celebrated in gossip columns for proving 'abilities in the field of Venus, as well as he had done in that of Mars'.[16] Others forged their reputations with their pens rather than their swords, like his 'evermore scribbling' great-aunt, whose greatest delight was seeking beauty and true love.[17]

The romance of both his ancestry and the Abbey itself bleed into George's early writing on love, death and liberty. Surviving family members are immortalised in his earliest verse – the ridiculous great-aunt, the dark-eyed cousin who 'looked as if she had been made out of a rainbow' – and their shared heritage is revived and embellished in long elegies.[18] During the years of his intermittent residence at the Abbey, between 1808 and 1814, he embraces its aesthetic of untamed decay.

'What you say is all very true, come what may!' he writes to his mother shortly after his arrival there, 'Newstead and I stand or fall together. I have now lived on the spot, I have fixed my heart upon it, and no pressure, present or future, shall induce me to barter the last vestige of our inheritance'.[19]

During George's own residence, the once elegant Great Dining Hall hosts uproarious young men playing shuttlecock or dashing about in a stupor dressed as monks. In the Grand Hall, where imposing portraits of his ancestors William, 4th Lord Byron and John, 2nd Viscount Chaworth once stood guardian, a lumbering wolf-dog and a tame bear pad around listlessly. When a gardener unearths the skull of a long-dead friar it is set in silver and used as a drinking vessel, prompting the poet to ask himself, 'And when, alas! our brains are gone, What nobler substitute than wine?'[20] To the epithets earned by his illustrious relatives – such as the 'very great Rogue', the 'Columbus-like' explorer, the 'Wittiest Widow in England' – George will add 'the bard who sang freedom', 'human tyger' and most famously, 'mad, bad, and dangerous to know'.

With the weight of its past and all its drama, melancholy and contradictions, Newstead could not have acquired a more appropriate lord. For George the Abbey is an inhabitable memento mori, both a testament to what he believes to be humanity's inevitable decline and a reminder of his own family's steep fall from grace. The story of that fall, which saw this once lively, beloved family seat 'swallowed in deep waves of black oblivion', began two generations earlier with the birth of a child.[21]

I

The Courtyard

Rebuilding a Dynasty, 1720–36

> Amidst the court a Gothic fountain play'd,
> Symmetrical, but deck'd with carvings quaint—
> Strange faces, like to men in masquerade,
> And here perhaps a monster, there a saint . . .
>
> *Don Juan*, canto XIII

1722

The baby is brought screaming into a world of fire and festivity. It is Thursday, 5 November – a day of peculiarly English celebration – and preparations for the evening are under way. Some are constructing crude effigies of the devil, the Pope or a long-dead traitor in old-fashioned clothes. At the Tower and on ships idling along the Thames others load their cannons for the salute at noon. From Newquay to Newcastle townsfolk set up their parades: guildsmen unfurl their flags, musical troupes test their instruments, innkeepers check they have enough ale to satisfy the crowds. The face of the country is pocked with piles of wood, old furniture and household debris, ready to be set ablaze when night falls. It is Gunpowder Treason Day – the anniversary of an old Protestant triumph over a failed Catholic plot – and toasts are proclaimed in dank taverns and at the glittering royal court.

Circling a bedchamber at Newstead Abbey, the groans of a young woman in the throes of agony. Her dark hair sticks to her face, her breath comes in gasps. The air in the room is thick with the smell of sweat, blood and the herb concoctions supposed to ease the labour. Servants dash about the house, muttering and carrying out orders. The younger maids summoned to the chamber might be alarmed at the glint of medical instruments, or their mistress's uncharacteristic loss of poise. Her name is Frances, and she is nineteen years old. As her torture seeps through the house, her husband – a peer of the realm – waits for news. He is fifty-two, and hardly a handsome man: a heavy wig frames his drooping dark eyes and prominent nose, and scratches at the sides of his jowled neck. He has been through this before. Five times, in fact, though only two daughters remain. As darkness descends over England, bonfires flicker into life and devour the lifeless effigies of her enemies, to roars of approval. The booms of something like cannon cut into the sky, illuminating it with cascades of sparkling fire that hover momentarily before fading to smoke. William, 4th Lord Byron, has received word from those attending his wife and looks ahead with new hope for the future of his dynasty. A boy, thank God! A boy.

Gazing back from 1805 is his seventeen-year-old great-grandson George, 6th Lord Byron. Embroiled in a row with his mother, the young man studies a painting of William and interprets his fixed expression as sympathy from beyond the grave. Catherine is 'pouring forth complaints', he writes to his half-sister, 'whilst in the background, the portraits of my Great Grandfather and Grandmother, suspended in their frames, seem to look with an eye of pity on their *unfortunate descendant*'.[1]

George has by now become swept up in a half-imagined history of the Byron family, pieced together from books, peerage lists, the tales of Old Joe and traces of the past clinging to the Abbey itself. He chooses to brood over the salacious and the heroic, and to skirt over the mundane. The carved overmantel in the green drawing room – surely evidence of valiant deeds undertaken during the Crusades? The heraldry hanging in plaster over empty Newstead halls recalls the fluttering banners that rallied his ancestors at the battles of Crécy and Marston Moor. Perhaps he has already concocted the outlandish tales of inherited instability with which he will terrify his friends. ('There always was a madness in the family', he remarks one day to a Harrow classmate, interrupting himself in the middle of a cheerful tune, 'My father cut his throat.')[2]

The ghosts that he first encountered at the Abbey assemble as one remarkable dynasty: this man a hero; this man a villain; and in their shadows, the women upholding the family name. Heirs, warriors, mothers and lovers – all acting out the roles they were born to play. Like those curious figures on the courtyard fountain, they present a parade of monsters and saints, and men in masquerade.

~

As the people of England cleared away the debris of their revelries, the child was given his name: William, after his father and grand-fathers. Still adjusting to his new world – all movement and noise – he was baptised in the private chapel in the underbelly of Newstead. His mother Frances took a glazier's diamond to one of the bedroom windows and etched his name alongside that of her daughter:

ISABELLA BYRON BORN NOVEMBER YE 10TH 1721
WILLIAM BYRON BORN NOVEMBER YE 5TH 1722[3]

Relatives, servants and well-wishers cooed over him, offering their gifts and congratulations. He had two sisters: Isabella, not yet one (too small to be bewildered by his sudden arrival), and eleven-year-old Frances, the only surviving child from their father's previous marriage, who was quite old enough to recognise the superior value of a son and heir.

While his existence brought some stability to his immediate family, baby William was born into uncertain and changing times. The kingdom of Great Britain itself was barely out of the cradle, having been formed following the Acts of Union of the Kingdom of England and the Kingdom of Scotland in 1707. Its new royal family, the Hanoverians – Protestants plucked from German ob-scurity to succeed the inconveniently Catholic Stuart dynasty – had been far from universally welcomed. During William's first winter the newspapers were filled with stories of the recent ill-fated schemes of the 'Jacobites', who hoped to restore the exiled James Edward Stuart to the throne. Elsewhere, understandings of the world itself were shifting as the ancient lure of magic and super-stition was slowly suffocated by the march of science. A Westminster election loomed, and the aristocracy continued to nurse its finan-cial wounds after the recent, devastating crash in South Sea Company stocks. A shocking new book – seemingly the tell-all autobiography of prostitute-turned-penitent Moll Flanders – preoccupied literate society, and was passed with winks and nudges around gentlemen's clubs. Though it had brightened the hue of the world for his parents, the birth of an heir for Newstead passed with little to no national comment.

As William learned to recognise faces and discovered the full force of his lungs, around him linens were washed and dust was whipped from marble mantelpieces. His mother slowly recovered her strength. Frances did, at least, have youth on her side. She was a slender woman, with dark features and long chestnut hair; sometimes it tumbled over her shoulders, at others she tucked it into a white pleated cap. She loved music, embraced the growing fashion for drinking tea, and had approached her new life at Newstead dutifully, even though it wrenched her so far from her old one. She came from a large family, being the fifth of seven children born to William, 4th Lord Berkeley of Stratton, and having a host of doting aunts and uncles on her maternal side (her own mother was long dead). Her voice may have betrayed a slight Somersetshire twang, picked up during extended childhood summers at Bruton Abbey, her father's country seat.

Her marriage had been negotiated as the crash of 1720 crippled the court, and it was entirely a matter of business. 'In the midst of these battles I am going to dispose of one of my daughters to My Lord Byron,' her father had written pragmatically to a friend; 'a disproportionate match as to their ages, but marriages not offering every day. I would not miss an opportunity'.[4] (Lord Byron was, in fact, a year older than himself.) She had performed as directed. On a Saturday evening in early December Frances Berkeley took her vows at her father's house in Kensington, and took up residence in Westminster as Lady Byron. By February she was carrying William's child. He could not have wished for a more auspicious start. Her own feelings go unrecorded.

Her new husband had always been more comfortable immersed in the arts than in the banter of the House of Lords. He shared her interest in music – his own youthful compositions for the harpsichord had found their way into the theatres of Drury Lane – and was a keen collector of books, antiquities, paintings and prints. Like any country gentleman, he enjoyed the hunt, and was perfectly placed to pursue the sport in his lands around Sherwood Forest. In middle age he had turned his hand to art and architecture, becoming a patron of painters Michael Dahl – whose portraits filled the Abbey walls – and Peter Tillemans, who was tutoring him in sketching and watercolours. But where his own cash-strapped father had been more concerned with dabbling in poetry than debt management, the 4th Lord was determined not to make the same mistakes. As his children learned to write and lisp out the name Byron (or Bi-*ron*, in the French style, as successive generations often pronounced it), he resolved to do his utmost to marry it to a reputation for good sense and the modern idea of good taste.

Though he had held minor positions in the royal household, he was not politically ambitious. Taking a cautious approach, he established cordial relationships with both the Whig and Tory parties and became known as a man whose vote 'might be had a certain way' (this being the means to fund his projects in Nottinghamshire).[5] He had been popular enough at court to secure three financially advantageous marriages: first, to Mary Egerton, sister of the Earl of Bridgewater, who had succumbed to smallpox just six weeks after the wedding; second, to Frances Bentinck, daughter of the Duke of Portland, who provided four children before her death aged twenty-eight. (Her downfall was caused, so the gossip went, by a venereal disease contracted courtesy of her wandering husband: "Tis said she died of a distemper her Lord gave her', Lady Strafford had hinted darkly.)[6] Although by the time of his search for a third wife the only surviving legacy of either union was one daughter – William had lost three sons – his alliances with both families held strong. When his brother-in-law Henry Bentinck was dispatched to a post in Jamaica – most likely never to return – he wrote with the wish that his family would 'hereafter live happily for the rest of yr days'. He closed with a message from little Frances to her uncle, the sole surviving fragment of her voice: 'my daughter desires her duty'.[7]

As Lord Byron set about rebuilding his dynasty with his third wife, his already shallow enthusiasm for politics dried up almost completely for the best part of five years. Though Frances had successfully provided an heir, her husband – painfully aware of how precarious these early years were – expected to repeat the enterprise as soon as possible. While little Isabella took tentative steps and baby William began to see the world in colour, their mother's belly again began to swell, and amid preparations for their birthdays it became clear that the arrival was imminent. On 8 November 1723, shattering the tranquillity of Newstead: another boy. They named him John, after Frances's eldest brother. The first useful act of the child's life was to provide his parents with an opportunity to nurture friendly relationships in high places. While Frances chose her sister Jane Berkeley to stand as godmother, Lord Byron wrote to his benefactor Thomas Pelham-Holles, Duke of Newcastle – the most prominent landowner in Nottinghamshire and a rising star in government – 'to obtain the Honour of yr being a Godfather to a Son newly Born'.[8] Upon his acceptance, a letter swiftly flew out from Newstead 'to returne yr Grace my thanks and my Wives for the great honour yo[u] have granted us', before concluding soberly, 'I hope my Son will live to acknowledg his obligations himself'.[9] With such an illustrious godparent, little John's start in life was promising. He was baptised at Newstead and his mother tenderly etched his name onto the bedroom window. But her duties were far from over.

Exhibiting a remarkable talent for regularity, Frances noticed the tell-tale signs of pregnancy for a fourth consecutive spring. But this time, as the birth approached and the Abbey grounds turned from lush green to bleak, wet orange, the atmosphere in the household was different. The children were ushered away from their thirteen-year-old half-sister Frances, who had begun to cough violently and grow feverish and frail. Consumption. She died on 21 September 1724 and was buried with her mother and brothers in the Byron family vault at nearby Hucknall church, severing their father's final link with his former family. Though she remained forever fixed in a playful pose at her elder brother's side in one of the Newstead portraits, it is unlikely that her younger siblings would remember her – Isabella was not yet three.

The lingering grief that hung about the Abbey was interrupted by Frances's labour pains and the arrival of a third son – Richard – who ruined the run of November birthdays by making his entrance on 28 October. The chaplain pressed water to his forehead; his mother took her diamond to the bedroom window.

'Unacquainted with the vicissitudes of fortune'

While their father busied himself with building plans and shot about the country bidding on antiques, the children gathered up their earliest experiences at Newstead, where the silver and silk of fashionable living collided with the rudeness of rural life. Silver rattles, their christening gifts of silver plate, silver-laced garments and the glint of silver pots steaming with cocoa or tea; red silk cushions, their mother's sweeping skirts, the sumptuous hangings billowing over four-poster beds. Elsewhere, the familiar barking and snuffling of their father's hounds, the feeling of delicate flowers pulled from the earth by their inquisitive fingers, and mud-flecked labourers spotted through windows, repairing fences and tending the gardens.

This undated watercolour, View of a Park with Deer, *by William, 4th Lord Byron may have captured something of the rural serenity of Newstead.*

The children found sights and sounds to fire their imaginations at every turn. They passed their days with those employed to raise them: nursemaids fussed about them in coloured skirts and flapping caps; men darted down the corridors and about the stables in bright red livery. Outside, there was a lake with a little rowing boat, rolling green gardens dotted with frolicking statues, and thick woodlands filled with plants and interesting creatures. Inside, the walls were hung with gilt-framed mirrors reflecting their own little faces, and countless pictures including skilful watercolours and sketches by both of their parents.

The walls of the Great Dining Hall were crowded with portraits: a gaunt old man dressed in black, with a huge, gleaming white beard (their four times great-grandfather). A greasy-haired soldier with a black scar on his cheek, pictured with his horse and his slave, pointing at nothing (a twice times great-uncle). Alongside these long-dead relatives were two large portraits of their parents, painted by Michael Dahl around the time of their marriage: their ageing father stern and sagging in his parliamentary robes, and his young bride posing by a harpsichord in a gown of pale pink and green. (Nearby, perhaps not alleviating Frances's creeping dislike of the place, were two portraits of her husband's short-lived first wife, and four of his second.)

There was an extensive library of ancient and modern books, one day bound to appeal to the romantic Isabella and the studious Richard. Sometimes the sound of the harpsichord, fiddle or wooden bagpipe echoed through the house from the Great Gallery (perhaps their father treated them to one of his old compositions, 'Ye Ld Byron's Scotch Tune'). Nods to history and heroics stood at every corner – a suit of armour in one of the upstairs passageways, and paintings of naval battles that were bound to appeal to the young boys. Some of the rooms were dominated by hunting trophies: the glassy eyes of a huge stag in the Grand Hall; an elk staring blankly in the Great Gallery; bucks' heads in the parlours and servants' halls. Had they stolen into their father's study, they might have coveted his model horses or, stowed away elsewhere, his collection of swords and guns.

Renovations whirled around them as their mother was permitted a (short) respite from adding to the nursery and their father focused on his secondary mission – the dull courtyard was transformed into an elegant turning circle for carriages; grimy ecclesiastical windows were bricked over and bright sash windows installed; dark panelling was swept away in favour of light, painted wood. The new, warren-like suite of apartments might have provided better hiding places than the creaking, high-ceilinged halls. Perhaps they caught snatches of servants' chatter about improvements made to the old bakery, brewhouse and kitchen.

While the children learned and played, their father's portly and asthmatic friend Mr Tillemans captured the Abbey's progress in oil and watercolours. He also immortalised those living and working there: the prized racehorses and their grooms; Lord and Lady Byron riding on the east front, old William in cream and Frances's red dress spilling over one side of her horse. His liveliest picture, however, was an intimate scene of the family and servants gathered together in the Great Dining Hall, including three of the children (either the three eldest or the three boys, depending on who made the cut). In it, a fiddler plays an energetic tune as people dance, chat amongst themselves or embrace one another. A beagle pads about the floor. The infants gaze around with wide-eyed curiosity or try to wriggle free of their nursemaids, while their father observes the festivities with a drink. This frozen moment of shared revelry gave a flush of delight to the servants who appeared in it – one later visitor described how the housekeeper showed him a number of paintings including this 'good pretty one of all his servants dancing together' and enthusiastically named every person featured.[10]

A fifth Byron sibling made his appearance in the spring of 1726, apparently a time of particular fruitfulness for Nottinghamshire's affluent families. As another record was etched on the Abbey window – CHARLES BYRON BORN APRIL 6TH 1726 – he was swiftly followed by an heir for the neighbouring Saviles of Rufford Abbey and a second son, christened William, for Mr and Mrs Chaworth of Annesley Hall. Notes of congratulation flew across the county as the fashionable world descended on their rural estates for the summer. There was little John's godfather the Duke of Newcastle at Clumber Park, plus two newly entitled teenage lords: William Bentinck, Duke of Portland, who inherited Welbeck Abbey following his father's death in Jamaica, and Evelyn Pierrepont, Duke of Kingston, of Thoresby Hall. As well as the Chaworths and the Saviles, the genteel families active in local politics included the elderly baronet Francis Molyneux at Teversall, Tory stalwarts the Willoughbys of Wollaton Hall and the newly married Montagus at Papplewick. The names and faces of this genteel if not exactly glittering set of neighbours gradually became familiar to the Byron children, who observed their manners at church and in flower-scented drawing rooms during the obligatory rounds of social calls.

News from across the country provided entertaining tattle – "'Rabbits or no Rabbits" has been the great dispute this week' cried the newspapers, as the nation was swept up in a story of a woman from Surrey who had allegedly begun giving birth to litters of them.[11] (It was later proved to be a hoax, but not before a number of prominent physicians unwisely staked their reputations on it.) But while the adult world turned on polite chitchat and petty disputes, the children merely judged it by its gilded coaches and handsome gowns, the flashes of silvery fish in the lakes around Newstead and the nursemaids tetchily prising their sticky fingers from things they shouldn't be touching. Life at the Abbey had provided a relatively gentle introduction to the intoxicating high society of the early Georgian era, but – to their mother's relief – they were about to become better acquainted with the dazzling lights of the city. The summer of 1727 brought some life-changing news. Their father was required in London: the old king was dead.

The servants piled the family's belongings – and the five squirming children under six – into carriages bound for their house in town: 15 Great Marlborough Street. After what seemed to be an age of jolting through the countryside, the city was a rush of noise for little ears: cries of street-sellers and ballad singers, yelping dogs and horses' hooves, voices chattering in unfamiliar languages, the jangling of coins in purses. Raucous laughter spilled from taverns. They rode past dirty children in drab, coarse clothes, who idled on pavements or darted across streets, narrowly avoiding the gentlefolk being conveyed around in sedan chairs (and the notoriously foul-mouthed men who carried them).

Eventually they clattered briskly down a spacious street in

Westminster, and modern townhouses stretched above them on either side. It was not as grand as a *square* or a *crescent*, but according to one tourist of the time it surpassed 'any thing that is called a Street, in the Magnificence of its Buildings and Gardens, and inhabited all by prime Quality'.[12] They drew up at number 15. The house was large, with several floors looking down onto a neat garden, coach houses and stabling. Though no plan for the building survives, an inventory of the property next door gives some impression of its likely interior: four elegant rooms on the first floor, a dining room, four bedchambers, as well as the garrets, kitchen, washhouse and pantry used by the servants. Their father had ensured the house was prepared and furnished for their arrival, dressing the rooms with antiquities and paintings, bringing over some card-tables and hanging the staircase with prints. Marking their return to town in style, he purchased a coach with red silk reins.

It was a fashionable Westminster address that allowed their father easy access to the House of Lords plus the city's prestigious clubs and assembly rooms. He had been letting the house to Henry Howard, heir to the Earl of Carlisle, and his young family – illustrious shoes to fill – and their neighbours included lords, ladies, military heroes and Members of Parliament. (Fashionable society was, for the moment, cloaked in black to observe the official mourning period for the late king.) Far from the leafy shades of Sherwood Forest, the children were thrust into the heart of one of the largest cities in the world. Just to the north was the thoroughfare Tyburn Road (soon to be renamed Oxford Street), along which condemned criminals were paraded on their way to Tyburn gallows. From the windows of the upper storeys the view to the south offered another reminder of the fleeting nature of life: the bright, bustling Carnaby Market a stone's throw from an old burial ground. Nearby St James's Park filled with well-to-do folk during the winter afternoons and warm summer evenings, while residents of the city's upscale brothels preened themselves around St James's Square and at the notorious Mrs Needham's in Park Place. Childish screeches rose from the yard of the prestigious Westminster School and those of the workhouses and charity schools springing up near the river. Peers and Members scurried between the houses of Parliament –

then held in the cluster of crumbling medieval buildings that made up the Palace of Westminster – its surrounding coffee houses and the royal court.

Further afield, the city of London itself – still emerging from the ashes of the Great Fire of 1666 – was in the middle of a building boom. People and money poured into the capital, descending upon the markets of Covent Garden or the brand-new development of luxury shops at New Bond Street. The children's parents might have been tempted by the booksellers and stationers or the millineries filled with ribbons and lace. Experimental confections and exquisitely crafted wooden dolls and toys were set up in shop windows, and by the doorways of certain establishments wafts of chocolate and coffee went some way to masking the general lingering smell of soot and sewers.

In October 1727 the city temporarily resumed its colour for the coronation of the new king – George II – and Westminster was transformed into a heaving mass of giddy spectators hoping for a glimpse of the parade. It was an extravagant event, seen only once in some lifetimes and in others not at all. Somewhere amid the solemn procession from Westminster Hall to Westminster Abbey – around halfway along – were Lord and Lady Byron, cloaked in their crimson robes and clutching their coronets. (The honour was not cheap – a fellow peer, Lord Ailesbury, had spent over eighty pounds (approaching £10,000 today) on the necessary robes, gloves, lace, gold ribbons and ermine.) The crowd sniggered to see a fatigued sixty-seven-year-old Dowager Duchess of Marlborough commandeer a musician's drum and plant herself on it during a drag in the procession. The Abbey doors opened – 'God save King GEORGE the Second! Long live King GEORGE!' – and afterwards a banquet in the packed Hall. It was a long day. Lord and Lady Byron returned to Great Marlborough Street hours later, wondering how best to court the favour of their new royal family.

Fortunately, the Byrons were not without friends in town. With the change in regime boosting their father's enthusiasm for actually turning up at the House of Lords, politics may have become a more common topic of conversation at Great Marlborough Street. The family attended the neat redbrick church of St James's on Piccadilly, where a congregation of the first quality discreetly eyed each other's dress, hairstyles and manners. The children were toddled about the green avenues of St James's Park, entertained by the ducks and the tame deer, while their parents dashed off letters to friends and associates of varying respectability. They remained on intimate terms with the Bentincks and the Egertons (in which family there were a number of children for the young Byrons to play with); among the less reputable were the debauched gambling enthusiast Sir John Tyrwhitt and cockfighting devotee Lord Lovell, both of whom owed their father significant sums. As for family, there were few relatives left on their father's side. The children had just two childless aunts in their late fifties – Catherine, Lady Ranelagh, who lived in Ireland, and the unmarried Juliana: their faces, at least, would have been familiar, since portraits of both women (plus Lord Ranelagh) graced the walls of Newstead.

Their mother's family was vast in comparison, and supplied more regular visitors. Lord Berkeley, their only living grandparent, was a smart-looking man with a tightly curled grey wig, who had not relished the burden of bringing up daughters and had a tendency to nit-pick. He observed with dismay that the last few years had done no favours for Frances's looks. He now preferred exploring grand country estates to the 'solitude' of London where, he wrote to a friend plaintively, 'most of my acquaintance are gone and the time past for making new'.[13] The children probably knew their mother's beloved aunt Elizabeth Temple, who wore a small ruby ring inset with their entwined hair. Their own six Berkeley aunts and uncles, all in their twenties and early thirties, were also familiar faces. Their uncles: John Berkeley, married but childless; Charles, the youngest; and William, who had followed family tradition into the navy. Two aunts unmarried: John's godmother Jane (destined to die a spinster) and twenty-year-old Anne (destined to be killed by childbirth). And finally their twenty-two-year-old aunt Barbara – her portrait also hung at Newstead (though it was not a very good likeness) – who had followed her sister's example and been married off to a fifty-nine-year-old widower, John Trevanion of Caerhays Castle. When not in Cornwall the Trevanions settled just a few minutes' walk away at Charles Street, providing the siblings with some new cousins and playmates: William Trevanion was born in 1727, followed by Frances in 1728. In 1729 the sisters fell pregnant within a few months of each other – as Barbara was unlacing her stays to accommodate the growing bump, Frances was already preparing for her lying-in period.

A fifth and final son – born at Great Marlborough Street on 22 May 1730 – was the only Byron sibling whose name was not etched onto Newstead itself. The family's recent efforts in courting favour had clearly reaped rewards: the baby's godparents were Scroop Egerton, Duke of Bridgewater (William's brother-in-law), Sophia, Duchess of Kent (William's sister-in-law and Frances's cousin) and – remarkably – King George II. Some newspapers even reported that the new monarch performed the baptism, and 'named him *George*', after himself.[14] (He certainly gave a gift of 110 ounces of gilt plate worth £65, around £7,500 in modern currency.) Having evidently struck up a friendship with the king, their favour at court seemed secure. If little Isabella was disappointed in hopes of finally having a sister, she might have been consoled by the arrival of another cousin – Sophia Trevanion – on 8 July. Sophia's baptism held two weeks later at St Margaret's, the old church nestled next to Westminster Abbey, was the last for either family. The Byron and Trevanion nurseries – which would be linked again in adulthood – were complete.

By the time of baby George's arrival his three eldest siblings, aged between six and eight, were already being shaped for polite society. Dark-haired Isabella was growing into a miniature of her mother, and fidgeted in restricting dresses, stays and petticoats. Both William and John had made the symbolic passage into adulthood that was being 'breeched' – most boys swapped the cotton shifts worn by all infants for boys' breeches at the age of five or six. It was unfamiliar and uncomfortable at first, but generally a moment of pride. The nursery, of course, remained a scene of childish things: screams and scuffles, scolding nursemaids, teething toys and the building blocks, hobby horses and picture books that made up the paraphernalia of upper-class play. Here the children jostled for their places in their own sibling hierarchy, forging the relationships that would provide the basis for their long lives. (It is perhaps here that William, if his character in adulthood is any indication, became used to getting his way.)

Keeping a brood of six healthy presented a challenge, and thoughts of the endless litany of illnesses that threatened fragile young lives were never far away. While the baby was almost certainly breastfed by a trusted nursemaid (aristocratic mothers at this time were, for the most part, distinctly hands-off in this respect), if they came down with minor complaints Frances would swiftly be able to administer the oils, herbs and spices of her inherited home-made remedies. They might have been one of the families to place trust in the new and pioneering inoculation against smallpox, though having a father approaching sixty may have steered them towards more old-fashioned medicine.

Though the day-to-day practicalities of raising a child – in all its messy, unseemly chaos – were more properly dealt with by servants, their parents were responsible for cultivating their minds. The prevailing wisdom about education maintained that children were to be considered 'as white paper or wax to be moulded and fash-ioned', making these early years crucial in determining a child's character, interests and abilities.[15] Physical discipline was acceptable, especially if the child's disposition seemed to require it. Before they reached an age for formal tutoring, the children went to church and became familiar with the teachings of the family chaplain, and were perhaps exposed to the moralising ballads and poems that constituted children's literature. Both girls and boys were encouraged to learn from touch, smell and sight, and explore the qualities of herbs, trees, metals and minerals.

The contrast between the bustle of Westminster and the serenity of Newstead – with its waterfalls, wildlife and seasonal cloaks of snowdrops, bilberries and yellow gorse – provided a useful intro-duction to both the natural world and urban living. As children of the aristocracy, the young Byrons were also obliged to learn how to speak, behave and present themselves in a manner appropriate to their social position. In their earliest years they were taught the rudiments of politeness – 'that when you answer *Yes* or *No*, you must always add *Madam* or *Sir*, &c.' – and were gradually introduced to the various branches of intellectual life.[16] (One parenting guide of 1721 declared that children should be given 'the relish, as much as possible, for the pleasures of the mind; such as conversation, news,

history, and some kinds of sports, which require industry and attention, and contain something instructive'.[17]) As their learning
progressed, their father's library offered glimpses into new worlds of
knowledge, and visiting tutors – usually older, respectable gentlemen
– taught them the rudiments of reading, writing and arithmetic
(with the happy secondary consequence of polishing away any
uncouth habits picked up from the servants).

Exposure to society provided valuable opportunities to widen
their vocabulary and observe the rules of the adult world – it was
perhaps here that little William developed his lifelong tendency for
posturing and his thirst for praise. They might be allowed some
missteps in childhood, but as adults an inappropriate comment or
peculiar outfit could instantly mark them out as vulgar or absurd.
'If from your position in life, you are destined to pass it among
those, who are called fashionable,' Isabella herself later cautioned, it
was necessary to 'arm yourself with a strong preparation of reason
and resolution'.[18] Negotiating the so-called beau monde was as much
a performance as it was a pleasure, but with earls, dukes and royals
as godparents – their mother never failed to mention that 'I have
the honour to be well known to the King' when seeking favours
– the children were beginning life on an excellent footing.[19]

Here, Isabella's education took a different path from that of her
brothers. She was eight years old when her youngest brother was
born, and facing a decade of training for the mission of her young
life: matrimony. (Her parents were perhaps already compiling mental
lists of eligible bachelors.) Though his finances were stable it was
unlikely that Lord Byron could tempt a potential son-in-law with
an especially substantial dowry, so they were relying largely on
whatever charms Isabella herself managed to cultivate. In case she
did not grow to be considered a 'beauty' – perhaps they glanced
nervously at the mole beneath her lip – it was crucial to demonstrate
the requisite accomplishments and social graces to make up for it.
Etiquette guides laid down a seemingly endless list of rules. Young
ladies should behave with modesty. They should not laugh too much.
They should not slouch, or dance with unbecoming enthusiasm, or
contradict gentlemen in conversation. Even where girls were
instructed that learning was more important than obsessing over

their appearance, they were warned that it was improper to flaunt it. 'Silence always becomes a young lady,' wrote the Marchioness de Lambert, who otherwise championed cultivating the intellect, 'the greatest prudence lies in speaking little'.[20]

In reality, however, a girl's education was not only coloured by but at the mercy of the personalities and priorities of her parents – especially her mother. Even decades later it was remarked that girls 'are taught what their parents or guardians judge is necessary or useful for them to learn, and they are taught nothing else'.[21] Isabella may have been reflecting on her own childhood when she later wrote that female education 'sometimes accustomed the mind to credulity, from the pleasure that the marvellous then afforded'.[22] That she grew to be impulsive, flirtatious and too eager to indulge the longings of her heart, she is more likely to have owed to the influence of her young mother than her conscientious father.

At eight, Isabella was just the right age to commence her social education, where a 'variety of good company' was rightly supposed to be 'of more use in forming a gracious manner from the ages of seven to fourteen than seven years after that'.[23] The most valuable opportunities for learning came with a rap at the door. She watched and listened as dazzling visitors were swept in to take tea or coffee and admire the house, and was occasionally brought before the company to practise her manners or display her accomplishments. Less illustrious visitors were more likely to be received with groans. Tutors. Though she shared some studies with her brothers – she needed to be literate enough to display sense in conversation, and master arithmetic in order to manage household accounts – Isabella's lessons were designed to render her interesting, attractive and graceful: dancing, sketching, singing and languages (she certainly had French and some Latin as a young woman). She took to art and music – inheriting the personal passions of her parents – and somewhere in this girlhood also blossomed a lifelong interest in the natural world.

Though the boys were encouraged to learn modern languages, the arts and how to dance (clumsy feet would not win the heart of an heiress), countless other opportunities opened up before them. Physical pursuits, such as horse-riding and shooting, had the benefit of eroding any lingering effeminate 'softness', an unfortunate symptom of being brought up by nursemaids. (William and John certainly inherited their father's passion for the hunt.) Unlike Isabella, they might read their father's books on military history, politics and geography with an eye to one day making their own mark on public life or exploring those distant lands themselves, if they wished. While their sister was polished for the marriage market, for them the country's top schools beckoned, at whatever age their parents deemed appropriate and for however long they wished to pay. Through interactions with their parents, servants, tutors and superior families they learned their place in the world: that William would inherit, and the four younger brothers might expect to take up roles in the military, politics or the clergy. That their aristocratic birth set them apart – somewhat indefinably but indisputably – from the scrawny, dirty-kneed children they saw running about the streets of Westminster.

In the spring of 1731, as the older boys contemplated the prospect of entering school, the routine of study and social calls was shattered with a new arrival: fever. Seven-year-old John and five-year-old Charles were confined to their beds – soaked in sweat, whimpering, their pulses racing – and the other children were ushered away. A creeping dread settled on the household as the physician was called. Long hours passed and no improvement; maids waited on them, sat up with them, attempted to cool them; windows were kept closed to keep out foul air. They might have been treated with cordials of common herbs, but if the fever was considered inflammatory the medical professionals would have encouraged opening their veins and draining blood to reduce the excessive 'heat' of their small bodies. Long, agonising days, and still no change. The household fell into prayer. They could only wait for the fevers either to break, or take their boys. On 16 May, a few weeks after his fifth birthday, little Charles's breathing grew increasingly shallow and eventually stopped.

Amid their grief, a mire of administration – medical bills and funeral arrangements – as John remained in a delirium. His brother's tiny coffin was privately interred at St James's church and the family shuffled back into the daylight – the rector had four more burials that day, three of them children. John remained 'at the point of Death'.[24] A vigilant watch was kept, and his days passed in a painful blur as the rest of the household made their pleas and promises to God. Finally, just over a week after the death of his brother, John opened his eyes and fixed his gaze more clearly on something – a face, perhaps, or a picture on the wall. He was out of danger. By the end of the month the *Daily Advertiser* declared that John was 'in a fair way of Recovery'.[25] It was the first of his many displays of remarkable resilience in the face of death.

The family spent the summer in mourning, and Lord and Lady Byron decided it was time to dispatch the older boys to Westminster School. It was a conventional but not uncontested choice, at a time when the relative merits of public education or private tuition were hotly debated among the fashionable classes. The lessons at the prestigious boys' schools – Eton, Westminster, Harrow and Winchester – focused on the ancient languages, in which a gentleman must be proficient if he wished to excel. Packing his son off to Westminster at around the same time, Lord Chesterfield advised him to 'mind your Greek particularly, for to know Greek very well is to be really learned: there is no great credit in knowing Latin, for everybody knows it'.[26]

But public education was intended to instil confidence and character as much as verbs and vocabulary, and it provided a boy with an invaluable opportunity to forge friendships that could serve him well for the rest of his life. Thrust into an ungentle world, students were forced to cut the apron strings of boyhood and were trained up to be the next generation of public figures. On the other hand, some parents feared – not without reason – that launching their impressionable boys into such an environment could be distressing and even dangerous. At best, new starters would be robbed of any lingering innocent ideas by the swaggering older boys; at worst, they were removed from the relative safety of their homes and voluntarily delivered into a potential breeding ground for disease. It was not an experience that suited those of a disposition 'where there was any gentleness', and many hated it.[27]

'If you don't let me come home, I die', wrote one suffering seven-year-old to his mother from Westminster, desperate to be rescued. 'I am all over ink, and my fine clothes have been spoilt – I have been tost in a blanket, and seen a ghost.'[28] In adulthood the poet William Cowper, a schoolmate of youngest brother George a few years later, declared somewhat bitterly that parents choose public schooling 'only because they want to get rid of their Little ones and know not where else to dispose of them'.[29]

The Byrons found some middle ground in choosing Westminster School, which was sufficiently distinguished but also within two miles of their own house – the boys may even have foregone the usual course of boarding during term time and returned to Great Marlborough Street outside of classes. In February 1732 nine-year-old William and eight-year-old John, the latter clearly recovered from his early brush with death, were dispatched there together and plunged into a boisterous crush of some 300 other pupils. They may, like their near contemporary Philip Stanhope, have been advised by their parents to be on their guard against picking up 'ill-bred, and disgusting habits' such as 'scratching yourself, putting your fingers in your mouth, nose, and ears'.[30] (Though his father Lord Chesterfield believed it to be the best place to teach a boy to 'shift for himself and bustle in the world', he had to concede that Westminster School specifically was also 'undoubtedly, the seat of illiberal manners and brutal behaviour'.)[31] Perhaps more taxing was the monotony of lessons: shuffling into cold classrooms, commencing and concluding with Latin prayers, staring at grammar books and hoping not to be picked for an impromptu test on the previous day's work. Happily for the boys, their headmaster, Dr Nichol, was renowned for his relatively benevolent reign, generally sparing the rod and relying instead on instilling a sense of honour in his pupils. Unfortunately, such sympathy could not be counted on among the students.

As the sons of a peer, the Byron boys may have felt some advantage when it came to finding their place in the pecking order. Either way, it was best to show one's mettle from the first day. John was later credited with having quickly established a reputation for physical prowess, throwing himself into boxing matches with his schoolfellows and emerging as 'champion of his form'.[32] (Though this dubious early history loses credibility somewhat with the false claim that he was eventually expelled after a sexual encounter with the girl who cleaned his bedchamber.) However well they adjusted to their new circumstances, reports of their early weeks must have met with their parents' satisfaction, as seven-year-old Richard was packed off to join them in June.

As their juvenile years passed in seasonal cycles of study and improvement – curtseys, bows, country summers and city winters – the five remaining siblings nurtured their individual talents and interests. Young William and John asked eager questions about riding and shooting, and perhaps about their uncle William's seafaring missions; Isabella and Richard sketched copies of Rubens and Rembrandts. As they learned, played and made mistakes – exercising all the naivety and optimism of those Isabella later called 'young persons, unacquainted with the vicissitudes of fortune' – their parents continued to dabble in public life.[33] While she was pregnant with George their mother had become one of the very first 'Ladys of Charity' to lend her name in support of a proposed Foundling Hospital in the city, and she followed the campaign for royal approval with interest. (This pioneering campaign, which aimed to take in abandoned or impoverished infants, was a bold choice – its critics declared that such kindness would simply encourage vice among the lower classes.)

Frances may simply have wished to ally herself with a fashionable cause, or perhaps hoped to distract herself from the fact that the years had taken their toll. Though she was only just in her thirties, when her father's friend Lord Strafford spotted her in town he barely recognised her. 'I do not wonder you should not know her', replied her father somewhat unfeelingly, 'for I hardly recollect her myself. What with children and an old husband she has quite lost her youth.'[34] It was probably lost on the children, to whom a mother will always seem something of a relic, whatever her age. Frances's sorrows were compounded with the death of her 'intrepid, gentle' brother Captain William Berkeley while commanding a voyage between Africa and Barbados.[35] He was just thirty-three. If his adventurous career had already inspired his nephews with ideas of a life at sea, his grave at the bottom of the ocean was a stark warning of its dangers.

In recent years their father – now approaching his mid sixties – had been increasingly active in politics. Drawn under the wing of his Whig patron the Duke of Newcastle, his attendance at Parliament had risen to a dizzying height of thirty-eight per cent in 1731 (perhaps in recognition of the royal blessing bestowed upon his baby boy) and had since settled at around thirty-four per cent. If it nagged at him that he was relying on a diminishing set of old allies, he was not sufficiently moved to cultivate new ones, though his deteriorating health increasingly confined him to Great Marlborough Street. He had grown old – to his children he must have seemed positively ancient.

'I do hereby give and bequeath'

Lord Byron passed the Christmas season of 1734 struggling with such a persistent and aggressive illness that the newspapers declared 'his Life was despaired of'.[36] It cast an unflattering light over his financial circumstances. An improvement in the spring prompted a flurry of letters to the Duke of Newcastle about the pensions promised to him by the late king (now in arrears to the tune of £2,000). 'It's but a bad excuse,' he wrote from Newstead, 'because I've no other friend left (about Court) but yr Grace'.[37]

When he relapsed during the whirl of November birthdays – Isabella, already fourteen! – the lawyers were called. His will, which had been drawn up after the death of his daughter Frances a decade earlier, prioritised preserving his estates for his dynasty over releasing immediate funds for those he left behind. His 'dear wife' was to be allowed 'all her Jewells and other Ornaments of her Person', plus a sum of £500 for her personal use.[38] Along with her father Lord Berkeley, she was appointed a co-guardian of the children and given control of the family assets until their son William turned twenty-one – providing she did not remarry. (The clause protected his fortune from the potential meddling of any new husband.) Any future sales or resettlements of the family lands would need to be agreed by the incumbent heirs. While he had originally stipulated that 'my sons shall continue with my wife till they be fit to put to school', another worrying bout of illness in December 1735 prompted him to appoint his trusted chaplain to assist with both the guardianship of the children and the management of the Nottinghamshire estates. (He perhaps did not entirely trust his father-in-law to exert himself on their behalf, or his young wife to take care of Newstead.) Legalities settled, he took a carriage away from the grime of London to the health-giving spa at Bath.

As their father slipped in and out of danger, life continued for the siblings. Isabella focused on her accomplishments, enjoying the hours spent sketching copies of grand, unreachable landscapes and avidly reading – she later declared that embracing books and her faith in early life was 'laying up a treasure for the latter part of it'.[39] After three years at Westminster School, Richard had been brought back home to continue his education with his sister – perhaps he had proved too sensitive for the boisterous environment (certainly his talents seemed to lie in quieter, more reflective pursuits).

Among their tutors was the esteemed artist and drawing master Joseph Goupy, who was an associate of their father's old favourites Tillemans and Dahl, and fashionable enough to have both taught the royal family and developed gout. The serenity of Great Marlborough Street was sporadically shattered by the return of William and John, with tales of scholastic misdeeds or new arrivals among their classmates – their Nottinghamshire neighbours, the two Chaworth boys, twelve-year-old Patricius and nine-year-old William, enrolled at the school in February 1736. (Little did they know then how tragically the two families would be entwined in their adulthood.)

Their mother, perhaps increasingly sensitive about her disappearing beauty, fell into talks with up-and-coming artist William Hogarth and commissioned a new portrait. She did not wish to be portrayed as a doting mother or dutiful wife to an old, ailing lord, but as a smiling and self-assured baroness. The painting captured a serene Frances in a cream satin gown and gloves, her hair modestly tucked into a white cap. She drips with jewellery: as well as a matching pearl choker necklace and earrings, she wears a ring on the little finger of her left hand. A scrappy terrier plays about her feet. It is not the pose of a woman concerned about the future, or even about the fact that her husband is lying on his deathbed.

In late July 1736 London was boiling over with anger and fear. A small explosion of gunpowder filled Westminster Hall with 'noise, flame and smoak' and left behind a scattering of seditious pamphlets.[40]

The Irish neighbourhoods in the east were targeted by resentful mobs – discontent about cheaper immigrant labourers 'stealing' English jobs had escalated into riots and shootings. Coffee-house waitresses caught snatches of conversation about uncertain alliances in Europe and recent sightings in Bermuda of a sea-monster with the tail of a fish and the torso of a raven-haired youth. The children's attention might have been caught by the news that the vicious highwayman known as 'Turpin the Butcher' had evaded capture yet again.

At Newstead, far from all of this, William, 4th Lord Byron struggled to keep up his spirits. He had travelled to the Abbey – presumably with at least some of his family – for a final summer. It was his master-piece. The house was not finished, exactly, but undeniably elevated to new heights of beauty. Visitors fell into raptures.

'We were yesterday at Lord Byron's, a Glorious fine park & a fine old house' – 'A fine library joins to the gallery and in it is a most noble collection of books' – 'In front of the house there is a fine cascade, that tumbles over about 30 steps' – 'I saw every Thing in the Neighbourhood worth looking at; but what pleased me most was Lord Byron's Abbey upon the Forest'.[41]

In the sixteen years since his marriage to Frances, he had also accomplished the second major project of his later life: his dynasty had been secured. His five surviving children had already made their own mark on Newstead. Isabella's bedchamber was a cheerful ray of yellow, with plaid curtains and tapestries livening up the walls. In the boys' room were feather beds draped in red, a scattering of old prints and a model of a ship. This success must have been some consolation as the apothecary, physician and surgeon hovered gravely at his bedside, dispensing advice and pain relief as other, more familiar, faces worked respectfully about him. His steward Mr Marks, Tom and John the footmen, Sarah the maid – all passed long, difficult nights 'sitting up with my Lord in his illness', but it only tightened its grip.[42]

Having spent the best part of two years intermittently incapacitated by bad health, William, 4th Lord Byron finally died at Newstead on Sunday, 8 August 1736, leaving Frances a widow at thirty-three. Four days later mourners assembled in black as he was interred in the Byron family vault at Hucknall church, and the *London Evening Post* printed a careless obituary that misnamed his daughter 'Arabella' and revived little Charles, who had been dead for six years.[43] Other notices more accurately recalled his history – some conquering ancestors, an old position in the royal household, a wife dead of smallpox, a family wiped out – but no heroic deeds to inspire national grief. His lasting legacy was for his family alone: Newstead Abbey.

The five fatherless siblings found themselves in a kind of limbo. Their bright gowns and suits were put away – the death of a parent usually required a child to wear mourning clothes for a full year. Some of their father's trinkets had been distributed among the younger siblings as a token of remembrance for him. John was allowed a treasure: his pocket watch. Though thirteen-year-old William – now 5th Lord Byron – took up the mantle as head of the family, there were seven years until he could legally assume control of its estates and fortune. Isabella, on the cusp of adulthood, would remain under his legal protection until she found a husband. Twelve-year-old John may have already set his sights on a life at sea, following in the footsteps of his ill-fated uncle. Richard, established more comfortably back at home, practised his painting and little George was only just of the age to be proudly graduating to breeches.

The will was read and at first it seemed conventional, if prudent. Jewels for Frances, plus the use of the London house as long as she remained unmarried. The estates, furniture and works of art to his eldest son, and set sums of money for his younger children. But in reality it left them with a restricted income – word quickly spread that William had 'very little to live upon while his Mother lives who is a very young widdow'. 'Lady Byron I am sure will do nothing that is disagreeable,' wrote one of the Duke of Newcastle's agents, with a hint of uncertainty, 'consistent with ye care she owes her family which wants all the assurance she can possible [*sic*] give them'.[44] At Great Marlborough Street, Frances surveyed the assets under her guardianship to ascertain what could be converted into cash. She made lists of those who owed her late husband money, and – on the advice of her family – planned to apply to the king for an annual pension of £500 on her son's behalf. Newcastle heard from his concerned local agents about her plans for her son's greatest asset,

Newstead. Frances's lack of affection for the place seems to have been common knowledge – when Lady North later visited the estate she remarked, 'I am amased [*sic*] how my L[ad]y could hate it so much.'[45] She certainly didn't waste time in attempting to dispose of it. By October, letters flew from Nottingham with the news, 'Newstead, the Seat of ye late Lord Biron is to be let'.[46]

With their father's sisters by now both dead – cutting them adrift from any other Byron relatives – and their mother already picking at the family estate, the young siblings were left to consider how to carve their own paths in the world.

2

Devil's Wood

The 'Wicked Lord', 1736–70

In thy once smiling garden, the hemlock and thistle
Have choked up the rose, which late bloom'd in the way.

On Leaving Newstead Abbey

1785

*There are devils lurking in the shades of Newstead: two grimacing statues
with horns and cloven hooves, half hidden in a small, wild copse. They
prompt whispers in nearby villages. Why would a gentleman keep such
fearful creatures? Has his lordship turned his back on God? Suspicions unfurl
in the blinking candlelight of rural taverns, as tenants idle at their fences
and prattling laundrywomen hang out their smocks. They nod at each other
darkly, knowingly, as a dreadful litany of long-buried, half-imagined former
crimes are resurrected in whispers – and then exaggerate or invent new ones
for good measure. Alcohol-fuelled orgies in the castle on the hill. His lovely
wife, brutally hurled into the Abbey lake and left to drown. An actress
abducted and threats of suicide if she did not give herself to him. And the
blood on his hands! He had once shot a postilion dead and silenced the
witnesses with money. And poor Mr Chaworth – his own kinsman – whose
mother's hopes that he might finally settle down were shattered on a cold
January day twenty years ago, when the news came that Lord Byron had
driven his sword through her son's belly. 'It has been said, and repeatedly
said', cried one hastily published account of the affair, 'that homicide and
murder are innate passions of his heart.'[1] And now, satanic worship? The
so-called devils gaze on.*

As an old man, William must occasionally think of those sickly, uncertain days at the Tower of London – of sleeping a stone's throw from the green where the heads of adulterous queens had rolled free of their necks in the time of Henry VIII. Perhaps he recalls the sight of his sword – now hanging grimly above his bed – as it was in the dim candlelight, dripping with blood. Perhaps he thinks nothing of it at all. He shambles about his rooms at the Abbey, spits rage about snooping neighbours and calls to Joe for more port, for his snuffbox, for more wood on the dying fire. He cannot escape his history, and the black seal already set on his reputation will long outlive him. He will ever be the 'Wicked Lord' – the 'Devil Byron'.

In September 1814, almost three decades later, twenty-six-year-old George, 6th Lord Byron, walks awkwardly towards the wood where 'th'oud laird's devils' cavort.[2] It is his last day with his beloved half-sister. They wander to a curious-looking tree, with two trunks that appear to spring from one root. A pretty metaphor. He takes a knife and carves their names into the bark: BYRON and AUGUSTA M. L. Augusta, the only surviving child of Jack Byron's first marriage, has in recent years become George's friend, his confidante – and his lover. Her newborn daughter Libby is most likely his own – certainly they suspect so.

After a childhood apart the couple have bonded over a shared sense of humour and a macabre fascination with their ancestors. George never met their notorious great-uncle but has soaked up his history – by now a fixed catalogue of villainies. One of George's schoolfellows from Harrow, the future prime minister, Robert Peel, later described how the 5th Lord's example had inspired his young heir, 'particularly on the subject of duelling, which he accustomed himself to connect with the name of Byron'.[3] (The idea also provided a comfort when meditating revenge on bullying older boys.) George has followed in William's privileged footsteps, taking up his seat in the House of Lords and walking the hall where he was tried for murder. The tales of his fond servant Old Joe coloured his vision of the man and he gloried in the inheritance – even signing off one letter as 'the *wicked* George Ld. B.'

The day is drawing on – it's time to leave. George and Augusta make their way back to the Abbey, leaving the mouldering statues grinning stupidly behind them. The spot will be known to history as 'Devil's Wood'.

~

With the death of his father in the summer of 1736, William graduated from well-heeled schoolboy to 5th Baron Byron of Rochdale at the age of just thirteen. His dominions were set down in ink and unrolled before him. In Rochdale, Lancashire – the seat of the barony – acres of mills, moors, mines and quarries. A vast stretch of Nottinghamshire: Newstead, Piper's Meadow, Limekiln Woods, Bulwell Forge and more. Unsurprisingly, Westminster School could not hold him for long. After the formality of passing – merely signing his name in Latin – he left in the early weeks of 1737.

His mother's plans had continued apace. Valuations were made of the Byron assets, from pictures and linens to farming equipment and estate produce. Bills were paid: the grocer, the bookseller, the hairdresser, repairs to the harpsichord. She fielded enquiries from potential tenants for Newstead, to the dismay of concerned neighbours. 'He will destroy the peace of the country which at present is extreamly disposed to be quiet', one complained, upon hearing she was in talks with Jacobite sympathiser Watkin Williams.[4] 'The Prospect of such a Neighbour has giv'n us some Alarm,' piped up another, 'as his Character is well known for a plentifull Way of Living [and] for a Spirit of Intrigue'.[5] Only when the queen herself intervened did Frances relent, eventually agreeing to turn down 'very advantageous offers' on the Duke of Newcastle's promises of future favour for her son.[6]

Somewhere amid this flurry of activity, William's path was settled. It was an unconventional choice. There were to be no long days causing mischief at one of the universities, Parisian coffee houses or Venetian masquerades. No jostling about Swiss towns with a language dictionary in his pocket and a fussing tutor trailing behind. It was not the usual tour of the European courts that would 'Make a Man of him', but a life at sea. He would sleep in a rough wooden cabin and take orders on a creaking deck, with brisk winds lashing his face. Quite how much involvement William had in the decision is unclear. The Berkeley family certainly had a long tradition of naval service – and Frances was never shy of calling in a favour. Unchecked by an artistic father who would surely have steered him towards the sort of European tour that had shaped his own life, William may have been easily persuaded by a schoolboy enthusiasm for adventure. Whatever the case, it was a potentially perilous time to enlist. As the globe was charted and newly discovered territories 'claimed' by rival European powers, simmering tensions between Britain and Spain were threatening to boil over into war.

In March 1737, fourteen-year-old William stepped aboard the HMS *Falkland* as a newly minted midshipman (the commission apparently bought rather than earned through the requisite years of service). It was a weather-beaten fourth-rate ship, captained by the debauched and unpopular Fitzroy Henry Lee. (William's title presumably shielded him from the worst of his temper.) Captain Lee was the governor of the Canadian province of Newfoundland – under British control since the reign of Elizabeth I – where they were bound on a voyage of business and trade. They sailed for Canada in June, spent the late summer overseeing the fishing season, and returned to trade in Europe for the winter. William spent his fifteenth birthday cruising towards the Spanish city of Cádiz, and within the year they anchored back at Sheerness. No hostile encounters, no heroic deeds performed – but how many other teenage lords could claim to have crossed the Atlantic and seen the things he had seen?

The newspapers attempted to follow his unusual career but gave wildly contradictory accounts: he simultaneously sailed for the Mediterranean and for Guinea; he served Captains Osborn and Symonds; according to one report he embarked 'for his travels' to Italy as soon as he left the *Falkland* and another gave him command of his own twenty-gun ship. When Britain finally declared war on Spain in October 1739 his military service was applauded – at a patriotic procession through the marketplace at Rochdale, the people cried 'Success to His Majesty's Fleet and Arms, and Prosperity to the Woollen Manufactories of Great Britain, and to the Right Honourable Lord Byron, Lord of this Manner [*sic*], and now on Board the Fleet under the Command of Admiral Norris'.

If Frances felt any pangs of concern at having her two eldest boys drawn into war – John had also been dispatched to sea – she distracted herself admirably with business at Great Marlborough Street. With no sign of the duke's promised favours, a tenant was finally drafted in at the Abbey until William came of age, and trees were toppled and sold to raise cash. She quietly disposed of more valuables: a gold watch, 'Some old Rings' belonging to her late husband, their chariot. A sale of furniture and paintings raised over £600.

Eventually, however, she took a step too far. Still only in her mid thirties – and having first dutifully married the man picked out by her father – it is hardly surprising that she should be tempted by another chance at happiness. After almost four years a widow she succumbed to the flattering attentions of Sir Thomas Hay, a Scottish widower in his forties and a captain in the Royal Scots Greys cavalry regiment. By June 1740 she was seeking favours on his behalf, describing him as 'a Man of Family Estate & Interest, [who] has served many years extreamly well'.[7] Though nothing survives to indicate if it was a love match, Frances must have been optimistic about their chances – her late husband's will was clear about what she stood to lose. In remarrying she forfeited the London townhouse, her guardianship of the children – all legally 'infants' until they reached the age of twenty-one – and control of the Byron estates. Perhaps she simply hoped it would pass by unchallenged. Frances and Sir Thomas married in Chelsea on 31 July, presumably in the company of some of her children, even if William himself was out of the country as reported.

Her eldest son was not best pleased at this encroachment on his estate during his absence. At seventeen, resenting his powerless status as a minor, he seems to have suspected Frances of pillaging his inheritance – he eventually accused her outright of withholding information about his financial affairs. With his elderly grandfather's refusal to assume his responsibilities as William's guardian, his uncle John Berkeley stepped up. He decided to embroil his mother in a lawsuit – the beginning of a long and enthusiastic career of legal battles – and by October the matter wound its way into court. Questions were raised. What exactly had been sold? What had been done with the proceeds? The courts declared in his favour just before his eighteenth birthday, and Frances was ordered to compile a full inventory of the Byron assets – from toothpicks to Titians, chimneypieces to chamber-pots – and account for all outgoings since her late husband's death. The newlyweds retreated to the Hays' seat at Alderston in East Lothian, and the children's grandfather Lord Berkeley's death shortly afterwards confirmed their uncle's role as their guardian and mentor (a kindness from which they would continue to benefit for another thirty years).

In the summer of 1741, family rifts were overshadowed by worrying news from abroad. Following rumours that Spain and France had formed an alliance, the inhabitants of English coastal towns nervously eyed the horizon for hostile French ships. Naval defeats in the Caribbean had been expensive and humiliating. In the Pacific, Commodore Anson's expedition to 'annoy the Spanish' – which had carried away their brother John – had been crippled by scurvy and storms. Perhaps emboldened by his legal victory at home, William re-entered the fray, acquiring a prestigious commission as a lieutenant aboard the new flagship of the Channel fleet. HMS *Victory* was the perfect home for a swaggering youth hoping to prove his courage: this first-rate, 100-gun vessel was adorned with elaborate carvings of Britannia in a chariot drawn by sea-lions and, according to one newspaper, was 'not to be match'd in the Universe'. William came aboard at Spithead on 24 June with his servant Robert Watkinson, and presented himself to his superiors. (Among them was the renowned Admiral Norris, a no-nonsense officer in his late sixties and – perhaps not insignificantly – an acquaintance of his uncle John, now Lord Berkeley.) After days hauling provisions about under brooding, thunderous skies, their orders finally came: to cruise the Spanish coasts and provoke the enemy to action.

Over the next two months at sea William doubtless hoped to fill his empty logbook with thrilling deeds of war, but the reality fell rather short. It was a muster of the mundane: deaths ('Francis Harvey departed this Life at 5'), geographical observations ('grey sand with shells') and sightings of other vessels.[8] A sailor was lashed for theft. A boy fell overboard. When visibility was low, the beating of drums floated through grey fog. The Articles of War were read and firearms exercises practised. Other crews pulled alongside to boast of plundering 'a great deal of Riches' from Spanish chapels, but there was no sign of battle.

The *Victory* returned to England without fanfare and William lost the taste for navy life – though he remained on the ship's books for another eighteen months he only reported for duty to request further leave. When he was finally discharged in February 1743, his captain merely scrawled a note to confirm that he had 'Complyed with the Gen[era]l printed Instructions Given' to allow him to claim his pay. With that, his decidedly undramatic navy career was over. It certainly paled in comparison to that of his brother. Some two years previously John's ship had disappeared into a storm in the Pacific, while William had been preparing to set sail aboard his flagship and Isabella embarked on her own mission – twirling her fans and fluttering her eyelashes at admiring suitors. William had been the first of the brothers to enlist. He had been to sea first, seen Canada and Spain first and sailed on a British flagship – but any brotherly rivalry seemed to have ended in tragedy.

When news of the disappearance reached England, though they continued to scrutinise the newspapers and question friends at the Admiralty, the Byrons made a fair show of carrying on. Isabella's efforts to attract a husband proved a resounding success – in marrying an earl she became a *countess* and suddenly outranked them all. William enjoyed a summer at the races, successfully lining his pockets at Reading and enjoying a ball at Burford. Eventually, the tenant's lease on Newstead expired and the most significant date of his life loomed. On 5 November 1743, as England blazed with its Gunpowder Treason celebrations, he finally turned twenty-one. With (most of) the restrictions of his father's will lifted, his life as a lord could finally begin.

'Little to boast of but a title, and an agreeable face'

William had spent years impatiently waiting for this moment, and during his extended periods of shore leave he had had plenty of leisure time in which to polish his baron's coronet. Like his mother he made the charitable (and by now fashionable) statement of pledging his support for the Foundling Hospital, which had finally received royal approval in 1739. By the age of twenty he was descending on the racetracks, competing against a horde of other wealthy young gentlemen 'of modish dissipation'. Three weeks after his birthday he made his first appearance amid the sea of white wigs and crimson robes at the House of Lords, along with four other new peers waiting to take their oaths. George II himself was briefly present, for just long enough to declare his animosity towards Spain, before leaving them to cover the pressing issues of the day – in the event, how to commemorate the birth of a prince, and complaints about the hackney carriages blocking up Westminster. It was a fittingly soporific beginning to William's apathetic political career.

He was similarly easily distracted from excelling in what his sister termed 'the theatre of the great world'. As a baron he may have lolled at the less distinguished end of the aristocratic hierarchy, but there was plenty of scope for improving his family's fortunes, as his father had. Any man with ambition needed to be skilled at both commanding respect and currying favour, and to be considered a man of honour he had to look and act the part – a gentleman's reputation was forged through social position, patronage and masterly performance. The first, he had the good fortune to have acquired through birth. The second received a boost from the favour of his benevolent uncle, and – if his promises were kept – his father's friend, the Duke of Newcastle. The third point was the hurdle at which William fell.

William had grown to be an attractive young man – one female acquaintance with no reason to flatter him allowed that, if little else, he could boast 'an agreeable face'.[9] Though he was a keen sportsman, he did not have a commanding physical presence. By his own admission he spoke with a rather 'low' voice and one employee later dubbed him 'a poor little lord', because he was 'not only poor, but of low stature'.[10] Nonetheless, the older ladies of Nottinghamshire were charmed by his politeness, and his stories of life at sea may have offered some novelty in courtly circles. In his early twenties he was thrown into an influential and thoroughly debauched circle through his initiation into the Grand Lodge of Freemasons and his insatiable enthusiasm for rural sports. Embracing at least half of one writer's opinion that the lives of all noble peers were 'divided between the brothel and the horse-course', he became a fixture of the races, both spectating and taking the reins, and the associated glittering social events.[11] Many names recurred in these matches – the Duke of Kingston, Captain Vernon, the debauched Earls of March and Ferrers – and some, at least, spilled into his personal life.

While William was (for now) enthusiastically keeping up the performance of affluent living, he felt no desire to seek any meaningful position in politics or society, and so failed to earn the admiration of the world at large. Within two months the novelty of attending the House of Lords had worn off, and he settled into a lifelong habit of turning up just a handful of times each year. He was judged by the company he kept, including that of one particular (sadly unnamed) earl identified only as 'a disgrace to nobility'.[12] He frequented Woodifield's tavern in Covent Garden – the less refined part of town – and dashed off inebriated notes to women who had taken his fancy. At the Devil Tavern on Fleet Street he indulged in elaborately ritualised, raucous drinking sessions with his masonic brethren.

The London he had known as a child was transformed: where it had once widened innocent eyes with prettily sculpted parks and gleaming buildings it now twinkled with the promise of headier pleasures. The theatre districts, hedonistic gentlemen's clubs, private gambling parties and houses of 'liquor and lust' within a stone's throw of Great Marlborough Street competed for his attention. With the summer heat (and the subsequent noxious smells) the genteel world dispersed into the country before returning in the winter with a more urgent taste for society and a new batch of wagers: twenty guineas on who could tempt the richest heiress into marriage, five guineas on who had the most attractive wig (to be decided by a special assembly), fifty guineas on which old lords might die this parliamentary season. As she nursed hopes that her own son William might settle down with a nice wife, the young Lord Byron's neighbour Mrs Chaworth commented mournfully, 'young Men are wild as ye World gos now'.[13]

While he revelled in the trappings of high life, William struggled to stop the mask from slipping when things did not go his way. He was perfectly able to act graciously when attempting to gain favour – both with political superiors and with women – but quickly turned bitter and childish if his requests or advances were refused. Like most men of his rank he felt a sense of entitlement when it came to the female sex, and laboured under the conflicting burdens of a large ego twinned with a gnawing insecurity about the opinions of others. If the name of one of his prized racehorses – Why Do You Slight Me? – is anything to go by, by the age of twenty-one he was already brooding churlishly over the accusations and insults laid at his door. (In later years charges of cowardice riled him the most, and they were levelled at him frequently.) On his return from sea, he had been faced with hordes of gentlemen more used to the etiquette of court, more powerful orators in the House, and more dashing officers in candlelit assembly rooms. Where, then, was his place?

As he tried to find it, dark national events cast a shadow over society's pleasures. As William was preparing for his twenty-second birthday, news came that the magnificent *Victory* – which he had left just eighteen months previously – had been wrecked in a storm, and his former captain and crewmates lay drowned at the bottom of the Channel. 'Not one man saved', wrote his country neighbour Gertrude Savile solemnly in her diary, including all the 'Noblemen and Gentleman's sons, Volanteers'.[14] He could so easily have counted among them. (If he mourned, he found solace on the racetracks of Newmarket, Nottingham and Lichfield.)

Elsewhere, the war on the Continent was twisting almost all of Europe into turmoil, and as political alliances shifted Britain's hostilities with Spain were overshadowed by engagements with France on the fields of Flanders. William invested in a new racehorse and played frivolously at the card-table. There were whispers of a new rebellion in the north. After three brooding decades abroad the descendants of the deposed Stuart dynasty were rekindling their campaign, hoping to unite the Highland clans under the banner of their 'King over the Water' and take back the thrones of both Scotland and England. Leading the charge, Charles Edward Stuart – 'the Young Pretender' or 'Bonnie Prince Charlie', depending on your sympathies – landed on Scottish shores in July 1745. The Jacobites were sharpening their swords, and England nervously called to arms.

In that summer of '45 the Byron siblings were scattered. After a trip to Carlisle, Isabella and her husband returned home to Yorkshire to hear that as the Stuarts assembled their army in the north, Spanish troops were ranging against the west coast and 'a body of French forces shall be sent up the Thames'.[15] Midshipman John Byron remained far beyond the reach of news, though tales of his remarkable survival against all the odds had begun to trickle back to England. Richard and George persevered with their respective studies at Oxford and Westminster with varying degrees of enthusiasm.

Their forty-two-year-old mother fretted on two fronts: first, as her husband was drawn into the conflict on the Continent, and second, as the Jacobites won their first battle at Prestonpans – just a few miles from her home at Alderston – and proceeded to capture Edinburgh. Could they really invade England? She was not alone in her fears. Unsettled, the northern counties emptied and voluntary anti-Jacobite regiments sprang up across the country. In Nottinghamshire the Duke of Kingston raised his own troop of cavalry and William saw another chance to prove his critics wrong. He pledged £210, lent his sword and added his name to the top of the regiment's declaration condemning this 'horrid and unnatural Rebellion formed and carried on by Papists and other wicked and traiterous Persons'.[16] By October 1745 he was assigned the rank of captain and a troop of men.

They awaited their orders as the rebels crossed the border and took Carlisle, and continued to wait as the enemy began to march south. The Jacobite army had already arrived in Lancaster by the time Kingston's Regiment of Light Horse finally assembled in Nottingham on 24 November, with light weaponry slung at their sides and curved swords clattering against their horses. They rode north to meet their illustrious general, the Duke of Cumberland, and after a week of travelling set up a station in the marketplace at Manchester. In early December relieved reports came that the rebels, after getting as far as Derby, had reconsidered their prospects of success and were on the retreat – Kingston's men finally received their orders. They were to retake vulnerable Carlisle and pursue the retreating force into Scotland.

Far from evoking the anticipated thrill of the hunt, it was a grim and muddy slog towards the border. The men grabbed snatches of sleep in fields 'in very cold and wet weather' and commandeered horses and supplies as they went (though Kingston himself had 'a tent-bedstead, which was put up by his beleaguered valet every night during the march').[17] They reached Preston just four hours after the rebels had left. William met with Kingston in his coach to discuss strategy; a skirmish with rebels at Clifton left a number of their men dead. After finally reaching Carlisle they spent Christmas laying siege to the small Jacobite garrison left defending it, barraging them with gunfire for nine days before the white flag was raised. The English troops felt at once triumphant and a little deflated at the lack of action. 'I wish I could have blooded the soldiers with these Villains,' grouched the Duke of Cumberland.[18] William's men moved on.

They rode for weeks – past Newcastle and Edinburgh, towards the bleak, beautiful Highlands – and arrived at their Aberdeen headquarters in early March 1746. The city filled with shivering soldiers, their red coats conspicuous against the heavy snow: some 12,000 men, preparing for the final battle. Weeks passed by in repetitive training exercises as they waited for the weather to improve. Some of Kingston's men put down a small party attempting to rescue their rebel prisoners. London was told that spirits were high, that Cumberland had 'the Hearts of the whole Soldiery', and that the troops were impatient to meet the rebels.[19] Scouting parties were sent out and plans were laid: secure the vulnerable Fort William and bring the Jacobites to action. But as Kingston's regiment prepared to head west and into combat, a certain twenty-three-year-old captain ducked out.

On 20 March – after weeks traipsing across the north, some minor skirmishes and a siege – William submitted his resignation to the headquarters in Aberdeen. His reason was vague: he was, he announced, 'by the present Situation of my private Affairs, absolutely obliged to be from the Army'.[20] Perhaps it was his brother's appearance in London after almost five years away, and four assumed lost; perhaps the prospect of imminent battle did not appeal. Whatever the case, his disappearance just before the action can't have improved the reputation for 'want of Courage' that already dogged him by his mid twenties.[21] Perhaps he simply took an excuse to run.

As his men advanced on Inverness, William was reunited with his long-lost brother at Isabella's fireside in Soho Square. While he made polite conversation about the cold weather in the north, the Kingstons were thick in gore on the fields of Culloden. With that pivotal battle on 16 April 1746 the Jacobite dream was extinguished. The murder of the wounded Jacobite soldiers during the battle's aftermath, in which the Kingstons played no small part, only haunted Scotland – the man *they* dubbed 'Cumberland the Butcher' was England's fearless hero. In York, William's old neighbour Mrs Chaworth had 'a house full' to celebrate his triumph, and in London one theatre staged a concert entitled 'The BATTLE near CULLODEN-HOUSE, Under the Command of our Glorious HERO, the DUKE of CUMBERLAND', to which revellers were admitted for the price of a pint of wine.[22] William had squandered his chance to share in the victory.

He had not, however, been completely idle – in the midst of this national fever William had been conducting negotiations of a more personal nature. At the age of twenty-three – still relatively young – he was thinking of taking a wife. Upper-class courtship in the 1740s remained largely pragmatic in motivation and highly mannered in nature, though the seeds were being sown for a shift towards more romantic ideals. The experience was not to everyone's taste. 'Shall I go to an unknown gentleman's house,' complained one reluctant suitor to his father in 1743, 'be introduced to the family and particularly to Miss, saunter about till one or two of the clock, go to dinner, drink the Ladies health, after dinner drink some glasses with the man of the house, then take my leave and trott home, like a fool, as I went, with my finger in my mouth?'[23]

William did not have to contend with his parents' wishes, at least, and lost no time in seeking a bride. Perhaps he had been spotted visiting a particular house on Albemarle Street, or had made boastful hints about his conquest. Either way, his choice was no secret. 'We hear a Treaty of Marriage is concluded, and will speedily be consummated,' declared one newspaper in July, 'between the Right Hon. the Lord Byron and Miss Shaw.'[24]

Elizabeth Shaw was a fair-haired teenage heiress later described as 'the best and loveliest of her sex'.[25] Crucially, as the only surviving child of a long-dead Norfolk landowner she would command a considerable estate once she turned twenty-one – the newspapers grew more effusive about her beauty as her fortune was exaggerated to an enormous £70,000. It was certainly sufficient to attract the attentions of numerous noblemen, including Viscount Coke (who outranked William). Miss Shaw was said to have a sweet temper, perhaps inherited from her parents: her mother was known for her piety and her late father was lamented as a 'Gentleman of Extensive Charity and Benevolence'.[26] Tedious legalities aside – Elizabeth's age meant that any marriage settlement required approval by an Act of Parliament – she seemed the perfect, pliable acquisition for an aristocrat looking to boost his fortune.

At White's club, gentlemen placed their bets: 100 guineas that William and Elizabeth would marry within two years; 50 guineas on six months. But while William had clearly impressed the Shaws there were other matters to attend to. First, the dregs of the Jacobite rebellion were being hauled before the courts and William was summoned to give his verdict. While the vast majority were commoners, four of the prisoners were lords and had to be tried by their peers in Westminster Hall. William sat through each case, drinking in the pomp and parade, bellowing with the rest of his fellow peers at the doomed men in the dock and finally adding his voice to the unanimous call for death: 'Guilty, upon my Honour.' Second, he was quite content indulging his usual regime of merriment – though one party was cut short when one of his coachmen 'tumbled out of the Box in ye Courtyard, they say Dead Drunk'.[27] Third, amid the tedium of matrimonial bargaining another woman had caught his eye.

During the winter of 1746, his last as a bachelor, William was drawn – again and again – to the theatre. He was not inspired with a sudden appreciation for the dramatic form, but that of the nineteen-year-old woman on stage: George Anne Bellamy. She was a dark-haired Irish actress much admired for her fine figure and 'soft' but alluringly confident manner (quite the opposite of his genteel, elfin heiress). When William resolved to seek her out off stage – how could she refuse a lord? – he was shocked to find himself rebuffed with the claim that she 'would not listen to any proposals but marriage and a coach'.[28] He persisted. By Miss Bellamy's account his vanity was sorely wounded by this display of 'feigned virtue' coming from an actress – actresses were stereotypically thought to be generous with their favours – and his gracious manner quickly deteriorated into anger.

Whatever the truth of William's relationship with Irish actress George Anne Bellamy, he later appeared in her scurrilous autobiography as a wheedling villain.

Feeling insulted, he meditated revenge. One Sunday in January, she later claimed, an 'ignoble Earl' with whom William associated bundled her into his coach and warned darkly that she 'had better consent to make his friend Lord Byron happy'.[29] She should be *grateful* for his attentions, she was told, and, indeed, once he was married to the wealthy Miss Shaw, she would be handsomely provided for! When Miss Bellamy's brother arrived at Great Marlborough Street to confront him, William asserted 'upon his honour' that he had no knowledge of any abduction, nor had he even seen her that day.

Though William's version of events is lost to history, his subsequent infidelities and displays of ill-tempered, entitled behaviour lend some credibility to Bellamy's account. Even if he did not resort to orchestrating an abduction, there was clearly bad blood between them. William escaped any real consequences – his interrogator trusted the word of a baron over that of his sister, and the matter was dropped. On picking up the story, the gossip columns were helpfully eager to imply that Miss Bellamy had merely been a willing party in a sordid elopement. Having apparently taught the unyielding actress a lesson – though still smarting over the rejection – he turned back to his heiress.

'They do not consider they are to live all their Days together'

On the evening of 28 March 1747 the wedding guests gathered at Mrs Shaw's house on Albemarle Street. Among the groom's party, dressed in their finest, were Isabella and her husband Lord Carlisle, his uncle Lord Berkeley and some Nottinghamshire neighbours including Mrs Chaworth and young Mr Montagu. In the bride's party were her mother, her Aunt Lawson and her 'uncle' Charles Gould (a distant cousin and close friend). William drew up in a stylish horse-drawn carriage with liveried servants, wearing a brown velvet suit richly embroidered with gold and decked in 'extream fine' lace.[30] Nineteen-year-old Elizabeth, in a stunning gown of white, gold and silver, took his hand and they made their pledges to one another.

After a short journey to Great Marlborough Street, Elizabeth changed into a dark dress shimmering with silver and the celebrations continued. Here the merry party of around forty-five guests played at cards and devoured a lavish meal laid on by the Carlisles (who received an honourable mention for the cherries costing a guinea per dozen). The coaches didn't reel into the crisp London air until midnight. William's bride was praised by his well-wishers – namely Mrs Chaworth, who loved a wedding – for her prudence, 'extream good character' and 'fine person'.[31] But others viewed the match with foreboding. From her lonely home at Rufford, Gertrude Savile commemorated Elizabeth's blunder in her diary: 'Lord Byron who has a sad charicter in everything and particularly most shamefull cowardess and with little or no Estate, marry'd to Miss Shaw, a very great fortune, pretty and agreable in her person.'[32] It seemed a dramatic mismatch.

The early weeks of their married life were eventful, for better or worse. Their courtship had played out as the common Jacobite rebels were hanged, drawn and quartered before baying crowds, and the wedding announcements were drowned out by reports of the notorious Lord Lovat's grisly beheading. For better, they 'kiss'd hands' at the courts of King George II and of his offspring the Prince of Wales and Princess Amelia. For worse, in April their home was targeted by a female-led mob that descended on a handful of affluent Westminster homes and began 'very grosly [sic] abusing and insulting' those they found there.[33]

At the end of the month, amid cheers and toasts from his friends, William was elected and installed as the Grand Master of the Freemasons at Draper's Hall at the age of just twenty-four. It was a huge honour, and the ceremony – featuring an elaborate feast in decadent surroundings, a throne, magnificent jewels and the receiving of 'the Homage of the Brethren' – couldn't have been better calculated to massage William's ego. Two weeks later the Lodge boisterously filled the front rows of Drury Lane Theatre, demanding that William's musical requests were incorporated into the performance. With his marriage settled, the actress crept back into his thoughts.

Within days he had procured a prominent box for Miss Bellamy's new play, the tragedy *Theodosius*, and (she later claimed) unnerved her with his unwavering gaze throughout. At the end of the performance he renewed his pursuit. 'Well, Rich,' he bellowed at the stage manager, 'I am come to take away your Athenais!' Though unsuccessful, according to Bellamy's account, he returned the next night and was overheard threatening violence backstage: 'I will speak to her to night, or I will shoot my [self]' – the words of a man not used to being denied.[34] He tried to force his way into her sedan chair, and hounded her with letters swearing to pursue her until she married. His schemes were only dropped on receiving a note from her friend James Quin, an intimidatingly stout actor with a notorious temper, warning that if he continued neither 'his title or cowardice' would protect him. Another attack on his honour. William was happy to push his suit on a vulnerable woman, but not a known duellist. 'Men in general are rascals,' Quin warned – William seemed to have proved him right.

While William seemed determined to break his marriage vows,

Elizabeth acted the part of model wife. Miss Bellamy herself wrote of the new Lady Byron generously donating to one of her charitable benefits (she perhaps hoped to lay rumour to bed). More importantly, just five months into the marriage, Elizabeth fell pregnant. It may have been some comfort that she endured this daunting experience at the same time as her sister-in-law Isabella, and the summer of 1748 saw the two births announced together. An heir, finally, for the Carlisles, and for the Byrons at first attempt: baby William was born at Great Marlborough Street on 7 June and baptised shortly afterwards with Lord Berkeley, Lord Carlisle and Mrs Shaw standing as godparents. Tragically, their joy was cut short before he reached his first birthday. The baby died the following spring during a visit to Besthorpe Hall – Elizabeth's family home in Norfolk – and was buried at the local church. It was their first, bitter experience of a sorrow that would become all too familiar, though the fact that Elizabeth was already carrying their second child may have provided some small consolation.

They returned to Great Marlborough Street for the winter – though William didn't see fit to attend Parliament once, or attend any masonic meetings despite being their nominal leader – and their second son was born on 27 October 1749, as the *London Evening Post* proclaimed, 'to the great Joy of that Noble Family'.[35] He was also named William. A new heir, and a second hope.

Contrary to the expectation of disgruntled neighbours, as they came to learn each other's interests and foibles the young Lord and Lady Byron did find happiness together at first. Both relished the glitz of town and the advantages of the country, where they enjoyed an elevated social status and the opportunity to drop the masquerade a little. They were both inclined to youthful exuberance (the less diplomatic termed it childishness) and were accustomed to affluent living to the point of carelessness. They were not shy of displaying their feelings and became quite wrapped up in themselves, encouraging each other in their less admirable qualities. 'I can't say they behave as I cou'd wish, have done some very rude things indeed,' wrote Mrs Chaworth after visiting Newstead, 'but her Ladyship is quite young, & he is turnd Child too (I can't help saying so)'.[36] 'The fond fitt seems to take up all their hours, & one is tired of hearing of itt,' she continued; 'they do not consider they are to live all their Days together'.

Despite his roving eye William seems to have kept up the charm, and the couple certainly kept up their matrimonial responsibilities – their first daughter, Henrietta Diana Byron, was born during their summer at Newstead in 1751. As Elizabeth recovered, William celebrated at the races in Newmarket and Chipping Norton. In truth, he was better suited to life as a big fish in a small pond. In London, Lord and Lady Byron blended into an endless parade of glamorous couples, outshone by those richer and outplayed by those more skilled at navigating the rules of court. In Nottinghamshire – aided by a new and long-awaited source of income – they set themselves up 'in near Style' and sparkled among the brightest.[37]

Elizabeth had turned twenty-one in March 1749, at which her fortune became the property of her husband. With the extra funds at his disposal William immediately set about putting his own stamp on Newstead. Ahead of the trend, he had rather more 'Gothick', theatrical tastes than his father. Where the 4th Lord had kept a rowing boat, the 5th Lord made plans for a working fleet of ships. Where his father aspired to elegance and order, William preferred a wilder aesthetic. 'The Park is very rugged', noted an admiring Lady Northumberland after one visit, 'with such a profusion of Bilberry on the ground as is amazing, a great number of Oaks sprung from Old Stools all very wild'.[38]

Almost immediately he installed a 'large and pretty Gothic tower' – later known as 'Folly Castle' – with four guns and room to entertain guests on the hill overlooking the upper lake.[39] The splendid view also took in a new stone battery with crenellations and parapets that snaked along the bank facing the house. In the Abbey itself William added to his father's art collection with skill and discernment, moving visitors to praise both the works themselves and 'the taste that is shewn in placing them'.[40] He constantly sought new acquisitions – at one Covent Garden auction he couldn't resist forking out £43 on a seventeenth-century Dutch painting depicting a courtesan 'ogling & offering drink to a young man'.[41] In the Grand Hall he evoked the spirit of the hunt with paintings of lions, tigers and stags as well as 'several stuff'd Beasts and the heads of others with wonderful

Horns brought home by Commodore Byron' as gifts from his travels around the world.[42] The rooms used for receiving guests were scattered with Rubens, Raphaels, Titians and Holbeins. For her private dressing room Elizabeth chose an amusing painting of grotesque monkeys and a 'very fine' portrait of Mary, Queen of Scots (perhaps feeling some affinity with her alleged marital stoicism).[43] William's tastes were predictably titillating – in his private quarters he opted for a sleepy-eyed portrait of royal mistress Nell Gwyn and a woman undressing by Titian. Most splendid of all was the Great Dining Hall, filled with his distinguished ancestors and now a scattering of Elizabeth's, suspended in gilt frames. In pride of place were companion portraits of the couple themselves – 'Wm the pres[en]t Ld Byron' and 'Wife of the pres[en]t Ld Byron & Daur of Shaw' – by Thomas Hudson, one of the most illustrious painters of the 1750s (they are now sadly lost, with no further description given).[44]

William passed his summer days in the country hunting, fishing, attending the races and rattling about the country roads 'on a very prity post-chaise'.[45] He dabbled in watercolours, took snuff from gilt boxes and added to his library: new poetry, biographies of men he admired (including Peter the Great and notable Freemasons) and annual racing records (no doubt enjoying seeing his victories in print). They took trips into the north, subscribing to the new Assembly Rooms at York, visiting Isabella at Castle Howard and taking trips to the sea at Scarborough. At home they socialised with the same families his parents had known thirty years earlier – the Chaworths, the Molyneuxes, the Montagus – and grew particularly close to William's younger brother George (another racing enthusiast) and his new young wife Frances, who lived at Nottingham.

Elizabeth cultivated her own female circle, making a fast friend in a Miss Elizabeth Booth, and enchanting teenage sisters Anne and Julia Molyneux, who fell into raptures over her fashionable dresses and shoes. 'To day we went to Newstead very Graciously received', one noted in her diary after a visit to the Abbey; 'Lady Byron gave me a Gown silver necklace & earrings'.[46] (The same noted that Lord Byron had an unsociable tendency to skip chapel.) By some accounts they were considered just as favourably by their tenants, and on at least one occasion William was thanked for his 'kind allowance of some poor cottagers what was not able to pay their rents as particulars'.[47] 'The Byrons were always reckoned good Landlords,' recalled the granddaughter of another years later, 'friendly with their tenants and willing to redress grievances.'[48] William was not entirely without charity, when his coffers were full.

But even in these early days they were not universally liked. William's quickness to take offence and inability to hold his tongue invited continual petty disputes with local gentlemen. His most regular antagonist was William Chaworth (who had inherited Annesley Hall after his elder brother contracted smallpox at school) – they were intermittently 'upon so bad terms' that old Mrs Chaworth felt unable to visit Newstead.[49] His performance of remorse could be perfectly convincing, but when bested he became tetchy. After a tiff with the Montagu family he wheedled into their good graces by attending them at breakfast. When the Duke of Newcastle quashed his deceptive attempts to seize a pack of hounds from another landowner, he slipped from flattery to whining: 'I think it is very hard on me [that] I can't have ye Hounds on such easy termes'.[50] His grudges festered. 'He told me He did not care who had the Hounds,' he moaned years later.[51]

Even Elizabeth occasionally relaxed her manners too far, offending Mrs Chaworth during one visit by sweeping in late, with seven dogs fussing around her and looking 'as Dirtey as the very Ground'.[52] When Mrs Shaw (who was uncharitably described as looking like 'a good sort of a House keeper') offered her apologies, Elizabeth *pshaw*ed them away with the declaration, 'Lord Madam, say nothing about it, for anything is good enough for the country!' William made matters worse by striding in looking 'soure and thin', and refusing to engage in conversation. Their neighbour left vowing never to repeat the visit, complaining, 'they seem to Study to [be] rude, to every body'. But, quarrels were quieted. When Chaworth asked to cross Byron's lands during a fox hunt William allowed it, and Mrs Chaworth was soon gushing to a friend, 'I always thought when you was once acquainted wth Lord Byrons politeness & good Qualitys you wou'd value the Acquaintance, & I don't doubt but Lady Byron is as deserveing.'[53]

While enjoying the high life at Newstead, William was criticised for ignoring his responsibilities in London. As well as routinely failing to turn up for parliamentary sessions he had neglected to attend a single masonic meeting in almost five years (on some occasions, even when he was in town). Many at the Lodge were unimpressed by his token gestures from afar and not only complained that he was causing a rift but threatened to illegally elect a new Grand Master. When he eventually reappeared at the Devil Tavern in March 1752, the minutes tactfully recorded that he was received 'with great Demonstrations of Joy' and explained his absence with the spurious excuse that he 'had been abroad for several Years'.[54] He eventually buckled to the pressure and stepped down, having forged a reputation as a man who enjoyed the pomp of the Craft but displayed no commitment to it, or his responsibilities.

It was no great loss. William had become consumed by his grand project – the Newstead model navy – and in September 1753 the day finally came. 'Ye ships came to day to Newstead,' wrote one of the Molyneux girls, a few days after noting excitedly that there were two new puppies at the estate.[55] (With the girls unable to resist the temptation of such delights, the family called by the following day.) The following year, incredulous reports of another 25-ton vessel being wheeled overland from the River Trent, on a carriage drawn by twenty-seven horses, even made the American newspapers. 'Every body & every Lettr tels me of the improvements at Newstead,' wrote Mrs Chaworth, 'always a charming place'.[56] Isabella's friend Lady Northumberland was charmed by the wildness of the grounds as well as the 'great variety of Boats and Ships'.[57]

New faces were also brought to the estate: a 'sailor', Barnard White, and a young 'sailor boy' named Joe Murray were hired to maintain and crew the ships.[58] Employed in the less weather-beaten but undoubtedly the more difficult to navigate role of steward was William Daws, who took on responsibility for the general management of the estates, including collecting rents and dealing with debts. Both the loyal Murray and Daws would be torn from the Newstead estate only by death many decades later. William's theatrical vision was a timely and increasingly fashionable one. In May 1756 a new war was declared with France, inspiring a patriotic taste for all things nautical. While his brother prepared to sail into the conflict, Lord Byron delighted guests with the boom and splash of cannon fire in the middle of Sherwood Forest. He was, finally, admiral of his own fleet.

While William indulged in his fantasies of military heroics, his wife had another daughter: Caroline was born at Great Marlborough Street on 17 January 1755. Though Lady Byron was only twenty-five, the child was their last. Perhaps four births had taken their toll on Elizabeth's body; perhaps the couple no longer shared a bed. Certainly, there was good reason for the 'fond fitt' of their early marriage to have worn off.

William had been steadily dismantling her ancestral estates ever since she came of age. He had immediately disposed of £4,000 and a few years later sold Besthorpe Hall (but not before plundering or selling the furniture, some of which belonged to Mrs Shaw, she complained, 'without delivering or accounting to me for any part of it').[59] Daws tried to balance the books by negotiating loans from banks, moneylenders and his lordship's friends, but he was fighting against a flood. Neither William or Elizabeth had good financial sense and they were incapable of controlling their spending – Isabella branded them 'ye worst managers I ever saw'.[60] Renovations at Newstead continued. To the south, another lake. Fences built, leaky roofs fixed, cannon-blasted ships repaired. If any particularly rare or costly artwork caught William's eye, he 'would order horses to his Carriage and set out at a Moments Notice to purchase them', Joe Murray later remembered, while bills were left unpaid for years.[61] Daws struggled to hold back a tide of disgruntled tradesmen, only to be summoned to London to bring 'cash for the jewels'.[62] By 1755 Elizabeth's inheritance was virtually exhausted, and William marked the birth of his second daughter by losing money at Epsom and then Burford races.

By now any efforts to maintain a semblance of fidelity to his wife had gone up in smoke: the novelty of marriage had long worn off and his wandering eye had become an outright embarrassment. Whiffs of scandal preceded them on a visit to the Carlisles in Yorkshire, where Isabella observed her brother's indiscretions at a ball. 'I let nothing escape me . . . I never saw any thing more Cavalier', she wrote with amusement to her friend Lady Grey; 'he really is so devoted to the Charms of Mrs Reynardson that it was with difficulty I could keep up my Gravity, nor could I have conquer'd myself to the end of the Scene, had I been Eyewitness

to the aff[e]ct[ionat]e salute he gave her at the Ball door at parting'.[63]
(Her hypocrisy in chastising his shameless flirtations would undoubtedly have raised eyebrows.) He was also linked to the beautiful Mrs
Scrimshire, a fellow horse lover and one half of a married couple
with whom they associated – it was later reported that they '*burned*
for each other'.[64] With William totally disregarding even a pretence
of matrimonial loyalty, gossip was inescapable. 'We have many Storys
at York, of their parting, & my Lord going to Live abroad,' lamented
Mrs Chaworth, adding, 'hope a falce report.'[65] The honeymoon
period was unequivocally over.

A decade in, and the only things causing ripples in the couple's
otherwise stagnant marriage were death and financial misery. In the
autumn of 1756 the Newstead accounts bore the cost of burying his
brother George's newborn twin boys in the family vault at Hucknall
(and, later, a baby niece). A year later their mother Frances died in
Scotland aged fifty-four, leaving what little she had to her second
husband. When William was called to the sensational murder trial
of Lord Ferrers in April 1760 – he had brutally shot and killed a
steward – he stood shoulder to shoulder with the rest of his peers
and sentenced his former racing companion to death: 'Guilty, upon
my Honour.' Just weeks later, their nine-year-old daughter Henrietta
fell into a 'violent Fever' at Great Marlborough Street and died
shortly afterwards.[66] Two of their four children lost. They buried
her on 3 June at St James's church, where her little uncle Charles
had been laid to rest a generation earlier.

In the autumn of 1760 the death of the king brought his twenty-
two-year-old grandson to the throne as George III, and the Byrons
prepared for the coronation while still in mourning for their daughter.
Robes, jewels and accessories. The procession, the music – 'Long
live King GEORGE!' – a lavish feast.

Back in black, they returned to their strained domestic life.
Mounting debts forced William to begin cutting down the old oak
woodlands at Newstead, spoiling the estate but raising cash – some
'five thousand pounds worth' according to Horace Walpole.[67] In 1762
Elizabeth's mother died after suffering a 'paralytic disorder', depriving
her of her closest ally and dashing William's hopes of further inheritance from the family.[68] Leaving her 'dearly beloved Daughter' her

choice of jewels and trinkets, Mrs Shaw had stipulated that all remaining assets were to be held in trust for her grandson, young William, and her furniture to her sister Mrs Lawson. 'I think I have a right', she had noted, recalling her son-in-law's plundering of her property at Besthorpe.[69] Their son's departure for Eton School at the age of twelve was another blow for Elizabeth, who clung to their remaining daughter Caroline and her friend Miss Booth for company. When Isabella visited Newstead in the summer of 1763 she wrote with concern to her husband, 'I find Lady Byron grown very thin.'[70]

There was one piece of good news that winter. Amid the scramble to impress the new king, William had secured his first and only post in the royal household: Master of the Royal Staghounds. It was a paid role and aligned perfectly with his interests, requiring the care and maintenance of the king's hunting dogs (he had perhaps bene-fited once again from the influence of Lord Berkeley, now Constable of the Tower of London and a member of the Privy Council). The honour was crowned four months later when the young king visited Newstead with a hunting party for a day of sport around Sherwood Forest. The entertainment was a great success, with numerous gentlemen approaching William 'to pay their Compliments to his Lordship' and the newspapers giving glowing accounts of the huntsmen in royal livery and the 'beautiful Pack of Hounds'.[71] Shortly afterwards William staged a deer hunt at Nottingham racecourse that attracted 'the greatest concourse of Gentlemen ever known on the like occasion'.[72] His talents clearly lay with sports and spectacle rather than the serious pursuits of government.

Despite this minor royal commission and an aptitude for aristo-cratic amusements, the good opinion of his peers continued to elude him. His snatches at military glory had fallen utterly flat, and humili-atingly so in the face of John's adventures. His inability to keep the royal hunting hounds under control exasperated his neighbours – the Duke of Kingston's prized herd of deer had to be destroyed when the dogs ran amok on his estate at Thoresby. 'His Lordship was not much beloved of the Duke, or any of his neighbours', Kingston's valet later remembered, noting that his master avoided events that Byron was attending with the words, 'You will excuse me, you know I do not like his company.'[73] Two decades after Gertrude Savile bemoaned his 'sad charicter in everything', Isabella's friend Horace Walpole called him an 'obscure Lord' and a 'worthless man'.[74]

Creditors had grown wise to his insincerity in money matters, all polite promises in person – *Ask my man Daws, the money shall be ready quite soon* – before disappearing into town. His mother-in-law had used her will to posthumously condemn him for prioritising his pleasures over the needs of his family, and a history of the Freemasons published in 1763 bitterly proclaimed that 'Grand Master *Byron* was very inactive'. During his reign, it claimed, the fraternity was so 'intirely neglected' that it caused a schism between the Lodges.[75]

Even Newstead, for all its elegance, had become shrouded in dark tales. The lavish private quarters of 'Folly Castle' were not merely a secluded retreat for sipping champagne and observing the ships: behind that forbidding oak door William and his dishonourable friends supposedly sank into depravity and staged drink-fuelled orgies. His disregard for his marriage vows sparked tales of domestic violence – an accident in which he sent Miss Booth reeling into the water cascades at Newstead was transformed into a furious attempt to drown his own wife in the Abbey lake.

But it was not until the New Year of 1765 that William cemented his place in history's catalogue of villains. To the titles 'coward' and 'adulterer' he added another that was even worse: *murderer*.

'My Lords, this is my melancholy Story'

On 26 January 1765 ten gentlemen hurried out of the wintry afternoon and into the Star and Garter in Pall Mall, sweeping past Fynmore the innkeeper and going upstairs to their usual room. The Nottinghamshire club – a set of landowners, politicians and gentlemen's sons brought together by their county connections – settled in for their monthly social meeting. William, the only lord in the room, was surrounded by familiar faces flushed with the sudden warmth and the excellent wine, from his twenty-something neighbours Frederick Montagu and Francis Molyneux to the mature and stern-faced Sir Robert Burdett. Three hours passed – *More claret!* – and the toastmaster Mr Hewett introduced a topic that 'often produced agreeable conversation': how landowners might best preserve game on their estates.

The question was taken up with interest. William confidently declared that it was best not to intervene too much, preferring to let nature take its course. William Chaworth loudly disagreed from the other end of the table, and he felt a pang of annoyance. They began bickering over who managed their estates more effectively, and William laid down a bet of £100 – around £10,000 in modern currency – that an acre of his land would boast more game. 'Pen, ink and paper!' called Chaworth, keen to set the challenge in writing.

A snappy exchange about estate boundaries followed, during which William misheard and took offence at an imagined suggestion that their neighbour Sir Charles Sedley owned Bulwell Park (one of his own estates). After waging a persistent, petty interrogation he sulkily hinted that certain lands could be recalled to his family if he wished it. A sharp word from Chaworth silenced him. The conversation moved on but each nursed his own grievance: Chaworth was irritated by Byron's childish inability to listen, and William felt he had been spoken to 'in a slighting and contemptuous Manner'.[76] The exchange hadn't attracted much notice – one attendee called it 'trifling' and another subsequently chatted with William in good humour. They were, after all, a little in liquor.

Stepping into the hallway an hour later, William was confronted by Chaworth who barked – perhaps a little sarcastically – 'Has your Lordship any commands for me?' William replied that he *would* like a few words, and a waiter ushered them into a private room lit only by a dying fire and a flickering candle. What happened next is not entirely clear. William later claimed he had simply asked, 'How am I to take those Words you used above, as an intended Affront from *Charles Sedley*, or yourself?'[77] Chaworth complained that he 'said something very rough'.[78] Either way, Chaworth – a 'strong stout man' with the clear physical advantage – went to close the door and perhaps turned back a little too aggressively.[79] William panicked and yelled *draw!*, unsheathing his sword. Chaworth, 'knowing the Man, imediately [*sic*] (or as quick as he could) whipt out his sword' and lunged towards William's chest, backing him against a table.[80] Stumbling, each thrust simultaneously. William felt a blade strike against his ribs as his opponent tried to grasp the tip of his sword. A groan as he missed – another as the sword pierced Chaworth's belly and ran him straight through. They drew apart, startled, hearts thumping. As the waiter decanted more claret to the guffawing gentlemen upstairs, blood oozed down William's sword and seeped quickly across his opponent's embroidered waistcoat.

'I am afraid I have killed you,' mumbled Chaworth, thinking he had also hit his mark. William pulled on the bell for help, still clutching the darkly dripping sword. His first thought was of himself. 'You might thank yourself for what has happened,' he declared. 'I suppose you took me for a coward, but by God I have as much courage as any man in England.'[81] He looked down to see an eight-inch tear in his waistcoat, but no wound. Mr Fynmore blustered in to find the two men hunched by the fireplace, Chaworth leaning heavily on William's shoulders. 'Get some help immediately'.

Chaworth collapsed into a chair. As the blood pooled around his feet the Nottinghamshire gentlemen piled in, quickly followed by a surgeon. The same questions over and over. Chaworth talked of a 'peculiar Kind of Faintness and Sinking' that convinced him he was done for. William convinced himself that he had acted like a gentleman of honour, that the situation had made it impossible to 'avoid putting my hand to my sword'.[82] He remained in the tavern until Chaworth was fit to be taken home, before returning to Great Marlborough Street with his clothes torn and covered in blood. (One account reported that he told Elizabeth he had caught them on a nail, or a chariot door.) As William laid his head to his pillow, across the city Chaworth hurriedly revised his will to provide for his mistress and their unborn child.

With the morning, news. Chaworth was dead. The enormity of the situation began to sink in. The law frowned upon duelling, of course, but wasn't this more like a panicked scuffle? On the other hand, he had to concede that both had considered it a matter of honour, that William had issued a challenge. With his opponent dead, the details were inconsequential. If it was deemed murder, he faced the death penalty.

Reports of the fatal dispute shot across the country. The accuracy of Horace Walpole's report – that Byron had challenged Chaworth and escaped with a tear to his coat – was quickly lost in the feverish accounts hurried to print. The rumours were inevitably coloured by the fact that the dead man was well liked and William was not. In one rare sympathetic account, Chaworth had issued the challenge, ignoring Byron's request to discuss the matter in the morning when tempers had cooled. More often, Chaworth was entirely defenceless. Some refused to believe that the cowardly Byron could have conquered his much stronger opponent in a fair fight. 'Mr Chaworth was a much more popular man than his adversary,' wrote a Miss Townshend, 'which I believe has inclined people to give hints which they had not much foundation for.'[83] Others believed that William's poor reputation had caused the trouble in the first place. 'Ld Byron has been a good deal refl[ected] on for want of Courage which might probably induce Mr Chaworth [to] treat his Lordship very Cavilierly', speculated one gentleman. 'I think he did fright when he did go out to make a duel stand for something and push home, had he been worsted he w[oul]d have been more reflected on.'[84] Walpole was certainly struck with the public's lust for blood: 'the bitterness of the world against him has been great, and the stories they have revived or invented to load him, very grievous'.[85]

William did not help his case by promptly disappearing off to Boulogne, seemingly joining his friends Lord March and Gilly Williams, to escape the publicity and – according to one newspaper – 'wait till his Friends on this Side of the Water shall inform him how Matters are likely to turn out'.[86] He was hiding – but couldn't do so forever. 'I suppose Byron has told you himself that he intends to surrender as soon as Westminster Hall is ready for him', Williams wrote to England. 'It will be a show for a day to the Queen and the foreign ministers,' he continued optimistically, 'but cannot possibly be attended with any ill consequences to the culprit.'[87] When the warrant was issued for William's arrest on 13 February he (eventually) stood by his word, arriving in London two weeks later to surrender himself at the House of Lords in 'seeming Composure, and dressed in mourning'.[88] He was conveyed to the Tower.

What was for the vast majority an unbearable experience was for William rendered perfectly tolerable by his rank (and the fact that his uncle John was still the Constable). He was at liberty to wander the grounds if accompanied by a guard, and the physician was called when he fell ill with 'a slight Cold'.[89] One of the warders relinquished his residence on the parade and his rooms – though 'closely Barricaded both within and without' – were comfortable enough to accommodate visitors.[90] 'A great many of the Nobility' were seen paying their visits, with friends joining him for dinner three times a week.[91] 'How different from the recluse life we have known passed within those walls', commented his friend Gilly Williams.[92] While Elizabeth and the children discreetly made their way to the Tower, the newspapers alternately declared that Lady Byron was heavily pregnant or dead. Sir William Musgrave, Isabella's new husband and a trained lawyer, helped him to compile lists of witnesses to attest to his usual 'friendly Intercourse and Civility' with Chaworth, on the assumption that the prosecution would drag up their long, quarrelsome history: among others, his brothers George and John (perhaps he had already fallen out with Richard), Musgrave himself, some lawyers and clergymen linked to Isabella's family and his teenage nephew Lord Carlisle.[93] The date of his trial was set for 16 April.

Though his friends remained confident there was 'not the least chance of either hempen or silken halter in Byron's process' – referring to the fanciful idea that aristocrats were entitled to a silk noose – public excitement grew ferocious.[94] The trial of a peer was a rare spectacle, and Gilly Williams predicted that this one would be attended 'as if the fate of the country depended upon it'.[95] Gentlemen placed 'great bets' on the outcome.[96] The prisoner perhaps cast a thought to the lords he had himself condemned to death. It was only five years since he had declared Lord Ferrers guilty of murder – within days the malefactor had dangled lifelessly before a bloodthirsty crowd at Tyburn. One especially slanderous pamphlet claimed that it had been 'repeatedly said that Lord B— is of a most overbearing, cruel, tyrannical disposition'.[97] Was William, like Ferrers, a violent lunatic?

Gilly Williams's prediction was borne out by the scramble for tickets allocated to peers. The Duke of Ancaster received petitions from prominent magistrates and musicians, and countless requests on behalf of wives, wives' maids and 'very pretty' ladies travelling from the country. While elsewhere proclaiming disdain for such a trifling 'puppet-show', Walpole begged tickets for his friends in Lord

Lincoln's gallery. Rumours of a 'cargo' of French gentlemen visiting expressly for the trial were outed by the newspapers as a foreign ruse to conceal some illicit negotiation. The days ran down. Scaffolding was erected in Westminster Hall, and a military presence requested. Two enterprising parliamentary coffee-house owners secured permission to remain open and take advantage of the extra footfall. As the trial approached, Westminster braced itself for the crowds.

At dawn on 16 April, a company of bleary-eyed soldiers stationed themselves around Westminster Hall with orders to 'prevent any riotous Proceedings' in the long day ahead.[98] By eight o'clock a swell of eager ticket holders assembled at the doors of the House and pickpockets prowled the procession routes. The Earl of Northington, lord high steward, set out in a carriage drawn by six horses fluttering with ribbons, along with a troupe of liveried servants. Across the city William's peers – his jury – donned their robes and descended on Parliament.

Just before nine o'clock William emerged from the warder's apartment dressed in a black suit of mourning and was escorted to a small carriage. Climbing in alongside him were one of his lawyers, the major of the Tower and the gentleman gaoler, with his ceremonial but ominous 'Ax of Death'. It was a slow, winding procession calculated to please the crowds. The carriage was flanked by ten Yeoman Warders and thirty Foot Guards.

Just before ten o'clock the horses were brought to a stop and the stony-faced men filed out. William straightened his suit as they met the Duke of Ancaster and was conveyed into a chamber. His warders shuffled into place along the corridor, lining the way to the bar. After a short wait, he could hear heavy footsteps beyond the locked door. He was required before the court. Silence settled on Westminster Hall as William was marched in behind the gaoler, who pointed the handle of his axe at William's chest. Rows of eyes burned into him as he stepped to the bar and bowed deeply at the gathered lords. They bowed back.

The room was packed. An arched wooden ceiling yawned over a fidgeting mass of velvet suits and tightly gathered skirts. Before him were a scattering of bishops and the peers with whom his fate rested;

further along the hall were the crimson-decked royal boxes and Lord Northington, sitting beneath a canopy. On William's right, his council; on his left, the prosecution. Ranged along the hall on either side, behind, and bearing down above him were benches packed with some 2,000 spectators. His witnesses were somewhere among the throng, though two of those closest to him were noticeably absent: his brother John, recently declared commander-in-chief of the East Indies, who had been at sea for over a year; and his sister Isabella – no stranger to scandal – who had taken refuge with her friend the Duchess of Portland until this particular affair blew over.

Lord Northington opened the proceedings with what Walpole described as his usual 'vulgarness and blunders'.[99] 'Your Lordship is unhappily brought to this Bar to answer a heavy and dreadful Accusation, for you are charged with the Murder of a Fellow Subject.' The clerk addressed him, 'How say you, William Lord Byron, Are you guilty of the Felony and Murder, whereof you stand indicted, or not guilty?' William spoke. 'Not guilty, my Lords.'

As the prosecution gave their summary of the events of 26 January, thirteen witnesses prepared for questioning: six members of the club, Mr Fynmore and two tavern employees, the medical professionals in attendance, Chaworth's lawyer and his uncle Mr Levinz, who attended him in his final hours. Mr Hewett was the first to take his oaths and give his account – a hearty meal, 'Pen and ink!', a pool of blood spreading beneath a chair. Though the snatched memories of the witnesses that followed varied slightly – phrases used, how much alcohol had been consumed – they agreed on the essentials. The room was dimly lit and the dispute was trivial – Chaworth himself died lamenting that the affair could 'have been explained and easily made up'.[100]

The lords chimed in with questions. Had either man taken up his hat, as if intending to leave? Had Byron overheard Chaworth talking ill of him on the stairs? Did Byron relinquish his bloody sword willingly or under duress? William was paraded to and from the bar as ceremony required. Just after five o'clock the Lord Chief Justice adjourned proceedings for the day. William was conveyed to the Tower as the chattering crowd spilled out into the streets to discuss their verdicts.

The next morning a new crowd gawked at the royal boxes, where a flock of curious princes and princesses (the king's siblings) took their seats. The procession entered and Mr Levinz begin a sorrowful but measured testimony of his nephew's final hours – '*Dear Billy, for God's sake, how was this, was it fair?*' . . . '*Good God, that I should be such a Fool as to fight in the Dark*'. He twisted the knife somewhat by mentioning Chaworth's declaration that he preferred to die as 'a Man of Honour' than to be responsible for another man's death. The prisoner had attacked, Levinz concluded, while Chaworth's back was turned. In short, he fought like a coward.

Following a swift cross-examination the Solicitor General gave the concluding speech for the prosecution. 'That he killed him, is a Truth beyond Dispute,' he declared – but this was no accident. It was premeditated murder. The cooling period between the altercation and William's challenge was too long for the fight to have been the mere 'Impulse of a present Passion'. He alluded to William's spiteful self-congratulation as his opponent bled to death – '*as much courage as any man in England*' – as evidence of his motivation: 'some secret Grudge, or an imaginary Necessity of vindicating his Honour, or of satisfying the World of his Courage'.[101] William was painted as scheming, bitter and weak. Throughout the proceedings William had behaved with perfect 'serenity and composure of mind', always appearing suitably 'shocked and mortified'.[102] Hardly the conduct of a madman. The prosecution closed.

Now it was William's chance to speak for himself. He faced the assembled peers. 'My Lords, I shall not call any witnesses,' he stated, having dispensed with his prepared list. 'I have reduced into writing what I have to offer your Lordships; which, as my voice is very low, I am apprehensive of my not being heard by your Lordships, and therefore desire it may be read by the Clerk.'[103]

'Read! Read!' came the booming response.

Absolved of the performance, William relaxed a little as the clerk took up his paper and read out his statement. A hush fell on the room, and benches creaked as spectators strained to hear. His version of events mirrored what had already been heard, but portrayed Chaworth as disrespectful and hot-tempered and himself as a humane estate owner subjected to undeserved abuse. 'I was of a different

Opinion, being for *gentler* measures,' he said of the dispute about dealing with poachers. Chaworth treated him with contempt, insulted his estate management and dredged up generations-old land disputes. He defended himself in a scuffle 'in which I received the first Thrust, at Peril of my own Life'. He convinced many of the spectators. His painstakingly prepared statement was at all times respectful to the deceased and deferential to the jury – perhaps his barrister brother-in-law had a hand in the wording – and he displayed 'unfeigned Sorrow for the Event'.[104] 'My Lords,' the clerk concluded, in William's own words, 'this is my melancholy story.' The House was adjourned and whispers rose to an animated murmur as the lords swept out to deliberate.

William waited under guard outside as the 124 attending lords strode back into the courtroom. One by one they raised their right hand to their chest and gave their verdict. The prisoner was brought in amid a call for silence. 'William Lord Byron,' Northington began, 'the Lords have considered of the charge and Evidence brought against you, and have likewise considered of everything which you have alleged in your defence' – William felt the heavy gaze of a judgemental crowd upon him – 'and upon the whole matter, their Lordships have found you *not* guilty of the murder whereof you stand indicted, but *guilty* of manslaughter.'

A breath of relief. The unanimity had been resounding, with 120 finding him guilty of manslaughter only. Four men cleared him of all charges, perhaps giving some insight into the company he kept: his friend Lord Falmouth, whose wife had visited him in the Tower; Lord Despenser, the now elderly founder of the notoriously debauched Hellfire Club; and Lords Orford and Beaulieu, both of whom were declared 'lunatics' in their later years. William was saved from the gallows. His rank even protected him from the usual punishment for manslaughter – being branded on the hand with a tell-tale *M* – through a sixteenth-century law that allowed him to escape with a fine. Lord Northington declared the proceedings over, ceremonially broke his white staff in two and gave permission for the peers to take their leave. The ordeal was over. William stepped into the Westminster air a free man, at which he 'took a Chair, and proceeded through St. James's-Park to his House'.[105]

If Lord Byron had hoped to emerge from the affair with a new reputation for fearless martial prowess he was sadly mistaken. Some supportive voices battled weakly against the whirlwind of gossip: 'in the Heat of Duelling who can always be collected?' asked one journalist.[106] Notes of congratulation flew in to Daws from agents and tenants: 'give me leave to congratulate you on the happy success of the house of Lords determination on Lord Byrons affairs with Chaworth'.[107] But in general, Chaworth was lamented as 'one of the most benevolent, as well as the bravest of men', and the blot on his own character was now immoveable.[108]

Walpole concluded that the trial had been 'a solemn scene for a worthless man, but whose former faults had given handle to ill nature to represent him as guilty of an event, which truly it had been very difficult for him to avoid.' 'He escaped with life and recovered some portion of honour, if that can comfort him,' he continued, 'after the publicity made of his character, and the misfortune of killing an amiable man'.[109]

In what could have been a fit of gratitude or defiance William attended Parliament an uncharacteristic four times the following week, while conversation began to turn on other things. The king was finally recovering after a worrying bout of illness, and Lord Abergavenny had been caught in a compromising position with a nursery-maid – his furious wife was busy revealing the sordid details to the world.

William immediately settled his thoughts on pleasure. Feeling they both deserved a break from their woes in England, he and Isabella arranged a summer trip to the German town of Spa (now in Belgium) with Lady Byron and three of Isabella's children. It was a perfect retreat. While his wife entertained herself elsewhere he rode out in the morning, played whist in the evening, and joined in the occasional wild boar hunt. When the opportunity arose to purchase a wolf pup he couldn't resist. Isabella was dubious. 'I own when he grows a little bigger, I shall be very loath to trust him', she wrote to her husband, 'tho they have broke his teeth and that he is at present innocent and full of Play and lies in Ldy Byrons lap.'[110] William did not even allow his pleasures to be interrupted by the unfortunate news that, amid a change of government at home, he had lost his position as Master of the Staghounds. 'He bears it very properly,' Isabella wrote, believing him to have 'fallen a sacrifice' to his friendship with a 'Lord H' who had slipped from favour.[111] The careless extravagance of both William and Elizabeth was undimmed by recent events – 'I am sure I could do ye same things at half the Price', Isabella commented – and the arrival of the Scrimshires afforded William an opportunity for equally reckless flirtation.[112]

Their return to England in the autumn of 1765 thrust him back into business. In January the peers were called to vote on measures for quashing the increasingly bothersome 'Riots and Tumults' in the American colonies. New taxes – in particular the recent Stamp Act, which levied a tax on all printed paper documents – had sparked both peaceful petitions to the king and violent protests. William (ultimately on the losing side) voted in favour of maintaining the tax. While dismissing the rights of British subjects overseas, he aggressively railed about preserving his own, having the guns and dogs of stray hunters on his land confiscated and becoming embroiled in legal disputes about his lands in Rochdale.

In a particular low point he dragged the brother of a recently deceased old woman into court on the grounds that her most recent will – which reinstated the brother as beneficiary rather than himself – was invalid. The defendant explained that an old dispute had been healed and the will legitimately amended, 'and so much the said William Lord Byron doth know and in his Conscience believe to be true'.[113] Desperate not to lose out, William insisted that the lady's illness must have 'brought on a Delirium' and that she 'continued delirious and was not during any part of the said time of sound Mind Memory or Understanding sufficient to make any Will'. (As he refused to back down, it took three years for the case to be dismissed.)

Newstead was constantly on his mind and when in London he stayed up late scrawling notes to Daws about gathering hay, fixing guttering and fretting about hard frosts. He somehow extracted another substantial loan from his wife's relative Charles Gould and commissioned a new pleasure boat, offering to pay with venison rather than cash. He continued to splash out at auctions and the horsetrack, arranging mysterious assignations with his steward in the secrecy of the booths at Nottingham races. By now – pressing on through their forties – his less incorrigible friends began to question their frivolous lifestyle. When his old racing partner Lord March went about flaunting a new mistress at Newmarket, Gilly Williams sighed, 'I do not think these frolics go off at our age as they used to do.'[114] But William had no intention of retiring. In fact, his grand scheme for restoring his old, carefree ways was about to come to fruition.

Towards the end of the decade William's debts exceeded £19,000 (the equivalent of over £1.5 million today), and the 'money'd men' Daws customarily approached for loans were politely declining further dealings with his Lordship.[115] Making things worse, his teenage son had embarked on his Grand Tour – William travelled with him as far as Paris, where he stayed for a few weeks – and was paying tribute to his father's influence by promptly racking up debts across Europe.

While he did at least attempt to patch up Newstead, William's other estates were suffering considerably. 'When you was over last you promised me that you would give orders for all necessary repairs to be done,' came a letter from Norfolk, 'but nothing has been done.'[116] Funds were also wanted in Rochdale, where his neglected properties were being used as taverns and brothels. Fortunately, Lord Byron had a plan. His son would turn twenty-one in October 1770, at which point they could legally resettle the inheritance and open up some lands for sale. All he needed was the young man's consent. And, the final card up his sleeve: his son's title. Being the heir to the barony, young William would be a tempting prospect for wealthy families looking to join the ranks of the aristocracy. As plans for a coming-of-age party proceeded apace, his father set about finding a bride to inject some much needed cash into the estate. Young William returned from his Tour in early 1771, and both men intended to celebrate in grand style.

In the months leading up to the event the Abbey and its grounds were primped and preened. Fencing and roofing were repaired and artworks and scientific curiosities displayed to their advantage: here, macabre animal specimens preserved in jars; there, an 'Indian spear' (perhaps picked up on one of John's voyages). The flag of St George fluttered proudly on the miniature forts and a new twenty-one-gun ship was brought overland as the party's spectacular centrepiece.

Adding some dramatic flair, his animals prowled the estate. The German wolf, which had grown to a great size but was 'so tame that it play'd with the Cows, & run about with the dogs', gained a new playmate when John returned from Canada bearing an unusual gift: a Newfoundland dog, 'shaggy, fierce, and almost as large as a two year old heifer'.[117] Invitations were sent out to family, friends and influential connections, indicating that open house would be kept for days.

Coaches soon jolted around the courtyard, their occupants spilling out to gaze at the beautiful ruins of the Abbey, still nestled in a cloak of woodland. Among them were William's three brothers, John, Richard and George, scrutinising the changes to their child-hood home. (Isabella was abroad, having left the country seeking her own excitement.) The Newstead navy put on a spectacular show as they engaged in battle, the boom of cannon reaching the farthest reaches of the county and beyond. Overall there were, as Joe Murray later fondly recalled, 'proud doings at Newstead'.[118] It may have differed from his father's elegant vision, but William's 'Gothicking' of the Abbey had a peculiarly theatrical charm.

The five Byron siblings, by now all in their forties, had produced a considerable brood of cousins. As well as William's two surviving children, there were Isabella's son and four daughters, who enjoyed the highest rank; John's six children, born and raised by the sea; George, settled with a surgeon's daughter in Nottingham, had three; and the newly married clergyman Richard had just welcomed his firstborn. It is probable that the younger generation attended the celebrations as some of the cousins were close – in certain cases their professional and personal lives would soon become somewhat *too* entangled. Had William and John been paying sufficient attention, it is possible that they could have prevented the calamity looming before them.

But William was too busy congratulating himself on securing a bride of suitably large fortune for his son – negotiations were well under way. His mistake was neglecting to consider that his heir might have a mind of his own. Young William was not obliged to approve his father's legal plan – it would, after all, mean a reduced inheritance – and parents could no longer expect to arrange their children's marriages without opposition. Another woman, much closer to home, had caught the headstrong young man's eye. As father and son proclaimed toasts to the very different futures they envisaged, that of Newstead teetered on the edge of disaster.

Since childhood, William's vision of the world as an aristocratic playground had crept into all aspects of his life: his family, his finances, his dabbles with the Freemasons and the military. While he maintained the trappings of rank, his reputation had been eroded by mounting debts and then permanently stained with Chaworth's blood. The Nottinghamshire estate was the only enduring jewel in the family's crown: 'Newsteade delights me', Walpole had written to a friend some years earlier, 'There is grace and Gothic indeed.'[119]

But while the dominion William had fashioned at the Abbey looked the part, it was flawed. Despite its picturesque appeal, one visitor remarked ominously that it seemed 'rather unfortunate that the cannon should be levelled at the parlour windows'.[120]

3

The Upper Lake

'Foul-Weather Jack', 1736–70

> I did remind thee of our own dear Lake,
> By the old Hall which may be mine no more.
> Leman's is fair; but think not I forsake
> The sweet remembrance of a dearer shore . . .
>
> *Epistle to Augusta*

1741

Seventeen-year-old midshipman John Byron is thousands of miles from home. He has spent eight arduous months at sea, and his heart thumps in his chest as he surveys the chaos now whirling around him. His ship, at the mercy of a fierce storm, has just suffered a violent blow – were they struck by rocks, or pitched over by a great rolling wave? He squints into the darkness, and the answer comes – they strike a second time and the ship skews wildly to almost ninety degrees against the swell of the sea. Men spill out onto the quarterdeck from below, and the breaking dawn reveals rocks jutting up menacingly on all sides. John fights to keep his balance, while those trapped in their hammocks below – crippled by scurvy, fever or injury – slowly drown as water surges into the bowels of the ship. The captain, confined to the surgeon's cabin by a wounded shoulder and a considerable dose of opiates, is tossed painfully against the wooden wall.

As another battering wave helps the ship to right itself, John is dismayed to see its useless wheel spinning uncontrollably. The men around him – feeling 'destruction at their very throats' – prepare for death with varying degrees of dignity. Here, a man falls to his knees and prays; there, others are thrown across the deck like dolls or (John thinks) like inanimate logs. Those preferring to face the end unencumbered by sobriety dash below to raid the liquor rations.

A tortured cry cuts through the general clamour – 'I am the king of the country!' – and John turns to see a raving sailor waving a cutlass above his head, skewering anyone who dares to come near. In the midst of madness, a lone voice rallies the men: 'My friends, let us not be discouraged!' It is the ship's mate, Jones. 'Come, lend a hand!' They haul to. As the rising sun casts a glow over the ocean, land is sighted! With renewed hope, the pain in their frozen fingers and soaked skins is forgotten – as John later recalls, 'We now thought of nothing but saving our lives.'[1]

Seventy years later, John's grandson George, 6th Lord Byron, is casting the hero of his new epic poem onto a stormy sea. He has no need to rely on invention. Proudly drawing from John's experiences, he writes that 'Strange sounds of wailing, blasphemy, devotion / Clamour'd in chorus to the roaring ocean'. Don Juan has suffered more than anyone on earth, he insists, and presses the point with the declaration that 'his hardships were comparative / To those related in my grand-dad's "Narrative"'. In 1816, the remarkable survival story of Midshipman Byron of the *Wager* is known across the world – rivalling the most spectacular fiction of the eighteenth century. But this dramatic adventure had been only the beginning for John, whose long navy career was pursued so relentlessly by tempests that he would go down in history as 'Foul-Weather Jack'. Though George never knew his grandfather, the poet feels a kinship in his 'inheritance of storms': 'He had no rest at sea,' he writes in an epistle to his half-sister Augusta, 'nor I on shore.'[2]

~

John Byron was twelve years old when his father died at Newstead, and seemingly fully recovered from the harrowing fever that had killed his brother Charles in 1731. He had inherited the softer facial features of his mother, with brown eyes and lighter brown curls than the unruly dark mop of his sister, but had already displayed his resilience of both body and mind – having not only endured but thrived during his four years at Westminster School. It had always been William who would inherit – barring any further fatality – and John was set on the conventional path for a second son: the military.

His elder brother had been removed from school within a few months of their father's death, and John had followed by the end of 1737. With his family's ties to the navy, it was natural that he would be steered in that direction – he was perhaps even primed for such a career during those early years surrounded by seascapes at Newstead.

By the age of fourteen John had swapped Latin and Greek for astronomy and trigonometry, and took his first appointment as an able seaman on the HMS *Romney* (a fourth-rate ship – no edge gained over his brother there). Having packed his trunk and travelled to Portsmouth, on 21 April 1738 he presented himself to his captain, Henry Medley, a distinguished officer in his early fifties. His scholarly and practical training would continue on board the ship – as well as mastering navigation and strategy, he would need to negotiate the dangers of enclosing hundreds of men into a large wooden crate and setting them adrift on it. In the summer, following the path his brother had taken a year earlier, the *Romney* set sail for Newfoundland and John was launched suddenly into an unfamiliar world.

His new colleagues were quite different creatures from the schoolboys he had boxed with at school – years at sea inevitably roughened the edges of even the most wellborn officer, even if only in the lines of his face and speech saturated with nautical colloquialisms. Though John wasn't quite among the officer class, his distinction as 'able' rather than 'ordinary' meant a higher pay grade and a place among the elite. There was another rising star on board, with whom he made fast and lifelong friends: twenty-year-old junior officer George Rodney, a man of poor background who would rise to become an admiral. Most of the 300-strong crew, however, were the rabble of the lower ranks, many of whom had been plucked forcibly from civilian life by a press gang or court order.

Here, onboard a 'man of war', the hierarchy preserved so systematically at home hung in delicate balance. Being an '*honourable*' gentleman provided no protection against fever, cannon or the gnaw of starvation as rations grew thin. Eight physically demanding weeks at sea would be a rude shock to the system of anyone accustomed to feather beds and a crackling hearth.

Young John weathered the challenge. Following a summer in Canada, the *Romney* traded in European waters before returning to

England in the spring. A few months, and a second season of fisheries and furs – this time with Medley as governor of Newfoundland – and on 28 February 1740, while they were stationed in Lisbon, John requested discharge. He returned to England to find his mother preparing to remarry and his eighteen-year-old sister eagerly seeking a husband of her own. The reunion did not last long. In his absence war with Spain had been formally declared, and he was to be sent into the fray. At sixteen, John was promoted to midshipman and assigned to a squadron commanded by one of Britain's most promising officers: forty-two-year-old Commodore George Anson. John loaded his trunk: uniform, books, navigation equipment; a red velvet waistcoat lovingly embroidered by Isabella, his father's watch. He set out for a new adventure, hoping to return in a year or two.

'So terrible was the scene'

Anson's mission was to lift Spain's stranglehold on the ports along the coasts of South America by 'taking, sinking, burning or otherwise destroying all their ships'. It was quite literally a golden opportunity for the men, who had hopes of 'returning to *Old England* loaden with the wealth of their enemies'.[3] At first sight, lying at anchor among 200 warships, HMS *Wager* was unimpressive: merely an old sixth-rate storeship heavily laden with the squadron's supplies of food, water, weapons and some ten thousand sandbags. John later gave a scathing review of both the ship and its men, describing the marines as 'decrepid invalids' who had to be hoisted aboard because they were too feeble to climb the rope ladders. Hundreds of the crew had been pressed into service, and as they idled in port even the prospect of Spanish gold could not lift the 'desponding' atmosphere. Eight men deserted. It was probably the best decision they made in their lives: speaking of the *Wager* years later, Anson grieved, 'perhaps History itself cannot parallel the many Hardships the poor Men laboured under, after the melancholy Fate of their Ship'.[4]

The eight-strong squadron finally sailed from the Isle of Wight on 18 September 1740. Strong winds on the first leg of the journey – to the colourful port of Funchal for supplies – kept them at sea for five weeks instead of two. Cheered by this short, convivial stay in Madeira, the squadron bobbed out of the harbour bound for South America, and John spent his seventeenth birthday at sea in good spirits. The merriment grew to a pitch three weeks later when they crossed the equator and the uninitiated were presented with the traditional choice: to forfeit a bottle of liquor and a pound of sugar, or submit to a ducking overboard (which meant, as one man aboard another ship in the squadron cheerfully put it, being plunged 'over head and Ears in the Water . . . till the Offender is as wet as a Drownded Rat').[5] John may well have been among them.

But as they sailed west, the revelries hushed and the air in the lower decks grew 'foul and nauseous'. Fevers began to prey on the men. When they docked at Santa Catarina – around 700 miles south of Rio de Janeiro – on 19 December, makeshift sick bays were hastily pitched on the shore and stocks of fresh beef were ordered. John got his first look at this extraordinary land as he was employed in repairs to the rigging and getting fresh water. Here he was, the son of an English lord, spending Christmas feasting on exotic fruits, and exploring forests that chattered with parrots and monkeys. The wildlife was strange. Mr Millechamp, the purser of HMS *Tryal*, another ship in the squadron, was often to be found wielding his watercolours, capturing the 'half Fish half Fowl' (penguins), 'what the Seamen call Hogs in Armour' (armadillos) and the baffling pink flamingos.[6] As weeks passed the climate seemed less wondrous, with thick mists at night and swarms of mosquitos during the day. On 16 January 1741, Anson announced his plan to continue south around Cape Horn, believing that the winter gales would have died down by the time they reached it. They set sail, straight into the storms.

Their first attempt to navigate the Cape scattered the ships. They were not reunited until almost a month later at the port of San Julián, where rumours spread that Captain Kidd of the *Pearl* had died presaging 'Vermin, Famine, Death and Destruction'. The subsequent reshuffle in command brought a new captain aboard the *Wager*: forty-seven-year-old Scotsman David Cheap. While Anson planned a second attempt at the Cape, the superstitious sailors brooded over ill omens – the *Wager*'s master gunner, John Bulkeley, observed that the sea around the harbour was so full of red shrimp that 'the Water appeared tinctured to that Degree that it look'd like Blood'.[7] In late February, orders to press on. One by one the patched-up ships pulled away from the safety of the harbour into the paths of curious Spanish ships, with the flagship *Centurion* at the helm to 'make timely signals of danger'.[8] But it quickly became apparent that the more pressing threat lurked within the ships themselves. The men grew weak – broke out in ulcers – began to spit out teeth. Scurvy.

Known for centuries as 'the Spoyle of Mariners', the disease was an inescapable companion to long sea voyages and epidemic throughout the fleet, with no known cure – treatment relied heavily on quarantine, potatoes and prayer. Richard Walter, chaplain of the *Centurion*, wrote of the men being reduced to 'rotten bones, and such a luxuriancy of fungous flesh, as yielded to no remedy'.[9] In its final throes patients were little more than breathing corpses.

In March the storms set in. Winds whipped the sea into mountainous waves, forcing the squadron to clamber tirelessly upwards before 'sinking into the most frightful valley'.[10] In perpetual danger of being 'dashed in pieces against the decks or sides of the ship', the men found it almost impossible to perform their duties.[11] Sails were torn to ribbons by piercing winds, or froze and snapped; the coat of ice on the rigging made it impossible to grip. '[O]ne of our best seamen was canted overboard and drowned', an officer of the *Centurion* later recalled; 'another dislocated his neck, a third was thrown into the mainhold and broke his thigh, and one of the boatswain's mates broke his collar bone twice'.[12] For six weeks his ship buried four or five men daily, and eventually eight or ten. As they approached the Cape in early April, the *Wager* narrowly avoided being wrecked on Staten Island – they limped on, though John could see the ship was 'in all parts in a most crazy condition . . . shattered and disabled'.[13] They drifted into a thickening mist and the weather worsened. A wave pitched Bulkeley, the gunner, right over the ship's wheel, and stove in some of the boats. On 12 April, midshipman Alexander Campbell was almost knocked overboard by a man falling from the rigging above. That morning the *Gloucester* and *Anne* disappeared into the fog – it was the last time they had sight of the squadron.

The men of the *Wager* found themselves suddenly alone. They had endured twelve long weeks since leaving Santa Catarina, and with Anson beyond reach their lack of faith in their captain became dangerously apparent. 'Now you have parted with the Commodore, by God, you will find the Difference,' one sailor muttered darkly to the steward. Captain Cheap, who was intermittently kept below decks by rheumatism and asthma, persisted in the charted course even though they had been cut off and visibility was virtually non-existent. He dismissed the warnings of his officers, and when the men's complaints turned to threats he simply provided each with a brace of pistols in case violence erupted. John tried to bat away his creeping doubts.

Gazing out from the quarterdeck early one morning, John noticed that something was different. The waves were tinted brown with clumps of bladderwrack. 'We can't be far off the Land by these Weeds,' he called to Cummins, the carpenter – but his observation didn't tally with their assumed position.[14] They heard the caw of birds. Some reported seeing land in the distance – on one occasion John himself thought he could make out 'an imperfect view of an eminence' – but Cheap dismissed the sightings with a wave of his hand. Someone suggested that the officers register their objections as a group, but it seemed improper to question their captain so openly.

On 13 May any further consideration on the subject was halted when violent winds wrenched the foreyard from its mast and brought it crashing down 'about our Ears'. In his rush to reach the deck, Cheap missed his footing on a ladder and fell heavily, dislocating his shoulder. As the small band of men still fit for duty struggled on against a gathering storm, their captain was carried to the surgeon's cabin and given a dose of opiates. (He later blamed the surgeon for rendering him virtually incapacitated, claiming, 'I knew nothing of what was doing in the ship from seven o'clock at night till half an hour past four next morning.')[15] At this critical moment, a clear sight of land! As the wind whipped into what John called 'a perfect hurricane', Cheap finally gave the order to alter their course. It came too late. That night, only twelve men were fit to divide the watch between them. In increasingly unforgiving conditions, John was charged with taking updates and orders between the deck and the barely sensible captain. 'All the first and middle Watch it blow'd and rain'd,' Bulkeley remembered later, 'and withal so very dark, that we could not see the Length of the Ship.'[16]

It was around 4.30 a.m. when 'a great and tumbling Sea' tossed the *Wager* sharply against a sunken rock. Midshipman Campbell, blearily dressing in his cabin, ran above and lost his balance in a violent second strike; for a few awful minutes the entire vessel buckled sideways until righted by another forceful wave. Within seconds the deck crowded with hands from below – John observed that the general terror mobilised men 'that had not shewed their faces upon deck for above two months' – but the ship's wheel was inoperable and desperate attempts to steer by tugging ropes dangling from tattered sails failed miserably. A final strike, and the ship lodged fast between two large jagged rocks: it could neither sail or sink. As the sun yawned over the horizon it became apparent that they were just a musket-shot from land. John stumbled below to acquaint the captain and was directed to get the men ashore as soon as possible. Cheap would stay aboard until the job was done.

As preparations were made to launch the boats, John and some of the other officers waded through the hysteria on deck and attempted to restore order. To their dismay, they were bluntly informed by the men that they would not go; the ship was lost, Cheap's authority had foundered with it, and everyone was at liberty to shift for himself. Hearing that the men were refusing to leave while there was alcohol on board, Cheap eventually decided to leave without them. Taking his cue, John made for the wardroom to save some things from his trunk, but as he entered a violent judder sent him stumbling and water spewed into the room. He was forced to retreat without saving 'a single rag but what was upon my back'.

One by one the boats lurched towards the shore. Yells drifted from the wreck, and as night fell gunshots were directed towards the camp. John despaired at the choice dividing the men:

Which ever way we looked, a scene of horror presented itself; on one side, the wreck (in which was all that we had in the world to support and subsist us), together with a boisterous sea, presented us with the most dreary prospect; on the other, the land did not wear a much more favourable appearance: desolate and barren, without sign of culture, we could hope to receive little other benefit from it, than the preservation it afforded us from the sea.[17]

A scattering of small huts indicated that the place – wherever it was – was not entirely uninhabited. Were they being watched? And if so, were the onlookers hostile? Soaked to the skin, the weary men tentatively crawled inside or sheltered under trees. John spent the night leaning against the pole of one hut, gripping his pistol. He awoke from troubled sleep to find that a man next to him had perished from the cold. As he shivered, listening to the distant whooping on board the *Wager*, the events of the past few hours revealed themselves for what they were: mutiny.

When the sun rose it was barely visible through the rain. Three men were buried. Their first meal for two days was a miserable soup cobbled together from wild celery, a seagull and a bag of 'biscuit dust', which turned out to have been mixed with tobacco and prompted violent retching.

Parties were sent aboard the *Wager* to review the situation. It seemed hopeless. The ship's papers had been torn up and the mob prevented them from salvaging much of use. After disorderly sailors had ransacked the officers' chests and commandeered the 'richest apparel they could find', the growing shoal of corpses floating between decks began to gleam with the finery of these inebriated 'imaginary Lords'.[18] Only a second tempestuous night aboard the wreck (and the eventual depletion of the brandy barrels) persuaded the mutineers to return to the fold. They did not escape punishment – their ringleader, boatswain John King, was 'felled to the ground' by a blow from Cheap's cane, and their weapons and stolen clothes were requisitioned (including, to John's relief, his father's watch and his now bedraggled cocked hat). But the sight of this hungover rabble with fine suits thrown over greasy trousers and dirty checked shirts provoked the first mirth in what seemed an age.

In the days that followed the initial furore subsided into squabbling about pay, food and – in more hushed tones – whether the officers could claim any authority now the ship was lost. The increasingly skeletal wreck was stripped of canvas, rope and nails, and barrels of flour and beef. The survivors were a motley crew of around 145 men: some, mere boys, another, an eighty-two-year-old cook; well-born officers and skilled tradesmen; and the chaplain, a man of God, among the press-ganged criminals. With most sick or injured, they were ill-equipped to deal with the combined threat of malnutrition, potential attacks and the unfamiliar climate of what they dubbed 'Wager's Island'. It was a land of marsh and rock, which John solemnly declared 'the most unprofitable spot on the globe of the earth'.[19] The bay, bordered by a dense forest, lay in the shadow of a mountain to the south and faced the churning sea to the north. The coast remained too volatile for exploration, and expeditions scaling what they dubbed 'Mount Misery' only revealed higher peaks beyond. On one such mission John was horrified to discover the corpse of the assistant cook Thomas Lark on the mountainside, 'stabbed in several places, and shockingly mangled'. The men were already resorting to murder.

One dismal evening the officers assembled in the captain's hut, where wooden planks from the *Wager* had been lashed together to serve as a makeshift table. The ship's lantern swayed gently atop a pole. Outside, rain hammered down on the miserable guards stationed at the rations tent. Cheap, animated by his new idea, held up a book. It told the story of the *Speedwell*, he said, wrecked at Juan Fernández in 1719: the crew had constructed a vessel with materials stripped from their crippled ship and had made their way home. The *Wager* crew had a carpenter, and an armourer – could they not do the same? John borrowed the book, fired with new hope. But when the men were told of the captain's plan – to continue north in search of Anson's squadron – the frustration was palpable. They had expected a boost in rations, not physical labour and some hopeless quest. The sentiment extended even to the midshipmen's tent, which John shared with fellow officers Campbell, Morris and the amiable (but somehow consistently inebriated) Cozens. An attempt was made to blow up the captain's hut. Men began to desert the camp.

Around four weeks into their project, John was salvaging materials aboard the wreck when a call went up signalling the approach of three canoes. Peering curiously at them were a group of short, black-haired indigenous people clothed in animal skins. John and his companion Lieutenant Baynes – Cheap's second-in-command – tentatively offered pieces of cloth as a sign of friendship. Their visitors appeared entirely unacquainted with Europeans and, to their relief, showed no hint of hostility. Having been conveyed to the captain, they were won over with gifts – officers' hats and a mirror – and reciprocated by offering a few mussels. They returned the next day with three sheep, before bringing their families and showing the sailors where to find fish. It seemed like the beginning of a life-saving economic and cultural exchange.

By the middle of July – almost two months wrecked – the men were shooting the vultures picking at their crewmates' corpses on the collapsing *Wager*. The surgeon Mr Elliot, a strong and active young man, was kept busy as the weaker boys fell sick. John helped with the longboat but, being handy with a gun, he was more often sent hunting. He returned from one trip into the woods with a 'poor Indian dog' trotting cheerfully in tow. Comforted by his company, John named the dog Boxer and constructed a small shelter to house them both. 'This creature grew so fond of me and faithful,' John later remembered, 'that he would suffer no body to come near the hut without biting them.'[20] He tried to remain positive.

The atmosphere was certainly growing antagonistic. The men entertained themselves with firing volleys about the camp, and mixed rations of wine and brandy to get drunk more quickly. New graves were dug each day as the weaker men starved. There was no consensus about the captain's plans, even among the officers. When 'warm with liquor', Midshipman Cozens openly criticised Cheap and started a physical fight with Mr Elliot. One afternoon, gunshots brought John dashing through the rain to find Cozens lying on the ground, blood weltering around his head – the skittish captain, on hearing a commotion, had flown from his hut and 'without asking any questions, immediately shot him through the head'. When the midshipman died two weeks later, accusations of murder mobilised Cheap's growing band of opponents.

When not out hunting with Boxer, John lived quietly and cautiously alongside the dissenters, politely declining Mr Bulkeley's invitation to join in the discussions held in his hut but seeing no reason to refuse his request to borrow the book about the *Speedwell*.

Having used it to devise a feasible route through the Straits of Magellan to the south – surely this was safer than persisting north? – they petitioned the captain to consider it. After a flat rejection both Bulkeley and Cummins (the carpenter) laid down their tools, refusing to build a vessel that would lead them to their deaths. The blossoming relationship with their indigenous allies also came to an abrupt end when a violent altercation broke out after a sailor had – as John delicately put it – 'endeavoured to seduce their wives'. With the visitors' departure went their most reliable source of food.

Four months since the wreck, and over a third of the ship's company had starved to death. The rations tent was fiercely protected. Those caught robbing the stores were flogged – receiving hundreds of lashes – and Cheap banished one offender to a distant rock without any sustenance. His corpse was retrieved the next day. Eventually an inevitable shadow darkened the entrance to John's hut, where he was resting with Boxer. They demanded the dog. John protested desperately, arguing for his usefulness in hunting and his 'faithful services and fondness' to no avail. They took him by force – and then he was dead. 'I was invited to a Dog-Feast at Mr J—'s tent,' Bulkeley later recalled; 'it was exceeding good eating'.[21] The grieving but practical John reluctantly joined in. Three weeks later he returned to the spot, and was 'glad to make a meal' of the rotting paws they had thrown aside.

Five months since the wreck, and mutinous whispers finally translated into action. At dawn one day in early October John was wrenched sharply to consciousness by the ringing of the *Wager's* bell. With Bulkeley's men assembled behind him, Lieutenant Baynes announced that the captain was under arrest for murdering Mr Cozens. As Cheap was placed under guard, the emboldened boatswain struck him repeatedly in the face. Things began to move quickly.

Their plan was already settled: they enforced a new rationing system and tested the longboat – which they christened the *Speedwell* – plus two other small vessels salvaged from the wreck. When everyone piled aboard to head south, John discovered that three men were being left behind: Captain Cheap, Elliot the surgeon and Lieutenant Hamilton of the marines. He struggled with the moral predicament. Should he remain behind with his captain, even if he did not entirely condone his conduct, or with the men, many of whom he liked and whose plan seemed more promising? There was no time to decide – they set off.

As they made their way south, John continued to be plagued by doubts and began to steel himself against the hardship to come. During one fishing excursion his hat was blown away by the wind, prompting an amiable Londoner named John Duck to plant his own on John's head. '*John!* I thank you', he responded, 'if I accept of your Kindness, you must go bare-headed; and, I think, I can bear Hardships as well as the best of you, and must use myself to them.'[22] He had resolved to go back. Under the pretence of retrieving more canvassing, he and the similarly conflicted Midshipman Campbell returned to Wager's Island – and their overjoyed captain – with a barge of nineteen men. Realising they had deserted, the *Speedwell* put to sea.

Almost six months since the wreck, and after weeks of eating almost nothing but weeds and celery, John spent his eighteenth birthday on Wager's Island almost crippled with dysentery. An unearthly shrieking awoke the men one night and brought them to the shore, where several swore they saw the figure of a man half submerged beneath the waves. They began to talk of ghosts. Were they being haunted by the marine from the rock? Or the cook murdered on Mount Misery?

Seven months since the wreck, and Cheap announced that the two small boats at their disposal were ready to launch on his original course to the north. Any initial optimism was quickly eroded by days of rowing on 'mountainous seas'. Making virtually no progress, the only way to save themselves from disappearing into the waves was throwing their precious provisions overboard. While his family defrosted by their London fires, John spent the night before Christmas laid upon his oars and soaked to the skin; he finally resorted to tearing apart and hungrily devouring his seal-skin shoes.

New Year 1742 began just as miserably. A vessel was lost, and with insufficient space for everyone, four marines were abandoned on a desolate shore – in practical terms, a death sentence. John later wrote of the deserted men stoically giving three cheers and calling out 'God bless the king!' as the remaining boats rowed away – however selective this memory might have been, the faces of the men would haunt him. After two months battling insurmountable seas the sixteen survivors gave up and returned to Wager's Island, expecting to 'linger out a miserable life, as we had not the least prospect of returning home'.[23] They were consumed with thoughts of death. A man deserted. Two more succumbed to starvation. Some superstitious sailors rushed to bury the body of Thomas Lark, convinced that he was wreaking his revenge from beyond the grave. When John closed his eyes he saw the faces of the abandoned marines.

Nine months since the wreck, a new and desperate scheme: some began to whisper of 'consigning one man to death for the support of the rest'. Just as the prospect of cannibalism reared its head, a new party of curious dark-haired visitors arrived in the bay. They were bolder than the last and clearly familiar with Europeans – Mr Elliot could just make out the laboured Spanish of their leader, 'Martin'. To their amazement he agreed to take them to a Spanish settlement on the island of Chiloé, in exchange for their barge. They gathered up their meagre possessions and left Wager's Island for good.

Even with their knowledgeable guide it would prove a difficult journey – first, more manpower was required. On the way to find it, Cheap refused to share his stash of seal meat, ignoring the pleas of two of his men as they slowly starved to death in the barge. John couldn't bring himself to follow the captain's example: 'I sat next to him when he dropped,' he wrote of one formerly stout sailor, 'and having a few dried shell-fish [in] my pocket, from time to time put one in his mouth, which served only to prolong his pains; from which, however, soon after my little supply failed, he was released by death'.[24] Six more deserted.

While the others rested, John and the captain were conveyed to an encampment where they received their first, extraordinary experience of life among an indigenous culture. It began auspiciously. The settlement was composed almost entirely of curious but friendly women and children. John's desperate signs for food were immediately understood – he was given fish and, after collapsing from exhaustion, awoke to find himself cloaked in a blanket of feathers. He bathed and washed his clothes in a stream, and watched the women perform amazing feats of deep-diving for fish. The serene atmosphere was shattered with the return of the men: around thirty warriors, who resented the kindnesses being lavished on these intruders. John watched in horror as the young woman who had housed him was brutally beaten. Once Martin had enlisted some help for the voyage to Chiloé they swiftly left and were reunited with their feeble shipmates. Their number was reduced to just five: John, Captain Cheap, Lieutenant Hamilton, Midshipman Campbell and Elliot the surgeon. Emaciated, the latter was fading fast.

In foreign territory and totally dependent on their new companions, the officers became familiar with the tribe's way of life. Both sexes hunted with astonishing dexterity, catching birds by holding torches beneath cliffside nests and spearing seal between the eyes from a remarkable distance. (Frustratingly, only the women shared their spoils.) John tried to avoid what he took to be their 'religious exercises' – though intrigued by their chanting, he was unsettled by the sight of them wounding one another with shells until smeared with blood. 'These orgies continue', he later wrote, 'till those who preside in them foam at the mouth, grow faint, are exhausted with fatigue, and dissolve in a profusion of sweat.'[25]

Another short venture north, and they landed at a small bay. 'Here', John recalled, 'Mr Elliot, our surgeon, died.' He had been their physician, translator and friend, and Campbell took the loss particularly hard. Though exhausted, the men 'scraped a hole for him in the sand, and buried him in the best manner we could', naming the spot Elliot Bay. They were reduced to four. They had to carry on. They rowed. They marched, barefoot and burdened with the provisions they had foraged along the journey. Weighed down by a bag of seal meat, John lost his footing and slipped into a swamp – his cries went unheard. Heaving himself from its grip, he sat muddied and hopeless beneath a tree, where he finally broke down and 'gave way to melancholy reflexions'. When he somehow summoned the energy to catch up with the rest, they merely grumbled about the food he had lost.

Thinking only of food, John no longer cared where he was taken. His guides, whose language he could not understand, offered him nothing and for two days he survived on the limpets he collected as they travelled. At night they were consumed by lice. Frustrated and in pain, John pulled off his clothes and beat them furiously between two stones 'in hope of killing hundreds at once'. Captain Cheap – bearded, emaciated everywhere but his bloated legs and with a body like 'an anthill' – seemed to be losing his mind. He slept clutching his bag of rotting seal meat and the names of his companions – on occasion even his own – began to elude him. Lieutenant Hamilton abandoned hope, choosing to try his chances in a different direction.

When the three remaining men finally arrived at Chiloé – just over a year since the wreck – it was snowing heavily. Whisked to a snug house with boiling potatoes and sheepskin beds, it seemed as if they were in a dream.

The Spanish authorities were quick to convey their new prisoners to the governor at the town of Chacao. After a considerable march – John picking at lumps of seal meat from his pockets as they went – they came to a small town consisting of nothing more than a scattering of buildings housing some people, and a greater number of pigs. A volcano murmured in the distance. The elderly governor was full of sympathy about their plight. Commodore Anson treated his Spanish prisoners kindly, he declared, and he would return the favour. While they awaited passage north to St Jago (now Santiago), they enjoyed their first taste of relative normality in a year. Though they were well fed, John made a point of befriending the cook and couldn't resist cramming his pockets with food whenever possible. He traded his ragged clothes for new breeches and the local 'puncho', and was amused by the tobacco-smoking women wading 'bare-legg'd, walking through mud' to get to church. He picked up enough Spanish to get by, and some of the language of the local people (which was also spoken in the town). The arrival of a 'wretched' Lieutenant Hamilton – rescued at the governor's orders – some three months later seemed little short of a miracle.

During these months in Chiloé, John's nearest brush with disaster was provoked by his own politeness. While touring the island with the governor he became acquainted with a rich old priest and his niece, who quickly became smitten with the young officer. (John's heart was less affected – he later wrote that though she was accomplished, she 'could not be called a regular beauty'.) John was surprised to eventually find himself ushered into a room and presented with the woman's fine clothes, and those of the old man – which, the priest declared, would one day be his if he would consent to marry her. He was momentarily seduced by the thought of fine linen shirts.

'I own this last article was a great temptation to me', he remembered, 'however, I had the resolution to withstand it, and made the best excuses I could for not accepting of the honour they intended me'.[26] All parties were spared further embarrassment when John swiftly returned to Chacao and received word that they had a place on a ship heading north, to Valparaíso.

The ship they boarded in January 1743 was manned by slaves. On arrival in Valparaíso a curious mob followed them to the residence of the governor, who merely condemned them to a small, flea-ridden dungeon. John contemplated his change in fortunes as he listened to the groans and clanking chains of criminals in the adjacent cell – the shuffling soldiers standing guard with their bayonets – the screeches of passers-by hoping for a glimpse of the English prisoners. After a few days, Cheap and Hamilton – having somehow kept hold of their identification papers – were released and sent to St Jago, promises of sending help falling from their lips as they left them behind. The prisoners' situation grew dire. When the governor declared that he would not fund rations for John and Campbell – they could starve! – for several weeks they were kept alive only by the charity of the townsfolk. Finally they were dispatched into the mountains towards the capital, escorted by a drover and his mules. With his parting words, the drover cautioned John not to linger in a place of such 'extravagance, vice, and folly'. It was perhaps the city that made a man of him.

Twenty months since the wreck, John arrived at St Jago and was briefly bewildered by 'the sudden transition from the most dismal to the gayest scenes in the universe'. They were reunited with Cheap and Hamilton, met the president and were allowed to write to England. When an invitation came to dine with Spanish Admiral Pizarro – Anson's nemesis – they worried only that 'we had not any cloaths fit to appear in'. They learned the fates of their commander's squadron and the mutinous *Speedwell*, which had successfully navigated the Straits of Magellan and reached Rio Grande a year earlier, after a voyage of fifteen weeks. While John had languished in the dungeon, the twenty-nine surviving mutineers reached England, spreading reports of Captain Cheap's brutality.

After so long pursued by illness, famine, vermin, violence and storms, this fashionable city seemed charmed. It was a hive of gilded churches and shopping piazzas, perfumed with orange trees and tropical flowers. Busy friars and well-dressed female slaves solemnly went about with their orders. John thought the climate the finest in the world – long, hot days and cool, refreshing evenings – but struggled to adjust to the spicy food, which set his throat 'on fire for an hour afterwards'. Among his new friends was his neighbour Donna Francisca *Giron*, who cheerfully declared that as their names sounded alike they must be related. He marvelled at the bullfights and admired local women at late-night 'fandangoes'. Perhaps unsurprisingly, he was so taken with their attire that he could describe it in minute detail twenty years later: 'Their breasts and shoulders are very naked; and, indeed, you may easily discern their whole shape by their manner of dress'.[27]

The months passed pleasantly and his bills racked up; in the spring of 1744 he wrote to his brother William asking that he cover his debts, signing off 'Your Most affectionate Brother'.[28] Campbell was so content that he converted to Catholicism and elected to remain behind. Almost four years since the wreck, and the three remaining prisoners finally received word that they were to be released and sent back to Europe aboard a French ship. In the spring of 1745 they set sail; by October they were in France. While they awaited permission from Spain to return to England, Cheap wrote to Commodore Anson with his account of events, signing off: 'Messrs Biron and Hamilton (my faithful companions and fellow sufferers) beg leave to Kiss your hand'.[29] In February 1746 they were finally bundled onto an English ship bound for Dover.

John couldn't wait to get home. While Cheap and Hamilton recovered their strength at Canterbury, he hastened straight to London on horseback – having no money for the toll-masters, he simply rode 'as hard as I could through them all, not paying the least regard to the men who called out to stop me'. The prospect of disgruntled debt collectors was hardly going to faze him.

His first port of call was Great Marlborough Street, but he found it shut up: William was in Aberdeen. He racked his brains. 'Having been absent so many years, and in all that time never having heard a word from home, I knew not who was dead, or who was living, or where to go next . . .'[30] Enquiring at a linen draper's shop his family used to frequent, he learned that his sister Isabella was not only alive but set up in grand style as Lady Carlisle on Soho Square.

'A home to rest, a shelter to defend'

The young man who presented himself at Carlisle House in February 1746 was not the same smart sixteen-year-old who had left aboard the *Wager* in the autumn of 1740. He was taller – at least two descriptions pitched him at 'near six feet high' – but years of starvation lingered in his figure and face. Confronted by this mud-caked stranger clad in a bizarre mix of French and Spanish hand-me-downs, the porter was ready to slam the door in his face. John desperately made his case. The astonished Isabella dashed immediately to meet him, with a whirl of questions and exclamations of disbelief. 'I need not acquaint my readers with what surprise and joy my sister received me', he later recalled. She introduced him to his brother-in-law and little nieces. He was supplied with generous sums of money for new clothes, and letters were dashed off to the rest of the family. Almost five years since the wreck, John was finally home.

After years of no contact, there was a deluge of news. He was an uncle, to Isabella's two girls; their grandfather Lord Berkeley was dead and Uncle John had taken up his title; William, now a bona fide peer, had been traipsing around the north in search of Jacobites. Richard had been accepted at Oxford University and George was itching to leave school. But it was his own story that everyone wanted to hear. In all, just thirty-six men survived the disasters that befell the *Wager* and the public had been gripped by their stories: of men swallowed by the sea or abandoned on unknown shores; of boys starving to death; of poor John Duck, born to a black father and a white mother, who had been forcibly 'adopted' by one indigenous chief on account of his skin colour and sold, probably into a life of slavery (he was never heard of again). Bulkeley and Cummins had set down their experiences in print shortly after arriving at Spithead in 1743, downplaying their part in the mutiny and painting Cheap as an idle, unbalanced commander. (John featured in their narrative primarily to abandon the *Speedwell* simply because 'he could not get any Accommodation aboard the Vessel that he lik'd, being oblig'd to lie forward with the Men'.)[31] In the summer of 1744 Anson's flagship had returned loaded with treasure and the commodore produced his own account of the dreadful conditions his squadron had faced. Now, Cheap's small party was charged with completing the picture. There would be a court martial.

It was unclear exactly what charges would be brought until almost the day of the trial, which was held aboard the *Prince George* at Spithead on 15 April 1746. An investigation was required into the loss of the ship, but there was also evidence of mutiny (which would see the ringleaders hanged) and allegations of murder (which would see Cheap hanged). The statements of the ten assembled witnesses were read out before questioning by the court. Facing the noose, the animosity between them seemed to evaporate. Cheap knew that bringing charges of mutiny would invite difficult questions about the death of Mr Cozens. Under interrogation, the boatswain – who had repeatedly struck Cheap in the face – testified that 'the Captain behaved very well'.[32] A stalemate. (It was, the Admiralty thought, perhaps for the best.) On the loss of the ship, only Lieutenant Baynes – who had failed to report a critical sight of land – was held in any way accountable. He escaped with a reprimand. John acquitted himself admirably throughout, giving a measured testimony and displaying a clear grasp of the technicalities of seamanship. His part in the *Wager* disaster had earned him the immediate notice and respect of the Admiralty – within two weeks he was at Sheerness taking up command of his own ten-gun sloop, HMS *Vulture*.

During the course of his first summer back at home, life settled into a routine. Isabella entertained friends at her Yorkshire mansion. William filed into Westminster Hall for the trials of the Jacobite lords. John was ordered to 'look out Diligently' for small Danish vessels (which had been ordered to carry the Pretender's son safely away from Scotland under the guise of trading), and then dispatched to carry messages to his superiors cruising Cape Finisterre.[33] Wartime was far from over – in his absence Britain's rivalry with Spain had been subsumed in a wider conflict drawing in almost all of the European powers (the War of the Austrian Succession).

John's record of professionalism and unwavering loyalty served him well. 'I am glad your Grace has Captain Byron in your thoughts for a post-ship', Anson wrote to the First Lord of the Admiralty. 'I think he will turn out well.' [34] By New Year 1747 he was formally promoted to captain and given command of the *Syren*; Anson, clearly taking John under his wing, promptly invited him to join his own fleet commanding the more considerable *Falkland*. Months passed uneventfully – an escort duty protecting convoys of silverware from Amsterdam, hosting enemy prisoners, cruising the Bay of Biscay – but threw him into positions of trust with influential superior officers and allowed him to get to grips with the difficulties of commanding a crew of 300 men. But when he returned to England in July 1748 there were entirely different waters to navigate. At twenty-four, with the path of his career established, Captain Byron was engaged.

John was not unpopular with the female sex. During his adventures abroad the kindness of those brave indigenous women had kept him alive; he had also received his first offer of marriage from a besotted Chilean heiress, and had been flirtatiously pinched by a veiled woman at a ball in St Jago. It was likely during his two-year residence here that he learned the rudiments of courtship, among sparkling-eyed women with (he later claimed) 'a strong disposition to gallantry'. He returned to England with an air of rakish charm, agitating female hearts in his favour with both his heroic history and promising future. He may not have been wealthy, but he was a dashing captain with stories of the icy Canadian winter, of bullfights in Lisbon and caves of the dead in remote Patagonia. Doubtless to the dismay of the ladies of Plymouth, his chosen bride was close to home – they had known each other since they were children.

Eighteen-year-old Sophia Trevanion was undeniably attractive, and a model of elegance. She was fashionably pale, with blue eyes and curling brown hair – a friend later remarked that her 'Style of prettiness' was such that 'Men would willingly run thro' fire' for her. [35] In an arrangement not unusual for the time, she was also his first cousin – the youngest daughter of his aunt Barbara – and during the London seasons they had lived just a short walk apart. When the Byron children were whisked to Newstead, Sophia passed her childhood summers with her brother and sister at the Trevanion country estate, Caerhays Castle in Cornwall. They seem to have influenced her character – she was later described as an indisputably 'Cornish lady', with all the 'native fire' the phrase implied.[36] She had a sharp mind and impeccable, expressive manners, and like her cousin Isabella she felt her emotions keenly. (Unlike Isabella, she would be admired for her ability to adopt a stoic and sociable front no matter what raged behind the scenes.) Taking comfort from the rules of high society, Sophia did her best to live by them and expected the same from others. She was an impressionable fifteen years old when her heroic cousin had returned from his adventure, and their acquaintance evidently renewed on a romantic note.

News of the engagement rippled through their social circle. 'Each might perhaps according to the estimation of the World have done better', wrote Sophia's neighbour Mrs Eliot – hinting perhaps that Sophia's beauty could have earned her a title, and John's good prospects a better fortune – 'but they whose only business that is do not think so, are both young agreeable people and as the settlement is to be *for Life* I heartily wish it may prove a happy one.'[37] They were evidently well liked but, more importantly, they had a genuine affection for each other.

The courtship had played out in part while John was away at sea – a taste of things to come – and within weeks of his return, Cornwall buzzed with excitement about 'Miss Sophia's and Captain Byron's Wedding'.[38] Guests began to arrive, and villagers were enlisted to help with the cleaning and catering. On 8 September, the couple took their vows in the private chapel at Caerhays – John probably in his captain's uniform – and locals strained for a glimpse as the couple emerged as the Honourable Mr and Mrs Byron. Good wishes poured in and the newspapers were peppered with announcements: the *London Evening Post* declared that Sophia's dowry was £12,000 (surely some consolation for the loss of those linen shirts). The marriage was crowned with more good news six weeks later: the declaration of peace.

The newlyweds set up their home in Plympton, near Plymouth, and in the eight years of uneasy truce that followed Sophia dutifully added to their family as John was assigned from ship to ship. Sophia either fell pregnant immediately or was already carrying his child – their first daughter Frances, known as Fanny, was baptised just under nine months after the wedding, on 4 June 1749. Though busy with his duties, John remained nearby – his ship, the *St Albans*, was stationed at Plymouth, and he was allowed to return home unless expressly instructed to remain on board – so Sophia didn't endure the early years of parenthood entirely alone.

John must occasionally have meditated on how close he had come to being cheated of this peaceful domesticity. A later poem attributed his survival solely to the power of his hope, which eventually led him 'o'er many a cliff sublime' to finally find 'a home to rest, a shelter to defend'.[39] Being already well acquainted, the newlyweds began on a more familiar footing than most. They both enjoyed horse-riding and reading, each hoped to live good, useful lives according to their Anglican faith, and made efforts to establish themselves as part of the community. And within three months Sophia was pregnant again.

Plympton was an old town clustered around a crumbling priory, a grammar school and the ruins of a motte and bailey castle, and the lives of its residents were coloured by the local tin-mining community and the naval might of neighbouring Plymouth. It might have been a little provincial for Sophia, but a new social world opened before her with the cluster of navy families by the ports: the Ansons – the Rodneys – the Boscawens – young Captain Barrington and John's 'great friend' Commodore Moore.[40] They also infiltrated the fashionable circle of a local young artist named Joshua Reynolds, who had painted John around the time of the wedding. (In the portrait he sports a rakishly buttoned-up frock-coat and silver-laced hat, gazing confidently forward with one hand casually planted in his pocket. Though there is little allusion to his nautical career – perhaps he did not wish to be defined by his one famous, disastrous voyage – the setting and his attire hint at his travel and outdoor pursuits.) Sophia grew close to Mrs Hannah Horneck, a young military wife immortalised by Reynolds as 'The Plymouth Beauty'. When Hannah suddenly found herself a widowed mother of three while still in her twenties, it was Sophia she called on to stand as godmother to her youngest, Catherine.

It was a bleak reminder of the uncertainty of their chosen path. As well a strong dose of courage, the qualities required of a captain's wife were discretion, good household management and an ability to uphold the family's social position while her husband was at sea. The new Lady Anson (John's patron had celebrated his elevation to the peerage by acquiring a wife) acted as her husband's secretary, unburdening him of tedious paperwork. Others, like literary hostess Frances Boscawen, were entrusted with official secrets.

As the Byrons entrenched themselves in Plymouth society, Sophia was increasingly sought out by friends and family looking for navy news, and junior officers looking to curry favour with John. Throwing herself into the role, she kept up with the comings and goings of the ships and her language gradually coloured with navy expressions. John was stationed near Plymouth when their second daughter Sophia was born in June 1750, and when she died ten months later. Sophia was already pregnant when they buried her at St Andrew's church (just one of twelve children interred there that month). Shortly after the birth of this third child in September 1751 – another daughter, Isabella – John received new orders: Africa. He sailed in December.

The mission to the Gulf of Guinea provided John with his first extended stay along the perilous African coast, and Sophia with her first real taste of life without him. In the event, it was devastating. Dispatched for 'the Protection of the Trade of his Majesty's Subjects on that Coast' – the trades operated by merchant companies being primarily gold and slavery – the squadron's task was to patrol the seas and prevent rivals from encroaching on British interests. John was warned against drinking palm wine and staying ashore overnight; he was told in no uncertain terms that any navy officers transporting West Africans 'to Barbadoes for Publick Sale' for personal profit (apparently a common trick) would be severely punished.[41]

Back in England, Christmas passed and Sophia took the children the fifty miles to her family at Caerhays. When little Isabella died there aged just four months, John was cruising off Cape Verde in pursuit of suspicious French vessels. With weeks between letters, he sailed the Ivory Coast, the Gold Coast (now Ghana) and the Slave Coast (around Benin) oblivious to his daughter's death. He marvelled at the towering trees – they reminded him of his years in Chile – and picked up a token for Sophia: a 'Gold twisted hoop Ring' made by an African craftsman 'who never saw a Tool'.[42] His sentiments about the human horrors he must have witnessed on the 'Slave Coast' go unrecorded – he certainly called at the port of Ouidah, from where thousands were forcibly shipped to the Americas, and the infamous Cape Coast Castle, a gleaming British-held fortress where governors lived in splendour above a lightless dungeon of bloodied captives awaiting their place on a ship. He had seen the galley slaves and bejewelled female slaves of Chile – this was unfamiliar territory.

After a relatively uneventful but undoubtedly eye-opening absence of six months he returned, settled his wife and surviving daughter Fanny in Plymouth – reputedly at what remains known as 'Byron House', a small, weather-battered villa overlooking the creek towards Mount Edgecumbe – and remained in English waters for two years. He took command of the *Augusta*, and Sophia fell pregnant. By the time the child was born in early 1754 – another daughter, Juliana Elizabeth – he was aboard the *Vanguard* awaiting sailing orders. Just two summer months away this time, conveying troops and their families to and from Gibraltar, followed by an extended stay in Plymouth that inevitably led to another daughter: Sophia Maria, known as Sophy, was born in autumn 1755. Seven years of marriage had produced five daughters, three of whom survived. But at thirty-two and twenty-five, they were still young. There was still a chance for sons.

On 22 May 1756, Captain Byron called the men of the *Vanguard* on deck to make an announcement. War had been declared with France, by now Britain's most troublesome rival on the global stage. A struggle over territories in North America had eventually exploded into chaos as the rivalry reached European soil. The delicate balance of power was destroyed and the resulting conflict – arguably the first 'world' war, but now known as the Seven Years War – divided Europe and spanned five continents. Britain had formally entered the fray.

Within weeks John was ordered to cruise French waters, and he took his leave of Sophia in characteristic fashion: she fell pregnant just before he left. As she suffered the inevitable sicknesses and pains – Sophia was an anxious patient – she scoured the newspapers: to her relief she found her husband successfully commandeering a handful of French ships.

Returning in January 1757, John may have been back in time for the birth of their long-awaited son, and certainly for his baptism at St Andrew's church in Plymouth on 17 March – the first record of his existence. He was named John, or 'Jack', and would be a fittingly unruly child for their first born in wartime.

As well as a long-awaited son, the spring brought the command of the *America* and another mission cruising French waters. John was abroad when his mother died in September and spent a profitable winter capturing enemy vessels, though the mood of general jubilation was dampened when a French ship loaded with Canadian furs accidentally set itself on fire and exploded before their eyes. 'Out of 70 Hands no more than 24 could be saved,' John wrote, 'and those so miserably burnt, that many of them are since dead.'[43]

Another stint at Plymouth resulted in a second son, who was born in November 1758 and baptised George Anson Byron in tribute to his father's old friend. Meanwhile, John continued to impress his superiors. As a commander he was attentive and generally benevolent but was practical about the custom of 'pressing' – or forcibly recruiting – men, and swiftly turned disciplinarian when required. Having witnessed the perfidious effects of insubordination aboard the *Wager*, he was not afraid to have men whipped for mutinous or riotous behaviour. Controlling the men was challenging, and he was occasionally presented with darker problems: he immediately incarcerated one 'Worthless drunken fellow' who had sexually assaulted the child of a fellow sailor on board the ship, writing solemnly, 'there can be little room left to doubt of his Villainy'.[44]

As France drew up plans for an invasion of England, John was given a new ship – the *Fame* – his own squadron and a new challenge. In March 1760, leaving Sophia in the condition she had come to expect, he sailed for Canada with his friend Captain Samuel Barrington in tow. The mission would earn him acclaim in the British press and a dark place in Canadian legend. His orders were to superintend the demolition of the fortifications at the port town of Louisbourg, to ensure that it didn't fall back into French hands. As the engineers went about their work, John prowled the coasts looking for the enemy. When he received word of suspicious vessels in nearby Chaleur Bay he reflected that 'an Opportunity like that of curbing the French should not be suffered to slip' and set out in immediate pursuit.[45] Within days three French frigates and over twenty smaller vessels had been burned and destroyed – along with a village of some 350 houses inhabited by Acadian refugees (descendants of the early French settlers). After months of work, in mid October one final blast reduced the last stretch of the fortifications to rubble, and the town to just a scattering of fishermen's houses. Having played their small but significant part in ending French dominance in Canada, the squadron left the next day feeling their duty had been thoroughly fulfilled. Accounts of John's own 'spirited behaviour' at Chaleur Bay already filled the newspapers back home.[46] (Behind them mournful tales of British destruction, of Acadian women and children callously driven from burning homes, began to take root.)

When John returned in November 1760, Britain was changed. There was a new king on the throne and, briefly, another daughter in the Byron nursery. The likeable young George III was the first 'home-grown' monarch the nation had seen for fifty years. 'Born and educated in this country,' he cannily declared in his accession speech, 'I glory in the name of Britain.' He also made quite an impression on his female subjects: 'Every body continued in speaking of the King's affability and goodness,' gushed Isabella to her husband from Bath, 'but Mrs Lane says his Breath is like Roses, and his Lips velvet'.[47]

Baby Charlotte, perhaps named in honour of the new queen, was baptised in the new year of 1761 – and buried in the same church on 17 April. Life carried on with the weight of three daughters lost. John was deemed an active and popular enough member of the community to be made a Freeman of Plymouth. Another pregnancy brought another daughter, baptised Augusta Barbara Charlotte on 28 November 1762. Sophia might have been relieved had she known that Augusta would be her final child. At thirty-four she had borne nine children, six of whom survived infancy: two sons, Jack and George Anson, to bring honour to the family name; and four daughters, Fanny, Juliana, Sophy and Augusta, to seek fortunes of their own. Fourteen-year-old Fanny was entrusted with the task of dashing off letters to family members when her father returned from his missions. ('I have [had] a letter from my little Niece Byron at Plymouth', Isabella wrote with relief after his Canadian mission, 'to let me know her Papa is arrivd safe.')[48]

When the brutal hostilities of the Seven Years War formally ceased in February 1763, Britain congratulated itself on a conflict well spent: territories had been gained in Canada, America and the West Indies, and France's supremacy in Europe was in tatters. John had escaped any real horror, though he had lost men – much of the nation was left mourning their fathers, husbands or sons. For his part, he had lived up to Anson's predictions – his Canadian endeavours had gained him a reputation as a bold and active wartime commander – and the family took up a peaceful country residence at Mortlake, in Surrey. But while the fretful Sophia welcomed the end of the conflict, it did not mean a new season of domestic bliss.

'And with Commodore Byron we'll sail the world round!'

With peace, the Admiralty discreetly swapped its cannon for its compass and meditated on ventures of a different kind: voyages of discovery. With swathes of the globe as yet uncharted and – crucially – 'unclaimed', the powers of Europe would inevitably begin jostling for control over new lands. Old navigators' journals hinted at Pacific islands glittering with riches and reported sightings of others that would secure control over the surrounding seas. There were rumours of a vast *terra australis* in the unmapped waters of the south. But, as one contemporary writer put it, nothing had yet been done 'to enable the geographer to fill up that wide-extended and opprobrius *blank*, so conspicuous in our maps of the southern hemisphere, without the assistance of mermaids, dolphins, and flying fishes'.[49] Plans for a mission to the Pacific were drawn up in the strictest secrecy – even government ministers were kept in the dark – and John was called to town from Mortlake. He had been chosen to take command and fill up that 'opprobrius *blank*'.

His brief was ambitious. With two vessels, the sixth-rate frigate *Dolphin* and the sloop *Tamar*, he was to find and claim the elusive Pepys' Island off the coast of South America – as well as any other unknown territories they happened across – before proceeding through the Straits of Magellan towards California to seek an as yet undiscovered North-West Passage. While the *Dolphin* was being equipped with an experimental copper-sheathed bottom (an attempt to prevent decay), John assembled his crews. He retrieved his favourite cook, Mr Stanley, and his boatswain from the *Fame*, William Baxter, whom he described as 'as good a Man as ever came into a ship'.[50] He dispatched a note to his friend Lieutenant Carteret from the *Vanguard*: 'If you should chuse to go to Sea with me, make all the Haste you can to Town as not a Moments time must be lost.'[51] It would be a long journey, and before sailing John requested a few days' liberty in town to settle his affairs and say goodbye to his family. Putting foreign spies off the scent, the Admiralty announced that he was bound for the East Indies and formally declared him commander-in-chief of that station to add weight to the deception. John repeated the story to his crew – and, presumably, to Sophia – before they set sail on 3 July 1764.

The usual stop at Madeira, and a cannon salute sent them reeling towards Brazil. Having witnessed the ravages of scurvy on his last voyage to the Pacific, from the very earliest days of the voyage John was vigilant about the health of his men. He ordered 'as much fresh meat and greens as they could eat every day', and on reaching Cape Verde lectured them on the importance of responsible behaviour and not sleeping in wet clothes.[52] His efforts were admirable but not always successful. Three days later they set sail accompanied by a 'large cargo' of goats and chattering monkeys, which the excitable sailors had traded for their extra shirts and bedding.

They anchored at Rio de Janeiro on 13 September and John took up lodgings on shore while the ships were repaired. Even he found the heat 'intollerable'.[53] Society only sprang to life in the late afternoon when the sun lost its sting and the marketplaces filled with peddlers and entertainers, their cries mixed with the sound of clanking chains as naked slaves were paraded for sale. The evenings provoked 'scenes of debauchery' as the women appeared and merchants conspired to inebriate, rob and dispose of unsuspecting sailors. (Five of the *Dolphin*'s crew were lost this way.) John enjoyed more genteel company, being hosted in the palace of the viceroy and entertaining aboard the *Dolphin* the illustrious Lord Clive, who had recently secured British rule in India. His arrival provided a glow of satisfaction for John. 'Upon our arrival at this place, to our great surprise, we found Commodore Byron', Clive wrote in astonishment, 'who left England nearly a month after us, and anchored here nearly a month before us.'[54] John noted in his journal that, unlike his own men, Clive's crew was riddled with scurvy.

On 22 October, having finally put to sea, John called all hands on deck to deliver a bombshell: they were not bound for the East Indies but tasked with a secret mission of discovery. Armed with the charts of history's fearless explorers – Magellan, Narborough, Anson – they were to seek out unknown lands and resources. (If this failed to fire enthusiasm, it was quickly inspired by his promise of double pay 'if they behaved themselves to my satisfaction'.)[55] And so they set off, in the scorching heat, in search of a new paradise.

While John was familiar with the whims and tempests of the South Seas, many of his men were not. When the swift change in climate presented a string of shivering, shirtless sailors – their monkeys, providing no protection from the cold, were no longer quite so amusing – he ensured they were properly dressed. He was unwavering in his patience, seemingly thinking of them as he might a rabble of unruly children: 'they are all now well provided again', he recorded in his journal, '& in all probability will not have an opportunity of selling these for some time'.[56] Curious creatures were brought aboard, including a 'fierce' little tiger cat that became embroiled in a 'tight contest' with John's own dog (though the men forewent further enquiry into the 'little ugly Animal that stunk so we could not any of us go near him').[57] During one landing party, the discovery of an old British musket – which began crumbling in his hands – transported John back twenty years: 'I imagine it must have been left here by the *Wager's* people,' he wrote, remembering the route taken by the *Speedwell*.[58]

As winter deepened, so nature seemed to conspire against them – their progress was marred by thick fogs and 'ugly swells', and clear sights of land promptly vanished before their eyes. The search for Pepys' Island continued, but John's charts were proving unhelpful: 'nothing was ever so confused as Sir John Narborough's description,' he lamented.[59]

Just before Christmas they were cruising a mile off the Patagonian coast near Tierra del Fuego when someone noticed smoke winding its way into the sky. A distant 'hallooing' drifted towards them. John looked through his spyglass and made out a group of local inhabitants some 500-strong. Unflinching, he took a boat of officers to the shore and gave them strict orders not to move or speak unless he gave them explicit orders to do so. He approached, alone. Clothed in animal skins and with their faces 'painted in the most frightful Manner imaginable', they were an intimidating sight for an Englishman – but most remarkable of all was their height. Though he never publicly specified his estimation of their size he was effusive in private correspondence, declaring, 'I never was more astonish'd than to see such a set of People, the stoutest of Our Grenadiers would appear nothing to them', who 'in Size come nearest to Giants of any People I believe in the World'.[60] The encounter was peaceful, with John communicating as best he could through gestures and signs and offering gifts of beads and silk ribbons. He retreated, pleased to have made contact and hoping to find them again; but when his crew returned, they had moved on.

Having passed into the Straits of Magellan, they spent Christmas at the 'second paradise' of the Sedger River, enjoying 'all that season of jollity and mirth could desire'.[61] For John, the celebrations were dampened by their failure to find Pepys' Island – they should have reached it weeks ago. Beginning to doubt that it existed at all, he resolved to turn back. After more fruitless searching, he wrote, 'We are well assured there is no such Island.'[62]

Violent storms kept the ship's carpenter busy for the next two weeks until land was sighted on 13 January 1765. 'Falkland's Islands'. John gave the order to send boats ashore. Though the land had been discovered by an English explorer in the previous century it appeared deserted – their only assailants were a few wolf-like creatures and flocks of curious geese. The land seemed habitable and fertile, teeming with birds, oysters and seals, and was easily cultivated (the surgeon of the *Tamar* even built a 'pritty little Garden'). For ten days John's men surveyed the area – taking the opportunity to fashion new waistcoats from seal skins – and he named the harbour 'Port Egmont' after the sponsor of his mission.

On 26 January – as his brother prepared for a fateful evening of carousing with the Nottinghamshire club – 'the Commo[do]re hoisted his Colours & went on Shore & took Possession of Faulklands Islands in the Name of His Majesty George the third'.[63] The Union Jack fluttered above the harbour, the *Dolphin* issued a booming salute, and the crews raised a tot of brandy to the king. They may have failed to complete the first part of their mission, but this was surely some compensation. The next day they set sail still celebrating their success, apparently unaware of the existence of a year-old French settlement on the other side of the island – subsequent centuries of simmering conflict invited by this oversight could not concern the oblivious John, who was already meditating his next move.

While his brother sat sniffling in the Tower, John was overtaken by a fit of rebelliousness. They had passed back through the Strait, but he did not give the order to turn towards North America. They had spent months at the mercy of bad weather and he considered this sufficient reason to take another route: 'Our Ships are too much disabled for the California Voyage,' he wrote to the Admiralty, describing the 'infinite deal of Fatigue & many dangers' they had faced.[64] With a touch of the melodrama the Byron siblings seem all to have shared, he continued: 'I protest for my self that I have gone thro' them with the greatest Chearfulness and I can safely say that in either Ship no man has had so large a Share of them as I have'. Where, then, were they bound? He informed Lord Egmont that he would 'run over for India by a new Track', hoping to fill in some uncharted waters on the way. Perhaps a little too opportunely, lying somewhere along his planned course were the much sought 'Solomon Islands' and a reputed bounty of treasures. An irresistible quest.

In the months that followed the *Dolphin* and *Tamar* cruised the Pacific, enduring piercing winds and spending crisp, icy nights under the stars. John wrote in his journal of 'every body continually wet to the Skin . . . however I thank God my People are all very healthy, & go through this fatiguing work with great chearfulness'.[65] When morale dipped, John distributed new cloth so that his men could make longer, more protective waistcoats, and successful surveying parties were rewarded with double brandy rations. As soon as they began to spit out teeth, he ordered fresh beef and vegetables – a measure not enforced, or even recognised, by many commanders of the time. His motivation was as pragmatic as it was compassionate – sickly mariners could not have withstood the violent gale that almost left both ships 'dashed in pieces against the frightful rocks' in March – but his attentiveness to those under his command earned him a reputation for 'great humanity'.

As they continued in their quest, the crews had varying degrees of success with the inhabitants of the islands on which they landed. John recorded one particularly friendly encounter in April: 'one of our Midshipmen plaid on the Fiddle & some of our people danced to entertain them'; in return 'one of them brought a bag of paint up, & daub'd one of my Officer's faces all over with it, & wanted to pay me the same complement [sic]'.[66] But John's initial positivity faltered as no significant lands – certainly none promising treasure – deigned to present themselves. Unluckily, in May he narrowly missed encountering the as yet 'undiscovered' island of Tahiti. The call of *land!* one day in June finally presented a small but beautiful haven of cocoa trees and slow-moving turtles. As John formed a design of establishing a sick bay on the shore – thinking of the limes and bananas he knew could help his scurvy-ridden crews – it became clear that both the coral rocks and the aggressive islanders would frustrate him. The inhabitants of neighbouring islands (now part of the Tuamotu Archipelago in French Polynesia) were similarly hostile, pelting them with stones or attempting to drag them from their small boats into the sea. Turning away in frustration and dismay, he dubbed them the 'Islands of Disappointment'.

Their search continued, and scatterings of small islands were added to their charts. The heat was intense, and there was no way of knowing if the approaching islanders intended murder or mischief. In one encounter their small landing boats were overrun by assailants, one of whom stole a sailor's jacket and another attempted to take a midshipman's hat, 'but not knowing how to take it off, he pull'd down, instead of lifting it off his head'.[67] On 'Coral Island', they found a human skeleton and the feathered corpse of a dog hanging from a tree; at 'King George's Island', the skies glinted with the greens and blues of tropical birds. But nothing matched the description of the Solomon Islands – John set down his old French maps with a sigh. Another lost cause. He might have been slightly cheered when they stopped at a 'delightfully pleasant' island, 'which my Officers chose to give my name to'. ('Byron's Island' is now Nukunau, in the Gilbert Islands.)

At the end of July, six months after leaving the Falkland Islands, the sickly crew landed on the uninhabited, mosquito-ridden island of Tinian. By now even John was suffering the swollen, bleeding gums, bruising and weakness brought on by scurvy, and he remained pitched on the shore for a month. Despite the relatively forgiving climate and plentiful food supplies it took weeks to restore everyone to health. One midshipman later recalled, 'all our thoughts ran now upon getting home', and John resolved to oblige them – but it was not an easy crossing.[68] Passing by Sumatra in November, the bread began to squirm with maggots, and in December a putrid fever broke out after a short stay in the sweltering, swarming city of Batavia (now Jakarta). ('I came in here without a Man Sick in either Ship', John wrote, later remarking, '[but] the Europeans die here like rotten Sheep'.)[69] After calling at the Cape of Good Hope they set a course for England. The *Dolphin* sailed into the South Downs on 9 May 1766, just over twenty-two months after leaving: John had achieved the fastest circumnavigation of the globe to date.

Though he had graciously declined to follow orders and failed to discover any lands of significance, Commodore Byron's expedition was hailed as a success. First, it was record-breaking as both a feat of seamanship and in its remarkably low mortality rate. The copper sheath was a triumph, and praised by John as 'the finest Invention in the World'.[70] Second, he had secured possession of the Falkland Islands – considered 'the Key to the whole Pacifick Ocean'– and added a new scattering of small Pacific islands to European maps.[71] Third, his detailed journals and charts would be invaluable for subsequent voyages – excitable journalists (prematurely) declared that he would command another before the year was out.

While he was praised by the Admiralty for his 'good conduct', a keener measure of his success as a commander came from his men. In early June the peace of Mortlake was rudely interrupted with the arrival of a gang of familiar faces at his door, clattering musical instruments and carrying 'a globe and colours'. At their entreaties he met them on the terrace, 'when they returned him thanks for his great tenderness and humanity to them on their late voyage'. The tribute was concluded with a raucous song of their own composition, with the whole crew joining in the chorus, 'And with Commodore Byron we'll sail the world round!'[72]

Readjusting to family life was an entirely different challenge. He was swarthier, his clothes battered, his looks perhaps altered by the scurvy. Little Augusta – just a baby when he left – may not have recognised him at all. Fanny had just turned seventeen and nine-year-old Jack, the man of the house for the last two years, was preparing for Westminster School. Sophia's hands had been full during his absence. As well as managing her own brood of six, she displayed 'proper and spirited Conduct' when her holidaying sister-in-law deposited her daughters Betty and Julia at Bolton Row, just as Betty was in the middle of a troublesome romantic tryst.[73]

Isabella herself flew the fourteen miles from her Surrey residence to welcome John home and regale him with the dramas that had unfolded while he had explored the farthest reaches of the world. William had killed Mr Chaworth, and been tried for murder! Their uncle Charles Berkeley had drowned in a freak boating accident on his estate, and they had a new nephew, Frederick George Byron, courtesy of George and his wife Frances in Nottingham. As for Isabella, she had been at the heart of the social scene at Spa, where holding a musical court for European aristocrats and royals had left her 'giddy as a goose'.

When the truth of John's mission was revealed, the 'inflexible Integrity and great Generosity of the Hon. Commodore Byron' came close to eclipsing even the notoriety earned by his brother.[74] But one particular element of his trip captured the public imagination: the talk of *giants*. How the reports began is unclear – perhaps the exaggerations of boastful sailors, or a leaked document – but within weeks the gossip spilled into sensationalism on both sides of the Atlantic: these towering warriors had dwarfed Byron's crew, and the women had breasts 'as large as cow dugs'.[75] Horace Walpole embraced the first opportunity to poke fun at the credulous and pass comment on the British colonial spirit: 'As soon as [the "giants"] are properly civilized, that is, *enslaved*', he noted archly, in the midst of America's protests about taxation, 'they shall not wear a Sheep's skin that has not been legally Stamped.'[76] (John himself emerged relatively unscathed, being described as a six-foot man of 'bold and sensible resolution'.) A gossip-mongering publication of 1767 (now attributed to one of the midshipmen) placed them at between eight and ten feet tall, with fifteen-foot horses and dogs with snouts like pigs. Keen to distance themselves from the book, several of John's officers took out an advertisement in national newspapers to declare that they had nothing to do with it. In the absence of an author's name, John was likely perturbed to find the outlandish claims attached to him, though he had barely said a public word on the subject.

A Patagonian Woman and Boy in Company with Commodore Byron
was printed shortly after John's return from circumnavigating the globe.
He is shown offering a string of beads as a token of friendship.

Thanks to John's voyage, interest in the Pacific had been thoroughly revived. Travelling in his wake, his colleague Captain Wallis assumed command of a second expedition with the *Dolphin* and a junior officer named Captain James Cook was preparing for his first mission aboard the *Endeavour*, 'following the course pursued by Commodore Byron . . . upon the same important business'.[77] It is likely that John was employed in some advisory capacity for these missions: no one was better placed to offer suggestions for new routes, and the search for a vast southern land was encouraged by the positive signs recorded in his journal. (Certainly, the foreign spies soaking up leaked information declared it to be 'Byron's second expedition'.) John, however, had another project on his mind. The public had for years weighed in with opinions about his life and career – why not tell his own story?

John may have been compiling his account of the *Wager* disaster for years – unless his memory for minutiae was remarkable, he must have made notes. With Captain Cheap long dead there was no longer any danger of causing offence, and he had secured some leisure time, having politely declined the post of governor of Pensecola (now Florida). Finally yielding 'to the desires of my friends' and breaking the professional silence he had maintained for over twenty years, John put pen to paper and found a publisher.

The resulting book showed that he was not merely a hard-headed officer, but an astute and a learned gentleman. His writing style – modest and clear, with an irresistible hint of romantic colour – mirrored the drama displayed in his *Dolphin* journal (in which he routinely declared that 'nothing could be more melancholly than our present situation'). It hinted at his commitment to his religious faith and included interesting notes about flora and fauna, geography and both British and foreign medical knowledge. He addressed the falsehoods of previous testimonies, cannily putting old arguments to rest by giving himself the last word.

In late April or early May 1768, *The Narrative of the Honourable John Byron* was unleashed on the world. The reviews began to trickle in. 'Our readers are undoubtedly apprised of the great services the Hon[ourable] author has done his country', declared the *Scots Magazine*, 'but, till this narrative appeared, they could have no idea of the hardships he suffered.'[78] The *Kentish Gazette* was succinct: 'Simple, interesting, affecting, and romantic.'[79] The public devoured the tales of murderous sailors, of his gentle, ill-fated dog Boxer, and of a poisonous spider that turned his face black at St Jago. 'I never before read of any who endured such hardships and survived them,' the Methodist preacher John Wesley mused in his journal. 'Sure, no novel in the world can be more affecting or more surprising than this history.'[80] The book's resounding success saw translations promptly begin to pop up across Europe. John's status as a man of action and courage was proven in both his youthful heroics and recent accomplishments: 'Columbus-like may Byron plow the main, For fresh discov'ries to the nation's gain,' gushed a poem published in one evening newspaper.[81]

It was not long before John, still buoyed by this new literary achievement, was offered a new commission: governor of Newfoundland and Labrador. It was not exactly an irresistible prospect. No enemy to pursue or distant lands to discover – just five months dealing with fisheries and trading complaints. But having already declined the post in Florida he perhaps didn't wish to seem apathetic, and on 15 February 1769 he kissed the king's hand in formal acceptance of the post. He coordinated his preparations from 56 Welbeck Street, a house he had leased in a neat new development in the West End of London (it perhaps afforded a little peace from Sophia and the ruckus of children at Bolton Row). Weeks passed as he assembled his crew – wresting his much needed secretary Mr Stacey from another ship – and gathered 'several valuable presents' as friendship tokens for the indigenous chiefs.[82] Meanwhile, Sophia and the children prepared for another long stretch without him.

As John knew from his very first voyage aboard the *Romney* three decades years earlier, Newfoundland – the most easterly province of Canada – was a valuable fishing and trading outpost. It could also be a violent place. The harbours crawled with illicit traders and the land was infested with 'barbarous furriers' and 'lawless vagabonds' who pursued their business by force if necessary – especially if those standing in their way were the local inhabitants, the Beothuk and the 'Mickmack' (Mi'kmaq). The latter had long fought against the creep of British colonialism, and relations with the former were deteriorating in the face of increasing violence from British settlers. As well as tightening controls on fishing, it was hoped that John's extensive experience of cross-cultural communication could smooth the disorder. He set sail aboard the *Antelope* in early June, bound for his administrative base in the town of St John's.

They reached the harbour just over a month later amid lightning and driving rain, and the ship fired an eleven-gun salute as he strode ashore on 8 July 'to take possession of my Government'.[83] First: the proclamations. Among them was a decree for the protection of the Beothuk, condemning those who had been wilfully murdering them 'without the least provocation or remorse' – perpetrators would be transported to England under pain of death.[84] From St John's he toured the 'Boisterous and dangerous Coasts' and the ports under his jurisdiction. 'From the general good Character of our present Governor, and his free affable Behaviour,' declared one sympathetic local newspaper, 'by what we can at present judge, have great Reason to suppose he will be generally esteemed.'[85]

Life at St John's was a far cry from the genteel bustle of Welbeck Street, and the weeks of grinding administrative duties must have worn on the spirits of an officer used to storm-tossed seas. He was flooded with complaints: of settlers 'wantonly setting fire' to the huts of French merchants, of rotting ships, of suspicious vessels, and masters paying in rum instead of money. Finally, November came. He left for Portsmouth laden with gifts for friends, including two large, shaggy Newfoundland dogs – one for his brother William (a friend for the wolf, perhaps) and the other for Lord Hillsborough, Secretary of State for the Colonies.

Leaving Newfoundland (temporarily) behind, his seven-month season at home was dominated by an entirely different kind of fuss – weddings. Two promising military officers had been lined up for John and Sophia's eldest daughters. For twenty-one-year-old Fanny, he negotiated with the family of Lieutenant Charles Leigh, a young soldier who had connections to the royal household and was later described as a man of 'accomplished manners, and never-failing suavity'.[86] A summer wedding was arranged. For sixteen-year-old Juliana, her parents selected Captain John Delap Halliday, whose father was a 'man of fortune' with significant plantation estates in the West Indies.[87] To the delight of Juliana (and Sophia) he swiftly professed his love. John also found some time for leisure, commissioning a couple of quaint hunting portraits: in one he sits, rather plump and genial-looking, astride his horse and with a gun slung at his side; in the other he is depicted 'hunting his own hounds', riding full pelt behind a pack of slavering beagles.[88]

His peace was, however, cut short when word came in that the Spanish had overrun the settlement John had established at Port Egmont in the Falkland Islands – he left for Canada amid difficult questions over the validity of his claim over it. (Unsurprisingly, the British press ranged itself squarely behind its home-grown hero.)

John was batting away the usual tedious complaints about fishing rights when Fanny took her vows at St Marylebone church to become Mrs Leigh on 11 July. He was still in Newfoundland on 6 October when the licence was secured for Juliana's marriage to Captain Halliday. He had likely set sail for England by the time Halliday deserted her and eloped to Scotland with Jane Tollemache, a sister of the Earl of Dysart. It was apparently an impulse decision. 'The Captain was just going to be married to Miss Byron, the coach and clothes were bought,' Lord Malmesbury heard from his gossiping mother, 'but he saw Lady Jane twice at the Richmond assembly, was captivated, wrote a letter to Miss Byron, to inform her he had changed his mind, and had set out for Scotland.'[89] Despite facing the wrath of both the Byrons and the Tollemaches – the lady's brother was forced to intercede and reconcile the two families – Halliday apparently felt no regret, insisting with startling naivety not only that 'I never meant any Injury of the sort to Mr. Byron's Family', but continuing:

> I confess that I have not the least Sense of the injury so grievously complain'd of, for what could have been more injurious than to have enter'd into the most Solemn of all Contracts with one Lady whilst the Other has Sole Possession of my Heart? Whilst I continu'd to love Miss Byron my Behaviour was Irreproachable. Why then has it been less so when because that Love cess'd (which unaccountable Effect I can impute to nothing but the Caprice of the human Heart), I had the Resolution to Declare it?[90]

There was talk that an overly meddlesome Sophia had been making unreasonable financial demands and was now threatening to seek legal redress for breach of promise. She was certainly furious, and poor Juliana was left broken-hearted.

On 17 November 1770, shortly after his forty-seventh birthday, John sailed back into Plymouth harbour. Had he taken a moment to reflect on his life, he could have counted himself the most outwardly successful of his siblings. William postured and plotted as he fell deeper into debt, his early happiness with Elizabeth eaten away by resentment. Isabella fluttered about Europe seeking solace for her woes in the 'romantick' surroundings of France (and, according to gossip, in the arms of dashing young officers). Richard and George followed their quiet but creditable lives in the provincial clergy and local politics respectively. Meanwhile, John had achieved uncommon success in both his personal and professional life. Sophia had borne him six healthy children and, though her nerves had suffered, she had proved an outwardly resilient navy wife. 'Dear Mrs Biron, she has the courage becoming an Admiral's lady,' sympathised her literary friend Samuel Johnson, as her spirits sank under the heavy trials brought by the 1770s.[91]

Hard work and level head had secured the professional esteem that had always eluded his commitment-shy elder brother. He had demonstrated a remarkable talent for survival during the *Wager* disaster, proved his mettle in war and stood literally at the helm of a new age of exploration. At home he was acclaimed in the press as a good man and as a man of action: a 'gallant, active Officer' who had 'greatly distinguished himself for his good Conduct' during his voyage around the world.[92] 'Though he made some of the greatest discoveries of this century', declared one flattering (if somewhat premature) biographical note of 1771, 'he scarce shed any human blood.'[93] Sailing in the path paved by John's expedition, Captain Cook had 'discovered' mainland Australia in 1770 and paid tribute to his predecessor by naming its easternmost point 'Cape Byron' (the subsequent settlement became known as 'Byron Bay'). It was a compliment mirrored elsewhere. Today there is Byron Island (beside Wager's Island), off the Chilean coast; Byron Bay in Newfoundland; Byron Heights in the Falkland Islands; and the former Byron's Island, in what is now the Gilbert Islands (though, admittedly, his men designated this one themselves).

Combating the dubious celebrity bestowed upon it by his reckless brother, John had made make the Byron name both deserving of admiration and truly international. 'Upon the whole,' surmised one reviewer of his *Narrative*, 'we think the author has suffered more in his own person than any man now living, and deserves the highest preferment his profession can admit of.'[94]

Unfortunately, if he looked to the future with the hope of having left the bad weather behind him, he was sorely mistaken. Though there was, as yet, little reason for pessimism, his most bitter disappointment lay ahead. The Americans were stirring.

4

The Great Dining Hall

Lady Carlisle, 1736–70

And sunk are the voices that sounded in mirth,
And empty the goblet, and dreary the hearth . . .

Newstead Abbey

1759

It is a Sunday evening in early September and Isabella weeps as her carriage rattles through the darkness towards Ferrybridge. Each moment wrenches them further apart. She thinks of his tender declarations, the touch of his hand, the lines of anxiety carving themselves into his serious face. Her bookish young baronet. She attempts to rally her spirits by closing her eyes and picturing the last few days at Halnaby Hall. They seem enchanted. An ornate old mansion nestled in perfectly sculpted grounds – in it their friend Lady Milbanke, whose kindness brought them together. The crisp air of the Yorkshire autumn. The three sweet Milbanke children: Ralph, John and Elizabeth. Laughter and the clinking of glass in the prettily stuccoed dining hall, as the sun disappeared below the horizon. The leaping heart at the exchange of a glance. Society will not think well of her. It is a year to the day since Henry died and she intends to return to town barely out of her mourning dress, with news of a suitor fourteen years her junior? She indulges her melancholy ideas and the inevitable tears, knowing they go unobserved in the dim light.

She reaches her lodgings and takes up her pen. 'What shall I say to my Dear Friend?' she begins. 'Weary, dejected, and sleepy as I am now and yet ye moments & thus employ are the first easy ones I have felt since I have quitted you.' She scribbles passionately, messily, with little consideration to style. 'Remember my health and spirits are so connected with yours, that the one must suffer if the other does, thought crowds on thought so fast that I cannot express myself could you but read my heart you would then discover the sincerity, and tenderness of my meaning to you . . .' She finishes with apologies for her handwriting — 'I have been blinded all day with Tears'. It is late. The world seems at once lighter, and heavier. Have these been the happiest days of her life? Are they now over? She climbs into bed feeling the bittersweet pangs of an ill-starred attachment. Isabella is in love.

In January 1815 George Gordon Byron sits at a desk in Halnaby Hall composing a letter. He is on his honeymoon. 'I don't dislike this place — it is just the spot for a Moon,' he scrawls. 'I have great hopes this match will turn out well — I have found nothing as yet that I could wish changed for the better — but Time does wonders,' he adds cynically, 'so I won't be too hasty in my happiness.'[2]

His bride is Annabella Milbanke — a granddaughter of Isabella's 'Lady M' — and his correspondent is his friend and her aunt Elizabeth, Lady Melbourne (who as a seven-year-old Miss Milbanke had politely curtseyed to a powdered and perfumed Lady Carlisle and the studious *Sir* who was in love with her). George calls his new wife 'Bell' or 'Pippin' — a tribute to her round, rosy cheeks — and she calls him 'Dearest Duck'. They have been prevented from venturing out by snow, and (he claims) consummated their marriage on the sofa.

But his attitude seems to change. Bell is confronted with his 'fit of *grumps*', including dark hints that he is 'guilty of some heinous crime' and that she has married into a family plagued by insanity.[3] They leave after three weeks and his new reality sinks in: 'the treaclemoon is over, and I am awake, and find myself married'.[4]

George passed the earliest days of his marriage in the very rooms where his great-aunt's intoxicating romance had blossomed — and like that of her great-nephew, the 'fairy dream' of Isabella's Halnaby romance did not end well.

~

Isabella was fourteen when her father died and the legal burden of her existence transferred to her younger brother William. While the boys were dispatched to a prestigious school, she was kept at home to practise her accomplishments, but she had no intention of confining herself to the sort of female education that could be reduced to 'a set of phrases learn'd by rote' and 'a passion for a scarlet coat', as the poet Swift had implied.[5] She studied French and Latin, and sketched and sang with proficiency. She was drawn to the poetry of Shakespeare and Spenser, and though her handwriting was not especially elegant – her feelings hurried her too much – she loved to write. She embroidered clothes for her brothers to take on their adventures across the seas, a comforting reminder of home. She studied mathematics in preparation for running her own household, and was especially inquisitive about botany and cooking: her mother Frances passed down generations-old recipes and remedies from her maternal family. If Isabella found interest in a subject, she was determined to master it. 'Be not repulsed by the first difficulties in learning', she later wrote, 'the roughness of the road to any science will insensibly decrease, as you approach the summit.'[6]

If her character as a girl resembled that of her adulthood, the young Isabella was restless, sociable and easily caught up in her passions – it was later joked that she 'always spoke of what was running in her head'.[7] She quickly grew bored without company and itched to be launched into the adult world. With an eye to this momentous event, the artist Michael Dahl was recalled to the Byron household to immortalise Isabella on the cusp of womanhood. This first portrait captures the direct gaze of a girl in a pale grey gown shimmering with bronze. She has striking dark features (and slightly dishevelled hair), her flushed cheeks are inclined to plump and there is a mole below her bottom lip; she clutches sprigs of a delicate white flower to her breast, perhaps alluding to her purity and faith. A model of wifely potential.

Isabella's heart fluttered as she was finally presented to the ballrooms of London and Bath as the *Honourable Miss Byron* under the watchful eyes of the Dowager Lady Byron and her uncle Lord Berkeley. She was eighteen when her mother remarried and William hauled the couple into court. By the time word came that John's ship had disappeared into the storms off South America she had turned twenty, and was living in an exhilarating whirl of candlelit ballrooms, card games, and flirtatious exchanges with eligible bachelors. She must marry, and marry well. Her entire education had been preparing her for it.

Among her suitors was forty-eight-year-old Henry Howard, 4th Earl of Carlisle. They may have met when she was a child – he was her father's former tenant at 15 Great Marlborough Street – or brought together more recently in the crush of society. He was already a grandfather and mourning three recent losses: a gambling-addict sister, an heir riddled with venereal disease and a much lamented wife. A connoisseur of the arts, he had powerful friends – among them the heir to throne, Prince Frederick of Wales – and was admired as a 'Man of uncommon Probity and good nature'.[8] Though he lacked the vitality of youth he certainly had style: his houses were filled with treasures from ancient Egypt, Rome, China and Persia, and his horse and saddle were eye-catchingly draped with leopard skin and silver trimming.

Most importantly, the Carlisles were among the wealthiest fami-lies in the country, boasting estates across Yorkshire, Cumberland and Northumberland. When Henry began to pay his attentions to Isabella, Frances was delighted. Lord Berkeley was drafted in and the families entered into negotiations. It hardly counted among the type of courtship condemned by one writer as 'mere Smithfield bargains, so much ready money for so much land, and my daughter flung into the bargain!' – Isabella had no father, after all, and no dowry worth flaunting in the newspapers (it was just over £3,600).[9] But she was young, vivacious and of relatively illustrious stock – and her new legal status was soon set inescapably in ink: 'Isabella BYRON [will] belong to the said Henry Earl of Carlisle upon the solem-nization of the said intended Marriage'.[10] As a wife, anything she owned would become the property of her husband.

'A good but inexperienced heart'

On the evening of 8 June 1743, twenty-one-year-old Isabella walked into Carlisle House, Henry's mansion on Soho Square, as a bride. The bishop of Hereford, a distant relative, performed the service. With a few short words Isabella suddenly outranked her whole family

– 'Miss Byron, only Sister to the Lord Byron' became Isabella, Countess of Carlisle. In practical terms she had made an excellent conquest. 'It is impossible for me to express ye sense I have of my daughter's happiness in being y[ou]r Lordship's choice,' Frances wrote ingratiatingly from Alderston shortly after the wedding. 'I pray God she may contribute as much to y[ou]r felicity as I am persuaded 'tis her wish & desire to do', she continued, 'tho it will not be easy for her to make a return any way suitable to ye unspeakable goodness with which you have acted toward her.'[11] Isabella's new life was about to begin.

Accustomed to being the eldest daughter in a house of sons, Isabella had to find her place in an already established family. As well as a husband, she acquired three stepchildren her own age: Arabella (a new wife and mother), twenty-year-old Diana and deli-cate eighteen-year-old Robert, who had suffered from fits since childhood. Her mother-in-law Anne lived in a house on the oppos-ite side of Soho Square, within spying view of their windows (and, according to myth, connected by an underground tunnel). She was presented to a new brother-in-law, Charles – a distinguished military officer – and two sisters-in-law in their forties: the unmarried Mary and the poetic Anne, Lady Irwin.

Innumerable connections opened up as they welcomed a stream of well-wishers, all curiously eyeing Henry's new young wife. 'I know the young Lady Carlisle,' Mary Wortley Montagu confided to her husband, 'she is very agreeable; but if I am not mistaken in her inclinations, they are very gay.'[12] Being mistress of the Howard family estates was cause enough for high spirits, and her enthusiasm for society breathed new life into a home overshadowed by grief. Carlisle House was modern and extravagant, with lofty ceilings and marbled floors – and just half a mile from her brother's house at Great Marlborough Street. Her arrival was commemorated with a pair of miniature portraits by Frederick Zincke: Henry wore a rose and gold waistcoat, his blue eyes accentuated by a pristine white wig; Isabella chose a white lace dress with blue bows and ribbons, and a string of heavy pearls. Her dark hair was pinned up, showing off a pretty, rosy face that had shed its childish plumpness.

Isabella and Henry quickly found they were companionable if

not consumed with passion – unlike some of her unfortunate friends, she was certainly not forced to endure a marriage dictated 'by the will and pleasure of an absolute Lord and Master'. Henry was a kindly mentor, and Isabella was a breath of fresh air. Though he had settled into maturity he was sociable, enjoyed a drink, encouraged her sketching and understood the joy she took from music. His tendency to fret about aches and pains was perhaps what prompted Isabella to begin compiling the book of home-made remedies and recipes that accompanied her on her travels. As a wife, she was expected to manage the household, support her husband and provide new heirs for the estate. As a countess, she was required to be a sparkling hostess, a jewel on his arm and a model of propriety. In all but one of these duties Isabella would be a resounding success.

Just a few weeks after the wedding she was introduced to her responsibilities in Yorkshire, where the family reigned as one of the county's most prominent families. Their carriage swept into the grounds of Castle Howard, her husband's glittering baroque mansion just north of York, to be welcomed by rows of servants in eye-catching yellow and blue livery. Henry's theatrical chateau was crowned with a golden dome and the interior was no less lavish: bedchambers draped in red silk and ostrich feathers, a grand painted antechamber, a chapel cloaked in purple and yellow velvet, marble statues at every turn. It was soon fitted out with her new possessions – one later visitor marvelled at the beautiful jewellery box she proudly kept on display in the drawing room. The gardens, dotted with follies, stretched into thousands of acres of woodlands and waterfalls. A bakehouse, brewhouse, slaughterhouse, poultry yard and kennels – it would take weeks to explore.

Isabella was allowed four months to adjust to the pleasures of married life before the sudden death of her only stepson, Robert, called her more urgently to her real purpose: to provide heirs. Fortunately, she inherited her mother's easy fertility – she was pregnant by the New Year. By March, Henry was already receiving notes angling for gossip. 'I heare my Lady Carl[isl]e is with Child', came one from Berkshire, 'I hope it is true'.[13] As they retreated to Yorkshire for another summer, polite enquiries turned to hopes that 'Lady Carlisle whenever it happens may have an easy & safe time'.[14]

It was a far from hollow sentiment – pregnancy was a dangerous time for women and especially frightening for those carrying their first child. A ladies' manual of the previous generation was blunt in its advice for expectant mothers: 'None ever repented of making ready to dye'.[15] Just five years earlier, Isabella's aunt Anne Berkeley had died following complications after childbirth, and the Byrons' neighbour Juliana Molyneux wrote fearfully to her sister of this 'fatal time' even when expecting her sixth child: 'how happy shall I be if I arrive to that and bring forth a live Child, sometimes I have hopes and sometimes I have none . . . Pray for me my Dear Sister, it is impossible for you to judge what my fears occasion'.[16] It may not have eased Isabella's anxiety that she passed much of the pregnancy at Castle Howard, far from the medical expertise of town. She prepared as best she could, perhaps testing the mixture of egg, water and sugar that she later recorded in her recipe book as 'the best Remedy to prevent miscarrying'.[17] Finally, in early September 1744, the arrival of their first child: a daughter, Anne. While Isabella recovered, Henry was inundated with hopes that 'tho' you was disappointed of a Boy, that you will have many a one, to continue your noble, and worthy family to Posterity'.[18] (Better luck next time!) They did not wait long before trying again.

In the troubled early summer of 1745 Isabella's delicate condition became apparent as they visited their estate at Naworth Castle – a picturesque medieval fortress near Carlisle, just a few miles from the Scottish border. The place was entirely calculated to appeal to Isabella's romantic spirit – 'I am very fond of that old Castle, and its Environs', she later wrote, despite it being so often deluged with rain – and she made lifelong friends in Henry's distant relations Philip and Anne Howard of neighbouring Corby Castle.[19]

They returned to Castle Howard, still in the flush of excitement at the prospect of another child, to receive good and bad news. The first came from Lord Winchilsea, with new intelligence of her lost brother John. 'Being perswaded it will give my Lady Carlisle & y[ou]r Lordship great pleasure to have a certain account of Mr Byron', he began, 'I could not help making the Enclosed Extract . . . I hope my Lady may soon have the pleasure of seeing her Brother return in perfect health after all his fatigues & distresses.'[20]

After all these years, proof that he was alive! The more worrying national news of Jacobite rebellion in the north was swiftly followed by the enemy capture of Carlisle just a matter of weeks after they left it. As they departed for Soho Square, Lord Carlisle wrote fretfully to friends in that city insisting they flee to his house in York, 'out of the way there of the Rebels'.[21]

As William marched to Aberdeen with Kingston's regiment, Isabella went into labour and a second daughter – Frances, after her own mother – was born at Carlisle House on 25 January 1746. (Better luck next time!) A muddy-booted John may have arrived at their doorstep just in time for the baptism three weeks later, followed by Lord Byron from Scotland – reuniting the three siblings for the first time in almost six years. As the Carlisles refitted John for society and the brothers swapped stories of valour (likely exaggerated on William's part, for how could his tales compare?), the city erupted into celebrations at the death of the Jacobite cause.

Her brothers were called back to their duties, Isabella's family spent a sickly summer in Yorkshire, and her brother-in-law and stepfather were dispatched together to the war brewing on the Continent. 'Thus we are tossed about in our way of life,' Charles Howard wrote miserably, 'and, instead of passing my time agreeably at Castle Howard, are we sent, when we least expect, to a life of care and anxiety'.[22] Isabella's youngest brother George, fresh from Westminster School, angled for a commission with Charles's regiment, the 'Green Howards', and was graciously accepted.

While the men fought their wars and her husband attended to business, Isabella kept the family home running. Her household accounts were meticulous, recording to the penny their expenditure on groceries, wine, candles and firewood. She ministered to her stepdaughter Lady Diana's cough – perhaps employing her favoured concoction of pearl barley, milk and 'one dozen of snails' – and kept their army of servants in check while her husband focused on business. While the city devised punishments for its Jacobite prisoners, she hosted suppers for the famous dancer Eva Marie Veigel, attended York Races and enjoyed all the 'diversions of the Northern Carnival'.[23] On 1 November, ten condemned men were dragged to the gallows at the racecourse, where the sporting applause of weeks earlier was replaced by 'loud Huzza's' as they were disembowelled and decapitated – two of the heads were set on pikes in the city. Three days after this grisly display the Carlisles left for the winter, perhaps already suspecting that Isabella was carrying another child.

By the time they arrived for William and Elizabeth's wedding at Albemarle Street – bearing expensive cherry desserts – Isabella had unlaced her stays to accommodate the growing bump, and within weeks her labour pains began. On 16 May 1747 a bustle of solemn excitement and another birth at Soho Square: a girl. Elizabeth. Three daughters. Still no heir. Lord Carlisle, now in his mid fifties, was growing impatient – Isabella was pregnant again by August, visibly so for the wedding of Lady Diana (by now her only surviving stepchild) the following February, and the 'fatal time' was upon them.

Isabella prayed for a boy as she retreated to Carlisle House for her fourth lying-in. Finally, on a Saturday morning, the moment her life had been leading up to – on 28 May 1748, a son. He was named Frederick in honour of his father's friend the Prince of Wales, declared Viscount Morpeth (a nod to Henry's estates in Northumberland) and his future was mapped out. Eton. Cambridge. The House of Lords. Bells were rung in the marketplace of his namesake town, where locals entertained themselves 'Drinking the Healths of Lord and Lady CARLISLE, and Lord Morpeth, and ordering Ale for the Populace'.[24] The baby was baptised at the family home in June, with Prince Frederick, Princess Augusta and his uncle Lord Byron standing as godparents. (Though Henry undoubtedly had royal approval, Isabella was less beloved by the prince's wife – when her friend Elizabeth Percy, the future Duchess of Northumberland, recommended her for the position of Lady of the Bedchamber in 1747 she was passed over in favour of her sister-in-law Lady Irwin.)

Whether Isabella's success secured her some respite from her childbearing duties is not entirely clear – a scattering of newspaper announcements for the birth of a second son in March 1749 are unverified elsewhere – but there was certainly one more addition to the Carlisle nursery: the family was completed with the birth of Juliana in Yorkshire in July 1750. Seven years of marriage had produced five healthy children – Anne, Frances, Betty, Frederick and Julia – including the all-important heir. She had survived the threat of childbed fever and defied the old declaration that the 'bringing forth of children, wastes women, wears 'em, shakes, spoils and destroys the very frame and constitution of them'.[25] Isabella was still just twenty-eight years old, and determined to enjoy herself.

For those with money to spend the mid eighteenth century was, as her brother-in-law termed it, 'an age of diversion'. Sparkling winters in town were followed by lazy summers in the country, punctuated by the occasional country tour, visit to the coast or business trip. But for a lively young wife it could be a solitary existence: 'If he should prefer the country during your earlier years,' Isabella later cautioned those preparing for married life, 'a period when diversions are most attractive, it may at first be painful.'[26] She made the best of it. York itself was a charming and bustling place to shop and meet friends. The Assembly Rooms held subscription balls on Mondays, and in August York Races provided the highlight of the social calendar. Flocks of gentlemen descended on Castle Howard for the shooting season, and others dropped in during their northern travels: the Ansons, the Yorkes, the Bentincks, the Thynnes. During one rambling journey from Alnwick to London, her friend Elizabeth commented: 'Of all the things I saw whilst I was abroad nothing pleas'd me so much as Lady Carlisle's Dressing Room.'[27] As well as boasting 'a most chearful Prospect of Water Lawns Cottages & Woods,' it had been crowded with pictures and antique mosaics. Isabella's name was even carved into the new wing at Castle Howard as it was finally completed: THIS STONE WAS LAID BY HENRY AND ISABELLA, EARL AND COUNTESS OF CARLISLE, 5TH OF JULY, 1753.

In London, Carlisle House was sold and a new home in Dover Street with 'every convenience for a large family' was soon dripping with Venetian landscapes and family portraits.[28] Unburdened of the obligation to provide an heir, Isabella seized the role of hostess – 'you know how I love a great Dinner', she thrilled – and became known for her musical soirees.[29] She established a weekly 'Musical Tuesday' before hosting great concerts 'where *the world* assemble' on Fridays, with performances from the leading opera singers and musicians of the day.[30] She filled her house with an assortment of instruments for visitors to showcase their talents, and was invited to sing at concerts laid on by other hostesses. She found a divinity in it – 'if you shall perceive that music exalts your sentiments, encreases your devotion, and harmonises your mind,' she later wrote, 'you may be assured of your vocation'.[31]

Isabella's open and gregarious nature allowed her to forge friendships readily and she struggled to hold a grudge. She loved to be loved. 'To one of my disposition with regard to my Friends', she wrote, a sincere apology 'can never come too late for forgiveness, unless I was in my Grave'.[32] She saw little merit in 'superfluous Ceremony' and happily filled her letters with what she called 'fiddle faddle'. This tendency to wear her heart on her sleeve earned devotion from some quarters and invited ridicule from others – increasingly the latter as she began to lose the excuse of youth.

Her social circle was a colourful mix of old money, politicians, intellectuals and artistic types. The Carlisles were firmly entrenched among the Whig political set and had a foot in the door of the incoming royal household. Before his premature death in 1751, Henry's friend Prince Frederick had urged his son – the future George III – to heed 'ye Opinions & advice of the Earl of Carlisle'.[33] Through calls and correspondence Isabella cultivated her own friendships: the great natural history collector Margaret, Lady Portland; Elizabeth, Lady Northumberland (cheekily branded by Walpole 'that great vulgar Countess'); the artistic Caroline, Lady Ailesbury; the talented harpsichordist Lady Milbanke; the chatty Howards of Corby. Poets, musicians, dancers and actors (including David Garrick, the most renowned thespian of his day and husband of her friend Eva Marie): all were welcomed to Dover House.

Isabella's accomplishments provided another ticket to fashionable company. Her sketches and watercolours of flowers, invented landscapes and copies of the old masters – signed 'Isabella Carlisle' or simply 'Isa' with a flourish – were admired by amateurs and connoisseurs. Though she couldn't boast the talent of her brother Richard – who had painted a remarkable self-portrait aged just sixteen and was a prolific etcher – one artist saw 'a good share of merit' in her copy of a Rembrandt, 'particularly in the spirit of the eyes', and Walpole snapped up a number of her drawings for his collection.[34] She subscribed to a prestigious new musical academy and her tutor – the Italian composer Giardini – dedicated a songbook of violin sonatas to 'Madame Isabelle,

Comtesse de Carlisle'. She found a place on the fringes of the blossoming set known as the 'bluestockings', a female network dismissing
the idea of women's intellectual inferiority and cultivating a space for
learning. The delight she took in unusual flowers, ferns and mosses
perhaps inspired her particularly close friendship with the Duchess of
Portland, and the botanical artist Mary Delany.

Isabella's undated sketch of the Rest on the Flight into Egypt,
after an etching by the seventeenth-century artist Cantarini.
Her signature can be seen at the bottom, centre.

Described as 'evermore scribbling', she also had literary aspirations:
Isabella swapped poetic verses with friends, taking inspiration from
Spenser and her 'belov'd Shakespeare'.[35] The summer of 1758 brought
some notable acclaim; she was the dedicatee of a verse by her friend
Frances Greville, which took the form of a melancholy plea to
Oberon the fairy to grant the blessing of indifference, and solemnly
concluded:

> *And what of life remains for me*
> *I'll pass in sober ease;*
> *Half pleased, contented will I be,*
> *Content but half to please.*

Readers scrambled to read the response of the notoriously romantic Lady Carlisle, who duly supplied a sentimental tribute to the passions in 'The Fairy's Answer'. There are, frustratingly, two candidates for her verse. The first (and more convincing) echoes her verbose poetic style, but was later reattributed to Lady Craven. It is voiced by the fairy:

> *. . . Tell her with fruitless care I've fought*
> *And tho' my realm's with wonders fraught*
> *With remedies abound;*
> *No grain of cold* indifference
> *Was ever yet allied to sense,*
> *In all my fairy ground.*
>
> *The regions of the sky I'd trace,*
> *I'd ransack every earthly place,*
> *Each leaf, each herb, each flower,*
> *To mitigate the pangs of fear,*
> *Dispel the mist of black despair,*
> *Or lull her restless hour.*[36]

The second, more widely printed under Isabella's name but only after her death, perhaps has a more baldly Byronic foreshadow:

> *. . . It never shall be my desire,*
> *To bear a heart unmov'd,*
> *To feel by halves the generous fire,*
> *Or be but half belov'd.*
>
> *Let me drink deep the dang'rous cup,*
> *In hopes the prize to gain,*
> *Nor tamely give the pleasure up,*
> *For fear to share the pain.*[37]

Whichever spilled from Isabella's pen, their debate about the human passions – anticipating that of Jane Austen's *Sense and Sensibility* –

drew in much of the polite world. 'I send you Mrs Greville's verses, they are exceedingly pretty indeed', Lady Holland wrote to her sister, complaining, 'Lady Carlisle's I have not nor do I know how to get them.'[38]

The eighteenth-century woman had many solitary hours to fill, and when not preoccupied with society Isabella deftly launched herself into domesticity. With five sniffling children and an older husband inclined to hypochondria, her book of home-made reme-dies and recipes became indispensable. The perils of the northern climate demanded cures for coughs, colds, chapped lips and sore throats; the state of the marital bed is alluded to in a medicine, tactfully noted in French, 'For a very common malady in men *of a certain age*'.[39] She was not afraid to get her hands dirty, nor was she squeamish about ingredients. For fever she recommended 'viper broth', a stock made from 'one chopped viper and a lean chicken'; for heartburn, lozenges made from chalk, sugar and crab's eyeballs. Alongside recipes for 'mince pyes' and 'Orange Flower Cakes *very good*' (evidently a favourite) she included instructions for calves' head hash and black pudding containing 'the Blood of a whole Hog'. She doubled the size of the kitchen gardens at Castle Howard, and when her successor later struggled with the grounds she confidently advised having 'some of it Ploughed & sown with Buck Wheat & other Corn, & perhaps it wants a little new draining'.[40]

In managing her staff, from housekeeper Mrs Marston to Henry's trusted servants Joseph and Lydia, Isabella learned to be kindly but cautious. The advice she later gave of the dangers of speaking freely in front of them – 'they will not fail to take an advantage of it at some moment or other' – and of hiring anyone with a tendency towards 'licentiousness', was perhaps learned the hard way.[41] Nonetheless, she was happy to lend books to servants if they showed an inclination for learning and preached that mistresses should ensure they 'diligently perform their religious duties, even if of a different persuasion from that of your own'. Like much of women's work, household manage-ment was often a thankless business, being invisible when successful: 'Conceal from the indifferent spectator, the secret springs,' she wrote, 'which move, regulate, and perfect the arrangements of your household.'

The happiness of Henry and Isabella's marriage is difficult to gauge.

Despite the age difference they were rendered companionable by their shared interests and her 'great taste for Antiquities and every other Branch of Literature' was encouraged and refined by her husband's influence.[42] They were both charitable – her cause of choice was the Marine Society, 'for cloathing Men and Boys for the Sea' – and on drawing up his will in 1754 Henry referred to her as his 'Dear Wife'. The children were raised in a household prizing arts and politics, and their minds were formed accordingly – Frederick knew from an early age that he was destined for influence in government, Frances had a talent for sketching flowers and Julia took to the harpsichord. But the family picture was far from perfect.

Isabella tried, but had occasionally – inevitably – been distracted from self-improvement by the pleasures of the world. 'Half the worthy intentions, flowing from a good but unexperienced heart,' she later cautioned, 'are rendered ineffectual by procrastination, or the interposition of alluring trifles.'[43] Acquaintances privately referred to Henry as a great 'Sott', and it may be no coincidence that Isabella's later advice for new wives included hints about disliking a husband's friends, growing bored in the country and being attracted to other men.[44] While her high spirits served her well as a countess, she had slipped into impropriety as a wife. Henry's friend Mary Wortley Montagu wrote scornfully of Isabella's 'folly' and numerous 'misdemeanours', bluntly declaring that he was too forgiving of 'a Lady he had no reason to esteem'.[45] Whatever truth lay beneath the rumours, fifteen years into their marriage Isabella had certainly earned some dubious notoriety: she was at best a flirt, and at worst an adulterer. But for now, she remained blissfully unaware of the black charges being laid at her door.

As she reached her mid thirties, Lady Carlisle's carefree, colourful lifestyle was regularly and rudely interrupted. In the spring of 1756 her brother John was drawn into the new war – she had every confidence that he 'should have something to say in this Business' but must have felt concern as it extended its reach across the world. Newspapers filled with reports of victories, losses and mounting death tolls across Europe and America.[46] In the autumn of 1757, a bereavement closer to home: word came from East Lothian that her mother Frances was dead. It is unclear when Isabella had last seen her, but the news doubtlessly unearthed memories of the woman who had shaped her young life. Her dark hair tumbling about pearl earrings, perhaps; her gorgeous, delicate handwriting; her hands fluttering across the harpsichord. The news travelled quickly. 'I designd writing to Lady Carlisle this post but hearing of Lady Byron's death makes me afraid it will be troublesome', her sister-in-law Mary wrote sympathetically to Henry; 'I am very sorry for any occasion yt [that] gives her concern wch I beg you tell her'.[47] The Dowager Lady Byron was brought to Twickenham to be laid to rest alongside her ancestors in the Berkeley family vault at St Mary's, a small and tranquil church on the banks of the Thames. It is unlikely that Isabella made a special trip down from Yorkshire for the funeral – her brother Richard certainly didn't feel compelled to attend. And then – within a year – the jolt that unhinged her life entirely.

Henry, now sixty-four years old, had long been intermittently confined to Dover Street, leg propped on a mahogany gout stool and listening to his brother's futile pleas to relinquish the 'fatigues' of his responsibilities. While attending York Races in August 1758 he eventually suffered an 'Apoplectick Fit' that left him unable to speak – word quickly spread that he was 'within a few hours of his end'.[48] Henry nonetheless lingered for a week at Castle Howard, before finally dying on 3 September. The obituaries were uniformly effusive – '*his innate Goodness . . . Affability to all Mankind . . . extensive, though private, Charities . . .*' – as the family descended in black on the mausoleum at Castle Howard.[49] Frederick – Isabella's 'sweet boy' with 'the best of hearts' – rose to become the 5th Earl of Carlisle at just ten years old.[50] Isabella had not only lost a mentor and friend, but her anchor in the respectable world.

Unsurprisingly, Henry's will left her a comfortable thirty-six-year-old widow. She was bequeathed a sum of £1,000, an annuity and her own estate in Cumbria – after provisions for other relatives and tokens for the servants, the rest was to be held in trust for Frederick. She was named co-guardian of the children with Lord Berkeley and their friend Robert Ord, for as long as she remained unmarried. 'I am to dine with my Lady Carlisle to-morrow, who is a melancholy Dowager', smirked the poet Thomas Gray, revealing that she was reduced to merely a substantial annuity, 'her jewels, plate, & a fine house in town excellently well-furnish'd'.[51] Uncharitable tongues could not help wagging about her flirtatious history. 'I am not sorry *Lady Carlisle* is to loose [*sic*] five hundred a year and the care of her children if she marries again,' sneered the Dowager Lady Irwin, whose son had married Henry's sister, 'it is believed in general that she will be comforted without loss of time.'[52] 'It was certainly the kindest thing he could do for her,' chirped Mary Wortley Montagu on hearing of the restrictions placed on her inheritance, 'to endeavour to save her from her own Folly, which would have probably precipitately hurry'd her into a second marriage'.[53] One politician's wife joked that Henry's efforts 'to restrain his Lovely Widow from Marrying again' had put paid to the efforts of young (and reputedly silent) MP William Gerard Hamilton: 'poor Mr Singlespeech's prospect is lost in the Clouds; you know he declared it a distant one last year'.[54] No sensible woman would rush to relinquish such a profitable independence to another man. But the vultures were circling, and Isabella was notoriously easy prey. Her weakness was not money or rank, but the prospect of finding love.

'If you are dispos'd to marry', the politician Henry Seymour Conway wrote cheekily to Horace Walpole, before Lord Carlisle was even dead, 'I can give you the earliest intelligence of the Youngest, Handsomest & Wittiest Widow in England, even the Countess of Carlisle.'[55] (Walpole proclaimed himself preoccupied with attempting to share a bed with Lady Mary Coke; 'I beg your pardon for attempting your constancy with the charms & perfections of the *New Widow*', came the reply.)[56] On hearing that Lord Temple would assume Henry's place as a Knight of the Garter, the MP Charles Townshend joked that 'if he would have been contented to ask first for my *Lady* Carlisle's garter, I don't doubt he would have obtained it'.[57] When she finally caught wind of the gossip, Isabella was stung. 'She has just discover'd too (I am told in confidence) that she has been long the object of Calumny, & Scandal', Thomas Gray learned before their dinner. 'What can I say to comfort her?'[58]

The legalities of her situation also weighed heavily upon her. Henry had left debts, and both Lord Berkeley and Mr Ord claimed that they lived too far away to assist with either the estates or the maintenance of the children. Hoping to release funds from the estate to pay for Frederick's school fees and support her daughters – 'who are now growing up to be Women the Eldest of the said Young Ladies being near Fourteen years of age' – she swept them to the courts.[59] Mirroring the considerably less amicable dispute between her mother and thirteen-year-old brother two decades earlier, William was drafted in to stand as plaintiff and guardian for his 'infant' nephew Lord Carlisle. The tedious process was not completed until the following spring, but in the meantime it was becoming clear to anyone who dared to take notice that Isabella had no intention of settling into a meek and retired widowhood.

Henry had been her rock but, at his sickly end, had he not weighed her down? 'When her autumn-season came on', ran one later account, 'that at which ladies who have been gay think it high time to draw in and become more grave, she surprised her acquaintance by seeming to relax, and grow gay'.[60] Dover House was sold and she took up residence in Whitehall, where she and her friend Frances Greville were observed to be 'the happiest of beings – little parties and suppers continually'.[61] Unfortunately, her open-hearted nature only encouraged new, impertinent schemes at her expense. Lord Pembroke and others managed to persuade her – 'without much difficulty to be sure' – that a Mr Stopford, son of the Earl of Courtown, was 'dying for her'. Lady Holland sent the full story to her sister.

> To complete the thing they sent him to see her t'other day with a long melancholy story of his passion for her; but, his father being alive and intending to make some great match for him, would not consent to his proposing himself to her; but his love was so great that – in short he was as rude to her Ladyship as could be, except to the last favour all passed that could on such an occasion. But she scream'd and expostulated and, in short, did and said everything to make him desist but what she should have done – which was to ring the bell and bid her servants kick him downstairs. However, she escaped, is convinced 'twas all owing to excess of love, and is mighty good friends with him again, and he goes about giving the men a description of all he saw. It's really infamous tho', and the poor woman's folly almost incredible.[62]

While Stopford laughingly boasted about their passionate encounter to all and sundry – everything except 'the last favour' – she flushed with the idea of casting such powerful bewitchments. Putting the incident behind her, she planned new entertainments and trips to see friends, among them a late summer expedition to Lord and Lady Milbanke at Halnaby Hall. Whether or not Isabella had romance on her mind when she arrived, by her departure her thoughts could fix on nothing else.

'I am and ever must be yours'

Sir William Musgrave was a twenty-three-year-old barrister and baronet whose late brother had married Lady M's sister. He was attractive in a willowy, studious sort of way, with a dimpled chin, an intellectual air and the curls of a neat wig hovering punctiliously above his ears. He had been brought up in Cumberland and unexpectedly inherited his title after the deaths of four older brothers. The intimacy into which he and Isabella fell at Halnaby during her first summer as a widow was rapid and intense. Quite apart from hardly knowing each other, they were not what society would call a good match. Not only did she outrank him considerably; she was fourteen years his senior. And yet, they felt a spark. Young Sir William was cultured and extremely committed to his work – as well as recently qualifying as a lawyer, he had plans for ambitious historical and biographical projects. Isabella was impressed with the 'superior talents' of his mind, his gentleness and his moral principles. Becoming wrapped up in a shared love of books and botany, they grew closer as Halnaby rang with Isabella and Lady M's impromptu musical performances. They spoke of a future together and declarations of love were made: they would meet in London before Christmas and marry. But when Isabella left on 3 September 1759, neither could help worrying that the other would change their mind.

In the weeks that followed the anxious couple exchanged furtive letters via friends, with constant reassurances about their feelings. 'My thoughts are extremely occupied by you, that I have not a wish but to make you happy', she wrote as she travelled south; 'every day of our separation confirms me in my opinion of you of y[ou]r passion y[ou]r Friendship y[ou]r Fidelity'.[63] Having received a long epistle of love – which she read so often she declared it 'wrote in my heart, on my Memory' – she assured him that 'a thousand thoughts in your Letter seemd only to return home to mine'.[64] Her feelings weakened her – her hand shook, she couldn't sleep and suffered such a 'flutter of spirits with ye agreeable thought of seeing you so soon, I cannot write sensibly and coherently'. *If I do change 'tis your own fault!*

'I am continually with you,' she wrote longingly from Oxfordshire, 'and can dream of nothing else.'[65] He sent new music and scraps of his writing; she recommended her favourite poetry and busily embroidered a purse for him. Still he seemed to have concerns about their compatibility – perhaps he had heard the rumours. 'You have so short a time been aqquainted [*sic*] with me', she wrote from London; 'I could not expect to be excepted from so natural a suspicion.' Doubting that the world would view their relationship with an indulgent eye, she nonetheless urged him to lock up her letters.

As she waited for him she was 'jovially attack'd allready with suspicions', but denied everything until his arrival in November prompted the tell-tale meeting with her uncle.[66] To her delight, Lord Berkeley seemed to approve: 'he spoke of my choice with infinite pleasure,' she assured her fiancé, 'and said everything y[ou]r Character deserv[e]d'.[67] (His lordship was perhaps relieved that her predictably hasty choice seemed, at least, to be a sensible man.)

The news was soon raising eyebrows across town. 'My lady Carlisle is going to marry a sir Wm. Musgrave, who is but three-and-twenty', Walpole noted with amusement, 'but, in consideration of the match, and of her having years to spare, she has made him a present of ten, and calls him three-and-thirty.'[68] Lady Blandford was less diverted. 'Well, I have not patience with that woman,' she scoffed, 'at her time of life, and with daughters grown or growing up around her, to go and marry a young fellow she must buy breeches for.'[69] Isabella merely declared that other people's opinions about her attachments were of no consequence, 'as I am authoriz'd to form any I please, and I am determined to pursue that which pleases me'.[70] They married at her house in Westminster on 10 December 1759, as London was plunged into the coldest winter it had seen for years.

Isabella and William entered society as newlyweds amid 'violent bitter' frost and fog. 'I saw Lady Carlisle presented at Leicester house,' wrote a Mrs Southwell to her son shortly before Christmas, 'with such an Air of innocence and modesty as must be very edefying to all the young Ladies; no Girl of fifteen could have put on a prettier confusion. You'l say that tis more proper for forty to be ashamed of marrying, and I agree with you.'[71] But the 'nine days' wonder' whipped up by their wedding soon bowed to other, less mirth-inducing novelties. Lord Ferrers was pleading insanity after callously murdering his steward and a 'black list' of illustrious ladies were succumbing to fatal fevers and sore throats. As death settled over the city, the newlyweds ingratiated themselves with each other's families and searched for new homes in London and the country. They eventually settled on a house in Cleveland Court (near Green Park, a favourite spot for duellists) and took a lease on Randall's Park, a rustic retreat in Surrey where they could rear cows, pigs and chickens. (Sir William was undoubtedly an old soul.)

Isabella would not be deterred from her pleasures by climate or contagion. She socialised with her usual set – the Northumberlands, the Portlands, the Howards, the Cokes – and in January 1760 she joined an excursion to the newly opened Magdalen House (a controversial establishment intended to rehabilitate penitent prostitutes) with a jovial party including the king's brother Prince Edward. In June she visited Lady Ailesbury in Henley, where spirits were high and the morose Thomas Gray sulked about having to live 'for a month in a house with three women that laughed from morning to night', during 'cards at home, parties by land and water abroad, and (what they call) *doing something*, that is, racketting about'.[72] The following month both Isabella and Sir William visited her dear 'Dutchess', Lady Portland, at Bulstrode Hall for a week, exploring her unparalleled natural history collections and twinkling shell grotto.[73]

Impeding her new-found happiness with Sir William, Isabella's health began to dip. She intermittently suffered from 'cholick' (pains in the stomach and bowels) and – like much of the leisured class – from complaints supposedly brought on by a 'delicacy of the nerves'. These exhausting digestive pains, bouts of sleeplessness and faintness were not always obvious to an outside observer; speaking of fellow sufferer Mrs Howard, Isabella wrote that 'she looks amazingly well, but we Nervous People are dutifull in that particular'.[74]

To aid their recovery the two friends spent an autumn season together in the fashionable, health-giving spa town of Bath. Isabella wrote to her husband within an hour of her arrival, imagining herself sitting by him, 'and am as little here as I can possibly be and when I do recollect my distance from you, tis so much the worse'.[75] How fortunate to have found such a love, but how painful the separation: 'it is neither the same Moon, or the same Sun to me', she lamented. Though her thoughts wandered continually to Sir William pottering about in his garden – she hoped (just a little) that he found Randall's dull without her – there was plenty to entertain her between consultations. She played cards, took the waters at the Pump Rooms – 'the Noise turn'd my Brains . . . I thought of you all the time, and how tir'd you would be' – and saw an art exhibition of 'some Pictures which are striking Likenesses done by one Gainsborough'.[76] An idea took root. Giving no hint in her letters, she decided to commemorate her new life with a new portrait – perhaps it was intended as a surprise. For the darkly furrowed portraitist Thomas Gainsborough, just making his name in the elegant world, the Dowager Countess of Carlisle was a prestigious client. A meeting, a sitting or two, an impatient wait – and the result was captivating. The mature woman of Gainsborough's portrait is elegant and self-assured, with her dark hair appearing almost lilac under a stylish dusting of hair powder and white cap. She wears her favourite colours, blue and white – reams of satin beneath a lace shawl – with clusters of blue jewels at her ears and a ribbon around her neck. The artist gallantly neglects to include the mole beneath her lip and her illness does not show, but her happiness seems to. She yearned to return to her husband: 'my heart and affections are your property my D[ea]r Friend'.

Seasons drew on and the children were growing up. In the autumn of 1761 the family was 'jump'd into the Bustle' of London just in time to see the young new king George III take a wife and his crown.[77] 'All the vines of Bourdeaux, and all the fumes of Irish brains cannot make a town so drunk as a royal wedding and coronation', complained Horace Walpole.[78] At the wedding Isabella fretted over her 'very humble gown indeed' – hearing of 'nothing but Five Pound a Yard' from the other ladies in attendance – but was proud to see her thirteen-year-old son take his place in the coronation procession (outranking even Lord Berkeley and Lord Byron) two weeks later.[79] She received regular reports from Frederick's tutor, Mr Ekins, about his progress at Eton, and was delighted to see him grow into an entertaining and affectionate boy. During a rainy day on a trip together, he chose to stay in with his mother 'because I seemd lonely'. Taking up his duties as stepfather, Sir William had been forced to abandon his own projects for the tedious business of the Carlisle family's political concerns – when the couple were bombarded with letters about support in the Morpeth election, Isabella merely resolved to answer 'no Election letters at all, for I really don't know how to proceed' and let the burden fall to her husband.[80]

The girls kept her company at Randall's Park, where she spent her time 'botanising' and reading, but still she grew listless and bored when her husband was away. They did, at least, provide an irresistible new source of entertainment just to Isabella's taste: bachelor watching. Each girl had her merits. The prudent Anne, on the cusp of being launched into society, was proving an elegant letter writer; Frances, who had grown 'very pretty, both in face and manner', inherited her mother's love for walks, flowers and art; Betty showed signs of becoming a great beauty.[81] Julia, just eleven, was shy and eager to please. The prospect of five match-making projects was a dream for Isabella – and a potential nightmare for their conscientious young stepfather.

In the summer of 1763, feeling the familiar pangs of her nervous illnesses, Isabella announced that she was going to take the waters at Derbyshire with the Duchess of Portland. As Sir William busied himself in his study, reports of the patient's adventures rolled in: card games and horse-riding; tours of grand houses; romantic streams and castle ruins; a rain-soaked expedition to the pioneering Manchester 'Manufactorys', where she marvelled at some new contraption used to make gowns. His annoyance might have eased with news that she was collecting ferns for his garden, or forgotten with that of a chaise ride turning to terror when she lost control of a horse and it began kicking at her head. 'I very fashionably flung myself out', she assured him, 'without the least hurt.'[82] A detour to her birthplace, Newstead Abbey, gave Isabella an opportunity to survey the state of both her brother's marriage and his improvements to the estate. The family had just returned from Scarborough – her nephew William was about to set out to join Frederick at Eton, and Elizabeth was looking too thin. They discussed the weather and the best routes home, and she toured the grounds. 'The Water is in the highest beauty', she wrote wistfully, 'and the Room in the Castle made very elegant.'[83] The art collection had only improved since her father's day and there was now something exquisitely theatrical and Gothic about the place. Her brother had done well.

Back to Randall's, and the usual regime: Sir William poring over dusty books and Isabella scribbling and dreaming up new entertainments. As the first flush of romance gave way to daily drudgery, the differences in their characters were becoming painfully apparent. She was a social butterfly, embracing each day as it came and living by the maxim that one should never 'suffer yesterday, or to morrow, to poison the present moment'; he was a solitary and economical creature seemingly more in love with the dead than the living.[84] She wilted without company; he disliked fuss in general and the frivolity of his wife's friends in particular. His correspondence was painstakingly drafted and redrafted; hers, a flurry of spontaneous effusion. He drank too much wine, and she preferred a sociable glass of ale. Both felt neglected, and misunderstood.

Unable (or unwilling) to curb her pleasures, she learned to hold her tongue and sought out merrier company elsewhere. They argued, and fell back into their old affectionate expressions. The problem stemmed from the fact that, since those intoxicating flirtations at Halnaby Hall, Sir William's behaviour had changed and Isabella's had not. She thought he appreciated her lively, romantic moods, when in truth he had expected that marriage would tame her. It was not lost on the children. Frederick later described their home as 'comfortless from domestic feuds; my mother having married a person to whose manners and habits she could not accommodate herself'.[85] When not at Eton – and, later, Cambridge University – he sought refuge at Holland House, the family home of his schoolfriend Charles James Fox.

Five years into their marriage, Lord Byron's fatal altercation with

Mr Chaworth at the Star and Garter suddenly hung darkly over them all. With the incident seeming only to confirm William's poor reputation, it was his siblings who benefited from society's sympathy: 'I feel for both families,' wrote Horace Walpole, 'though I know none of either, but poor Lady Carlisle'.[86] Both Isabella and Sir William leapt to her brother's defence – the former desperate to support her brother, the latter perfectly placed to offer legal expertise. He carried messages to and from the Tower, went through his predictions for the prosecution's arguments and helped to compile his brother-in-law's list of witnesses. Yet another headache courtesy of his wife's family, but it was the honourable course of action. Isabella tried to help but was pushed aside. 'In the subject of my Brother's Affairs,' she later complained, 'nobody was more disposed to have shar'd ye pain of them, but that I was taken up and reproved so sharply whenever I venturd my sentiments that I determined to say nothing and to remain in ignorance.'[87] Feeling shut out, she gratefully accepted her beloved duchess's invitation to Bulstrode at what Mary Delany called 'a time when it must have been shocking to her to have been in town'. 'I am glad the affair has ended to her satisfaction', she remarked.[88] Unfortunately, Lord Byron's acquittal did not remove the wedge that had been driven into the Musgrave marriage.

One day in April 1765 Isabella returned to Cleveland Court to find that Sir William had disappeared to Randall's, leaving a letter loaded with accusations. She was ungrateful for the laborious efforts he had made on behalf of her brother. She claimed to be ill and yet sortied out 'at all times and Hours' with her friends. She had humiliated him at dinner by chiding him in front of company. Furious, Isabella picked up her pen. If she did not seem ill it was because she did not wish to worry her friends, and she tried to appear well when 'very few would have spirits to have done'. As for her supposed neglect, *he* refused to go out, and made no secret of looking down on the *whole world*. 'If you would please to recall the days the weeks during ye course of our Marriage, in which I have scarcely been spoke to,' she scrawled, 'and this arising from some trifle of discontent beneath ye notice of an understanding like yours, it were not much to be wonderd at that I should seek that satisfaction which arises from ye Society of them who have a regard for me, where I can not find it at home.'[89] 'I wish your happiness', she continued, 'but I have tried too often to hope ever for success; because when I have thought myself the most secure it has been in the power of ye commonest occurrence to disorder your temper and to make me miserable.' Smarting from his insults, she resolved to pursue another adventure without him.

Though the way to a reconciliation was paved when she wrote that her doctor had advised her to visit the German town of Spa – and that she would return in August 'if I live' – she pressed on and did not invite him to join her. After settling Betty and Julia with her sister-in-law Sophia – John was away, sailing around the world – the party set off: Isabella, Lord and Lady Byron, and her elder daughters Anne and Frances.

Isabella's first taste of Europe was balmy and intoxicating. While William amused himself with gambling, buying wolves and hunting boar, she became the beating heart of the music scene, introducing new songs and teaching dances to an illustrious company of European aristocrats and royals. Finding the German countryside 'excessively Romantick', she determined to see as much of it as possible, riding out despite the hot weather and the foreigners' twittering about sunburn. To Anne and Elizabeth's delight there were balls three times a week. While Isabella's stomach was eased by taking the waters, she rejoiced to see her daughters making effortless conquests – Frances in particular was deluged with gentlemen valiantly 'walking out' to find flowers for her to paint. She pestered Sophia for news of Betty's blossoming relationship with a brother of Lord Shelburne, and was galled when the gentleman's mother – 'ye Old Woman', she spat – put an end to it.[90] The arrival of seventeen-year-old Frederick added to their merriment. 'Ld Carlisle has his usual Spirits and we have a continual laugh', she wrote; 'he has been amusingly prudent about Cloaths' (a trait he would swiftly outgrow).[91]

During the prolonged separation, the warring Musgraves returned to their former affectionate wishes: 'I am giddy as a Goose, with writing, mais que faire? Adieu my D[ea]r ever y[ou]rs most affectionately . . .'[92]

'I must be thinking of new Bustles'

Returning from her first European adventure in the autumn and with her own love life settling back into a strained peace, Isabella cast about for what she called 'new Bustles' to keep her occupied. Needing no encouragement, she promptly threw herself into the romantic affairs of her children. Betty's first promise of marriage had fallen through, but no matter. The five Howard siblings were fortunate that both their mother and stepfather held the modern opinion that they should be at liberty to bestow their hands as they wished (within reason). Less favourably, Isabella embarked upon the mission with a little too much enthusiasm – Frederick later despaired that 'it was my lot, not my good fortune, to be launched into a wide and too gay World at the Early age of 17'.[93] In the spring of 1767 he returned early from his first attempt at a Grand Tour, having succumbed to the charms of the irresistible Lady Sarah Bunbury in Paris and followed her (and her husband) home. An amused Lord Holland, something of a father figure to Frederick, wrote a comic verse about his new habit for moping about and lying in bed until noon, beginning:

> Sally, Sally, don't deny,
> But for God's sake, tell me why
> You have flirted so, to spoil,
> That once lively youth, Carlisle?[94]

Nonetheless, Frances, Betty and Frederick – who Lord Kildare called 'certainly a pretty man' – seem to have had no trouble in setting the hearts of the opposite sex into a flutter.[95] The whole family were constantly 'out': at Almack's assembly rooms and private balls, around Ranelagh gardens and crowding themselves into the opera. Though by now forty-five years old – when most dowager countesses might retire gracefully into the role of chaperone – Isabella stayed out dancing until four o'clock in the morning.

As her children made their first attempts to traverse the difficult terrain of courtship, Isabella's talents as a mentor quickly proved woefully inadequate. When Frederick made his second attempt at a Tour – hoping to conquer his infatuation with Sarah Bunbury –

she cheerfully wrote with regular updates on the lady's whereabouts and of seeing her at chapel looking 'like an angel'. 'She need not have told me that', he sighed to his friend George Selwyn.[96] She was overjoyed when she gazed across Almack's ballroom one glittering March evening to see Frances dancing with Lord Anglesey, and their engagement was swiftly announced as duchesses and viscountesses clucked over which family benefited the most between sips of tea. The triumph was short-lived. Within days it was declared that Anglesey was to marry Lord Lyttelton's daughter, and he flatly denied having ever thought of Frances at all.

If the injured Frances had hoped to lick her wounds privately she underestimated the fury of a prospective mother-in-law scorned – in a rash move that could easily have embroiled Frederick in a duel over his sister's honour, the incensed Isabella marched to Lord Lyttelton's house clutching Anglesey's letters as proof of his duplicity. Watching the affair unravel, Lady Mary Coke wrote that she would have been 'far wiser to have kept the whole affair a secret, & by that means not exposed her Son's life, nor have made herself & her Daughter the talk of the Town'.[97] Instead Isabella marched her daughters back to Almack's, where Betty raised eyebrows by joining the Duke of Cumberland and doing 'nothing but dance cotillons in the new blue damask room, which by the way was intended for cards', Selwyn commented sardonically.[98] If not the ballroom, then it was the opera, the pleasure gardens or the royal court – Anne was chosen as a new Lady of the Bedchamber for Princess Amelia, an aunt of the king. A grand assembly thrown by the Duchess of Norfolk, and then Almack's again, where even Sir William made a rare appearance.

By the winter of 1767 a wedding was finally in sight. Into the humiliating void left by Lord Anglesey stepped John Radcliffe, a thirty-year-old aspiring politician with a good name and a freshly inherited fortune of a reported £150,000. By December he was referred to in family correspondence as 'Lady Frances's Mr Radcliffe'.[99] Frederick's enquiries from abroad elicited reassurances that he was 'very well spoke of' and eager for a political place. 'What you and all my friends say in regard to my sister's marriage, and concerning Mr. R's character, makes me a very happy being,' he wrote to England with relief.'[100] '[I] shall think him a bold man to undertake a contested election and a wife in the same year,' Sir William quipped.[101] The house at Cleveland Court was prepared and a licence secured; Lord Byron dropped by to check on the date, and suddenly it was upon them. On 14 April 1768, Frances became Mrs Radcliffe and mistress of High Down in Hertfordshire. One down, four to go.

Eyes turned immediately to Betty, who had unwittingly made a conquest of another young and affluent (but apparently not especially easy on the eye) politician, twenty-one-year-old Peter Delme. Frederick received conflicting reports, with Isabella's feverish excitement somewhat undermined by her husband's clear-sightedness: 'Lady Betty is at present so young as to think of beauty in a husband, and does not seem to relish this overture.'[102] No matter, thought Isabella, another prize in sight. On hearing that Lord Percy was on the brink of divorce she was characteristically indiscreet in flaunting her prettiest daughter before him, 'who She invites him to meet in some party every day, &, as I am told, does not scruple to say with what intention'.[103] Whispers even followed the Howard sisters to church: *Is it her, that Lord Percy is so much in love with?* Faced with this unattractive and sickly peer, Betty suddenly didn't think Mr Delme quite so unappealing after all. The Delmes were respectable, in any case, and rich. His father was a 'quiet placid Man of Business' with 'unruffled Passions' and – not insignificantly – such wealth that he was known about town as Peter the Czar.[104] Isabella and Sir William held their breath. 'I think she ought not to be teased into it', the latter suggested, 'but left entirely at liberty to make her own choice.'[105] As negotiations proceeded apace Isabella followed his example and stepped back: 'tho I w[oul]d never persuade her, I own I think her very Prudent, & Wise, to accept it'.[106]

Yet while Isabella and Sir William were caught up in the romantic entanglements of the younger generation, by spring 1768 something between them had turned sour. Perhaps her insatiable hunger for society had simply worn him down; perhaps she took a flirtation too far. He made barbed comments about infidelity and she grew defensive and cold. In May 1768 the tenor of her letters changed for the final time – he was not her 'Dear Friend', but merely 'Sir'. She was no longer 'Ever, ever yours', but an 'Obedient Humble Servant'. A separation usually softened their hearts, but when she took a summer trip to Corby Castle the habit persisted. As she attended dinners and engaged in lively debates – struck by her Whiggish politics, one host remarked that 'her dress was blue and I think her principles are of the same colour' – Sir William dissected and brooded over her correspondence.[107] He finally resolved to address it directly. He could not fathom, he wrote, why she persisted in calling him 'Sir' when she lavished the slightest acquaintance with a profusion of affectionate salutes: 'I cannot help thinking it looks rather awkward'.[108] He closed with arch hints that fashions in writing should not make any woman 'ashamed or forget to subscribe themselves Dutyful Wifes' – even if 'we have lately Had but too many Instances to the Contrary' in some 'of the first Rank'.

Isabella received this thinly veiled censure a week later and did not react well. 'I am mighty sorry that my attention in writing, was spoilt, by ye manner of it, w[hi]ch was so little thought of by me,' she declared. She refused to address his final charge, 'w[hi]ch seemed to be drawing parallels, and giving hints that, knowing I do not deserve, I do not take'.[109] Far from rushing home, she extended her trip to visit the country homes of the Duchess of Northumberland, Lord Sussex and her daughter Frances, and their letters withered to dispassionate reviews of the weather and family goings-on. Corby is intolerably rainy; Alnwick Castle is in high beauty. 'I must be thinking of new Bustles, as soon as I get home', she declared breezily, 'as Ldy Betty's Marriage with Mr Delme is pretty much agreed'.[110] Their correspondence never regained its former warmth.

The intimacy that had been lost over their nine years of marriage is achingly apparent in their last surviving letters, from the winter of 1768. 'Mad[a]m', he began on 12 November, offering solemn congratulations on Betty's imminent marriage, 'I do not Hear of any Weddings going forward here nor any other News but what I dare say you will Receive earlier & in a more entertain[in]g Manner from your other Correspondences.' He began to offer an update of his health – 'I have at last got rid of my Cough' – before crossing it out and replacing with '& therefore shall not detain you longer'.[111] Where she once felt she would burst with impatience to meet and 'tell you over and over how very faithfully and aff[e]ct[ionat]ely I am y[ou]rs', she could no longer abide the idea of sharing his bed.

Her final letter, dated 7 December, offered condolences for the death of a friend before noting her imminent arrival in town: 'I have no requests to trouble you with on this Subject, but that I may be in Bettys Room, and that you will remain in y[ou]r own, as it is much properer that I s[houl]d be on that Floor, with my Daughters'.[112] Isabella might have been addressing her past self when she later outlined the dangers of being swept up in romance at the expense of everyday concerns – you finally risk, she cautioned, 'to be awakened from your fairy dream, by some sad, but common event'.[113] She had simply been too much for him. When Lady Betty Howard stood in a glittering gown before Mr Delme and made her vows of marriage on 16 February 1769, Isabella and Sir William had given up trying to save their own. Those polite, anxious, thrilling days with the Milbankes were long behind them now.

The collapse of their relationship had been gossip fodder for weeks – Lady Mary Coke heard it from Sir George Macartney at a ball. They were pursuing a legal separation. The alternative – divorce – was an expensive and very public affair, requiring a brutal airing of the couple's dirty laundry in the courts and an Act of Parliament. (As a result it was very rare – only 132 divorces were granted in England up to 1800.) They could hardly afford, or justify, it. There was, however, one drawback: as the ruling was not recognised by the Church, neither would be free to remarry while the other lived.

Sir William sat at his desk, writing and rewriting a characteristically unrevealing separation agreement. 'I Sr Wm Musgrave & I Isabella Countess Dowager of Carlisle intermarried in the Year 1759 for certain Reasons & Causes are now disposed to separate & live asunder . . .'[114] She kept her residence at Cleveland Court, Randall's, and the estates bequeathed to her in Henry's will. He claimed nothing from her family's assets, specifying only that he would not be liable to pay her debts and drawing up a short list of his personal possessions to be removed from Cleveland Court as soon as he found new lodgings: 'Furniture in my parlor', 'A Small Quantity of Sheets & Table Linnen to serve till I can purchase others', 'a few Blue & White plates', bottles of port. The minutiae of separation.

Having been passed from her father and through two husbands, the burden of Isabella's maintenance fell now to her son. She urged

Frederick to wrap up his Tour – 'my mother seems to wish my return', he sighed, feeling a new weight about his shoulders.[115] Two of his sisters were settled under a husband's protection and Anne had her royal position, at least. The separation papers were signed on 15 March 1769, with Frederick agreeing to act as guarantor for his mother's debts (an act of generosity he would come to regret). 'Sir William Musgrave and Lady are parted, Worgan the organist, & the Duke of Grafton divorc'd', babbled the world, packing the ruins of their marriage comfortably among those of other illustrious failures.[116]

Frederick's return was a great source of pride. Isabella's little boy had grown confident and devastatingly fashionable – an acquaintance abroad commented that 'the ladies were very much inclined to be in love with him'.[117] He celebrated his coming of age by throwing a gentlemen-only party at Naworth Castle and commissioning a full-length portrait by Sir Joshua Reynolds. He took his seat in the House of Lords, drank all night at Almack's, joined a string of gentlemen's clubs and planned a masquerade at hostess Teresa Cornelys's prestigious premises, his childhood home, Carlisle House.

To Isabella's joy, he had also fallen in love. Sixteen-year-old Caroline Leveson-Gower was a modest creature with chestnut hair and blue eyes – and the daughter of an influential earl. Frederick asked for her hand at what was celebrated as the most extravagant masquerade of the age, as the candlelight played on his diamond-encrusted footman's cap. It was quite a gesture, among a bevy of Vestal virgins, medieval monarchs and men in drag (plus one Captain Watson, who scandalised the assembly in a skin-tight 'Adam' costume that appeared to be just a well-placed cluster of leaves). Isabella herself was a 'white slave', a doubtless glittering take on the Europeans snatched by Barbary pirates and delivered into slavery in the Ottoman world. 'Lord Carlisle this night made his proposals to the beautiful Lady Caroline', Lady Northumberland recorded, 'and was accepted.'[118]

They were married in March 1770 and roundly proclaimed the model couple: he was stylish and rich, she was pretty and polite. 'Everybody says it is impossible not to admire Lady Carlisle,' raved Lord Holland.[119] 'I rejoice sincerely he is so happy', Isabella wrote, 'I believe L[ad]y Carlisle to be a most excellent young Woman.'[120]

Her relief was all the keener as Frederick's success came as the scales were already falling from Betty's eyes. In April her new father-in-law 'on some pretence or other sent out his Wife & Daughter [, went] into his Garden & shot himself' – it soon transpired that his fortune had been frittered away.[121] (The obituaries were tactfully vague: 'suddenly, at his house in Grosvenor-Square'.) Her mother-in-law followed him to the grave within two months, providing a dramatic and devastating start to an ultimately unfortunate marriage.

The summer of 1770 was dry, windy and uninspiring. Isabella's forty-ninth birthday was approaching, she had formally taken the title *Dowager* Lady Carlisle (making way for her daughter-in-law), and the prospect of grandmother-hood was hoving unchivalrously into view. She found little joy in England and had grown tired of the arrogance and hypocrisy of the *bon ton*. 'Be neither vain of your birth, nor your present rank', she later warned; 'they are accidents, not always acquired by merit'.[122] Her past misdemeanours kept re-appearing like weeds, strangling her peace. With the escalation of unrest in America – British troops had fired on a crowd of protesters in Boston – the political world breathed nothing but war.

As her spirits sagged and her nervous complaints flared, she thought wistfully of her friends abroad. The Howards lodged in southern France and a certain baronet to whom she had taken a shine – Sir Edward Swinburne, a widowed father of six – had taken up in Vienna. Why shouldn't *she* ride through the French countryside, walk among the ancient ruins of Rome or climb the Swiss glaciers? Her mind was swiftly made up. She would set out to meet the Howards at Aix. In private, gossips scoffed at her avowed motive: to improve her health. 'Some people think She has another, the person you mention'd to me', smirked Lady Mary Coke, thinking of Sir Edward, 'but I hope it is not so.'[123] Isabella had evidently learned little from the errors of her baronet-chasing ways. Ostensibly offering information about Aix (but in truth hoping to judge her friend's intentions for herself), Lady Mary dropped by on 26 September to find her 'very busy preparing for her journey'. The following week, armed with her baggage and her adventurous intentions, Isabella set off for Paris. It would be almost fifteen years before she saw England again.

5

Folly Castle

The Scandalous 1770s

And Ruin is fixed on my tower and my wall,
Too hoary to fade, and too massy to fall . . .

Newstead Abbey

Cologny, Lake Geneva, 1772

Isabella gazes into the howling dark. Dramatic flashes of lightning 'like the most brilliant Fireworks' fleetingly illuminate the rippling water stretching out before her – and she is plunged again into blackness.[1] Rolls of thunder compete to disturb the mountains yawning about her on both sides of the lake. Her villa rattles and strains against the wind as rainwater begins to pour into every room 'in rivers' – after weeks of stifling heat the air has finally yielded to the gathering tempests. But while the servants squawk in terror, clinging to window shutters in a vain attempt to stem the flooding, she is transfixed by what she later describes as 'the Most Violent Storm I ever saw, or heard of'. In truth, it is a welcome interruption to her long, uneventful evenings. She is lonely. Mrs Howard has written that they miss her in France – I am sure I miss myself, Isabella thinks. Even the finest, most romantic views in the world cannot cheer her like being surrounded by friends.

As the storm gives vent to its furies her thoughts turn to her family, and Betty's delicate condition in particular. The baby will be named Isabella, if a girl – she hopes the name might prove luckier than she has found it. Letters from England have been routinely filled with bad news: patched-up scandals, professional misfortunes, mounting debts, deaths. John's notes are steeped in melancholy and William shows no sign of learning from his mistakes. 'There is a Planet overrules some Familys & blasts every Prospect', she lately lamented to her daughter.[2] The Byrons seem cursed. She passes her days with sketching, writing and trimming gowns, watching with envy as intrepid gentlemen depart to scale the glaciers she longs to see. They say it is an inappropriate excursion for a woman. As ever, her heart's desire is just beyond her reach. The dust she has kicked up in France refuses to settle, lingering stubbornly about to provide scandal for her acquaintances – 'I never thought travelling a safe thing for her', they hint, shaking their heads.³ Her children wish her home, but she has places – and people – to see. He will be here soon, she reminds herself. Her spirited 'capitain' in yellow and blue.

She stays up to watch the storm for near three hours, renouncing her bed until the spectacle is over. In the morning the garden is strewn with the lifeless bodies of dozens of 'poor little birds', struck down dead from their comfortable perches in the trees and bushes. They are hurriedly cleared away by the servants.

In the summer of 1816 a bored Lord Byron is holed up in a pretty villa at Cologny, looking out over the same lake. His companions – fellow poet Percy Shelley, Shelley's clever wife-to-be Mary Godwin, the desperately flirtatious Claire Clairmont and moping physician John Polidori (whom Byron unkindly dubs 'Childish Dr Pollydolly') – regret their spoiled excursions but cannot help admiring nature's formidable display. 'The thunder storms that visit us are grander and more terrific than I have ever seen before', Mary writes.⁴ Cooped up indoors, these radical friends amuse themselves with dreaming up new horrors: stories of the dead reanimated by electricity; of darkness consuming the world; a new species of 'vampyre', reimagined as a depraved aristocrat sucking the lifeblood from young maidens (a veiled tribute to Byron himself). The monsters they create will haunt the literary world hereafter.

In the weeks that follow he unthinkingly drinks in the sights – glaciers, waterfalls and Alpine forests – that had been denied to his great-aunt Isabella. But, like her, scandal pursues him at every turn. He receives word that a scornful former lover has decided not just to 'kiss and tell' but 'f— and *publish*'.⁵ The collapse of his marriage has broken his heart, he writes – 'I feel as if an Elephant had trodden on it' – and even the beauty of his surroundings cannot dispel his gloom: 'Neither the music of the Shepherd – the crashing of the Avalanche – nor the torrent – the mountain – the Glacier – the

Forest – not the Cloud – have for one moment – lightened the weight upon my heart'.[6] He seems to be cursed.

~

As Joe Murray and the rest of the Abbey servants cleaned up the debris of young William's coming-of-age party, the Byron siblings were plunged back into business as usual. In the spring of 1771 the Dowager Countess revelled in the varied society of Aix (inviting coy hints that 'there may be other things besides the climate that makes it so agreeable').[7] Her brother William made his final appearance at the House of Lords – probably feeling compelled to attend by the debate about his brother's contested claim on the Falkland Islands – and eagerly awaited the spoils of his namesake son's imminent marriage. At Welbeck Street, the commodore brushed off the furore surrounding his voyage of discovery – surely it would pass soon – and prepared for his third crossing to Newfoundland: clothes, orders, gifts for the local chiefs. Richard, the clergyman of the family, had settled into his post near Durham, and George was fixed in Nottingham, where he had been made a burgess of the city council.

Unsurprisingly for a brood of five siblings with almost as many decades behind them, their shared history smouldered with its own wars. The sermonising Richard in particular struggled to stomach his siblings' misdemeanours. He had 'not always been upon the best terms' with Isabella, whose family – he suspected – considered themselves superior.[8] When his nephew Frederick forgot to address a letter to the 'Honourable' Reverend Richard, he responded with a tirade about 'the Name of Byron (in my opinion) carrying with it an Idea of *real* Honour at least as that of Howard & making something a better figure in History'.[9] Isabella had neglected to send her congratulations after his marriage, and on hearing good reports about his new wife Mary did not exert herself beyond politely 'express[ing] herself extremely glad that her Brother had so fair a prospect of Happiness'.[10] Wrapped up in his pastoral sketches and pious Latin verses, he clashed with the hedonistic William and viewed George's persistent money troubles with distaste. Only John seems to have been willing to overlook personal differences and lend a hand – every one of his siblings came to him for legal, financial or professional help at some point, and he obliged even when struggling himself. It would be a challenging decade for them all.

The 1770s were an exciting time to be young and a potentially exhausting time to be a parent. As the affair with Captain Halliday had painfully demonstrated, a revolution in ideas about love and marriage – fuelled by these new sentimental novels, a disgruntled older generation complained – emboldened the young to reject parental control over their love lives. Radical cries of liberty wafted in from the Americas. A boom in trade and consumerism brought new luxuries within people's reach: porcelains from China, gorgeous fabrics from India, sugar and tobacco from the West Indies. Britain was growing fat, and its households were sprinkled with exotic 'baubles' from around the world.

The masquerades of Carlisle House became legendary. Sailing in John's wake, Captain Cook's voyages gave titillating glimpses of the cultures of the Pacific – even reputedly inspiring a Tahiti-themed erotic event at one affluent Westminster brothel – and provoked questions about human nature and the natural world. Travel across Europe grew cheaper and easier. The family heirs – young William and Frederick – returned from their European tours with a newly continental swagger, joining the horde of gentlemen who, in Frederick's own words, 'drank lemonade and ate macaroons, in short were perfect fops, only they were Italian fops'.[11] Hair grew taller and more elaborate, ladies' buttocks were padded out with fashionable cork rumps and frivolous young gentlemen – with Frederick topping the list – were accused of whisking themselves to France merely to purchase the latest stylish waistcoats.

The Byron siblings, slowed by both depleted purses and nervous complaints on the unforgiving approach to their fifties, did not escape this new stage of parenthood unscathed. The younger generation was growing up, and providing the first grandchildren – John's first, George Leigh, and Isabella's, the short-lived John Delme, were born in 1771. But still they tested the bounds of filial obedience, and of their parents' patience.

Accustomed to getting his way, Lord Byron still presumed to dictate how his children disposed of their money and their affections wherever possible, and they had grown resentful about his selfish motives. Isabella's emotional outbursts and permissive approach to motherhood – 'I wish your Happiness but cannot dictate to you' – was not always appreciated by her own children. Though she received long letters from her unmarried daughters, Betty was busy and Frances had long been silent – 'I believe I am not, nor never was agreable to Mrs Radcliffe,' she lamented, '& I am wean'd from all Expectation of more than common duty in that quarter.'[12]

With six children raised by a highly strung, interfering mother and an intermittently absent father, John and Sophia's family danced in and out of their squabbles. The more extroverted, rash-thinking Fanny and Jack were close, and generally pleased themselves; the pretty Juliana was seemingly beloved by all; the romantic young Augusta doted on the gentler Sophy and George.

Each household clung to its unsteady peace. At Great Marlborough Street, dust settled on chandeliers and servants patted down the beautiful French rose-pink and pea-green drapes, as William's antique clocks sombrely observed the passing summer days. Lord and Lady Byron were looking forward to their son's wedding, eager both for the irresistible pomp and the prospect of a wealthy bride – named in one later source as a Miss Danvers – removing his profligacies from the Newstead accounts. The groom's clothes were chosen, the invitations sent and entertainments prepared. And then – betrayal.

By Joe Murray's account, young William abandoned his father's chosen bride 'on the very eve of the appointed wedding day'.[13] He not only 'ran away' with but *married* another woman. Disbelief turned to rage when her familiar name reached the family's ears: Juliana Byron, John's sixteen-year-old daughter and the groom's own cousin. His father's painstakingly constructed house of cards came tumbling down. If they had made it to Edinburgh or Gretna Green, there was nothing to be done – the English laws requiring parental consent for those under twenty-one did not apply over the border. It was too late. The fortune was lost.

The couple's exhilarating stolen hours were followed by those of an anxious return. They were met by a furious William. The dishonour of a broken engagement paled in comparison to the havoc it wrought on his financial plans. His son had explicitly disobeyed his commands and this girl, his niece, brought nothing of value. The news travelled across the sea to John, who cannot have relished the report that his reckless daughter had been seduced by a young man set to inherit a crippled estate. She was undoubtedly stung by the disastrous broken engagement he had negotiated just months ago – if Halliday had abandoned her and run off to Scotland, then why shouldn't she do the same? It had all happened so quickly, and any attempts to part the couple were in vain. Though the exact dates are unclear, by the time the initial English legalities were scrambled together in mid October – declaring that 'a marriage had been lately had & solemnized' – Juliana was already some weeks into pregnancy.[14] By any stretch of the imagination it was a bad match, and the way in which it was conducted was nothing short of scandalous. Even Isabella – ever on the side of true love – wrote that she was 'grieved at the unfortunate Marriage of my nephew, as I know my Brother's Circumstances must suffer by it'. 'Perhaps you may hear whether or no they are coming to France', she hinted to her daughter, grasping for ways to help.[15]

Having wrapped up his final, tedious season as governor of Newfoundland, John sailed back into Spithead in November and braced himself for an almighty row with his brother. The marriage agreement would have to be negotiated amid financial chaos, and they had very little to offer one another. The resettlement of the Byron estates was not yet formalised but William's ill-advised promises were being called in. 'I must insist upon being paid my money immediately' – 'his Lordship takes no heed towards securing the repayment' – 'unless his Lordship pleases to take my miserable condition into consideration I must inevitably go to prison'.[16]

Finally, as February blanketed the woods at Newstead with snowdrops, it also brought 'the prospect of a reconciliation between my Lord and his Son and the Commodore'; the following month William openly declared that 'his affairs was or would very soon be settled'.[17] In the meantime he resorted to desperate measures to raise cash: the dismantling of the Byron collection began. First, the art. He surveyed the contents of the Abbey and selected some 460 paintings and miniatures to be packed up and dispatched to Christie's auction house in London. A catalogue was compiled, announcing a five-day sale of pictures 'collected by his Lordship and noble Father during the Course of a great Number of Years with great Speculation and vast Expence'.[18] Holbeins, Rembrandts, Titians, Lelys, Van Dycks; valuable hunting and religious scenes, nautical battles, Italian landscapes and a 'very perfect and undoubted' Da Vinci of holy infants embracing.

The vultures eagerly descended. The sale raised almost £3,300 – and for the first time in generations the walls of Newstead began to look bare. The arrival of young William and Juliana's baby in May – the tactfully named William John Byron, after both of his disapproving grandfathers – at least brought a new heir to secure the dynasty. In June, as the final deeds for the unfortunate marriage were prepared, William placed 'his whole reliance' on his brother and prepared to leave town.[19] Temporarily flush, he was leaving his wife to deal with the estate and spending the summer in France with the extravagant and disreputable Lord and Lady Kerry.

'There is a Planet overrules some Familys & blasts every Prospect'

By the time Newstead's masterpieces were gradually scattered across the country in the spring of 1772, Isabella had been in France for eighteen months. She and her daughter Julia had spent the winter with the Howards in the pretty town of Aix, mixing with local dignitaries and studiously avoiding the other English tourists, 'who grumble & growl so much at every thing'.[20] (Her friend Lord Warwick was of the same mind, wishing his countryfolk 'at home again with their own Beef & Cabbage'.) No sight of Sir Edward Swinburne – 'tho' as a certain Countess is not famous for her constancy', remarked Mary Coke, never one to miss taking a swipe at her peers, 'perhaps some Gentleman at Aix has already supplied his place'.[21] Romance was certainly on Isabella's mind. She teased a friend about taking 'a good Wife of my chusing' and rejoiced on hearing that twenty-seven-year-old Anne was finally on the brink of an engagement.[22] In France, there was no shortage of dashing regimentals to coax female hearts into a flutter. When they had moved to Beaucaire for the summer of 1771, two entirely unsuitable gentlemen had swiftly caught Isabella's eye.

With the scent of orange blossom and nightingale song drifting on the air, mother and daughter were enchanted by their new picturesque surroundings. Almost immediately they were thrown into company with the Regiment de la Marck, a German arm of the French infantry, 'the officers of which are the politest men in the world', Isabella gushed.[23] Among them was a Monsieur L'archer, who was proving a particularly entertaining and attentive captain. Though ancient, Beaucaire was a lively place. The Rhône tumbled its way between two medieval castles and provided a marvellous centrepiece for the renowned local fêtes, when its banks were taken over by booths and entertainments of all kinds – it reminded Isabella of York racecourse in her youth. At dusk the officers mingled with the beau monde on a flower-decked meadow and danced until midnight 'by the brightest of moons' – Isabella thought it 'the prettiest ball in the world'.[24]

In such a place, who could help but fall in love? Unable to resist a flirtation, Isabella was charmed by a Monsieur Beaulieu, a Corsican officer stationed over the river, until she noticed that he and Julia were growing close. At a picnic in Peyrolles she was amused to see the poor man's face drain when her daughter announced her aversion to garlic – just after he had helped himself. Such despair!

By September word reached England that 'an extraordinary marriage' was afoot, and the blame fell roundly on Isabella.[25] 'A more prudent person than L[ad]y Carlisle might have been of use', reflected Mary Coke, 'but unhappily She is so indulgent to the passion of Love, that it makes her a bad adviser on these occasions.'[26] 'If any thing can justify the most explicit Disobedience to a Parent,' railed another acquaintance, 'it would be L[ad]y Carlisle's behaviour in fobbing off her cast off Avanturer upon Lady Julia.'[27] Still reeling over the elopement of their Byron cousins, Frederick sent exasperated letters and Betty branded it 'the very worst match that ever was'.[28] With true Byronic melodrama, Isabella wilted under this filial persecution: 'I felt I believe exactly as King Lear did.'[29]

By the time the broken-hearted Julia was summoned back to England – much to her mother's chagrin – in October, the intentions of another officer fell under suspicion. The Dowager had a suitor of her own. Jean-François L'archer – who styled himself Monsieur de Weinheim after his purported hometown – had hovered like a moth about Isabella's flame during the summer, but first appeared in her letters in November acquiring a violent cold. His true history is uncertain, though he was later declared to be the spurned son of a respectable lawyer living in Cologne or near Alsace. He was not an attractive man, being dubbed an 'ugly, broken-nosed fellow' and a 'boar' in less charitable circles. One acquaintance's complaints about this 'Hounnuyhm (or how do they spell it)' suggest there may have been a horsiness about him – the Houyhnhnms were a fictional race of horses from Swift's *Gulliver's Travels*.[30] Nevertheless, he was talkative and amusing and quickly made himself indispensable to Isabella. 'It is Impossible for any Woman to subsist at a reasonable rate', she wrote defensively to her daughter Julia, 'without somebody of Spirit to interpose for one.' With no husband or brother to assist her, Weinheim filled a convenient void. The opinion of the world, however, was unequivocal: 'one shou'd have thought at her age, & with no great pretension to beauty, few temptations wou'd have offered to have disgrac'd herself', Mary Coke wrote cattily, 'for it was always to be fear'd if they did present, they wou'd not be resisted.'[31]

Isabella spent the winter of 1771 in a frosty Montpellier lapping up Weinheim's flattery, playing whist at Madame de Perigord's 'monstrous' assemblies and holding her own musical concerts on Sundays. In her letters she alternated between laments that 'the little things that pass here, are exactly as if the Ants could speak' and – apparently forgetting herself – dizzy declarations that 'I seem to live in a great Bustle & you will think me a great rake'. News trickled in. Anne's supposed engagement came to nothing, her suitor having changed his mind after a mischievous rival sent a note warning that she was a gambling addict. 'There was no foundation for this Accusation', wrote Isabella's friend the Duchess of Northumberland, who described Anne as 'a very prudent deserving young Woman'.[32] Julia spent a miserable winter being lectured by her siblings, as Betty and Caroline vied to provide more grandchildren. Isabella's usually sympathetic sister-in-law Sophia had fallen unusually silent and she sought revenge – 'the way to punish Mrs Byron is to write to her Husband' – but John's melancholy letters provided little comfort.

When Weinheim was called to Grenoble in the spring, Isabella was bereft. 'He has managed all my Commissions so cleverly here,' she lamented, 'I shall not only be helpless, but half ruined where I am going.'[33] She wished to see Switzerland and convinced him to join her after his posting – but by the time she reached her villa on the shores of Lake Geneva she already felt 'very triste' without him. For weeks she watched the farmers of Cologny harvest corn beneath the glare of an unforgiving sun. She waited. She envied the gentleman tourists scaling the glaciers, where 'they say no woman can go, as no Carriage can, but there is nothing I wish more to see'.[34] He sent gifts – gloves, wine and prints of local curiosities, including a wild boar named 'Mad[ame?] Pauline'. She daydreamed about finding a mule and escorting herself. She waited, she sketched. Locals came to catch frogs around the shores of the lake. She rallied as soon as there was company – when the Duchess of Northumberland passed through she leapt at the chance to take a trip in the chaise across bumpy, difficult roads to see Crest Castle. (She did not mention such expeditions in her letters home, perhaps remembering that she was supposed to be gravely ill.) During the solitary evenings her spirits sank. The storms set in and she declined an invitation to meet the philosopher Voltaire. Where was her fond *Monsieur*?

When they were finally reunited in August they planned a tour of Italy, armed with her physician's recommendation to visit Rome 'for the air'.[35] Reports of her 'unhappy attachment' resurfaced with a vengeance at home: 'at her time of life', Mary Coke wrote scathingly, 'an affair of this kind admits of no excuse'.[36] 'There is so much more to be seen', Isabella scrawled to George Selwyn.

Her first sight of Italy did not disappoint. The couple passed through Bologna in November, exciting other tourists with rumours of a 'beautiful young Countess travelling alone!' before they realised it was only 'the Dowager Lady Carlisle & not her Daughter in Law'.[37] In the terracotta shades of Florence she impressed guests with her sketches, and was declared by one British diplomat to be 'very ingenious'.[38] On to Rome, where they were admitted to the court of the Princess Corsini, and toured the city's ancient ruins and new baroque masterpieces as the city gradually burst into spring. She later took lodgings on the Piazza di Spagna near the gleaming

Spanish Steps, where she was counted among the vast 'English company who keep excellent tables'.[39]

But who was this odd-mannered fellow with her? As their relationship was subjected to constant scrutiny, Monsieur L'archer discreetly elevated himself to the German aristocracy and assumed the title *Baron* de Weinheim. Though they had their own rooms and all decency was publicly observed, one landlady later commented that 'to be sure people talk'd a good deal'.[40] Isabella had either been utterly taken in or was a willing participant in her own ruin – remembering her relative indifference to rank and the pride she took in her schemes during her engagement to Sir William Musgrave, it could be that she suggested the deception herself.

Back in England, the unrest in the American colonies was beginning to impact on trade and the government was toying with the idea of a war with France. The aristocracy guffawed over their amusing masquerade costumes as starving workers drew up their desperate petitions. In Isabella's absence the Byron siblings had continued to be rocked by sorrows and scandals. First came the deaths. Their aunt Barbara Trevanion – Sophia's mother – died in the spring of 1772, leaving some money and heirlooms for John's family, including portrait miniatures, pocket books and silver candlesticks (Juliana and Augusta seem to have been her favourites, receiving emerald rings and a gold and diamond watch respectively). The childless Lord Berkeley – an uncle to them all – suffered a stroke and died the following spring, temporarily alleviating their financial woes with a final act of service. Richard, George and Isabella received set sums and shares, with which the latter wisely paid off a fraction of her debt. William received nothing – presumably on account of already possessing a title, or perhaps he had fallen from favour – though money was set aside for his son. John inherited his uncle's hunting estates in Yorkshire and Hampshire plus legacies for all the children, and was able to invest in a 'neat and elegant' villa with adjoining farm at Pirbright in Surrey, around thirty miles from London. With this flurry of financial activity and a season in mourning the siblings bid farewell to their uncle John Berkeley, the most dependable ally of their young lives.

Second came the unfortunate revelations about their private

pleasures. They might have excused themselves with the prevailing idea that it was not an age of fidelity. 'When I came into the World', Frederick later commented, 'I found no Lady who might be said to move with any splendour in it, or to lead it, but had an avowed Lover, and no Husband cared what path his Wife trod, provided he was unmolested in following his own'.[41] However exaggerated, he captured the mood of aristocratic insouciance that Sir William had held accusingly against Isabella as their own marriage fell apart. Though it was increasingly fashionable to suggest that marriage should spring from affection, it was quite normal for a husband to conduct affairs or even fund a separate household for a mistress. For a privileged man, protected by the law, the female world was something to be conquered. Women of all classes – servants, shop girls and naive neighbours' daughters – could be coerced with flattery, presents of varying value, or simple intimidation (though as a matter of honour other men's wives were, ideally, off limits). On the other hand, a married woman – on whose fidelity and honesty a man's lineage depended – was kept under close scrutiny. In the words of a contemporary *History of Women* (written, incidentally, by a man), the female sex were 'disgraced beyond all possibility of redemption by the commission of faults, which in the men are hardly considered as anything but acts of gallantry'.[42] While a husband 'may riot with impunity in adulterous amours,' it continued, 'if the wife retaliates, by copying his example, he immediately procures a divorce, and may turn her out without subsistence'. Whoever the perpetrator, the indiscretions of the *bon ton* provided sufficient salacious fodder to fill reams of cheap chapbooks and gossip columns. Divorce cases were hurried into print, and the 'Tête-à-têtes' feature of the newly launched *Town and Country Magazine* exposed a high-society sex scandal each month. Frederick himself featured in the spring of 1773 picking up the strategically dropped fans of 'a number of French beauties' during his teenage tour, though as these amours predated his marriage he emerged relatively unscathed – a few months later, his adventuring uncle was less fortunate.

As letters and gifts poured in from Isabella as she travelled across Europe, Sophia struggled to keep her household in order. John did not involve himself overmuch, leaving to his wife 'the doing every thing that is to be done'.[43] She did not find it easy – what Isabella called the 'secret springs' of her household laboured quite visibly, and the servants took advantage. A dishonest housekeeper had run them into debt. The family had caused a few waves as they settled into London life after the more provincial society of Plymouth. Sophia's childhood friend Anne Egerton confessed that since moving to the capital 'her way of life & manners have been so opposite to mine', and she had heard such convincing reasons for 'disliking any intercourse with her daughter, that I have been as quietly as I have been able withdrawing myself from any intimacy in that family'.[44] Sophia made her home at Bolton Row in Piccadilly, apparently leaving the house at Welbeck Street as John's retreat. No further active employments had been forthcoming since his return from Canada, and his misery was obvious even to his distant sister: 'I have had a very kind but melancholy Letter from the Commodore', Isabella told her daughter. 'I hope after all he has gone through he will not utterly be neglected, tho' hitherto he has met with much hardship, I am persuaded by what he says that he is very unhappy.'[45] Frustrated professionally, he found he could not (or did not want to) find the domestic comfort he craved in the arms of his fretful wife of twenty-five years – and so he looked elsewhere. He did not look far. One day Sophia walked into a bedchamber and found her gallant husband under the sheets with her teenage chambermaid. Perhaps worse than the betrayal was the very public fallout.

As Christmas 1773 approached, if Sophia had dared to peruse the latest issue of *Town and Country Magazine* she would have been faced with a pair of crude portraits: 'Pretty Betsy G—n' and a frowning officer dubbed 'The Nautical Lover'. It was a poor likeness but as the excruciating detail quickly made clear – 'the brother of a noble lord, whom an accident made very conspicuous some years ago' – it was her husband.[46] Reducing his entire history to a string of liaisons, it made John's sex life the talk of the town: a cleaning girl at Westminster School, a determined landlady at Plymouth, a beautiful Italian seductress during his duty abroad, the titillating princesses of the South Seas. The constantly pregnant state of his 'most amiable' wife only confirmed those insatiable passions that 'so often agitated him at home'. And now, nineteen-year-old Betsy Green. According to 'Tête-à-têtes', this 'captivating' farmer's daughter had quickly impressed both Sophia and John with her politeness and intelligent conversation. It was not long before the commodore began to press his suit and convinced her into his bed, until Sophia discovered the affair and dismissed Betsy from her service. At this, they reported, John merely installed her as his mistress in 'an obscure part of the New-buildings, near Marybone' where – despite Sophia's frantic complaints – 'our hero still pays her his constant visits'. (The description offers a neat match with Welbeck Street, a Marylebone townhouse built just a decade earlier.) However close it was to the truth, John emerged almost heroically, being described as 'emulous even in his youth for bravery', but for his painfully proud wife the humiliation of such a sordid *exposé* was a new low.

While John wallowed uncharacteristically in disrepute, the wider family (Richard perhaps excluded) did little to improve on his example. In Nottingham, his brother George had his own affair that resulted in demands for maintenance of an illegitimate daughter. (In the event, this amounted to twenty-four weeks of payments, plus funeral costs.) Meanwhile in Italy, Isabella's tour turned sour after Princess Louisa of Stolberg – wife of the exiled Jacobite leader Charles Edward Stuart – refused to admit Weinheim to her court, repulsing him 'with ignominy, as not being a gentleman, in the German acceptation, and consequently no baron'.[47] Their audacious pretence was detected. Having 'exposed themselves there shockingly' they decamped for Paris, where Isabella distracted herself from the gathering disgrace by hosting lavish dinners for the local officers.

In the aftermath of the Newstead picture sale William did not attempt to preserve the remains of his legacy by trying his hand at economising. As he attended charity dinners and the Prince of Wales's extravagant twelfth birthday party, it became clear that he could no longer afford to pay the rates at Great Marlborough Street. By the time of John's fall from matrimonial grace, number 15 stood empty and William's chaplain was drafted in to take residence. Father and son were at least approaching a resettlement of the family estates, which would allow William to sell the residue of his wife's Norfolk estates and a sizeable portion of his lands in Nottinghamshire. Though their debts meant that most of the funds were already spoken for (just £1,200 of the £50,500 raised by the Nottinghamshire sale was at William's disposal), he continued utterly incapable of moderating his spending. As Elizabeth found a more peaceful retreat at Petersham in Surrey, dismayed that he continued to take advantage of her few friends, he enjoyed a grand dinner at the launch of a warship in Deptford and then took a 'tour of pleasure' to Portsmouth with a large, disreputable band of gentlemen.[48]

In the new year of 1775, Sophia was at home on Bolton Row. An elegant street inhabited by politicians, baronesses and bluestockings, it lay in the shadows of two of the grandest mansions in the city – Devonshire House and Lansdowne House. She was fretting about money. 'I have on coming home so many things – alas – to pay,' she wrote anxiously to the family's financial agent James Sykes, 'it distresses me – nay near makes me mad'.[49] The children – now aged between twelve and twenty-five – were on the road to adulthood, but not exactly off her hands. Sophy and Augusta were perhaps still young enough for romantic ideas, despite the fact that though the elder girls were both married mothers, neither seemed happy. The outgoing Fanny, now Mrs Leigh, was a little too popular with the opposite sex. A poem recently published in the *Westminster Magazine* 'To Mrs Lee [*sic*]' raved:

> *The God of Wine grows jealous of his art,*
> *He only fires the head, but Lee the heart:*
> *The Queen of Love looks on, and smiles to see*
> *A dame more lovely than a Deity.*[50]

Whoever the author – a mysterious 'T.' – it was clearly not her husband Charles.

The boys were both set on conventional military paths. Sophia's beloved George Anson had recently enlisted in the navy. Jack had been in the army for almost three years, after being dispatched from Westminster to a French military school (perhaps Monsieur Lochée's private academy in Chelsea). The eighteen-year-old had grown into a handsome young man and his early military career had brought some bragging rights. Shortly after enlisting as an ensign with the 68th Regiment of Foot (a troop of light infantry) aged fifteen, he seems to have been posted – albeit briefly – to Antigua as part of the conflict with the Carib inhabitants of nearby Saint Vincent. (Certainly the regiment shipped out an officer named Byron in 1773.) On his return he had transferred to the Coldstream Guards and was now making a nuisance of himself at Bolton Row between recruitment duties. When in town he alternated between lodging with an Eliza Keele – who also made shirts for him and did his washing – and staying with his mother. Like his uncle, aunt and cousins, he had already developed a spending habit: having convinced his father to release the funds, he had already distributed the majority of his £3,000 inheritance from Lord Berkeley among the city's tailors, hatters and sword makers before he came of age. Sophia was aware of her son's profligate ways but let things slide. 'I have pretended *to be angry* you let him have *even that*', she wrote to Sykes, on hearing that Jack had just extracted five guineas out of him. 'Be so good to call here about twelve with my money', she continued, 'but if he should be in the room not give it me while he stays.'[51]

The family – and their agent – gave a collective sigh of relief in March 1775 when some good news (finally) rolled in from the Admiralty. John had been promoted: he was now *Rear Admiral* Byron.

'If their Treason be suffered to take Root'

This illustrious new appointment came amid intensifying national fever about America, where unrest over taxation had spilled over into decisive action. A protest in Boston during which the cargo of a tea ship had been raided and destroyed – now known as the 'Boston Tea Party' – had provoked further punitive British legislation, which in turn inflamed new outrage across thirteen rebellious colonies. The Americans were calling to arms. In April 1775, just weeks after John's promotion, a local militia faced the British army at Lexington, near Boston, and the first shots of battle were fired. Revolution.

As all eyes turned to their leaders, John's health failed him. 'The Admirals appointed to conduct the war in America,' declared the *Royal Gazette* cheerfully, 'are said to be Byron, Gambier, and Arbuthnot'; but when he was offered the position of second-in-command of the navy's North American station in the autumn, he had to decline: 'I should embrace this offered me now with infinite satisfaction, did my health permit; but in its present impaired state, I am much afraid I should not prove equal to the task.'[52] The king was disappointed but sympathetic, commenting, 'he is too gallant an officer to pretend illness without sufficient reason'.[53] As Rear Admiral Howe was appointed in his stead, a frustrated John struggled through an English winter. Sophia had also fallen sufficiently ill to be dispatched to Bath and fright her husband with an express requesting his urgent attendance – it was a false alarm, but not without consequences. 'I left her much better,' he informed Sykes, 'but the journey has half ruin'd me.'[54] He was eager to join the war effort, but he needed more time.

In London, the revolutionary summer of 1776 was sultry and tense. There was no consensus about the troubles in America and a suspicion in more pacific quarters of the House of Lords that 'full and authentic information' was being withheld in order to secure funds.[55] In any case, it was all so far away. Newspaper reports that New York was 'consumed to ashes' sat beside breathless descriptions of the beautiful courtesans gracing the latest masquerade at Carlisle House. John paced the halls of the Admiralty, and his son George Anson proudly received his first lieutenant's commission; Jack was lumbered with the 'sad work' of travelling the country attempting to drum up new recruits. Quite apart from the meagre wages and poor food offered by the army, many were deterred by the nature of the war: 'all our young people are averse to it', declared the *Edinburgh Advertiser.* 'The officers have been told, that they will not enter into the service of the ministry, who want to employ them in cutting his Majesty's subjects' throats. Had we been at war with France and Spain, they would have found many here ready to enter.'[56] With the three men of the family poised on the brink of overseas conflict, even Sophia's generous capacity for anxiety was stretched.

Across town, Elizabeth was enjoying a summer to herself – William had taken a jaunt around Scottish waters in one of his vessels, the *Mermaid.* Their twenty-six-year-old son had fallen ill with a consumptive illness and was confined to his house in Pinner, but the doctors seemed optimistic. The young man hadn't had much luck of late – after just five years of marriage he and Juliana had separated, and his political career had begun in truly humiliating style. Despite having his cousin Frederick's support and advancing bribes to 'Real Friends' and 'Half Friends' to the tune of £1,000, his election as MP for Morpeth had prompted the disgruntled populace to attack the bailiffs with sticks. On 21 June, Lady Byron took a trip to Ranelagh pleasure gardens with her young friend Julia Molyneux, and as they walked she opened her heart. She spoke of her son's illness and other misfortunes, but 'did not seame to think him in any danger'.[57] Conversation turned to other things.

That night, Elizabeth had just climbed into bed when an express arrived requesting her immediate attendance at Pinner – when she arrived her son was saying his goodbyes. His wife Juliana had also rushed over, in time to hear him rasp that he 'hoped she wou'd forgive him as he forgave her'. Within a few hours he was dead. Elizabeth was devastated – and furious. 'Lady Byron is much affected,' grieved her remaining friend Miss Molyneux, 'as to my Lord he is at Sea and she wishes never to see him again.' (She certainly had no support from her associate and William's supposed lover, Mrs Scrimshire, who 'turn'd Cat' and scurried off gossiping into Nottinghamshire.) Three children lost, and the breach between husband and wife was wider than ever. William did not trouble himself to return for his son's funeral, which took place just over a week later at the family vault at St Mary's in Twickenham. As young William's possessions were auctioned off, his father was preparing to sail from Stromness to Stornoway.

In Philadelphia, the summer of 1776 sparked with talk of liberty. It was a young city, and though it was by far America's largest it could easily be walked in a day – away from the port the dense commercial district gradually gave way to green parks and gardens. A clamour drifted up from its neat blocks and wound around the city's spires: laughter from taverns and coffee houses; shouts from the docks; the clattering of carts by day and bonfires and drunken brawls by night. But the jubilation of previous months was becoming more muted. There were clashes between British and American privateers. The British reports of 'People over Head and Ears in Debt, and ready to tear each other in Pieces' may have been exaggerated, but this shot at revolution was certainly a huge risk.[58]

On 4 July, just five days after the grieving Elizabeth arrived at

Twickenham to bury her son, the newly established Continental Congress ratified their 'Declaration of Independence' and rejected British rule. In London, Parliament was divided. Smarting from the insult, George III pressed for punitive action and in his first parliamentary speech on the matter insisted that 'if their Treason be suffered to take Root, much Mischief must grow from it'. A young, fashionable peer was the first to express his support. It was Frederick, and he did not hold back. He spoke of 'vigorously exerting ourselves in the course of the ensuing campaign', and could not help remarking that these hostilities 'would never have happened, if that disobedient, traitorous spirit had not been nourished, and strengthened by a set of men in this country'.[59] Following weeks of debate about money, military strategy and the ungratefulness of the American rebels, the king's argument for war won out. Poised for action, the Byrons awaited their orders.

The first six months seemed promising for the king. New York fell under British control. Philadelphia drained of people – including the new Congress – as morale dipped. Britain puffed out its chest and sent more troops across the sea. Among those drafted over in March 1777, amid the sea of red coats and black cockaded hats, was twenty-year-old ensign Jack Byron of the Coldstream Guards. With five years' experience he was promoted to lieutenant and quickly took up duties as a secondary captain. Even at this distance his parents could steal a glimpse of his activities through his dealings with Sykes. In September, Philadelphia was seized and Jack – apparently with little to do – plunged rather too heartily into the pleasures of the city. By Christmas he owed over £100 (more than £8,500 today) to one Daniel Smith, including something Sykes marked as 'Charges for Act of Honor'.[60] (That a Daniel Smith managed the renowned City Tavern, one of the most popular resorts of entertainment in town, may not be a coincidence.) If he performed any acts of valour or value they went unrecorded, but he did impress (or at least charm) his superior officers. In February 1778, after a relatively uneventful year away, he was given leave to return to England with new responsibilities for the administration and discipline of the regiment.

As Jack sailed home the political tide was turning – the American rebels had formed an alliance with Britain's old enemy, France – and his cousin Frederick was to be sent into the fray. A conciliatory commission had been drawn up in hopes that the rebellious colonies might withdraw their demand for full independence if offered the chance to self-govern. Controversially, twenty-nine-year-old Lord Carlisle was named the chief negotiator. Entrusting such an important task to a young peer with more experience in fashion than diplomacy provoked a slew of mocking prints and verses. 'Let *gentle* Stormont threat intriguing France! You shine, my Lord, *unrival'd in the dance*,' jibed one poem, 'What real praises then become your due! For who can dress and dance so well as you!'[61] France's recent hand of friendship to the enemy had also seriously undercut any chance of success. Undeterred, Frederick leapt at the opportunity to prove himself – he arrived in the blistering heat of Philadelphia on 8 June 1778, complaining that the threat of gnats as big as sparrows had forced him to the necessity of wearing *trousers*. Flitting about Paris, his mother waited impatiently for news.

John, now Admiral Byron, was hot on his nephew's fashionable heels. By the new year of 1778 he felt sufficiently recovered to finally accept a significant command: 'I [am] ready to go to any part of the world I may be ordered to,' he informed the Admiralty with conviction.[62] Having received instructions to assume the prestigious post of commander-in-chief of the East Indies, he shipped his belongings to his new station. But on the brink of his departure, news from France changed everything. A messenger arrived at Pirbright late on 30 April requesting his attendance in London – he had been personally chosen by the king for a new mission. During a 'long conference' with His Majesty the following day, John was told that intelligence had been received of a French squadron bound for Boston, with orders to attack the British in North America and the West Indies. A reliable officer was required to 'vindicate the Insulted Honor' of the British crown by 'attacking and defeating the said French Squadron'. The king had chosen John. Honoured by this royal confidence, he accepted with enthusiasm and learned what he could about his new nemesis: the French admiral, Charles-Hector, comte d'Estaing. His orders were necessarily vague: he was to pursue d'Estaing's ships whatever their destination, and conduct himself in whatever manner he thought best until they were destroyed.

With time of the essence he prepared as best he could, though with his things halfway across the world he observed, 'I think I have a chance of going to sea with only a purser's kit'.[63] 'He made no kind of difficulty when I broke the matter to him,' wrote the Admiralty's First Secretary, 'though to be sure it does put him to very great inconvenience to set out so suddenly and without having made any preparation at Plymouth for such an expedition.'[64] Nonetheless, John was grateful to have finally secured a meaningful commission. Unsure when – perhaps even if – he would return, he bid his family farewell. As he sailed on 9 June 1778 with a squadron of thirteen ships and one frigate, the thought may have nagged at him that during his last long absence his sixteen-year-old daughter had eloped. If he hoped that this stretch overseas might pass without further domestic disaster, he was sadly mistaken.

As John launched into the conflict from which he would emerge as 'Foul-Weather Jack', William set the seal on Newstead Abbey's unhappy fate. With his chaplain paying the rates on Great Marlborough Street, he took up a (presumably cheaper, but likely not cheap enough) lease at 11 Queen Anne Street. Unlike his nephew Frederick, he had showed no interest in attending debates on the American question since voting to keep it in submission by retaining the Stamp Act. While his peers discussed navy expenditure and lives lost as a result of the ongoing 'unhappy Contest', as it was called in the House of Lords, William was preoccupied with his own 'pressing Business' at Newstead.[65] His only son was dead, and the six-year-old grandson left behind was of little use until he was old enough to legally negotiate another resettlement. But money had to be raised, and quickly. In the six years since the art auction William had continually picked at the family inheritance – hearing that his Lordship was 'dismantling the Whole' in 1775, a local clergyman gladly parted with his cash in return for orange and lemon trees, as well as 'Lord Byron's strong beer for my Parish, & his Brass Eagle for Southwell [Minster], at very good bargains.'[66] But it was not enough.

In the summer of 1778 the entirety of Newstead's moveable assets were surveyed, divided into 429 lots and printed in a catalogue for an auction house at Mansfield. The listings for this 'Great Sale' gave an intimate picture of his family's private life. From Caroline's bedroom – draped in red and white plaid – went the curtains, carpets, feather bed and mirror. The blankets, dressing chests and armchairs from long-neglected nurseries. The medieval and modern masterpieces that had survived the first auction were torn from the walls and ten 'very fine Plaister Statues' were toppled from their niches in the Grand Hall.[67] There were William's packs of 'Lisbon toothpicks' and collection of swords and pistols, along with bird cages, fishing rods, backgammon tables and books. For two days the curious public tramped and gawped around the Abbey, and for another six they chattered cheerfully as the gavel fell and the Byrons' childhood home was stripped to a skeleton. In the Grand Hall, previously crowded with hunting pictures and paraphernalia, the vaulted ceiling gaped in shock over a barren space. Where fifty years earlier the Byron siblings and their parents had gathered to dance with the servants, only a scattering of family portraits remained.

The funds were siphoned off to the most demanding creditors and, significantly, to William and Elizabeth's lawyers. Weighed down by thirty-one long years – the loss of three children, rumours of adultery and cruelty, a bottomless pit of extravagance and a murder trial – their marriage was finally over. Unwilling or unable to secure an expensive divorce, the terms of their separation were drawn up. He agreed to settle £500 per year on their sole surviving child, Caroline, and £100 per year on his estranged wife. They were clearly an allied force and wished to remain together – Elizabeth declined his offer of another fifty pounds a year if she lived separately from her daughter. While the two women melted into the company of their friends, the widowed Juliana and little William John, Lord Byron turned back to his money-making schemes. He pestered Daws about pawning Newstead's chimneypieces, brass locks and flooring. '[T]ho I cant pull down the House', he wrote, 'I have a power to sell all the materials in the inside also the Game', implying that – had he been legally permitted – he would have been quite willing to utterly destroy the Abbey.[68] His desperation to recoup his losses was not a matter of restoring his family legacy, but merely of extricating himself from a crippling hole of debt. The hard work of his father's latter years had been entirely undone.

'My heart is so sorely afflicted'

While her brother and sister-in-law went their separate ways, the Dowager Countess and her cherished counterfeit 'Baron' revelled in the delights of Paris – the beautifully sculpted gardens, the lively promenades, glittering palaces and squares. From her lodgings at the Hôtel de Dannemarc, just south of the Seine and around a mile from Notre-Dame, she hosted modest dinners while Weinheim cosied up to potential moneylenders and dropped imprudent hints about Isabella's diamonds. She formed an acquaintance with the formidable Maréchal de Biron, with whom she believed there must be some distant kinship – the English *Birons* had come over with William the Conqueror, of course – but she didn't win over all of his countryfolk. 'What do you think of the Countess of Carlisle . . . ?' asked the antiquated hostess Madame du Deffand of their mutual friend Walpole. 'She comes to see me sometimes; I don't know if she is a very sensible woman.' 'She talks a lot, and in good French', she concluded, but contributes 'nothing shocking or interesting'.[69]

As she scribed and dined her way through her late fifties, Isabella was feeling her age. Her hair was turning grey and she was increasingly reliant on her spectacles. In a world where a woman's beauty was her most valued possession, it was a devastating blow to her vanity – 'I hate to be look'd at & as I grow older I must more & more entertain that Opinion', she complained – but may also have inspired her latest project.[70] It was a remarkable one: having stirred controversy and criticism for over thirty years, she was putting together an etiquette guide for young women. During the course of her travels she had been composing a manuscript of 'maxims', with nuggets of advice for all stages of life: early education, adjusting to marriage, negotiating fashionable society and coping with the approach of death. She clearly spoke from painful experience when she warned that 'the decay of beauty is perhaps one of the most sensible trials that female temper can experience'.[71]

Unsurprisingly, her companion – who had been a part of her life for eight years and whose livelihood was now entirely subsidised by her ill-advised generosity – was viewed with growing hostility by her friends in England. He appeared to be nothing but a parasite. Their subtle hints that she should return – *alone* – finally turned to schemes to forcibly separate them. Enough damage had already been done to her reputation. 'She does well to stay abroad,' declared Lady Rivers, John and Sophia's neighbour, 'for no mortal would go near her if she were at home.'[72] The Countess of Berkeley scoffed that 'She has no taste, to take such an ugly broken-nosed fellow', but 'had it been the tall footman' – who were notoriously hired on the merit of their attractiveness – 'she could forgive her'.[73] Having established a reputation for inheriting the unfortunate romantic sensibilities of her mother, Isabella's daughter Julia was caught up in her own miseries, being once again roundly (but this time unfairly) condemned for contracting an engagement with an undeserving 'basket maker'.[74] The sympathetic Sophia was one of the few whose letters offered any support.

When a talkative and deferential clergyman in his forties arrived in Paris to pay his respects, Isabella had little reason to suspect he was a spy. Dr John Warner had been dispatched by George Selwyn to befriend the couple and contrive a way to bring Isabella home. He was soon dining with them twice a week and sending back reports on 'the old lady'. He found her at once outwardly fragile and utterly intimidating. 'She was sitting at work between the window and the fire, the Baron on the other side, with a table on which were the papers before her;' he reported after one early visit, 'her head dressed very close in a tight little mob, as if prepared for battle.'[75] She spent another evening reading theatrically from her 'maxims', 'taking her eyes ever and anon from the paper, and sometimes the spectacles from her nose, to see how I relished the gobbets as she gave them'. He formed a disconcertingly strong opinion about the true nature of Isabella and Weinheim's relationship – their repeated and unsolicited protestations that 'there was nothing improper' in their attachment, which 'was nothing but mere virtuous friendship' only convinced Warner they were lovers.[76] She batted away all suggestions of returning to England with a string of excuses – the climate, the expense, her health: 'the respectable dame could never bear the jolting on the *pavé* from hence to Calais', Weinheim chimed in.[77] To her friend and benefactor Sir John Lambert she flapped her hands and cried 'don't mention England, for thither *I will not go!*', and when Warner enquired again whether she would depart soon he wrote that she 'tipped me the wink, nodded her head, looked very cunning, and cried significantly, "Ay!" which, if I were to translate it into genteel language, I should say was "So they may think, but they will be mistaken."'[78] 'As for the Baron,' Warner regretted, 'the lady is besotted to the fellow, and I am convinced will never be brought alive to England, unless he should desert or die.'[79]

As winter deepened the city was laced with frost and the freezing Seine slowed its march. The bells rang for the birth of a princess at Versailles, a daughter for Louis XVI and Marie Antoinette. Technically in enemy territory, Isabella couldn't help fretting about America and was 'very uneasy on account of her son, and of her brother' as she scoured the newspapers and examined her maps to follow the movements of John's squadron.[80] She pored over Frederick's updates from New York and no doubt fell into a characteristic 'fidget' when she heard that he had been challenged to a duel by the renowned French general Lafayette. Wildly conflicting accounts about the admiral and d'Estaing surfaced each week: John's ship was lost in a storm – he was killed by a stomach complaint – no, it was d'Estaing who perished, and John had achieved a glorious victory – or had he suffered a terrible defeat? It was all groundless rumour.

Letters about her own affairs brought little comfort, being increasingly barbed with innuendos and ultimatums about Weinheim. 'This Baron Hounnuyhm (or how do they spell it) is but a Yahoo', Warner finally declared to Selwyn in January 1779. 'We thought so once, but now we know it.'[81] His investigations had uncovered their humiliation at the Jacobite court in Rome and Weinheim's humble origins as the outcast son of a '*petit procureur*' living in Cologne. When Selwyn eventually wrote with open contempt for '*votre ami le Baron*', she dug in her heels and Weinheim indignantly demanded a duel. 'Such insinuations upon a man of quality and honour!' she railed at no one in particular.[82] Though her reluctant hostess Madame du Deffand was unaware of these gory details, she was unequivocal in her opinion: 'It is important that this lady leaves the country.'[83]

Feeling cornered, Isabella resorted to desperate measures – when pressed too far on a subject she did not like, she appeared to faint away and fall into some kind of fit. It was roundly presumed to be a ruse. She either remained steadfastly blind to the truth about Monsieur L'archer's origins or – to use one of her own colourful phrases – truly did 'not care two skips of a louse' about them.[84] At the very least, she must have been convinced that his intentions were good and his feelings for her were genuine (her entire history does attest to her weakness in this area). Weinheim, for his part, continued to pour forth inventions about his lands in Alsace and valiantly swore to Warner that he 'had a very sincere attachment for the lady, which death only should break' – just the sort of romantic oath to fire Isabella's heart. Her own conspiracies against Selwyn were foiled by the fact that 'she cannot harbour a thought of attempting it without letting it be known'.[85]

Her openness with the duplicitous Warner was her undoing. To her dismay the separation was finally effected in the spring – though it was Weinheim who was escorted to London (where Warner wrote miserably, 'My only hope is, to get rid of him by taking him to a city party, and stifling him with tobacco').[86] Some old acquaintances, the Robinson family, gossiped that the Howards had resorted to auctioning off her possessions: 'Jewells, Wardrobe even old shoes & books amongst which were a good many Spanish, of the Dowager L[ad]y Carlisle, who now lives at Paris, where she is much in debt'.[87] Everything she treasured was being taken away. When asked by Selwyn what he thought of the business, a mutual associate in France painted a melancholy portrait: 'I think that she is unhappy and lost, and it is no matter how much she suffers.'[88]

While Isabella avoided her prying countryfolk, Sophia felt critical eyes burning into Bolton Row: twenty-two-year-old Jack had kicked up a scandal of his own. He had returned from Philadelphia the previous spring – just in time to see his father leave – as an acting captain. Taking up residence in Pall Mall, he had enthusiastically embraced the life of a rakish young bachelor and was promptly swept up in an affair that would alter the course of his life. It was later declared that he first laid eyes on Amelia Osborne at the crowded summer festivities at Coxheath military camp in Kent. She was undeniably beautiful – one gossip column credited her with 'one of the most angelic faces, and elegant figures, that can be seen in the circle of a drawing-room' – and, like himself, full of laughter and levity.[89] She was also spoiled, with a particular reputation for ungracious manners towards her long-suffering mother; but these were not qualities to deter Jack Byron, who cheerfully subjected his own parents to similar torments. As Lady Carmarthen she outranked him considerably, and had inherited an independent fortune upon the recent death of her father, Lord Holderness. The irresistible pull of their attraction could not be stifled by the inconvenient existence of her husband, Lord Carmarthen, or even her three infant children – their sexual relationship reportedly began 'from the time of their first acquaintance'.[90]

By November their brazen exploits while her husband was away had turned her house at Grosvenor Square into a web of spies – the almanac of the appalled housekeeper was blackened with evidence of their indiscretions. Jack sallied about the house in his scarlet coat and cockaded hat, and perused the library in the middle of the night; he was spotted peeping his head out of her bedroom and – eventually – undressed and snoring in Amelia's bed. Maids pressed their ears against their mistress's door as the couple slept in until the afternoon, heard them laughing 'a good deal . . . as if they were very merry', and scattered when he eventually emerged whistling and singing.[91] One later recalled that he strolled out the front door 'perfectly easy, as if he had been master of the house', and they looked knowingly at each other when they found the bedsheets 'very much tumbled'. On Carmarthen's return to London, Amelia began feigning illness at social gatherings so that she could return home to meet her lover.

On 13 December, after around a month of these reckless secret trysts, Jack was visiting his sister Juliana when Amelia's footman appeared to request his immediate attendance at Bolton Row, where she was waiting for him. (Fortunately for everyone concerned, Sophia was not at home.) Their affair was discovered. Fleeing, they were pursued to lodgings near Brighton by Lord Carmarthen's footman – he found them in bed together, 'her Ladyship with a Pen in her Hand, sitting up in Bed, with Mr Byron between the Sheets'.[92] (Jack was no doubt incensed with his own servant, John Kates, for letting the man up simply because he recognised his face.)

The scandal exploded onto the public scene and Amelia did not fare well. 'Lady Carmarthen ran away yesterday with a young officer', revealed bluestocking Elizabeth Montagu to her sister; 'if he is wise he will soon desert her. I am glad she has rid the prettiest young man in England of the most vicious and detestable creature that ever disgraced the Race of Womankind.'[93] 'Lady Holdernesse is truly miserable at her daughter's conduct', gossiped the Robinsons. 'She was aware of great levetys in her conduct, but did not think her capable of such a publick scandalous unprovok'd *l'esclandre* as she has committed.'[94] The cuckolded husband himself was 'thunderstruck'. 'My heart is so sorely afflicted, that God knows if I write sense or not', he grieved to his errant wife; 'as to the leaving of Grosvenor Square, it is an inevitable consequence of the fatal business'.[95] He urged her to consider spending some time in a convent in Antwerp rather than casting herself irrevocably into the arms of a young captain whose only merit seemed to be his handsome face. But she had made her bed. She was pregnant, she informed him, and felt obliged to tell him the child was not his. Having thrown her mother Lady Holderness into despair, Amelia quickly became 'sensible of her utter ruin', but still she clung fast to Jack.[96] The depth of the couple's disgrace lay in her husband's hands.

Following the initial shock, Lord Carmarthen was more civil than Amelia deserved. Just a week after the elopement he signed his letters as 'your sincere well wisher' and offered his hope that they could avoid the courts, as 'we both wish to go thro' this melancholy business as quietly and expeditiously as circumstances will permit us to do'.[97] 'I am told norm requires that I should bring an action against Mr B.', he wrote just before Christmas, reassuring her that 'unless I am forced to it (which I dare say I shall not be) he may rest assured I shall insist upon no bail, nor will I accept one farthing damages'.[98] He would by no means prevent her from seeing her three children – as was his legal right – though Jack must not accompany her on any visits. He sent over her jewels, but kept some rings 'as ever valuable tokens of our former happier days'.

In January, as a matter of honour, Carmarthen took out an order against Jack amounting to £516 for 'Damages which he sustained by occasion of a certain Trespass and Assault' on Amelia, 'by the

William, 4th Lord Byron, painted here in his twenties, was a keen hunter, collector and amateur composer. Forced to begin his family anew in his fifties, he spent his remaining years making improvements to Newstead Abbey.

Frances, Lady Byron (née Berkeley) dutifully rescued her ageing husband's dynasty; after years of childbearing even her own father remarked, 'she has quite lost her youth'.

As well as becoming a committed scholar and successful clergyman, Richard Byron was a talented artist; he completed this self-portrait aged about sixteen.

Heiress Elizabeth Shaw's marriage to William began with a 'fond fitt', but he squandered her fortune and rumours of adultery and domestic violence clouded their later years.

This view of 1760 shows Newstead Abbey from across the Upper Lake and includes one of William's prized replica warships.

'Ld Byron's Household at his Seat Newsted Abbey' by Peter Tillemans, 1726. A later marginal note identifies his lordship seated on the far left, with Frances (in blue) dancing and the three infants to the right as William, John and Richard.

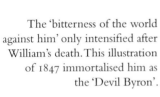

The death of Mr Chaworth by William's sword put an abrupt end to both of their pleasures. The subsequent murder trial of 1765 sparked a scramble for tickets.

The 'bitterness of the world against him' only intensified after William's death. This illustration of 1847 immortalised him as the 'Devil Byron'.

The shipwreck of the *Wager* in 1741 was just the beginning of the harrowing survival story that made John's name. This illustration depicts survivors landing on an unknown Patagonian shore, with the wreck behind them.

Sophia Byron (née Trevanion) was admired in youth for her prettiness, and later for her comic stories and refusal to let poor health (or her family's misdemeanours) disrupt her 'chatting parties'.

John's career at sea was so chequered by storms that by the 1770s he had earned the nickname 'Foul-Weather Jack'. The lurching ship and gathering black clouds perhaps allude to this unfortunate reputation.

On marrying in 1743, Isabella became mistress of Castle Howard. Her friend Horace Walpole later commented, 'I have seen gigantic places before, but never a sublime one.'

This portrait, likely commissioned during Isabella's visit to Bath in autumn 1760, captures her in the flush of new love, and with a fashionable dusting of lilac hair powder.

Young Sir William Musgrave was attracted to Isabella's passionate nature and intellectual curiosity – his hopes that she would adjust to his moderate lifestyle were quickly dashed.

Assuming his title aged ten, Isabella's son Frederick, 5th Earl of Carlisle, grew to be a leader of fashion and prominent Whig.

The American Revolutionary War saw John dispatched across the world in pursuit of his nemesis Admiral d'Estaing – in July 1779, the Battle of Grenada offered a final stab at glory.

Catherine Gordon, 13th Laird of Gight, married 'scapegrace' Jack Byron in 1785. This portrait depicts the widowed Catherine after their only son inherited the Byron barony.

Joseph Murray – or 'Old Joe' – was employed at the Abbey in 1755 and remained linked to the family until his death in 1820. His nostalgic tales saw him dubbed 'a walking & living Legend of Newstead'.

Visiting in 1814, the poet's publisher was surprised at his affection for the dilapidated Abbey, thinking it merely 'a perpetual memorial of the wickedness of his ancestors'.

said John Byron with force and Arms' (though it does not seem that he claimed the money, nor can he have believed the charge).[99] As negotiations proceeded, the couple took a house together just south of London, where Amelia laboured through anxiety-induced headaches. 'Crime should be punished and could you know what I have suffered for these six weeks you would be sufficiently revenged', she wrote pitifully to Carmarthen, calling him 'the only friend I have left'.[100] Life with Jack was evidently not living up to her expectations. Though the depth of his attachment goes unrecorded, as the talk of desertion implies, he had no legal obligations towards her. Either he truly loved her, felt a real duty to his unborn child, or – perhaps most convincingly, considering the tenor of her letters – there was a simple financial reason why the scandal was worth enduring. He certainly stood to benefit if Carmarthen filed for divorce: 'Lady Carmarthen lives at Chislehurst with Mr Byron', the Robinson family gossiped; 'her fortune when divorced will be very considerable so he will probably marry her'.[101]

The Capricious Marchioness. The Boisterous Lover.

Jack Byron and Lady Carmarthen's scandalous affair appeared in the gossiping Town and Country Magazine *in February 1779, as her divorce proceedings began.*

Like his father and cousin before him, Jack secured a starring role in 'Têtes-à-têtes' as 'The Boisterous Lover' to Amelia's 'Capricious Marchioness'.[102] (Their good looks were not particularly well represented in the accompanying portraits, though he does sport his tricorn hat and a neat white wig.) The venom was saved entirely for the lady – Sophia might have snorted at the assertion that her son's conduct had 'hitherto been entirely irreproachable, having always sustained the character of a soldier and a gentleman'. '[A]fter a divorce has removed all connubial ties,' it continued, 'the captain will offer his hand in an honourable way.' Jack fared less well in the *Westminster Magazine* – apparently a friend to Lord Carmarthen – which agreed only with the appellation of 'boisterous': '*Inclination* would have picked out a Gallant of sense and appearance – *Revenge* fixed on Jack B—n. Jack is the laughing stock of his companions, and furnishes more occasion for mirth, than any young fellow of the age. – He is boisterous in his manner – aukward [*sic*] and clumsy in his appearance – poor and unpleasing in his conversation'.[103] The scandal was only uncovered, the magazine declared, because 'he was too much elated with his conquest to keep his tongue within its limits'.[104]

The process took five months. The legalities were set in motion in January and court appearances made in February – Amelia attended but 'controverted none of the Allegations; nor did she examine any Witnesses'.[105] The servants presented damning evidence of the couple's repeated 'criminal and adulterous conversation', with one newly emboldened footman claiming to have chastised Jack with the words, 'Every servant in the house will be bound to curse the day, or hour, when you first came into this house'.[106] The petition was finally approved by Parliament in May. Ensuring their dirty laundry was not only aired in public but torn to shreds by it, the case was printed in a salacious catalogue of 'Adultery, Fornication . . . &c' which cost just sixpence and was 'very avidly purchased by the Ladies'.[107] Amelia had lost the respect of her peers, her lavish lifestyle and guardianship of her children – but she was finally free to remarry.

In the last seven years, the Plymouth set had furnished the gossips with one extramarital affair and two badly patched-up elopements between them. It got worse. To Sophia's dismay, as Jack was dragged through the courts his sister Fanny was accused of following suit, and the world prattled that 'Mrs Lee [Leigh] who was Miss Byron has run off with a Son of the late S[i]r C Whitworth'.[108] (Whether or not there was any truth to this supposed affair, it does not seem to have lasted, as Mr Whitworth is not mentioned again.) When a small wedding party gathered at St George's church in Mayfair on 9 June 1779 it was clear that the bride was heavily pregnant (gossips noted that the 'father hath not been ascertained').[109] Their voices rose above the clattering of carts in the street outside as they took their vows. Jack intended to resign his military post to focus on his new responsibilities or (perhaps more likely) to enjoy the advantages of being married to a marchioness. The service ended. Jack and Amelia – now Lady Conyers, having assumed her father's titles – presented themselves to the world as man and wife, and awaited the arrival of the baby.

'The most unlucky fellow that ever was'

On Jack's wedding day, his father had been at sea in pursuit of d'Estaing for exactly one year. Since the beginning of his mission nature's forces seemed to have formed an alliance with the French. The first debilitating storm came three weeks into the journey, around halfway across the Atlantic. When the violent gales and rains finally lifted, John despaired to see his squadron of thirteen warships reduced to just four – those left were 'shattered'. (Though he did not then know their fates, one staggered to England, another to Lisbon, and the rest towards America or Canada.) By the time his flagship the *Princess Royal* approached Newfoundland in mid August 1778, thick fogs and a scouting mission gone awry had deprived him of the remaining three. In this vulnerable position, he got his first glimpse of the enemy on the approach to Sandy Hook. Spotting a twelve-strong squadron lying at anchor, he made the private signal established through the British fleet – it went unanswered. It must be d'Estaing. If only he had his full squadron, he thought – it would be suicide to approach with just one ship. He steered north to the safety of Halifax while the French huddled into Boston.

The storms had left him weeks behind schedule. 'Admiral Byron's appearance would gild the face of affairs resplendently', lamented Admiral Gambier in New York, 'God send him to heave in sight.'[110] Eventually, the scattered squadron began to limp into Sandy Hook in a 'mutilated' state and raging with fever. Still no Byron. 'No news yet of my uncle', Frederick wrote to his wife in early September, 'we are very apprehensive for him.'[111] Those at home worried that his notorious bad luck had finally caught up with him: '[P]oor Byron,' sighed Lady Louisa Conolly to her sister, '[I] think him so unlucky that I almost feel sure of his being lost, though I sincerely hope not.'[112] Reports that the *Princess Royal* had been swallowed in a storm gave hope to George Washington – the American army's commander-in-chief – until it was finally sighted off Sandy Hook in mid September. He correctly guessed John's plans to 'take a Peep at the French fleet' in Boston.[113] John was itching for battle and both sides waited with bated breath. When Lord Carlisle's commission – dripping with anti-French sentiment – provoked the hot-headed General Lafayette to challenge him to a duel, Frederick politely declined with the remark that 'all national Disputes will be best decided by the Meeting of Admiral Byron and the Comte D'Estaing'.[114] A resounding victory was required.

Unfortunately, the treacherous passage to America was only the beginning of John's misfortune. Bad weather prevented him from drawing the enemy out and on 2 November his fleet was crippled – in John's words – by 'as violent a gale of wind as I think I ever remember to have been in'.[115] As his ships pressed on in vain against unruly seas, d'Estaing sailed 'with a fine Wind' towards the West Indies: 'They must have passed within a few miles of us', John grumbled.

He retreated to Rhode Island and was promptly trapped by storms. He vented his frustration in a letter to Frederick, who was about to head home: 'I heartily wish you a good passage and happy sight of your family; for my part, I look upon myself as the most unlucky fellow that ever was, and shall have no thoughts of home till I have had one fair meeting with D'Estaing.'[116] His nephew left with the hope that 'it may be still reserved for one of the family to return to his country with the satisfaction of having restored her affairs'.[117] 'Some good fortune must attend us at last,' he concluded cheeringly.

After several attempts Byron's squadron sailed for the West Indies on 14 December, meeting almost immediately with 'an uncommonly high & confused Sea in which all the Ships rolled & pitched exceedingly'.[118] Both the vessels and the men suffered considerably – in the melee John himself was hurt (the subsequent false report that he had 'died of an Inflamation in his Stomach' may hint at the nature of the injury).[119] The blow became a personal disaster as he struggled to recover. A few miserable weeks at sea carried them to Saint Lucia, 'torn to Pieces with Storms, and wasted by Sickness'.[120] As the British press heard of his struggles, the vision of John as a gallant hero plagued by storms captured the public imagination. 'The ill luck which has constantly followed the very deserving Admiral Byron, attends him in every instance', lamented the *General Advertiser*. 'On the instant of his arrival in the West Indies, the most tempestuous weather took place, and the sailors actually distinguish him by the name of "Foul-Weather Jack".'[121]

John's sickly squadron arrived at the island of Saint Lucia – recently wrested from the French by his valiant friend Admiral Barrington – on 6 January 1779. He had missed d'Estaing by ten days. As per his orders, he reluctantly assumed command of the Leeward Islands station from an officer 'who has done his Duty with singular advantage to his Country'.[122] He was pleased to see a trustworthy face – his new surroundings wore an altogether less friendly aspect. The Leeward Islands encompassed a string of lands including Antigua, Grenada, Barbados and Saint Christopher (or Saint Kitts), which were divided between British and French occupation. As Byron's men recovered, d'Estaing awaited reinforcements in French-held Martinique. Thanks to the European colonists it had become a beautiful but brutal part of the world. Saint Lucia itself was a verdant tangle of coves, bays and mountains. Its woodlands were now increasingly fringed with fields of sugarcane and dotted with the mansions of plantation owners. European grasps at new wealth had transformed it, along with much of the West Indies, into a land of captivity – according to one report of 1776, the island's total population of around 14,000 included almost 11,000 slaves. But even white skin and high birth could not guarantee survival. There were no hospitals, supplies were waning and the tropical climate was intolerable: one French spy described it as 'the Grave of Europeans'.[123]

John settled in. A hurried French attack was quashed. Requests for supplies and sightings of suspicious vessels poured in from the anxious governors of nearby islands. The 'arrival of Admiral Byron hath set our hearts at rest', wrote one merchant in Grenada.[124] But his crews weakened as the weeks drew on. Medical tents were crammed with 1,200 sailors debilitated by exhaustion, fever and scurvy. 'Messrs Byron & Barrington are still at St Lucie', reported one spy, 'and are paying for their Imprudence by the burial of from 12 to 15 Soldiers every day.' He continued: 'The two fleets are watching each other, & both keep their Stations.'[125]

As d'Estaing clung to his port, the anticipation of battle rippled across the sea. 'No accounts from the West Indies,' Frederick sighed to Selwyn in April, 'Byron's situation is a very hard one, for ignorant people conceive it is as easy to hinder D'Estaing from coming out of Martinique as it would be to hinder the Duke of Northumberland driving out of his gate.'[126] Victories and defeats were invented. Tales of 'the honourable, the polite Admiral Byron', whose impeccable behaviour aboard the *Wager* had 'made him the favourite of the whole crew', were retold in a biographical feature run by the *Westminster Magazine*: the little dog at Wager's Island, enemy ships boldly captured, his humanity during the *Dolphin* expedition.[127] Excitement grew, and the world expected a new feat of courage.

At this critical moment John's squadron wilted under the tropical summer. His letters were filled with disintegrating ships and sailors who were dying, deserting and driven mad. Eventually – devastatingly – he was forced to face the question of his own ability to command. '[Y]ou will please to inform their Lordships', he wrote to the Admiralty on 3 April, 'that my health is so much impaired by a Hurt I received in a violent Gale of Wind on the passage here from Rhode Island, that I find myself unable to support the constant fatigue which necessarily attends the important command I am entrusted with.'[128] The sleeplessness and anxiety of a 'nervous fever' – perhaps some form of post-traumatic stress – gnawed at his strength. He awaited their response.

John was anchored at Saint Kitts on 10 June when a call went up signalling the approach of a storeship: the *Sphynx*. He felt a flush of pleasure as its commander requested an audience – it was his son.

Twenty-year-old Captain George Anson Byron came bearing dispatches from the Admiralty. They were months old and – probably to John's dismay – did not contain permission to return home, but a promotion: he had been appointed commander-in-chief of North America. Father and son had some time to swap personal news – of Jack, perhaps, as George left England during the divorce proceedings – but normal duties were quickly resumed.

Five days later John was escorting a trade convoy from Saint Kitts to Saint Lucia. Choppy seas prevented him from calling at Barbados as planned – he pressed on. Finally landing on 1 July, he picked up a panicked, two-week-old message from the governor of Grenada: while he was at sea d'Estaing's fleet had left port, captured the island of Saint Vincent and was now ranging at Grenada. 'I am endeavouring to provide for our Defence,' read the scrawl, 'but hope to receive assistance from you without Delay.'[129] John scrambled for intelligence about the size of d'Estaing's fleet, which was estimated at between thirteen and nineteen warships plus frigates. With Barrington's reinforcements, he had the advantage. On 3 July he sailed with twenty-one men-of-war, one frigate and transport ships – carrying soldiers and supplies – to recapture Saint Vincent. When John received word that d'Estaing had already stormed Grenada, he changed course to meet them head on. Finally, this was his chance.

It was night when Byron's ships approached Grenada, where d'Estaing's force was anchored in a cluster at St George's Bay. The French flag fluttered from a fort. Moonlight streamed down on the red union flags and ornate gold at each stern, as men hung from the rigging and scurried around below decks waiting for John's instructions. In the early hours of 6 July, having spotted the enemy's advance, the French began to file out of the bay. Their modest fleet – fourteen, perhaps fifteen ships of the line? – seemed to be 'in great confusion' and the low winds slowed them down. As daylight broke over the island John issued his orders.[130] Leaving some ships to protect the transports, he made the signal for a general chase. The three ships heading up the squadron, including Barrington in the *Prince of Wales*, were thrown into the thick of the action. Amid the whistle, crash and splash of fire, a strong breeze finally drew the enemy fleet out from its cluster into a line of battle. Far too late, the devastating truth of d'Estaing's force was revealed: some twenty-six or twenty-seven ships – many of great force – plus a band of frigates.

After months of waiting, John was not about to be beaten. He renewed the order for close engagement and pursued. To his surprise, instead of returning his enthusiasm for a fight his stronger opponent merely manoeuvred just out of reach: 'they did us great damage in Masts and Rigging,' John reported, 'when our shot would not reach them'.[131] A necessary but scrambled change in formation brought three more ships under heavy fire; two more left in protection of the transports were almost crippled after swooping across 'in a very gallant manner' to pre-empt an attack. 'We lookers-on were full of admiration', wrote Major-General Grant from the transports, 'at many handsome things which we saw done and attempted in the course of the day.'[132]

By mid afternoon the two forces had formed almost parallel battle lines – detached from the centre of the action, John's view was obscured by the smoke and the spray. Shots tore through sails. Hours dragged on. Injuries on the *Princess Royal* were minimal, but he could see that aboard a handful of battered ships his men were dying. Yells rose into the air and a mast crashed to the deck. Still d'Estaing avoided open battle, still Byron's ships pressed on. At around 3 p.m. the French bore away – there was no chance of a pursuit. Taking cover from the descending darkness, John's squadron limped back to Saint Kitts expecting the French to attack the next morning. Both sides had suffered – though the French ships had fared better, they had just as many men killed and twice as many wounded – but the strategic loss was evident. Hampered by faulty intelligence and leaping too eagerly into battle, John had failed to destroy d'Estaing and knew his health would not allow another attempt.

When John compiled his account of the action at Grenada, he praised the 'brisk' and 'determined' behaviour of his men: 'such as became British Seamen zealous of the honor of their Country, & anxious to support their National Character'.[133] D'Estaing's superior sailing capabilities alone defeated them. The injured Barrington would return home to lay 'the true state of the Squadron' before the Admiralty, while he would hand command to Admiral Parker in Barbados. Major-General Grant supported him, writing that 'nothing could exceed the determined bravery and gallantry of the whole squadron' and optimistically declaring that 'the French, though superior in numbers, must at last give way to the intrepidity of the British squadron'.[134]

Unsurprisingly, the enemy were more damning. George Washington received reports of a decisive victory and Benjamin Franklin, the American ambassador to France, was told that John would 'return to England a disgracd officer'.[135] The *Pennsylvania Packet*'s declaration that 'the French have undoubtedly drubbed the English' was at least founded in truth; less so the *Martinique Gazette*'s claim that d'Estaing's victory was 'the most distinguished which the French navy has ever obtained'.[136] Amid expectation that the West Indies would now bend to France, the allied force basked in 'the smiling Aspect our Affairs begin to put on'.[137] John's loss was a huge morale boost for America.

Eight months after his injury and four since his request to be relieved of command, John finally received permission to return to England. On 4 August he responded in no uncertain terms: 'for some time past I have been so much afflicted with a nervous Fever that I find it impossible for me to discharge with propriety the important Duties of this station'.[138] Questions over his mental health later moved one sympathetic colleague to comment that 'I learn that this unfortunate man was struck with disorder and disease that deprived him of his reason'.[139] When John finally began his long journey back, on 29 August, he may have suspected that his active role in British warfare was over – the roar of extraordinary courage that had begun his career had been worn to a dull, pained moan. Yet as he sailed home he had no idea that the real sting would come not in his failure, but from a sneering public's reaction.

On 21 August 1779, as her husband prepared to leave Barbados, Sophia relieved her aching heart by opening it to her friend Hester Thrale. 'I wish I had any chearfull intelligence to give you – but it is all gloom with *me*', she sighed: 'In my Bed Gown + night Cap at this very moment – all yesterday in my Bed in such pain – + in so much danger – they did not know what to think of me'.[140] Only Augusta, full of her own complaints that she had 'grown fat', remained at her side: Fanny and Jack led their own lives, George Anson was at sea, and she and Sophy – who had inherited both her mother's blue eyes and her impetuous spirit – had quarrelled so violently that her daughter had marched off to live with Juliana. Sophia had pleaded with her physician not to make her go to Bath – *Mr B. will be home soon* – but fell silent at the answer that 'if I did not He would probably find me one half dead not unlikely quite so when He came'. The tide of criticism rising against her husband threatened to overwhelm them all. When rumours of triumph in the spring were contradicted, Walpole wrote that 'they who invented them, now declaim as bitterly against Byron, as if he had deceived them'.[141] News of the actual defeat brought a flood of pessimism – one peer wrote that Britain was 'baffled [in] every quarter of the Globe, our Empire Dismemberd, & Britain itself trembling to its Centre'.[142]

In France, Isabella saw her brother subjected to crueller insults – one grotesque print portrayed *L'Amiral Biron* as a gaunt and hook-nosed coward, and another as a chubby, childlike officer 'weeping with rage' over an upturned cooking pot. And then there were the songs. Madame du Deffand was highly amused by a rhyme beginning: 'While D'Estaing and his troop, / Trounce the poor Byron, / While the great Washington, / Has the English under his thumb . . .'.[143] Another, presenting the battle as a dance, finished with a snide '*Allez coucher Byron*' ('Go to bed Byron').[144]

When things grew so heated that John's honour was called into question, Sophia was mortified. 'Her Husband is supposed to have forborne fighting', Hester wrote in her diary, '& She is wild with Grief.'[145] Gossip that he had refused to support Barrington during battle and then spinelessly declined his subsequent challenge to a duel quickly filtered into the papers and there was talk of a court martial. His wife's distress was eventually calmed by a letter from the Admiralty confirming that 'the reports she may have heard to the prejudice of Admiral Byron are malicious, scandalous, and void of all foundation' and quashed by the arrival of Barrington in mid September, who attested that 'Byron did every thing that man could do'.[146] In the eyes of the fickle public, John's defeat suddenly became more reasonable: the French 'manoeuvre their Ships too well' – the sickly British had 'hardly a ship fit to keep the Sea' – 'Nothing but British Ardour and Enterprize could have saved them'.[147]

It could not undo months of slander. And, amid all this, the death of a granddaughter: Jack and Amelia's first child – named Sophia Georgina Byron, perhaps in some attempt at reconciliation – was born at their London home just weeks after their marriage, but did not live beyond two months. She was interred at Twickenham on 18 September 1779. 'Poor Mrs. Byron is a feeler,' Sophia's new friend Samuel Johnson commented on hearing of her distress from Hester. 'It is well that she has yet power to feel. Fiction durst not have driven upon a few months such a conflux of misery.'[148] Such was the unhappy family portrait that awaited the already suffering admiral.

From its auspicious beginnings – an imminent wedding, the promise of new money, an exceptional military reputation and new European adventures – the scandalous seventies had wreaked havoc on the Byron family. After embroiling her daughter in an outrageously misguided romance, Isabella had incurred both the wrath of her children and the ridicule of society by gallivanting across Europe with a man who appeared to be nothing but a swindler. William had suffered the sting of his son's disobedience and death, the total collapse of his marriage and – perhaps worst of all, in his eyes – the destruction of his delicate financial schemes. Clutching at straws, he interrogated Daws about his neglected estates in Lancashire – 'read the inclos'd & acquaint me if Chatburn is in my manour' – and rebuked the poor man if he was unable to drop everything and do his bidding.[149] Their childhood home had been stripped of its treasures and then of virtually everything else, right down to its toothpicks. In October, as the nation awaited his brother's return, William commissioned a search 'for a vault or cellar' beneath the cloisters, hoping to unearth buried treasure.[150] (He did not.) The younger generation were constantly tangled up in scurrilous affairs, and even the esteemed John had lost his relatively unblemished reputation in both his personal and professional life.

After a decade of false steps and failures, they could no longer lay claim to the fawning tribute that had so pleased their grandfather, the 3rd Lord: 'Is't not enough the Byrons all excel, As much in loving as in fighting well?' Having once enjoyed the family's enduring reputation for their exploits in the bedroom and on the battlefield, they appeared to have lost their touch.

6

The Great Gallery

In and Out of the Beau Monde, 1780–86

> Into a gallery, of a sombre hue,
> Long, furnished with old pictures of great worth,
> Of knights and dames heroic and chaste too,
> As doubtless should be people of high birth . . .
>
> *Don Juan*, canto XVI

1784

In stately homes across England the lifeless eyes of painted Byrons gaze blindly out at empty rooms, unmoved and unchanged by the passing years. A girlish Isabella still holds her white flowers and hopes for a husband; a bewigged and silk-clad William stands proudly, dreaming of actresses and a Newstead fleet; a storm gathers behind a commodore with crossed arms and rosy cheeks; wrapped in blossoms, the beautiful teenage Sophia looks forward to a glittering future. But life has marched on – the country is altered and the Byrons are slowing down.

It is the age of the heady musical genius of Mozart, of breaking chains and the birth of new nations, of mankind conquering the skies for the first time. But in the beau monde (or what Isabella calls the 'great and critical world') people of fashion must continue to abide by its rules or slip from it entirely – in this the family display varying degrees of enthusiasm and success. Tucking herself away in the heart of London, Isabella dwells on cherished moments with Monsieur de Weinheim and counts the days until she can escape back to the anonymity of France. 'We have almost to every one of us, some part allotted in the chain of society,' she laments, 'that will not permit us to detach ourselves entirely from it.'[1]

A letter flies from Pirbright to Paris, where John's daughters are enjoying the sights. 'How I envy you, or how much I wish to be with you to see Monceaux, the Tuileries, &c &c', he writes nostalgically, and a popular tune flickers in his memory. 'I shud sing Oh the Days when I was Young. I must now make myself contented upon this wild Heath.'[2] His wife sets out from a 'Stinking hot' Grosvenor Square for appointments with perfumers, physicians or philosophical friends – she recently distinguished herself by throwing a courtesan out of one of Hester Thrale's literary salons, 'to the Horror & Amusement of them all'.

Across town William is excavating the grounds of his new villa on Hampstead Heath, causing the press to sneer that it must be 'a grave to bury Taste, Propriety, and every elegant idea in'.[3] His list of friends has grown thin. 'One feels hostile to such a fellow as Lord Byron', writes Lord Fife. 'Thank God, we have few of these.'[4]

In 1820 the poet scrawls a riposte to a new, scathing review of *Don Juan*. A 'filthy and impious' poem, it slams, by a 'cruel and heartless' man.[5] Even at this comfortable distance (he has been in Ravenna for months) he feels the blow. His fall from grace has been spectacular, thanks in no small part to the vengeful crusades of his estranged wife Annabella and spurned mistress Caroline Lamb. His notoriety is, he feels, unmatched by all precedent and parallel, and he bristles as he reflects upon the public mood that had pushed him from England. 'I was accused of every monstrous vice by public rumour and private rancour; my name, which had been a knightly or a noble one since my fathers helped to conquer the kingdom for William the Norman, was tainted.'[6]

Noble it may have been, but the name *Byron* had been whispered conspiratorially in drawing rooms and coffee houses for decades. His grandmother's confidante Hester, so well acquainted with the torments of his relatives, ponders what her old friends might have made of him. 'I knew his grandmother most intimately and she was a favourite with Doctor Johnson', she had written in the early years of his fame. 'He would have been glad that her grandson was a poet, and a poet he is, in every sense of the word.'[7] She has followed his career through his marriage, separation and exile with interest, writing to a friend near Bolton Row in 1821: 'Poor Mrs Byron, who used to inhabit it, would have enjoyed her grandson's reputation, would not she?'[8]

~

The house on Bolton Row was empty when John finally stepped in and shook off the October chill. He was relieved to avoid fuss. Sophia returned from Bath the next day to find him dispirited by 'the abuse he unfortunately had heard the *good natured* Publick had so lavishly bestowed on his conduct', but he was soon buoyed by reassuring meetings with the Admiralty and the king.[9] Within a few days, though still 'shattered in his Nerves from a bad Climate and infinite fatigue', she reported that he had grown 'vastly well and chearfull'. After almost eighteen months apart Sophia had hoped for a warm reception, but their reunion was decidedly lacklustre. He wanted to rest and didn't exert himself to help with household management. '[H]e does not love trouble *more* than he used to do', Sophia wryly observed, as she was left to deal with rental leases, finances and even his prize money.[10] '[H]e sees me such an Object', she complained, 'he wants to pack me off somewhere immediately'. John felt harassed, and Sophia felt unappreciated. His world had changed. He was accustomed to hardship – he was not accustomed to failure.

Weeks passed as he became reacquainted with his family and his country. The war carried on without him, though wherever possible the fashionable world acted as if it was barely happening at all: 'Our common practice is to be alarmed for two or three days,' Frederick commented wryly, 'and then to go to all the balls and operas, as if the country was in the greatest safety.'[11] Suffering from its isolation in Europe, Britain suddenly found itself at war with Spain as well as with the American rebels and France. Elsewhere, the nation mourned for Captain Cook as the news broke that a hostile encounter with the inhabitants of a distant Pacific island had brought his latest voyage to a brutal end.

At home, the Plymouth set proceeded down their own paths. The widowed Juliana was struggling to support herself and her son on the meagre provisions of her marriage settlement – Lord Byron refused to offer a penny more. Jack was recruiting around Sheffield and providing 'much wonder and conversation to the neighbourhood' by lodging with his new wife in a Yorkshire parsonage – tormenting its poor owner with ideas of their dissipation and wantonness.[12] 'As Lady Holdernesse asked it', the reverend grumbled, 'I could not decently refuse'.[13] (The fact that Amelia fell pregnant with Jack's second child around this time suggests that his suspicions were not entirely unfounded.)

The return of George Anson from the West Indies in the spring of 1780 would have been a happier occasion had he not arrived with an undistinguished teenage bride on his arm. Born in Jamaica, eighteen-year-old Henrietta Charlotte Dallas was the fruit of an affair between a surgeon and another man's wife. They had met and wed in Barbados in a whirlwind romance that might have shocked even his aunt Isabella – he 'knew not this girl he has married till ten days before he left it!' exclaimed his 'romantically partial' sister Augusta to her friends.[14] Unable to conquer her snobbery, Sophia eyed their new daughter-in-law with shock and then furious distaste. George – whose gallant exploits in the war were already gaining notice – could easily have tempted a woman of some fortune. Their obvious affection for each other did nothing to soften Sophia, who remained steadfastly mortified that her 'darling, but ungrateful' boy had married such a 'little low dirty Girl'.[15] But he was twenty-one, and had carried Henrietta halfway across the world. There was nothing they could do.

After a long separation and haunted by professional disappointment, John and Sophia could hardly claim to be a shining example of wedded harmony. In the words of one of Sophia's old friends, 'Happiness in the matrimonial state is so precarious a gift, that with all the fairest prospects & after doing the best in ones power, one can only humbly hope for the blessing'.[16] Even a marriage founded on childhood kinship was not immune to difficulties, and the admiral and his wife struggled to readjust to each other's company. Her hurries and flurries proved draining for a man who preferred a steady, moderate way of living – Sophia was the first to admit that she had 'a large share of impetuosity in my temper'.[17] He valued circumspection, and her friends complained that she was utterly unable to keep a secret. Though they both suffered a litany of illnesses – gout, stomach spasms, rheumatism – their preferred cures were similarly incompatible: he favoured retreat where she found solace in the company of others. Their peace was constantly eroded by financial demands – money was required for hiring horses, tailors' bills, Augusta's dancing master – and the management of it fell to a flustered Sophia. If Sykes presented an unexpected payment, John blamed his wife for not keeping up and snapped at her. While he was happy to entertain their old navy associates – Lord and Lady Rodney, Admirals Barrington and Parker, Captains Mouat and Frodsham – he couldn't muster the energy to meet her new friends in the city. Writers, artists, Shakespeare critics, music historians. He never could feel at home in the endless rounds of 'chatting parties' his wife hosted and frequented.

After years confined to the society of Plymouth, Sophia had finally found her place in the world. Run aground by chronic illness and with little prospect of a new mission, John had lost his.

'Nothing so disagreeable as staying at Home'

In April, an ailing Sophia and excitable Augusta left for Bath, leaving John to a peaceful season of gardening and partridge shooting at Pirbright. Clattering up to their lodgings at the Belvedere, they gazed out over the magnificent view of the city and wasted no time in finding out who else was in town. The clever hostess Hester Thrale, who showed Sophia so much kindness; twenty-seven-year-old Frances Burney, whose novel *Evelina* was receiving rave reviews; Mrs Lambert, a chatty army widow; the charming dean of Ossory and his family; and John's navy friend Lord Mulgrave. The revered actress Sarah Siddons was engaged at the theatre and the Assembly Rooms would be fit to bursting. It would be a fine summer.

During her husband's recent long absence Sophia had found consolation in her new set of friends in town. In an attempt to relieve her own sufferings she dipped her toes into the world of medicine, befriending high-society physicians and herself gaining a reputation as someone worth consulting about new-fangled treatments. When a Mrs Gast was advised to try electrical therapy, her brother first begged of Sophia 'whether in *rheumatic cases* she thinks People may *electrify* themselves?'[18] On being mentioned to the Kembles, a renowned family of actors, they 'said every sweet & respectful Word in the Dictionary'.[19] Sophia's ticket into such illustrious company may have been her blossoming friendship with Hester Thrale and subsequent introduction to her literary salons at Streatham Park in the summer of 1778. Attendees included writers Elizabeth Montagu, Samuel Johnson (now most renowned for his *Dictionary*) and Hester's protégée Miss Burney, whose book had been devoured by the Byron household. 'I pronounce she will be an interesting as well as an accomplished Woman', Sophia had declared, 'and I value my self on having *read* her early.'[20] (Though John also enjoyed *Evelina* he jokingly questioned 'the Captain's being such a brute'.)[21]

Sophia, who was full of anecdotes and relished an 'amicable spar', proved a comic addition to their soirees, where she was playfully called Mrs Bi-*ronne*, 'always, after the French manner'.[22] When Hester amused herself by ranking her female associates in her diary, Sophia earned high scores for 'Useful Knowledge' (18/20), 'Good Humour' (17/20), 'Person Mien & Manner' (16/20) and 'Conversation Powers' (15/20).[23] (That she only achieved 5/20 for 'Ornamental Knowledge' – 'Singing Dancing Painting & suchlike' – she perhaps owed to those years of pregnancy in Plymouth.) Though Sophia initially found Dr Johnson's heart 'impregnable' he was swiftly won over with her cheerful chatter. He evidently considered her something of a project. 'You and Mrs. Montagu must keep Mrs. Byron about you; and try to make a wit of her', he encouraged Hester. 'She will be a little unskilful in her first essays; but you will see how precept and example will bring her forwards.'[24] But, unlike her sister-in-law, Sophia preferred to comment on the works of others over creating her own. Her particular enjoyment of innuendo-ridden poem 'The Geranium' reveals a bawdy sense of humour, despite her public insistence on propriety:

> Let but the dew of thy soft hand
> Refresh the stem, it straight shall stand:
> Already, see, it swells, it grows,
> Its head is redder than the rose! . . .

She lent the verse to Hester, who thought it 'Ingenious' but 'so obscene I will not pollute my Book with it'.[25] As well as discussing politics, philosophy and the arts, the Streatham set amused themselves with parlour games: when assembling his preferred female government, Dr Johnson appointed Sophia 'Head of the Admiralty'; when each person was represented by a meal, she was declared to be 'Provincial Toast'; when each was assigned an animal, she was 'the Zebra' (surely more complimentary than 'the Cow' bestowed upon poor Mrs Pepys).[26]

In 1780, at the heart of Bath society, Sophia seemed at once fragile and full of fire. Though described as 'far from well' she was a master of putting on a brave face: 'her charming spirits never fail her,' observed Frances Burney after one visit, 'and she rattled and shone away with all the fire and brilliancy of vigorous health.'[27] Mending visibly, as days passed her young friend marvelled at how she bore up 'against all calamity, and though half mad one day with sorrow and vexation, is fit the next to entertain an assembly of company; and so to entertain them as to make the happiest person in the company, by comparison with herself, seem sad.'[28] She took an awkward tea with Sidney Lee – the sister of Charles Lee, one of America's most prominent rebel generals – held court to officers who had served under John's

Sophia Byron and her sister-in-law Isabella sought solace for their woes in the spa town of Bath. This print of c.1785 shows a group of invalids and their companions socialising and 'taking the air' on the North Parade.

command, and watched the younger generation dance and flirt from the upper end of the glittering ballroom. Hiding their hangovers behind feathers and fine muslins, the older ladies winked as Augusta and Miss Burney were ambushed by hopeful young officers at the theatre. *Why then, he is in for it!* They promenaded about Spring Gardens and drank the waters at the Pump Rooms. Most days she pottered past Bath Abbey, oblivious to the fact that it would one day be her final resting place.

The summer brought turmoil both for Sophia and for the nation at large. With the alliance between Spain and France seemingly on 'very delicate and dubious terms', a minister was dispatched to Madrid to negotiate a peace which, it was hoped, would improve prospects in the American war.[29] In London, a new wave of anti-Catholic vitriol was being whipped up by the disputatious politician Lord George Gordon: though ostensibly a response to legislation relaxing the restrictions on Catholics, it was easily fanned by general discontent about the war, the government and high taxes. In Bath, Sophia was plagued by debt-chasing lawyers demanding her presence in town – she evaded them with a note from her apothecary insisting that she couldn't travel 'without great danger and Risque to her health'.[30]

It was just as well – the city had erupted into violence. In early June a Protestant mob covered in blue cockades – by some reports 60,000 strong – descended on Parliament brandishing a petition. The protest fell swiftly and spectacularly into violence. MPs were attacked. Newgate gaol was raided and prisoners marched out 'with all the humours of war'. The skies over the city were illuminated as Catholic neighbourhoods, chapels and businesses were set on fire and the homes of figures of authority gutted. Lord Carlisle braved the journey to the House for the first two days, though there was a 'tumultuous Assembly' of protesters at its doors; the thought of attending had probably never crossed his uncle William's mind.

Sophia caved in to her anxieties in correspondence with Sykes: 'I suppose we shall have no Westminster Hall – no law – no property – God have mercy on us – I am so terifyed with the dreadful disturbances – I have no peace – I wish you would write me how matters go.'[31] To her horror, riots sparked in Bath that very night:

'The disturbances began here last night much mischief done', she scribbled; 'a Troop of Horse marched in this morning its hoped will prevent further – if it should continue I will order my Horses and March out'.[32]

With the deployment of the military, the chaos quelled. The Gordon Riots – the fiercest week of mob violence the city had ever witnessed – saw almost 300 Londoners shot dead and hundreds more wounded or arrested. The fires were extinguished and Sophia's letters filled again with concerns about the price of sugar and how she might acquire some 'curious little Birds' from India for a friend. But the capital was shaken and its authority undermined in the eyes of the world. Amid whispers about 'the downfall of London', the 'government whelmed in ruin' and 'the rebellion of America transplanted to England', Catholic Spain began to lose faith in any budding alliance.[33] It was a heavy blow.

By the autumn life was more settled. Sophia returned home. In recognition of his efforts in the war, John was promoted to vice admiral, and he took a new residence at number 8 (now 9) Grosvenor Square: a neat, four-storey corner house in the heart of the city's fashionable quarter (if, a little awkwardly, just five doors down from the scene of their son's adultery at Lord Carmarthen's). Finding her husband in a better humour than when she left, Sophia renewed her entreaties to introduce her new friends and promised the favour to Miss Burney, who noted that it must be 'a great thing, as he always avoids seeing any of her female friends, even Mrs. Thrale, from some odd peculiarity of disposition'.[34] Eventually, success. By February, Hester wrote of her new conquest: 'Mrs. Byron rejoices that her Admiral and I agree so well; the way to his heart is connoisseurship it seems, and for a background and contorno, who comes up to Mrs. Thrale.'[35] Though generally discomfited by female conversation, he respected those with whom he shared intellectual interests.

In the absence of Admiralty duties, and while Sophia threw herself into society, John found his hands full with distressed family members. In February 1781 he wisely allied with his only relative of means: Frederick. 'My Lord,' he began, 'Nothing has been done for either my Daughter or her son' (the widowed Juliana and 'little William'), adding, 'My brother George is in the same distress'd situation he was in except now & then from the trifling relief I can badly afford him.'[36] On a similar application their 'charitable & Revd brother' Richard had merely sent a letter 'full of bitter invocations but not a single sixpence.' (While declining to help George, Richard felt no qualms about soliciting a place in the navy for his son – John, of course, acquiesced.) When Frederick secured an annual pension of £200 for the Newstead heir's education, John visited Castle Howard to express his gratitude and meet his nephew's own growing family (six children and counting). There was one other problem to discuss: Isabella. Avoiding the society of England entirely, she had been reunited with Weinheim in France and was making and breaking the same old promises. 'The Baron is a Monster,' railed her creditors in Avignon.[37] 'The Dowager Lady Carlisle after arriving almost at the waterside, changed her mind and is returned to France', reported Mary Coke; 'considering all things her family has no reason to lament her not coming to England.'[38] On the contrary, they were desperate to keep an eye on her. The sympathetic Sophia did not help, apparently strengthening Isabella's resolve to remain abroad with small loans and probably encouraging her to do what was best for her health – while known to be 'kind to all people in sickness or Misery', she would never have encouraged a relationship with a bogus aristocrat.[39] Her interference was not viewed kindly. After bumping into John, George Selwyn declared that he displayed 'great good nature and reason' about his sister, but 'said that the corre-spondence was between his wife and her, and seemed to hint, if he was himself consulted, he should advise her better'.[40] '[T]he greatest obstruction', Selwyn warned Frederick plainly, 'will come from that insinuating Bitch the Adm:'s wife who is her Counsellor.'[41]

For their part, the admiral and his wife settled into an unsteady peace that played out at Bolton Row, Grosvenor Square and Pirbright Place. John preferred the latter, on the edges of the wild Bagshot Heath – a notorious haunt of highwaymen, murderers and duellists. The villa itself, with an adjoining farm, was nestled beside a two-acre garden where he busied himself 'Planting & Making of Ponds &c', including exotic plants and an avenue of pines that became known as Admiral's Walk. Enjoying the seclusion, he rode his horse, went shooting and was visited by friends bringing news of the war. (It was not going well – one consolation, perhaps, was that d'Estaing had performed no feats of brilliance.)

Unhappily, this rural retreat couldn't protect them from their continuing personal troubles. Poor Juliana required more money. Jack's wife Amelia gave birth to their first and only son – he drew breath for just an hour, and was not given a name. Sophia's severe 'tutoring' of her less illustrious daughter-in-law Henrietta finally prompted her son George Anson to vow he would 'never see his Mother more'.[42] When he promptly disappeared, John was 'almost raving Mad' and Sophia became convinced he would 'either be broken or shot' for deserting his post. Augusta's meek suggestion that he had 'only gone off in a *pet* to his ship' proved correct, though John learned that Henrietta had followed: 'his Officers curse her from morning till night . . . as he is totally lost by it'. 'Hope George will be sent to America as long as the War lasts', he mused wearily to Sykes.[43] He grew nostalgic for adventure. 'I am happy to find you are pleased with your situation,' he wrote to Juliana and Sophy when they took a trip to visit Isabella in France, '& often wish myself with you for a day or two'. '*Adieu my Dearest girls*'.[44]

The magic of Pirbright was lost on Sophia, who grumbled, 'my being here is so visibly disagreeable to *Him* – he shewed it by such sourness – I determined to say I would go – the declaration has had a wonderfull effect – the humour is changed to good – and there-fore I see I am right'.[45] She had not, at least, entirely lost her sense of humour. 'Poor Mrs Byron, to solace herself by giving some variety to her sufferings,' wrote Frances Burney, 'said she would go to Spence to have a Tooth drawn.'[46] As their uncle used to say, 'to some People' there was 'nothing so disagreeable as staying at Home'.[47]

Away from her husband's bad moods there was plenty to enjoy among the beau monde, even if she increasingly felt the weight of her age. She climbed the sweeping stone staircase at Grosvenor Square, had the dining room prepared – it could seat around fifteen guests – and entertained novelists, actors and wits. She benefited from the sea air at Margate with her widowed daughter Juliana – whose '*sweetness of manners*, attended by *elegance* and *beauty*' continued to capture gentlemen's hearts – and gave comic reviews of the society gleaned by a new season in Bath: 'the Girls here are pretty – the

Men all shabby'.[48] Her enthusiasm on hearing of Hester's imminent arrival in town caught the messenger off guard: 'I almost wonder I did not *kiss* him – word – how surprized and shocked he would have been at so comically being saluted by an old Lady.'[49] '[I]f confined in your Summer House', she genially threatened, 'I should break the windows to get to you', promptly making a string of plans that she declared 'must be according to a Navy expression, wind + weather permitting'.[50] She displayed what Miss Burney called her 'native fire' by throwing the notoriously foul-mouthed courtesan Letitia Smith out of Streatham Park – perhaps in an attempt to defend the honour of her niece Betty, whose profligate husband Mr Delme had been the lady's recent slavish conquest. ('Ha, Ha! Ha! Admirable Mrs Byron!' laughed her young friend on hearing of the incident from Hester.)[51]

John, on the other hand, only intruded on town with notes requesting tobacco, wax candles and hampers of 'good port'. She worried that he was hiding himself away. 'I see no prospect of His being employed as he wont ask', she informed Sykes, 'besides we are to have a Peace directly – we must therefore make & scrape all we can'.[52] The long war was drawing to a disappointing close – America was all but lost.

Three years since John's return, and the family's prospects seemed more hopeful. Amelia had borne Jack their third child at a house on Audley Square: Augusta Mary Byron was born on 26 January 1783 and baptised at the same church where they had hurriedly wed. John's eleven-year-old grandson William John had been dispatched to school at Uxbridge – a respectable if not especially prestigious choice for the heir to a barony – and shortly before Christmas Juliana received an offer of marriage. 'How much do I regret, at this moment, the not having it in my power to do as I could wish on this occasion', John responded to the news, giving his blessing; 'the time will come when you will be much more at your ease'.[53] He was hardly about to object. Thirty-one-year-old Sir Robert Wilmot was a baronet and commanded an impressive Derbyshire estate at Osmaston Hall. 'I have heard lately that Sr Robert is a Man of very good fortune as well as character,' he reported optimistically, 'so that I hope they will do very well to-gether.'[54] He gave his daughter a final £100, 'for it would certainly appear very mean to go to him without a single shilling in her pocket', and they were married at Pirbright Place on 24 September.

When Juliana left as Lady Wilmot, both John and George Anson – who had been chasing employment 'to make some Money, especially for my sister' – felt a weight lift as the responsibility for her maintenance fell to her husband.[55] After an abortive engagement and an elopement, surely it would be third time lucky? Jack was less convinced, later grimacing, 'she never loved him & only married to hinder herself from being a burthen [burden] on my Father'.[56]

'Recluse in pride and rags'

While John and Sophia held their family affairs together, Lord Byron exerted little effort to tighten his grasp on anything but cash. At the dawn of the new decade he was fifty-seven years old, with little to show for all the privileges into which he had been born. He had made no mark on the political world – a dissipated youth had led to a disaffected middle age, and now increasingly desperate autumn years. Friends had fallen away as his funds depleted; he could no longer keep up with the extravagant habits of his rakish associates, or the promises made to those trusting enough to lend him money. He no longer spent his days with dukes, earls and beautiful courtesans, but with those he paid to do his bidding: Daws, Joe Murray, Betty Hardstaff and his legal advisor Robert Aisley. Another casualty of his downturn in fortunes was any lingering generosity of spirit. Where he once pardoned tenants struggling with the rent, he now pushed for higher rates. There is no record of any friendly contact with his wife or daughter, and he had proved utterly uninterested in supporting his grandson – his only heir – beyond the minimal terms dictated in his son's marriage settlement. (Until William John turned twenty-one, over a decade away, he was of little use. Another tedious wait.)

By this time, Lady Byron and Caroline had taken a house in town and lived in quiet domestic comfort, attending concerts, visiting the pleasure gardens and exchanging gifts with friends and family. Though neither woman had the security of a loving husband, they found some happiness in their relative liberty and circle of friends. Caroline was close to some of her cousins, especially the gallant George Anson and some of her uncle George's children, Isabella, John and Frederick George. She doted on her two little godchildren – the fruit of an elopement between a nobleman and her friend Frances, a clergyman's daughter – but had inspired no offers of marriage herself. Approaching her late twenties, and with no secret made of her father's debts, it was unlikely to happen now.

Money slipped through William's fingers as he continued to pay for his reckless past. His agreed payments to the estranged Elizabeth, Caroline and Juliana amounted to £915 annually, on top of the mass of unsettled debts gradually accruing interest. Having very little to live on, William's days were consumed with concocting new money-making schemes with Daws and Aisley. In January 1782 an auction was held for the 'superlatively elegant Houshold Furniture' from Great Marlborough Street – china, musical instruments, kitchen stoves and chandeliers.[57] He took a harder line with poachers, declaring in local newspapers that anyone caught shooting on his estates would be prosecuted. He advertised his house on Queen Anne Street and gave up his lease on a 'cottage-stile' home he had been keeping as an out-of-town residence on Walton Heath in Surrey (boasting a quite unnecessary five bedrooms, coach-house and ten-acre meadow). In Nottinghamshire, more trees were torn down to create new plots of leasable farmland. His estates in Lancashire were (unsuccessfully) scoured for mining interests and he persisted in his lifelong habit of firing lawsuits at anyone who obstructed his self-seeking plans. On being unable to locate some old deeds, he accused a former steward of 'conniving and confederating to and with divers Persons at present unknown' and 'contriving how to wrong and injure' him.[58] Viewing the world through thoroughly embittered eyes, any obstacle was evidence of a conspiracy.

For all his mounting resentment towards the world, William did not wish to retreat to his Abbey. (It was by now so stripped of comfort that William had to dash off notes to have the road cleared and bricks set up about the hall fireplace, 'that I may have a fire there' before his arrival.)[59] In the spring of 1783 he snapped up an elegant, Italian-style villa on Hampstead Heath – recently built for

Mrs Lessingham, an actress and magistrate's mistress – for just £560. Described as a 'most amiable retreat to a person whose avocations may require an attendance in town', the sale included the picturesque three-storey house with pleasure grounds, a kitchen garden and views over the heath.[60] His reputation for neglect preceded him – on hearing the purchaser's name, the *Whitehall Evening Post* sarcastically commented, 'if he displays there the *same sort* of taste that he has done in Nottinghamshire, [he] will make this place, like Newstead, the wonder of the neighbourhood'.[61] Sure enough, it was soon confirmed that 'His Lordship, both in this place and at Newsted Abbey, shews an imagination negligent of art, and addicted to the *wilder beauties* of nature.'[62] When he did attempt to make improvements by adding a pond, they snidely reported that he had 'dug a hole in the front of Mrs Lessingham's villa big enough to bury most of the wood he has cut at Newstead Abbey'.[63] William wallowed in a mire of criticism over everything he did – or didn't do.

He kept Newstead Abbey itself from total dereliction with the basic repairs he could afford, but any real hope of recovering its former magnificence was beyond reach. It seemed incredible that so much damage had been inflicted in a few short years. 'Lord Byron should restore the long lost Perfection of Newstead Abbey,' one journalist suggested, as if its noble owner had merely forgotten to maintain it. 'Before the house was dismantled, and the Plantations most unaccountably destroyed, this fine old Place was one of the most beautiful in England.'[64]

Instead, William hatched a new plot: he installed new dams and floodgates in the Newstead lakes, endowing himself with the (questionable) powers of control over the flow of the River Leen. His reasoning was simple. By rendering the nearby mills and villagers dependent on his magnanimity, he could hold them to ransom by charging higher rates for access to the dams, or even threaten to open the sluice and risk flooding. It was his right, he felt, indignantly. The water ran through *his* park. The people of Papplewick, who relied on a steady stream for both their businesses and their bread, nervously followed his progress. Stories of his former misdemeanours were dredged up in local taverns – poor, affable Mr Chaworth – and supplemented with sinister new ones. His lordship had brought some dubious new inhabitants to the Abbey, who surveyed the grounds from towering pedestals: two cloven-hooved figures, frozen in lead – a grimacing male and a smirking female with an infant – had been set among a wild grove in the gardens. William's grotesque taste in statues had the advantage of deterring potential intruders, but as word spread, dark suspicions took form. The locals began to whisper that the lord at the Abbey was filling his gardens with devils.

At the same time, in the parks and parades of London respectable wives and daughters were ushered away from as fiendish an example of female impropriety as France could possibly have delivered. She was pale and delicate, and not nearly as richly dressed as her former friends remembered. After thirteen years abroad, the Dowager Countess of Carlisle had finally returned. In November 1783, Isabella set foot on English soil, like her brother John, to find that the public had not been kind in her absence. The stories of her adventures in Europe had fatally sealed her reputation for careless behaviour in general, romantic folly in particular, and an inability to consider how her actions reflected on her family. Lady Rivers spoke of gentlemen refusing to let their wives be seen with her in public. In private, Dr Warner called her Weinheim's 'grey mare'. Frederick's friend Charles James Fox had included her in a recent poem poking fun at older women whose 'short-liv'd sway' was over:

> Come, Marlborough, brooding o'er your bags,
> Carlisle, recluse in pride and rags . . .[65]

Arriving in town, she attempted her most winning smile and opened arms of friendship to her former allies. Though Sophia wrote kindly and Mary Coke visited – probably inspired more by curiosity than affection – few others returned the favour. Feeling the sting of rejection and of the English winter settling on her bones, she decided to follow her sister-in-law and settle at Bath. 'I think she judges right', remarked Mary Coke, 'for considering her extraordinary conduct during her stay abroad she would probably find people in general rather shy of her.'[66] Her last few independent years had been spent in a characteristically unwise fashion.

Since being separated from her baron and dispatched to southern

France in the spring of 1779 – 'without debts, but with a reduced income', courtesy of Frederick – Isabella had done her best to live peacefully, but could not regulate her spending. Settling in Avignon, bound by an agreed annual sum of £500, she took up residence in an opulent seventeenth-century hotel and soon made new friends. She bonded with her physician Dr Calvet, who had the twin advantage of being a keen collector of curiosities and an unabashed flatterer. Presenting her with some unique fossils during one of her visits, he attempted a barely veiled compliment about her own rare qualities – though she pretended not to have heard, it cannot have failed to provoke a flutter of pleasure. Calvet was genuinely taken with this inquisitive and clever *comtesse*. Between medical consultations they occupied their days pleasantly, discussing ancient Syrian queens and the antiquities of Avignon, and attempting a French translation of her brother's *Narrative*. During the summer she took a 'pretty country house' on the island of Barthalasse, where one dinner prompted an awkward toast in her honour from Calvet:

> *Si fermeté d'esprit, sagesse, grandeur d'âme,*
> *Parmi nous avaient des autels,*
> *A vos pieds, brillerait la flamme*
> *Que l'homme doit aux immortels.*[67]
> [*If firmness of mind, wisdom, greatness of soul,*
> *Among us had altars,*
> *At your feet, would shine the flame*
> *Man owes to the immortals.*]

His flattering attentions kept her occupied until the reappearance of Weinheim, who couldn't be stalled in England forever. She fell into old habits, drawing bills for 'more than the Money then in hand belonging to your Ladyship', as her son's agent Mr Gregg gently warned her.[68] Defying her son's express instructions she hired one of her own old agents, obstructing his efforts to track her spending, and began to complain that payments were not being made. She enjoyed pleasant days out, paying for Weinheim as well as herself. Eventually, in the words of her frustrated son, her 'embarrassments increased, untill they arrived at that degree of magnitude, that required the interposition of some extraordinary remedy'.[69] The experiment had failed, and Dr Warner was dispatched once again to bring her home.

Warner arrived at her lodgings in Avignon shortly before Christmas 1780, and Isabella was quickly riled with indignation. Her debts would be paid, he confirmed, but she must return to England *without* her companion. Her furious protests to Mr Gregg – having been appointed lord lieutenant of Ireland, Frederick was preoccupied with his new duties – were characteristically hurried. She could not consent to being carried away 'in the midst of the severest seasons who has not stirred even in a Carriage but once in a whole Twelvemonth leaving a Person of the highest Quality a half years Rent unpaid her Servants poor people desolate; in the midst of a reputable Society torn on a sudden from them like a Criminal'.[70] Her excuses were endless: the climate would ruin her health, the cost of living would be so much higher, she could not abandon her servants. But the real issue loomed large in Frederick's eventual, exasperated response to her angry letters. 'What may be a familiar custom in one Country,' he wrote, with tactful restraint, 'can not always be reconciled to the manners of another; & it was not possible for me to avoid hinting the necessity of coming <u>alone</u>.'[71] With no other means of keeping the wolves from her door, Isabella was forced to relent.

Seemingly standing true to her word, Isabella, Weinheim and Warner begrudgingly travelled north as France burst into blossom. By May she complained from Lyons of the wounds the journey had inflicted on her character, her health '(& probably my Life)'; the whole presented an unqualified 'Scene of Sorrow'.[72] Still her letters to Sophia and Betty gave those at home every expectation of her imminent arrival. 'What a *fracas* we shall have when my Lady Dowager arrives;' Selwyn wrote to Frederick, 'and if she does not, I see no end of her vexations.'[73]

But when the party reached Metz, something changed. Perhaps Isabella finally realised that she and Weinheim couldn't wheedle out of the separation – whatever the case, she dug in her heels. By June Frederick's agents were receiving furious letters from Avignon, filled with demands for payment, calling to have the Baron arrested and preaching that Frederick should never have 'given a sous to Madame'. 'The end of this tragedy will be that Madam will die of hunger in some French town,' one creditor predicted, and 'the Baron will abandon her'.[74] For everyone's sake, they advised taking a notice in the *Gazette de France* and publicly declaring that *Madame de Carlisle* was not to be lent any more money.

Isabella painted quite a different picture: her money was being withheld, Frederick's rules held her a virtual captive and her loyal companion was being unjustly attacked. Everyone's conduct was unfeeling to a barbaric degree. A letter from Lady Rivers advising her to 'send away her Baron, and to return hither' put an end to their friendship.[75] Frederick's weary response to her litany of accusations was unhelpfully patronising: as usual, her passions were blinding her to the obvious common sense of the agreed plan. If she calmed down she would see. 'A cool & deliberate revisal of every occurrence since your melancholy separation from your Country, & your Family,' he concluded, 'affords me the comfort of thinking that I have never acted towards you but with the respect & affection a Son owes his Parent'.[76] It did not have the desired effect. At an impasse, after almost a year of fraught negotiations Warner returned laden with her usual promises of complying the next spring. (They were trusted only because Isabella had mentioned the same to a relative of the chaplain at Newgate prison, who had passed it along. 'To such she will speak *à cœur ouvert!*' wrote Selwyn in disbelief, '*Hélas!* My dear Lord, there is no help for these things'.)[77]

Feeling the relief of a reprieve, Isabella took a house at Moulins, near Metz. Here, at least, she would not be hounded out of her independent style of living. Though it lacked the elegance of a grand hotel, she had a 'vast and well cultivated Garden', and employed eight servants: a cook, three maids, two footmen, an upper servant and a coachman. Hearing that Dr Warner had quite cavalierly declared to the world that she was ruined, she dreaded her reception in England and made no secret of the fact that she would leave as soon as she could. 'If you mean [that] I must live without Servants and be a Boarder in a provincial Town or gather the Crumbs from any one's Table,' she informed Gregg, 'I can venture without any Sentiment of Pride to say, I never can submit to it.'[78] '[A]fter seeing my Friends and settling my Affairs in England,' she continued, '[I] should prefer to live out of it as a Gentlewoman, tho' a poor one,

rather than as a beggar there.' The designated spring of 1782 came
and went, as did the summer; in the autumn two nieces, Juliana
and Sophy, were dispatched to her with the secondary inducement
of introducing the Byron heir, little William John. The women were
perhaps considered more likely to elicit cooperation than Warner.
'I am glad my sister & you have clear'd up certain matters', John
wrote with relief, but they could not prevail upon her to return.

In February 1783, Lord Carlisle resorted to the desperate measure
of dining with Weinheim in Paris, a meeting that persuaded the
impostor his case was being heard – 'what you told me did not surprise
me, my Lord, on the contrary it has relieved my soul' – and convinced
Frederick that the man must never be permitted to stay with his
mother in England.[79] His insistence that he had never had dealings
with either 'barbarians' or 'Americans' did not suffice. *Monsieur*'s
deceptions had long since been revealed – those at home spoke darkly
of 'Monsieur Larcher, who calls himself the Baron de Wenheim [*sic*],
but is not so'.[80] Another spring – another summer – and Isabella
gave Weinheim the power of attorney to settle and sign off on her
financial accounts. Perhaps it was this bold move that convinced
Frederick to act. Having delayed the inevitable for four and a half
years, Isabella was forced to undergo her 'few Months of humiliation'.

She eventually arrived on English shores shortly after her sixty-
second birthday. The eyes of the world turned on her. At the
beginning of her travels she had declared to Selwyn that 'I must be
absolutely out of the world in England to be well'; the frosty reception she received when she appeared confirmed it.[81] Hearing of her
arrival, her old friends the Duchess of Portland and Mary Delany
shared (apparently unflattering) anecdotes of her until near midnight.
'The Dow[age]r Lady Carlisle is come to England', their new
companion Mary Hamilton recorded in her diary, 'to ye great distress
of many who formerly knew her.'[82] (One point of contention may
have been the duchess's continued friendship with her estranged
husband Sir William Musgrave, who had by then been appointed
a fellow of the Society of Antiquaries, vice president of the Royal
Society and a trustee of the British Museum – their separation had
clearly worked wonders for his productivity.) In Bath, even Sophia's
enthusiastic attempts to ingratiate her with the Streatham set fell flat.

'I used all the evasions I could to excuse meeting Lady Carlisle', sighed Frances Burney on 18 December, 'but as I could not say my motives, I have been obliged to leave it as a thing to be done some-time. That, however, must not be the case.'[83]

Isabella's flirtations were no longer viewed with amusement, but disbelief and disgust. Here, yet again, she felt the disadvantage of her sex. 'Men are never old in the eyes of the world,' she complained, 'who are polite and have spirit and wit enough'.[84] Without beauty or wealth she was merely a disgraced dowager, ridiculed for her romantic ideas and cripplingly dependent on her son. It was a painful adjustment for someone who drew so much pleasure from society. Instead, with her grey hair swept up away from her face and her spectacles perched on her nose, she sought solace in her projects. Writing. Embroidery. It may have been this unhappy interval that inspired her forlorn 'maxims' about the sorrows of losing one's position in the world. 'Lament not the desertion of certain persons, whose friendship and opinion you once relied on', she advised, perhaps as much to herself as any potential readers. 'You are better without them, if their former attentions were derived from your opulence or connections.'[85] She lamented the illiberal habits of the 'young and unthinking' towards the 'old and unhappy'. To this unfeeling world she urged kindness above all things: 'Abstain from all uncharitable comments on the reports of the misconduct of the world; be grateful to that Providence which hath conducted you into the harbour; and commiserate the storms your fellow-creatures are exposed to.' She retreated into the gentle regime of the wintry spa town and awaited her orders. With few friends and fewer funds to support her, England seemed a bleak and unforgiving place.

Fortunately for Isabella, the autumn of 1783 furnished the news-papers with plenty of other things to bleat about. Having broken from its allotted place, a new nation was being built overseas – isolated and without allies, Britain had failed and the war was over. In September – as her brother John was distracted with final wedding preparations for Juliana and Sir Robert Wilmot – a peace treaty with the new United States of America had been formally signed; shortly after Isabella's return, the last of the defeated British troops were evacuated from New York and the parliamentary factions began to squabble instead about deals for commerce and trade. From France came the unbelievable news that – in the wake of a promising experiment with a sheep, a duck and a rooster – the human race had conquered the skies and experienced *flight* for the very first time. Travelling in a gondola-like basket dangling below a huge taffeta balloon, two men had soared over Paris for more than five miles, to the 'rapture and admiration' of spectators below. (This remarkable feat would give a kickstart to the artistic career of her Nottinghamshire nephew Frederick George – George's second son – whose painting of the first exhibit and flight of such a balloon in Britain the following year was subsequently engraved and widely distributed. He dedicated it to his cousin, Lord Carlisle.)

Back at home, the king's controversial dismissal of his government led to the appointment of twenty-four-year-old William Pitt as prime minister. (Known to history as Pitt the Younger, he retains the record for being the youngest person to hold the office.) While critics poked fun at this 'school-boy' and his 'Mince-Pie Administration' – on the assumption it wouldn't outlast the festive season – his premiership would continue for the next seventeen years, and was the last the three eldest Byron siblings would see.

'A blasted Fame forever must be mourn'd'

The first winter of a disappointing peace was miserable and sickly for most of the family. Amelia was staying with her mother and baby daughter in London, apparently avoiding her profligate husband Jack. 'There is a noise in town', reported her friend Queen Charlotte, 'that a separation will be made between her and her husband' – the passion that had fired their relationship had diminished to flying sparks of a more hostile kind.[86] Their nomadic life and the loss of two children had taken a heavy toll, and despite her considerable inheritance Jack's constant spending had left her painfully reliant on the income from Carmarthen's lawyer.[87] Even worse, it looked likely that she was about to inflict one final sorrow on her long-suffering mother by 'dying of a consumption'.[88] 'She is always ill', worried the queen, 'and becomes thinner day by day.'

Neither Pirbright Place nor Grosvenor Square were temples of health: John was prevented from venturing out by snow and a violent attack of gout, and Sophia's sudden relapse panicked her friend Hester into a renewed fit of tenderness. John Radcliffe, the 'charitable honest Man' who had married Isabella's daughter Frances, died shortly before Christmas, leaving her a childless widow (he did, at least, leave her the house at Highdown, her jewels, and his considerable stock of 'all my Wines and other Liquors'). Caroline Byron seems also to have fallen ill, or been presented with some other reminder of mortality – at just twenty-nine and with no dependants, in January she made a will. The little she had was divided between her mother Lady Byron, her less affluent cousins and her godchildren.

On the evening of 26 January 1784, little Augusta Mary's first birthday, her mother Amelia succumbed to her illness at the age of just twenty-nine. (The poet later surmised that she fell ill after 'imprudently' accompanying her husband on a hunting trip before recovering from childbirth, though contemporary records give no such specifics.) Jack was not with her when she died. She was buried at her family vault at Hornby Castle in Yorkshire two weeks later, and her estates and income were diverted to her eldest son from her first marriage. Jack was left with a helpless infant daughter and none of the financial consolation a man might usually expect from marrying a marchioness. Amelia's scandalous life attracted comment even as she lay in her grave, and nowhere was her husband granted the sympathy of the press – theirs was evidently not considered a grand love story. 'The Death of a Lady of Quality, which took place last Week, is a striking Instance of the Misery which fashionable Manners have introduced among the higher Ranks', declared the *Derby Mercury*. Having fallen 'an early Sacrifice to the basest Arts', she 'died literally of a broken Heart . . . Remorse for what she had done, soon laid her low in the Dust.'[89] Where Jack *was* mentioned, he was offhandedly called 'George'.[90] His own family was less pontifical. His uncle Richard dispatched his commiserations to Grosvenor Square: 'If any thing can alleviate Mr Byron's pain at this event it must be to see the Child in a good state of health & too young to participate in ye common distress.'[91] '[A]ssure him from us', he continued, 'that the best part of our House (such as it is) is at any time at his Service when he shall have occasion to come into the North'. As the heartbroken Lady Holderness took the baby under her protection, Jack seems to have kept himself busy and managed a flying visit to his father in February. 'He did not stay with me more than an Hour', John reported to his daughters, 'he looked Ill but ate more cold roast Beef in that time than would have sufficed me for a week & told me he could have devour'd as much more if he had time, so that I hope he will do well.' [92]

Wherever possible, John directed his professional and personal correspondence from Surrey, away from the eyes of the world. He kept up with navy gossip, and grieved to hear that Lord and Lady Rodney had separated – the two men had been thrown together on John's first ship, and she had often stayed with Sophia at Pirbright while their husbands were at sea. Thanks to the interposition of Admirals Parker and Barrington, he was spared attending court for disputes about his war prizes. Though he was a military man with military manners, his correspondence with his daughters was warm and informal – full of nostalgic musings, hopes for the future and gentle rebukes for scruffy handwriting.

When Sophy and Augusta visited their brother George Anson, John lamented that '[I] have often wish'd myself of the party but that would have put him to too much inconvenience'.[93] 'Your letter dated Wednesday I did not get till this day all covered with dirt + grease', he wrote when they took a trip to Paris with Henrietta in the summer. 'But how could you expect my Dearest Sophy I should write where neither you nor Augusta sent me your address.' After long updates about the family – George Anson was struggling with low spirits; Fanny was stricken down with flu; little William John was quite accustomed to his new 'Papa'; Lady Wilmot seemed 'the happiest of women', having been treated to a flock of exotic birds and 'the prettiest Terrier she ever saw, with her name in the Collar' – he signed off: 'God Bless you – Ever Your Affectionate Father'.[94] Pleased to find his family so settled, John acclimatised to the stifling serenity of an English country summer. The once great adventurer tended his garden and grew melancholy as he struggled to traverse even the 'wild Heath'.

In the bustle of London, Sophia and Jack seemed to be getting on well together at Grosvenor Square, though his bereavement had not humbled him into moderation. 'He goes on as usual but where the money can come from excepting from one quarter I cannot imagine', John wrote, suspicious about his wife, 'for she declares he is her only darling.' Sophia may have been especially susceptible to her son's apparent tenderness – she had fallen out with Hester, perhaps over her renewed intimacy with Isabella; in July the hostess remarked unkindly to Lady Keith, 'reject all Offers of Kindness from Mrs Byron, as you value your Reputation'.[95]

Isabella was staying just a few doors away, waiting for Frederick's agent to comb out the bewildering tangle of her finances. She had contracted debts of over £3,500 'in France and elsewhere' and granted several annuities amounting to almost £2,300, on top of sums owed to Dr Warner and her servants. She had even convinced her maid Jane to sell her own shares 'at Isabella's special instance' and for 'Isabella's use'.[96] Finally, a resolution – in return for payment of her debts she relinquished her claim to the Cumbrian estate bequeathed to her by her first husband; the ever-reliable John stood as witness to the final settlement. Like her brother William, she struggled to adjust to her new situation, feeling trapped and unfairly maligned: 'Victim to slander thence my sorrow flows', ran one of her poems, 'A blasted Fame forever must be mourn'd'.[97] There was no escaping the gossips and she *longed* to return to Europe. After staying briefly with her daughter Anne, still unmarried and dutifully serving Princess Amelia, she took a house in Lower Brook Street and steeled herself against the world until the humiliation was over.

The year ended as it had begun – with the death of a young woman. Lady Byron had watched with concern and then horror as her daughter Caroline's condition deteriorated. One by one she had watched her children slip away: her first baby boy, buried far away at Besthorpe; feverish little Henrietta; their unhappy, reckless heir; and now her closest companion. Perhaps that cheerful yellow nursery at Newstead had been cursed. She dashed a pitiful note to her lawyer requesting his attendance the next morning to look over her daughter's will – 'Poor Miss Byron is Exceedingly Ill'.[98]

There was nothing the physicians could do. Caroline died in November at the age of twenty-nine, and was interred in the family vault at Twickenham. Elizabeth rewrote her own will while her grief was still fresh, and it shows that – though she had lost so much – she was not entirely alone. The majority of her modest income was to be held in trust for her grandson William John, by her brother-in-law the admiral and cousin Charles Gould – clearly her estranged husband had done nothing to regain her faith. Generous sums and tokens of affection were set aside for six servants and four close friends. Among them was her Nottinghamshire companion Elizabeth Booth, who came to live with her at Somerset Street, just north of the Tower of London, and helped her through her grief.

There is nothing to suggest that Lord Byron had played any meaningful role in his daughter's final years beyond the small allowance he was legally bound to provide – if he hoped to recover this at her death he was mistaken. Her will included the not unusual but in this case entirely understandable stipulation that none of her bequests should be 'subject to the debts control or Interference or any claim or demand of the said William Lord Byron'.[99] There was no leeway for misinterpretation. While his brother John drew some comfort from his children in his old age (the less unruly ones, at least), there is no evidence that William shared the sentiment. His sole heir was still at school – nine years left to wait. Dynastically speaking, in comparison with his siblings he fell distinctly short. Isabella already had eleven surviving grandchildren, and John had six; between them Richard and George had seven young, unmarried children with every prospect of carrying on the bloodline. While Elizabeth lived, William could not remarry or produce further legitimate heirs (though the power of his charms at the age of sixty-two – with no funds or friends to recommend him – cannot have been overwhelming in any case). His thoughts still occasionally wandered to Mrs Scrimshire and other ancient gallantries, but it was one of the Newstead servants, Elizabeth Hardstaff, who occupied his later years. She was generally assumed to be his mistress, and their intimacy raised sufficient eyebrows in the neighbourhood to earn her the facetious nickname 'Lady Betty'.

In the weeks after his daughter's death, the spectre of forty-year-old misdemeanours came back to haunt him. George Anne Bellamy, the actress who had once inspired such passion, had written a tell-all autobiography. In the years since their acquaintance, Bellamy's income had dwindled with her looks, and the public interest in her salacious life offered some prospect of ready cash. It is possible that its 'revelations' were not a complete surprise to William. Similar ventures maximised profits by blackmailing those who featured in return for a kinder portrayal – those who did not pay up were dealt with ruthlessly. If such an offer was put to him, he did (or could) not cooperate.

An Apology for the Life of George Anne Bellamy was published in six volumes in the new year of 1785 and pulled no punches in its portrayal of Lord Byron. He had orchestrated 'deep-laid plans of villainy and deception' – he was '*practised* in the arts of seduction' – his 'vanity was hurt at my rejecting him'. Having masterminded the scheme by which his detestable friend had abducted her, he plagued her with notes, promised her his new wife's fortune and threatened to kill himself unless she submitted. 'Could you have formed any conception that there had been men of his Lordship's cast?' the author asked, 'Of those who break their marriage vows *so soon* after they have been made . . .?' '[F]rom such false ones may Hymen preserve you', she concluded, invoking the Greek god of marriage ceremonies, 'and every other worthy woman.'[100] The book provided another nail in the coffin of his claims to being a gentleman of honour. By February it had already run into a second edition.

At Newstead Abbey, where the two grimacing satyrs stood guardian and rot crawled up the walls of the nursery, William powdered his wig and pondered his options. Daws was interrogated about obscure corners of forgotten estates – Aisley was consulted about devising more tenuous lawsuits. When word arrived that a local mill owner was *disputing* his activities on the lakes at Newstead, William was furious. The owners of the cotton mills at nearby Papplewick had noticed with alarm that William was using his control of the river to the detriment and even destruction of their business. When William ordered the floodgates to be stopped up, the water supply was cut off and their employees left idle; when they were partially opened the 'sudden and violent' surge threatened to damage everything in its wake.

Lord Fife, who had socialised with William and Isabella at Spa during that baking summer of '65, heard the specifics from mill owner

Mr Robinson himself. In return for access to the floodgates William had demanded an extortionate payment of £10,000, plus an annual rent of £6,000 – quite a hike from their previously agreed sum of five guineas per year. With William protected by his inherited privileges, and apparently immune to any appeals to his good nature, Robinson's options were limited. 'He has spent all his estate so there is no laying hold of this,' Lord Fife mused, 'and he has no principles, but what can you expect from a desperate, bankrupt, bad-hearted man.' He concluded, 'I most heartily wish Mr Robinson may lay him on his back.'[101] He was not alone – even the long-standing steward Daws, who was also owed money, agreed to testify against his employer.

When the news came in May that an injunction had been obtained, it was received by the local community 'with the greatest pleasure, and the two following Days were spent in Expressions of sincere and decent Joy'.[102] If Lord Byron was thought a kindly landlord in his affluent days, his true colours were showing – the newspapers cried that the valiant efforts of the mill owners promised to restore 'to many Hundreds of Industrious Poor – THEIR DAILY BREAD'.[103] Lord Byron was taking the very food from their mouths. He called on Aisley, and prepared for another legal battle.

Possibly sobered by his daughter's death and his own decline, or perhaps merely at the urging of his solicitor, William wrote his will. The entailed estates would, of course, fall to his lawful heir – William John – but his personal effects could be distributed as he wished. He considered who deserved remembrance. Robert Aisley, to whom he owed significant sums, was given permission to sell the remaining household effects at Newstead and Hampstead Heath – furniture, linen, china, carriages – to reimburse himself, plus £50 for a ring 'as a Token of the Sense I have of the Friendship Attention and good Offices . . . to me and my Concerns for a long Series of Years'.[104] Of all his sprawling and struggling family he honoured just two with any legacy whatsoever, leaving £25 apiece for his brother George's two eldest sons: John, a struggling junior officer in the 12th regiment, and budding caricaturist Frederick George. (Both living locally, they were among his most frequent visitors.) In what he must have known was a token gesture, he decreed that anything left over was bequeathed to Elizabeth Hardstaff 'as a recompense for her faithful and long Services'. His longest-serving servants, William Daws and Joe Murray, received no mention (the former had, in any case, fallen dramatically from favour). Likewise his siblings, his wife, his many other nieces and nephews and even his grandson received nothing – no sentimental token, or even a kind word.

William's world had grown small. His hand shook as he signed his name and set his black seal to the document on 27 May 1785. It would not be revisited.

'Still the Birons are irresistable'

As their aches and pains rendered the Byron siblings increasingly unable to escape the idea of their mortality, for the younger generation they presented a burden, or at least a problem to be solved. The now childless William grew reliant on his Nottinghamshire nephews, who otherwise immersed themselves in their militia duties and their boxes of paints. The Plymouth set could see that their poor father was ailing, and their stubborn mother continued to whip up all sorts of fuss. The Reverend Richard's three fond boys looked forward to steady, respectable careers. As Isabella drew closer to the end of her English season of penance, neither the advice nor the affairs of her children – by now slipping into their forties – persuaded her to stay. Frances, never particularly close to her mother, had settled into a comfortable widowhood. Anne, whose life revolved around her ageing royal mistress, was about to fall 'intirely Out of the great World' with the princess's death.[105] A long, active spinsterhood stretched before Julia, who flitted between her siblings, with a preference for enduring society belle Betty: 'L[ad]y Julia lives with the Delmes as indeed does every body else that chooses it,' one acquaintance reported, 'that house & L[ad]y Melbournes being perfect Coffee houses.'[106] Though her husband had proved a philanderer and a drunk, Betty continued to increase their family and their eighth and final child – Edward – was born while Isabella lodged in Bath. (The maternity contest with the delicate Lady Carlisle proceeded apace, as Caroline fell pregnant with her ninth shortly afterwards.)

In the summer of 1784, as soon as Frederick and Mr Gregg settled her debts, Isabella melted with relief back into the glittering embrace of Paris, probably travelling with her nieces Sophy and Augusta. While John imagined their tours enviously back at Pirbright, they practised their French, gazed in awe at Notre-Dame and visited the immaculate, enchanting gardens of Monceau and the Tuileries Palace. They read of a breaking scandal about the French queen Marie Antoinette, whose name had been (unfairly) attached to the fraudulent purchase of a diamond necklace and stood accused of frivolous spending at the people's expense. It did not take long for Isabella to sink into difficulties of her own, thanks in part to her soft spot for her most profligate nephew.

Jack had made no effort to control his spending since Amelia's death. Depositing little Augusta with Lady Holderness, he had promptly left for Frankfurt and then Paris, where he skipped between hotels, evaded creditors with claims of illness and fell out spectacularly with his parents when they stopped bailing him out. He called on Isabella, and fed her tales of his father's fury and the deep shame he felt at troubling his family further. As liberal as ever with money she did not really have, she gave him fifty pounds. He extracted help from his sister Fanny while declaring miserably to moneylenders that his mother-in-law was 'the only Friend I have'. He drove a wedge between his parents by hinting in his letters at Sophia's promises, while reassuring those chasing money that his father would settle the matter soon: 'till this moment we never fell out before, & have always lived like Friends'.[107] He had clearly inherited his uncle William's wheedling financial habits – whatever money he received was immediately swallowed up. Isabella's fifty pounds did not go far and her intervention embroiled her in rows on two fronts. First, Frederick was not going to be pleased, especially as forgotten debts from Metz were beginning to raise their ugly heads. Second, she felt a responsibility to smooth things over between John and Sophia.

Hoping to lessen the rift caused by Jack's irresponsible behaviour, she dispatched a note to John's agent Sykes. 'I cannot express enough the concern I am under to find the dreadfull Effect yt [that] my unhappy nephews Errors have had on my Brothers mind', she wrote sorrowfully in January 1785:

I have the strongest reason to believe that most indiscreet inflammatory and designing Letters have push'd him to such extremity of
Resentment as to involve Mrs Byron in a most unmerited Indignation,
of whose conduct I have such testimonys in the Affair as must & I
am sure will clear her in the End. I hope in God not too late.[108]

Contrary to Jack's hints, Sophia had always strongly urged Jack to
return to England, Isabella insisted, and if anyone was to blame for
giving him hope of further assistance, it was his sisters. 'Had it not
been for me, and my means,' she explained, he would have 'not got
away at all'. She begged Sykes's help in softening the admiral:
'he was ever compassionate and forgiving after the first moments of
anger were pass'd and nothing but the Poison of Malice could force
its continuation in a Heart so formd'.

Whether or not Jack deserved such compassion, he did eventually
return to England, having realised – perhaps with Isabella's help –
the surest way to contrive an escape from his vast hole of debts. He
landed in the spring, on a quest for a wealthy wife. Having set him
on what she must have hoped was the right path, his aunt made for
Boulogne.

The spa town of Bath was at its most beautiful in the spring –
tulips and daffodils brightened the parks, pink blossoms cascaded
over pale stone townhouses and dandelion seeds idly sailed through
the air. Here, at a safe distance from his debts in London, twenty-
eight-year-old Jack Byron provoked female hearts into a flutter. In
some cases, the attentions of a handsome captain with a dangerous
reputation can drive all other thoughts – riches, titles, propriety –
from a woman's mind. Excelling at the performance of politeness,
he pulled a mask over his natural arrogance and turned on the
charm. 'Still the Birons are irresistible [sic],' he later remarked to his
sister Fanny, 'you know that . . .'[109] Laughter in the theatre, bows
and curtsies in the Pump Rooms, jokes told and compliments paid
– he drew women into his orbit. It was the dashing figure he cut
in a candlelit ballroom that struck the final, fatal blow.

Twenty-one-year-old Catherine Gordon, also known as Kate, was
an orphaned heiress visiting Bath under the protection of a gout-
ridden great-uncle, Admiral Duff. She stood out somewhat from the

delicate English beauties lining the Assembly Rooms. She was fun-loving and boisterous – described as a 'romping, comely, good-humoured girl' fond of running races and swinging between trees – and spoke with a strong Scottish twang.[110] She was also the 13th Laird of Gight, having inherited the Gordon family estates in Aberdeenshire and a total fortune of around £23,000. She was proud of her lineage and aware that her assets would draw suitors even if her manners weren't exactly polished. (She had, according to one evidently unimpressed acquaintance, 'a mind wholly without culti-vation and the peculiarities of Northern opinions, Northern habits and Northern accent'.)[111]

Unfortunately for Catherine, her tragic history and romantic ideas made her easy prey for fortune-hunters. Her early childhood had been affectionate and enchanting, living with her parents and two younger sisters at a Scottish castle cloaked in tales of monsters, witches and ghostly bagpipers. Catherine was twelve when her smallest sister died, and fourteen when her devastated father followed – when his body was pulled from the River Avon at Bath, talk of suicide hung on everyone's lips. Another year took her sister Peggy, who was interred with her father in Bath Abbey, before her mother died at Gight in the summer of 1782. At eighteen, the newly en-titled Catherine was being passed between a flock of aunts, uncles and her grandmother. She may have accepted the Duffs' invitation to join them in Bath in 1785 intending to visit the memorial for her father and sister at the abbey, or was perhaps just eager to find love and start a family of her own.

Struck with admiration for his fine dancing, Miss Gordon's eyes followed Jack across the ballroom, and he found out what he could about this lively, artless heiress. She was worlds apart from the beau-tiful Amelia, but it was not love he was looking for. Catherine fell under his spell without hesitation – a marriage settlement was hastily drawn up and on 13 May they stood before the altar of St Michael's church. He could not muster the time (or inclination) to inform his parents, though he named John as a trustee and asked Sophia's friend Dr Hay to stand as witness. It passed in such a whirl that Catherine could later barely recall anything of it: 'I was married however on the 12th or 13th of May, I don't know which 1785 at

St Michael's Church', she confirmed years later on being interrogated about her husband's family history, '. . . and this is all I can inform you about it'.[112] For now, Catherine gazed disbelievingly at her handsome new husband, impatient to embark on married life. He was warmed by a new glow of vanity with the expectation of becoming laird of Gight.

Exactly when John and Sophia learned of the match is unclear, though it was announced (with little fanfare) in the *Bath Chronicle* within the week: 'Friday was married John Byron, Esq. to Miss Catherine Gordon'. Any immediate relief at his finding another heiress to fund his lifestyle quickly dissipated as further enquiry revealed that the money was tied up in land – their annual income would be very modest. After hearing the news from Sophia herself, Charlotte Lewis – one of the Streatham set – wrote to Hester scathingly about Jack,

> for whom they have paid and paid again, till I think they have been obliged to go into a small house and put off their carriage. He crowned it all by marrying without her knowledge, he said a fortune of £6 or £700 a year. But I fear that don't quite answer and all this mortification will be of little use to him, who is going on just in the same way.[113]

The hint that Jack's debts had cost John and Sophia their house seems founded in truth – in the summer of 1785 they gave up their prestigious address at Grosvenor Square. The identity of its new occupant may have piqued John further: his house was taken up by one John Adams, America's first ambassador to Great Britain, to be used as its first ministerial office on British soil. (In 1797, Adams would go on to become the new nation's second president.) During the war Adams had warned Congress that Byron's fleet would 'ravage the Coast, and bombard and burn the Towns' – now he was taking over his home and making demands about having the parlour repainted and windowpanes replaced. The incoming family described it as 'a descent [sic] House, a little out of repairs, but such a one as you would not blush to see any of the Foreign Menisters [sic] in'.[114]

The Byrons fell back to Bolton Row and Pirbright Place, where John distracted himself with business. In July he followed his brother's example by revising his will – reducing provisions for Jack and Juliana, who had already drained his pocket – and began negotiating another wedding. The marriage of twenty-three-year-old Augusta and navy captain Christopher ('Kit') Parker was prudent and measured where Jack's had been hasty and ill-judged. Kit was just a year older than his bride and the son of Admiral Peter Parker, John's trusted colleague during the last war. Two ceremonies were required – when the couple took their vows in Takeley, Essex on 29 September 1785, the couple were described as 'Already married (Catholic)' – and she happily settled in as mistress of nearby Bassingbourn Hall. (She fell pregnant almost immediately, beginning a career in motherhood that later moved her nephew William John to comment, 'I think her family is almost large enough now'.)[115]

Two weddings should have induced an immense relief – but as Jack left to take up his new estates near Aberdeen, John worried that too much damage had already been done. In December Sophia responded to an extortionate account from Sykes, disputing expenses for wine and travel and quoting the words of a captain to Lord Howe: 'You seem to have forgot you was not always the great man you are now become – and that you have heretofore wanted money still more than I do.'[116] She signed off, furiously, as 'the much injured by you, I might add the much insulted SB'. Before the year was out, a note arrived from Scotland asking if they might advance a little money.

As the Byron siblings were compelled by illness or ignominy to retreat from the unforgiving glare of public life, an excitable tourist took in the sights of England on her way north to Scarborough. Passing through Nottinghamshire, she was charmed by the Montagus' little manor at Papplewick and the beautiful parks at Clumber and Welbeck. Then, Newstead Abbey. 'There is every where an Appearance of past Magnificence, but such a Scene of desolation I never beheld', she informed her correspondent at home.

> The Hills which a few years ago were cover'd with timber are now plow'd up & sow'd. The Walls of the House are falling In, & It will soon be a compleat Ruin If it is not repair'd. There is a very fine Piece of Water & I can conceive it to have been when In its best State one of the most Capital places In this Country. [117]

Continuing on to Yorkshire, she stopped at Isabella's long-avoided matrimonial mansion, Castle Howard. Finding herself unequal to the task of forming a description of such a 'Princely thing', she contented herself with the breathless declaration that 'it pleas'd me beyond any thing I have ever seen'.

It was almost fifty years since William, 4th Lord Byron retired for the final time to Newstead, having devoted the final phase of his life to rebuilding both the Abbey and his dynasty. His wife Frances had been in her grave for almost thirty years, and the five children who mourned for them had grown old. Though divided by their differences, battered by sickness and subdued by financial distress, one principle seems to have guided them all, for better or worse: an unwavering pride in their ancestry. Richard had railed about the Byron name 'carrying with it an Idea of *real* Honour'.[118] William clung to the comforting idea of his family's ancient rights, muttering about the dignity 'derived to him from his Ancestors' and threatening anyone who wronged him with jail.[119] Isabella had been unkindly dubbed a 'recluse in pride and rags' and even his enemies' celebratory verses about the war credited John – 'the proud Byron' – with having '*une tête hardie*'.[120] But now, deprived of inhabitants and ornament, their childhood home stood sombre and still.

Somewhere in the south-east wing the 5th Lord shuffled about his chambers, taking pinches from a silver snuffbox with a trembling hand and brooding over what he had lost. He had given Daws permission to bring in a little money by allowing locals 'the privilege of laying corn in some of the low rooms at the Hall', and the smell meandered along the cold corridors.[121]

At Boulogne, in a little house opposite the church, Isabella pushed those unpleasant months in England to the back of her mind by busying herself with her manuscript. '*Let each year, which shall steal a charm or grace, the companions of your youth, add a virtue in return.*'

Smoking a pipe of tobacco in his gardens at Pirbright, John may have felt he was less deserving of his misfortunes. He had always tried to do his duty, and support his impulsive relatives. Finally driven from the sea by the epithet-making 'Foul Weather', he was sinking amid debts and demands. His heroics had not been forgotten

– the newspapers still occasionally singled him out as the best candidate for a new command in the East Indies, or Canada. But he was not well enough to accept such a post, nor could he bring himself to tell his family the truth of how much money he owed. He gazed over the heath and thought nostalgically of his youthful adventures, unaware that the coming winter would be his last.

Taking up a pen to write to his daughters, a song drifted into his mind:

> *O the days when I was young,*
> *When I laugh'd at fortune's spight,*
> *Talk'd of love the whole day long,*
> *And with nectar crown'd the night . . .*

7

The Chapel

The Fall of the House of Byron, 1786–98

And the step that o'erechoes the gray floor of stone
Falls sullenly now, for 'tis only my own . . .

Newstead Abbey

July 1789

In Paris a braying mob has released the prisoners of the Bastille and tipped its country into revolution. London nervously eyes its own king, whose good health and spirits can't erase the uncomfortable fact that he spent the winter wearing a straitjacket and babbling until he foamed at the mouth. Amid the grey stone of Aberdeen, a child with a deformed foot bawls out for his mother. In Bath, where the fashionable retire to depart the world with grace, a fifty-nine-year-old widow is convinced she is dying. In between visits from the doctor, Sophia Byron seeks solace in the small red prayer book stamped with her mother's initials. She thinks of those she will leave behind. Her friends, her god-daughter, her servants 'Little Betty' and Charles (whose real name, Jeremiah, she never much cared for). Her sweet granddaughters. Her children, wherever they are. Only George Anson has proved a diligent friend to his poor mother – 'my dear and best of Sons' she calls him, with little effort at subtlety – but he is thousands of miles across the sea. Her will has just been settled. 'Whenever it please God to take me out of a world I have experienced much sorrow in', she dictated, 'I request to be buried with the least possible Expence'.[1] There is not much to spare, in any case.

She thinks of where she is going. To her parents, her brother and the poor admiral, a lock of whose hair she keeps in a black mourning ring. To God. Why is it that He should bless some lives and plague others?,

226

she wonders. Now, a new terror consumes her: the thought of being buried alive. Her dear Dr Farquhar has promised that, once she is gone, he will cut into her stomach a little to be sure – 'if any life [is] left in me', she reasons, 'the operation of a lancet would soon make me discover it.'

Days pass as she prays, takes her pills and powders, and slips in and out of consciousness. That insolent new maid – Ellen, is it? – appears to grow more cheerful as she declines. She hopes to get my wardrobe once I am gone, Sophia thinks. She will not.

It has been raining. Beyond her window the pale city takes on a gloomier aspect as it soaks up the weight of the weather, and lights from the Pump Room and the Abbey are reflected in the glimmering pavement. Its ailing residents limp, cough and bleed their way through a fateful summer. Sophia feels pain in her stomach, in her head, in her legs. Little Betty, a truly good faithful girl, scurries to her side.

Animated by the pleasure of entertaining a visitor, Old Joe – still going strong in his late seventies – escorts an inquisitive gentleman around Newstead, chattering about 'what it had once been & what it is now'.[2] It is an afternoon in early October 1814 – the air is sharp and the grounds are blanketed in sodden leaves. John Murray, the poet's publisher (and no relation to his guide), is unsettled by the old man's memories. Deer frolicking in the woodlands and the gallery crowded with 'three hundred of the first people in the county'.[3] Hunting horns and flashes of royal livery for the visit of the young king – now old, blind and raving mad – back in 1764. The old lord's fleet of warships and his beautiful, dishevelled wife sweeping through the halls, surrounded by dogs. The poet's study, adorned with relics of the dead. The tour takes two hours. 'I can not describe to your Lordship the anxiety, & instant vexation, with which I viewed every spot & heard Mr Murrays description', he declares later, 'to have seen it in all its antique splendour and to have experienced, inch by inch, all its sad changes, as he has done, reflected to my mind a picture of human existance [*sic*] so miserable that I was thrown into a state of despondance [*sic*] which I could not shake of [*sic*] until the day after'.[4] He confides to his wife his amazement that George should ever have wished to live there, thinking the miserable place could 'present nothing but a perpetual memorial of the wickedness of his ancestors'.

~

In the spring of 1786 a feuding couple crashed into another argument about money. Jack and Catherine's marriage was falling dramatically short of their expectations. Hoping to assume the privileged life of a laird, Jack took his wife's name so that their heir might remain a Gordon, as per her father's will, and they had arrived at her estate – *his* estate – at Gight Castle in summer 1785. It was a far cry from Grosvenor Square. The old L-shaped tower house was a hunk of stone and fortifications that looked sturdy rather than splendid, sticking out rudely amid the scenic surrounding woodlands, wild flowers and winding river. It was twenty-five miles to Aberdeen – where fifty years earlier William had stood in the snow, debating whether to abandon his regiment – and Jack came and went as he pleased. To him, it was a city of pleasure: gambling, pretty women, thoughtless spending on clothes, alcohol and horses. By July – mere weeks after their marriage – rumours were already circulating. 'Rumour has gone thorrow [*sic*] in the town that Capt. Byron and his lady were parted', one of her relatives heard, 'which I am afraid is too true, for late last night Mr Byron arrived here in a chaise and four without any other person.'[5] But the frustrated Jack kept coming up against closed doors. Catherine's trustees were clearly wary of him, and it transpired that he could not claim the title 'laird of Gight' through marriage. On hearing that there were debts on the estate of some £5,000, he dispatched a note to his father requesting the sum in return for an annuity. He did, at least, convince his wife to confer on him the power to sell her lands and baronies, but he was disappointed again in February 1786 when his vote in the local elections as 'John Byron Gordon of Gight' was disallowed and he was mocked in a political song:

> . . . *an Englishman, married in haste*
> *To an Heiress that suited him, just to his taste,*
> *Yet his right of attendance at Court was not clear,*
> *So they sent him to dance it at home for a year.*[6]

Having married believing that her affection was reciprocated, Catherine was bewildered by her unhappy reality. She had drifted away from her family – one distant cousin wrote that she 'ever since her marriage and indeed since the Death of her Parents kept herself aloof from most of her relations'.[7] If Jack asked for money she could not resist. He lied, and showed flashes of his temper. She snapped at him, perhaps hoping to shock him into his former charm. He turned penitent – and then asked for more. During a visit, one of Catherine's impressionable teenage cousins was 'much struck by the extravagance of the establishment, and much impressed by the descriptions of society given by Captain Byron'.[8] His host's habits were less edifying – the young man spied an open copy of *La Nouvelle Héloïse*, a bestselling novel of temptation and sin – and music and dancing were kept up until dangerously close to the Sabbath. The community rallied around its heiress. Before she had laid eyes on Jack, a local composer had written a lively Highland reel for the dance-loving 'Miss Gordon of Gight'.[9] Now the balladeers played a different tune, with lyrics penned by 'a Scottish bard, who had been dissatisfied with the marriage':

> *O whare are ye gaeng, bonny Miss Gordon?*
> *O whare are ye gaeng, sae bonny and braw?*
> *Ye've married wi' Johnny Byron,*
> *To squander the lands o' Gight awa'.*

> *This youth is a rake, frae England is come,*
> *The Scots dinna ken his extraction ava;*
> *He keeps up his misses, his landlords he duns,*
> *That's fast drawn the lands o' Gight awa'* . . .[10]

Jack's charms were proving utterly ineffective on the Scots, and for the first time his father refused to bail him out. This had not gone to plan.

Elsewhere, the Byron family's struggles drawled on. In Boulogne, Isabella's attempts to moderate her outgoings came too late, while demands for forgotten debts continued to roll in from Paris: '*This cannot be eternal, I must be paid* . . .' Meanwhile, in a neat house in the shadow of the Tower of London – a looming reminder of her heartless husband's most famous transgression – Elizabeth lived quietly with Miss Booth. Once a carefree heiress, she now relied on a government pension of £300 a year. Her estranged husband William was dragged into the Mansfield courts to face charges about the water dispute – the cash-strapped Daws gave his evidence and after a six-hour trial all justifications for obstructing the river were declared 'groundless' and the verdict was given in favour of William's opponents, 'to the satisfaction of a crowded court'.[11] Furious that they should presume to dictate what he could and could not do on his own land, he stormed back to Newstead to plan his counter-attack.

'The favourite of the whole crew'

As William nursed his rage, a darker shadow crept over Bolton Row. John was dying. On 17 March, the day before his brother's latest trial, he dispatched an uncharacteristically pained note from Pirbright and Sophia urged him to come to town. Within days he was installed at their London home, being examined by old friends Dr Farquhar and Dr Hunter. It was a disorder of the liver. He had never entirely recovered from his last journey into the West Indies, and gout had compelled him into an increasingly sedentary life – those solitary days at Pirbright, suffused with wine and port, may not have been entirely restorative. (He had also been known to treat his wife to a bottle of wine and promptly drink half of it himself.) Turning his thoughts to the business of death, the pragmatic John immediately amended his will to include £100 for 'my friend J Sykes' and £140 for a servant, Sarah, and her husband. He instructed his wife that 'Farquhar might be handsomely paid whether he lived or dyed', and wanted to keep his illness as secret as possible – as George Anson later lamented, 'he did not wish to see any of his Children (as I suppose for fear of distressing them)'.[12] Still he kept up his spirits, perhaps recalling the countless times it had pleased God to save him when all seemed lost. But after two weeks he could no longer deny the devastating truth. 'He did not entirely think of death', wrote his grieving son, 'until two days before he departed this life.'

During his long and perilous career John had lost friends to tempests and flying bullets, and seen them eaten alive by disease and vermin or starve to death in his arms. He had explored corpse-strewn mountains in Patagonia, bartered with African craftsmen, fought battles in Canadian bays and survived deadly fevers in the Pacific. He had been among the first Europeans to see the farthest reaches of the world. But it was here, at home in the heart of London, that Admiral John Byron finally succumbed, at the age of sixty-two – in pain but 'sensible to the last moment'.[13] On Saturday, 1 April 1786, with his wife of nearly forty years somewhere nearby, he drifted away from the warmth of Bolton Row and the familiar shuffling and worrying around him faded into nothing.

A haze of grief and grievance followed. Those he left behind were enveloped in a world of black – black skirts and veils, black jewellery, black-bordered letters. Sophia commissioned a large black mourning ring adorned with a small diamond rose and containing a curl of John's hair. A miserable George Anson arrived three days too late – 'My Poor Father', he despaired. 'I wish I had been sooner to have seen him.'[14] Jack sped down from Scotland sniffing about for money. A heavy-hearted Sophy inscribed two poignant eulogies in her copy of her father's *Narrative*. The first was from a poem titled 'The Shipwreck':

> *Tho train'd in boisterous elements, his mind*
> *Was yet by soft humanity refin'd . . .*

Another, taken from a tragic play, evoked his lengthy career of suffering:

> *Had some good angel op'd to me the book*
> *Of Providence, and let me read my life,*
> *My heart had broke, when I beheld the sum*
> *Of ills which one by one I have endur'd . . .*[15]

If William mourned the death of his brother it goes unrecorded – if he maintained any correspondence at all with his siblings, it goes unpreserved. The only thought that certainly *did* occur was whether he might benefit from being a trustee of John's financial concerns. Isabella received the news in France, and undoubtedly grieved for a younger brother and friend with whom she shared an unhappy tendency towards disappointment – she once lamented that John 'had my fortune in establishment and money matters'.[16] He was finally laid to rest in the family vault at Twickenham, with his mother, on 10 April and the nation at large mourned for 'Foul-Weather Jack': notices of his death sprang up across England, Europe and America, and his adventures were laid out in a long obituary in the *Gentleman's Magazine*. The last survivor of the *Wager* wreck of 1741, a war hero, and a father of six. An enviable legacy.

The days that followed were a blur of administration. Avoiding 'the pain of it when I am in the House', Sophia kept out of the way as inventories were taken of the furniture at Bolton Row and Pirbright.[17] She drew up 'a little list of People there are I believe debts owing to on the Adl's account'.[18] A cup of cocoa – or a glass of madeira – for her nerves. Dr James's Pills for her sinking health. More ink, more letters – some composed and grateful, others feverish and frustrated by the constant, petty demands. Friends took her out for a half-hour's 'airing' every now and then. The reading of the will at Bolton Row left some severely disappointed. A comfortable annuity for Sophia, after payment of debts. Equal shares for four of their children, and single sums to the two who had already drained his pockets: £2,000 for Juliana and just £500 for Jack. When he discovered that he had also been disbarred from inheriting his father's properties and estates he was livid. Soon John's executor and relative Sir John Wodehouse was at Sophia's door accusing her of destroying documents, 'because I had so much money I did not chuse it should be seen', she griped to Sykes.[19] 'I find I have to thank Jack for it', she concluded, before finishing with a theatrical flourish: 'I wonder when people will be w[e]ary of persecuting your humble Sert, SB.'

John's final wishes quickly became common knowledge. On bumping into Jack in town, Lord Fife noticed that though 'his father has disinherited him' he still cut a fine figure parading about 'mounted on two fine steeds'.[20] Sophia's friend Mrs Lewis wrote disdainfully of 'that scapegrace Jack who has behaved in a most shocking manner to his Mother, & goes on as usual like a Rascal'.[21] It was no exaggeration. On 5 May he pleaded with Sykes to pay a debt of £150, promising to relinquish any part of his (i.e. Catherine's) estate for the favour: 'such is my necessity that I must go to prison if you do not relieve me'.[22] By mid May he had been conveyed to the King's Bench prison and was bailed out by his *tailor*, who was presumably not yet wise to Jack's habit of false promises. For Sophia, the shame must have been acute. To her mortification, it was also becoming clear that her income would be significantly less than hoped – John's debts far exceeded what any of them had expected. 'I believe there never was a Will made to equal it', George Anson later lamented. 'And I always thought that my Father did not owe a Farthing. When au contraire Sykes Bill alone was seven Thousand Pounds.'[23] Pirbright would have to be sold. Disputes arose over the lands at Crondall and Blansby. The annoyed Jack loped back to Scotland, where the locals hoped that the loss of Gight would finally dash his hopes of political influence.

Despite his behaviour, Catherine remained infatuated with her husband. Painfully aware of her inability to refuse him, she asked a friend to help secure some money that 'would be out of Mr Byron's power to spend, and out of my own power to give up to him'.[24] With Jack determined to sell Gight 'as soon as possible', their nomadic life began. In summer 1786 they left Scotland and fitted out a house in Hampshire, conveniently close to the Crondall estates, and Jack arranged a money-seeking excursion to his mother's family at Caerhays. After Catherine fell pregnant the following spring they promptly sold their effects and moved to the Isle of Wight, having uncharacteristically collected his toddling daughter from Lady Holderness. At some point during the year Gight was finally sold to Lord Aberdeen, raising around £18,000 – which was promptly reduced by their debts and outgoings to, at best, £5,000. (One agent estimated their expenditure in their first eighteen months of marriage at £8,690 – approaching £700,000 in modern currency.) Jack hired a boat and departed for Boulogne – a new venue for his immoderate spending – followed by Catherine (by then 'big with bairn') and shy little Augusta in September.[25] They dropped by Chantilly to see George Anson's family – surely his brother would back his claim on the family estates? – and then Paris. Jack's last stay here had furnished him with a fuller pocket and a plan to find a new wife – this time, his tender-hearted aunt was not there to succumb to his charms.

Isabella's second attempt at an independent life in France had not proved as pleasant as she had hoped. It was here that she received the melancholy news of her brother's death – the ever-dependable, ill-starred John. She grieved for herself and for his poor, wilting widow, who had ever been her friend. Returning to Paris for the cheerless winter of 1786, she underwent painful cupping treatments to reduce her swelling legs and developed a cough that made it difficult to bear the night air. The location of her hotel, being within earshot of the lively Jardin du Palais Royal, must have provided some torment. There is no record that Weinheim joined her – gone were the fraught reports of Selwyn flying to France with a pistol, hoping to 'blow his brains out', and of Frederick's plans to have his mother 'forced to England and shut up'.[26] She had funded Weinheim's spending for years – even once bailing him out of prison – but the strength of his protests about their 'friendship' had faded as the money ran out.

Unable to keep within her budget, Isabella was reduced to just two footmen and her much-put-upon maid Jane. As her sixty-fifth birthday loomed she came to a painful decision. She had always hated uncertainty and this, at least, put an end to it. She wrote to Frederick – full of apologies, of thanks, of 'the greatest humility' – to explain *how* the money had run out, skirting over the sums lent to her nephews (including Jack) and friends in Paris, and hoping that her new resolution would placate him. It may be that without Weinheim the real spark behind Isabella's desire to stay abroad fizzled out – whatever the case, her fire had died. 'It is my Intention in Spring (or April even) to go over to Eng[lan]d', she assured Frederick, 'and there to Remain.'[27] This time she kept her promise, and in the spring of 1787 she said goodbye to the lights of Paris for the final time.

On arrival in England, Isabella retreated almost immediately to Bath. With Frederick's assistance she procured a 'singularly elegant' house adjoining Sophia's old haunt at Belvedere, boasting 'a full command of view of the river, the London road, and the surrounding country of great extent and beauty'.[28] Her sister-in-law was in town in the autumn, in all likelihood prompting a reunion. Isabella quickly discovered that, for most, her former crimes were not forgiven. Her attempts to renew her acquaintance with Lady Middleton were coldly received and provoked mirth among other fashionable ladies. '*What baron attends upon her now?*', they quipped, teasing Lady Middleton for being singled out. Isabella's reported adventures with 'one *baron* after another' remained notorious; 'it had become a bye-word', one female acquaintance remembered many years later.[29]

Stung, Isabella sought solace in her writing, her needlework, her family and her faith. Frederick, Anne and Julia visited, and she met some of her grandchildren – so far, at least four surviving Delmes and six surviving brown-haired, blue-eyed Howards – perhaps for the first time. She continued to add to her manuscript. '*If you desire to continue agreeably in the world, in the latter season of your life, rather promote, than restrain, the innocent amusements of younger persons, that the echo of chearfulness may reach your ears.*'[30]

She was careful with her diet, afraid to tip the balance of her health. She looked forward to a visit from Weinheim, which was planned for the following spring (and would no doubt bring further criticism on her head). It would be his last recorded visit – by 1792 he had rejoined the armed forces on the Continent. Another love lost, but she tried to rally her spirits. '*If ever you should have been a sufferer from ingratitude, (and who has not more or less?) do not permit the recollection to harden your heart.*' Her little book of 'maxims' helped her to navigate the pain of her fall from grace, and though it had originally been intended for friends and family she began to indulge hopes that it deserved a wider readership. She made contact with a publisher at Grosvenor Square.

The winter of 1787 was quiet but fretful. At Newstead, a storm smashed three windows in the Great Dining Hall, drove in parts of the roof and blew large sheets of lead across the Abbey gardens. Another impossible expense. In Bath, the fashionable world complained that the Assembly Rooms were allowing in 'all sorts of *riff-raff*' and began to hold their own parties at home.[31] In December a heavily pregnant Catherine arrived in London, without her husband, to deliver Augusta back to Lady Holderness and await the birth of her own child. Her rooms at Holles Street were far from luxurious. Anxieties nagged. How painful would it be? Who would help? How long could she afford to stay? There were no relatives to whom she could turn; a last-minute midwife came recommended by the wife of London solicitor John Hanson, a contact of her Edinburgh agent. It was not an easy labour. The child was born on

Tuesday, 22 January, leaving poor Catherine herself 'far from well' – and the baby seemed to have a deformed foot.[32] Jack had scurried past town up to Scotland without visiting, and on hearing the news their agents sought measures to protect themselves. Two days after the birth they discussed the careful steps that were needed 'to prevent total ruine to the Lady and her Child', and how 'persons who run so fast to ruine' tend to subsequently blame mismanagement.[33] Everyone knew that any money entrusted to Jack would never reach her. When he wrote to them from Edinburgh with the happy news (and to request money), he got his son's date of birth wrong.

Catherine waited. For word from Jack – for his arrival. For her baby to be strong enough to travel. As the weeks passed her letters became desperate. She wanted a cheap house in the country – Wales or northern England, she did not care. Most importantly, she needed funds: 'I must have it as if Mr Byron gets it it will be thrown away in some foolish way or other.'[34] In Jack's absence she decided to name the boy after her father and grandfather, writing to her agent Mr Watson, 'my little boy is to be named George don't show Mr Byron this'. (The agent's earlier note that their son was born '21 Jany 1788' and was '(to be christened W[illia]m Gordon Byron)', implies that Jack had imparted the information and wished to call the baby William.)[35]

The baptism was held in Marylebone on 1 March – *George Gordon Byron* – and two of Catherine's relatives were named as godparents. Still no Jack, and the end of her lease on Holles Street loomed. '*Pray how am I to leave it without a farthing*' – '*I don't know what I shall do or what will become of me*' – '*For God's sake make an end of this business . . .*' From Edinburgh, her husband merely complained to his sister Fanny that he was constantly cheated out of money by 'Rascals': 'my income is so small and what there is of it is settled on Mrs Byron & the Child. Therefore I am obliged to live in a very narrow circle'.[36] Sophia's reaction to the news of her ninth grandchild is unknown, but she might at least have been pleased by the name – soon afterwards she hired a servant 'who She said She liked because his Name was George'.[37] Unfortunately, any joy sparked by the baby's arrival into the family was quickly overshadowed by two unexpected deaths.

The first cast even Jack into despair. 'My Dear Fanny,' he wrote on 21 March, 'I should have answer'd your Letter before, but I have not been well & I am now sorry to be obliged to tell you that poor Lady Wilmot is dead.'[38] Juliana's death at Osmaston Hall on 15 March, a little after her thirty-fourth birthday, was a shock.[39] The cause is unclear, but her brother nursed some uncharitable suspicions about Sir Robert. 'I have been much affected notwithstanding I have not seen her for some years . . . I am certain she was not happy & fell a sacrifice to her own unhappy situation, as he totally secluded her from her own family', Jack concluded, '& living with him, whom I believe not the most pleasant temper in the world.' Sophia was inconsolable – Hester Thrale later grieved that it 'broke her up, & She c[oul]d never recover to be what She was before'.[40] Lady Wilmot was buried at Osmaston Hall, leaving behind two sons: three-year-old Robert Wilmot and fifteen-year-old William John Byron, who was perhaps already contemplating an army life. Though Jack comforted himself with the thought of his sister's fate – 'I am sure she is happy at present as she was a very good Woman & a good Sister' – his grief betrayed a self-absorbed foreboding. 'My Father & now my Sister dying within a few years really makes me reflect that it will be my turn soon', he grieved, '& I am quite depressed.' Had he known how efficiently the next decade would ravage his family, he might have given up entirely.

The loss that swiftly followed was almost as devastating for the young Newstead heir. After the spring took his mother, the summer claimed his devoted grandmother, Lady Byron. Elizabeth had settled into a quiet but not entirely solitary life in the four years since the death of her daughter Caroline. Her house on Somerset Street bustled with servants – Mary, the two Sarahs, Chadwick and James – and Miss Booth, her friend of some four decades, remained with her. She kept up contact with her cousins, their children, and her indefatigable ally Mr Gould. But age – and long years of grief – finally caught up with her. She grew weaker, and began to have trouble with her eyes. She amended her will to ensure generous legacies for former and current servants, sums for Miss Booth and her Nottinghamshire nephew John, and her few gold and diamond trinkets to a cousin's daughter, hoping to keep them in the Shaw family. Everything else – the meagre shares that had escaped her husband's clutches – were to be held in trust for her grandson. Elizabeth, the long-suffering Lady Byron, died at home on the morning of Saturday, 5 July, aged fifty-nine. As per her wishes, she was buried at her childhood estate at Besthorpe, 'in the same Vault my late father and mother are deposited'.[41]

'Declining life is a very awful scene'

The pains of age gnawed at the remnants of the older generation. Four Byron siblings remained: Isabella, William, Richard and George. Their sister-in-law Sophia was by now a shadow of her former self, forever railing against the unfairness of fortune and even occasionally questioning her religion: 'I have as much faith and I hope devotion as any Body', she had once lamented to Hester, 'yet the uninterrupted Felicity I have in my life observed attend some Individuals has always puzzled me.'[42] Eight long years had passed since her friend Dr Johnson had heard her woes and grieved, 'Declining life is a very awful scene'.[43] He was now in his grave. John had been killed by an illness of just two weeks, and the once vivacious Elizabeth lay in a cold vault in Norfolk. At a twinge, a faintness, a spot of blood, thoughts of mortality would inevitably intrude. Those in the grey realm of 'old age' were expected to abandon their garters and gold for prayer books and medicinal powders, and settle into a season of repose and reflection. For the sake of both propriety and health they were advised to forego youthful pleasures such as dancing, lavish dinners, fashion and amorous behaviour. Bad weather and late nights became hazardous; meats and rich foods gave way to plain soups and broths; they walked in clouds of ointments, baths, vapours, milks and perfumes designed to combat the 'driness' of the elderly.

Sophia was ever on the lookout for new treatments – perhaps justifying the established drinking habits of Bolton Row, alcohol was considered medicinal: one navy physician endorsed a health-giving four glasses of wine per day at the age of fifty, and up to six per day at sixty. (It was a happy coincidence, then, that she eagerly enjoyed the comfort to be found in the bottles from Hester – 'such excellent Wine to my Greedy Stomach'.)[44] Hair greyed or disappeared – teeth loosened – eyesight failed – bodies unceremoniously began to droop. Growing vulnerable and increasingly irrelevant, the Byrons were at leisure to reflect on the decay around them. 'The amiable Woman you remember tall, active & elegant tho' never handsome is now chained to her Chair by infirmity,' Sophia heard of an old friend.[45] In private, Hester was candid about the decline of Sophia, who retained an innate elegance despite having long since lost her looks:

> How differently Age affects different Women! Mrs Byron and Mrs Cholmondeley – of the same Rank in Life, much about the same Degree of Beauty too – a Style of prettiness that inspired Passion more than symmetrical Proportion is ever found to do, in short two Women for whom their cotemporary Men would have willingly run thro' Fire – how they look now! Mrs Byron has lost all Face, but retains that elegance of Form & Manner – that still strikes you with the Idea of a decay'd Belle, a Lady of Quality more battered by Sickness than subdued by Age . . . Byron was *born* a Woman of Fashion, Cholmondeley became one at 15 Years old – yet you see *that* was not early enough.[46]

Nevertheless, Sophia stoically 'whirled round the Town' amusing friends with comical stories and irritating them by pilfering their servants.[47] She grew closer to her formerly maligned daughter-in-law Henrietta as her own daughters distanced themselves. After the sale of Pirbright she divided her time between Bolton Row and 3 Prospect Row in Brompton, Kent, a country retreat overlooking a park and the river beyond. Urging her friend to rest, Hester poked fun at her own nomadic life, putting words in Sophia's mouth: 'what a different Life do my Cat & I lead at Brompton!'[48]

Isabella, on the other hand, approached the winter of her life with a new meekness, and after Weinheim's visit retreated to a village outside Bath. Years of anxiety had affected both her health and her spirits: 'One must have a heart of Adamant not such an one as mine,' she had complained, 'to support such a Position in the decline of Life and when Peace at least should Kiss ones latter day.'[49] She struggled with her legs, her eyes, her old nervous complaints, and gave way to her melancholy turn of mind – but at least the uncertainty she so hated was over. In the words of one of her poems:

Thrice welcome said she is this horrid gloom,
Security in thee at least is found . . .[50]

Trying to follow her own advice, she yielded to pursuits befitting an elderly, scandalised dowager countess. '*When time, sorrow, or other causes, shall have abated your love of diversion, make your retreat silently, and without censure on the taste of others.*'

For William, who had been estranged from his wife by law for a decade and in affection for much longer, there was an obvious silver lining to his new status as a widower. In theory, he was free to marry again. 'He might have taken it into his head to do so,' remarked one of the many later fed tales by Joe Murray, 'more particularly as he appeared to be living in a very lonely & recluse way in the old Abbey'.[51] At sixty-five, there *may* even have been the chance of more children. But, as an insolvent and by all accounts unpleasant old man, he was hardly an irresistible prospect. No, no more wives. Instead he retreated into Nottinghamshire, relying on the attentions of 'Lady Betty', dwelling on his legal battles – he was still fixated on the Newstead river and now wrangling too with Sophia over John's will – and studiously ignoring his grandson's requests for help in purchasing military supplies.

One unhappy sentiment festering among the elder generation was a sense that the younger folk had neglected, cheated or forsaken them. 'What Children some people have!' Hester declared in her diary. 'Mrs Byron is now old & infirm, & apparently in her last Stage of Existence . . . but not a Daughter ever goes near her, & the only Son that should be her Comfort, is in India.'[52] Isabella had spent years convinced of her son's needlessly cruel behaviour. In these suspicions they were far from alone: the winter of 1788 presented the most illustrious example of filial impiety of the age. The fifty-year-old George III's sudden and devastating descent into a baffling illness saw him promptly ushered to Kew Palace and forced into a straitjacket; Sophia's young friend Frances Burney, now lady-in-waiting to Queen Charlotte, wrote in her diary of his 'positive delirium', his benevolent ramblings, and 'Heart unbridled [by] sober reason'. Amid these whispers of madness the twenty-six-year-old Prince of Wales made an undignified grasp at power. Supported by his champions, including Charles James Fox and Lord Carlisle himself, he pushed for legislation to appoint himself regent. Though he tactfully 'lamented the melancholy cause of their discussion', Frederick 'declared himself a strong advocate' for an amendment to the law. For all her Whiggish principles, it may have pained Isabella to see her son side with the prince's efforts to overthrow his suffering father. 'Your journey, if you live,' she warned readers of her manuscript, 'will be more speedy than you imagine to the same period, and render you equally dependent on the compassion and patience of a younger race.' The king's unexpected recovery in February was a sharp check to the scheming.

With a national crisis apparently averted, another spring brought another death close to home – this time, fifty-nine-year-old George, the youngest of the old Byron siblings and godson of the old king. Growing up in the shadow of his brothers, he had never managed to extricate himself from his financial difficulties. His professional life could be reduced to a brief army career – courtesy of Isabella's connections – and a flirtation with local politics. His marriage had produced seven children, of whom three sons and one daughter survived. Like John he died amid a London spring, at a house in Paddington on 6 May 1789, and was interred four days later at Twickenham, leaving little imprint on the world. His obituary writers found it easier to focus on his son Frederick George, whose caricatures about high life, low life and political affairs were by then achieving considerable success: 'Hon. Captain Byron, brother to Lord Byron, and father to the Gentleman whose comic pencil has lately enlivened the polite arts.'[53] The siblings were reduced to three.

The Byrons' grief was swiftly hushed by the rumblings of what would develop into one of the most dramatic upheavals in European history – the summer of 1789 would change everything. The prospect of a mad king paled in comparison with news from across the Channel: 'REBELLION AND CIVIL WAR IN FRANCE'. Revolution had come to Europe. On 14 July the Bastille prison in Paris was stormed, its inmates released and its officials beheaded – a symbolic victory over the tyranny of an unpopular and antiquated form of government.

A divided England looked on. There were reports that the French capital was plastered with handbills offering 500,000 livres for Marie Antoinette's head. That a nobleman had invited his tenants to celebrate the new 'national freedom' at his estate and had them massacred. Dreadful rumours of 'tumults in Paris – of the streets running in blood – of 12,000 being slaughtered – of the King and Queen being beset' were eventually dismissed as fabrications (though in fact they were merely premature).[54] Isabella scoured the news-papers for names and places she knew – just two years after her departure, that glittering world had danced itself off a precipice.

Sophia heard the news from what she thought was her deathbed in Bath. She hurriedly settled her will and awaited God's pleasure. 'Are you thinking of the French Government at all?' Hester wrote breezily just before the fall of the Bastille.[55] Sophia's thoughts must at least have wandered to her children Fanny and George, who were living across the Channel. By August she had returned to Bolton Row and her friend's letters were quite different. 'But these Frenchmen! these frantic Fools!' Hester declared. 'May their madness be of short duration I pray God – when one reads of their Cruelties, & reflects on that theatre of Gayety & Good humour – Paris – made a Scene of Sorrow & Bloodshed in this dreadful Manner.'[56] 'How one ought to thank God that has removed the black Storm from over *our* apparently devoted Heads,' she continued, recalling recent royal events and perhaps even the riots of 1780, 'and suffer'd it to break just near enough to impress us forcibly with the Idea of our *own* Deliverance.'

Undeterred by the charged political climate, Jack continued to view France as a means of escaping his problems. His second stab at domestic life in Scotland had been a storm of lies and squabbles. Perhaps in a vain attempt to stem Catherine's tirades about money, he told her that his nephew William John was dead (thus making himself the heir to Newstead) – 'he told me he was dead & till the time he went away persisted in it,' she wrote, 'not that I ever believed him'.[57] Passing through London – friends of the Holderness family gossiped that 'the wretched father' was 'skulking in Town under a feigned name' – he took up lodgings in Sandgate, near Dover, where he spent some time with his supposedly deceased nephew and made plans to skip across the Channel.[58] 'We had a very fine Lugger all the time', William John wrote excitedly, 'so that we were at Sea a great deal and in France.'[59]

Jack enjoyed the chance to show off and his presence undoubtedly caused a stir. 'Captain Byron is said, by the World, to be at Boulogne,' gushed the newspapers, 'and "as *handsome* as ever."'[60] His spending continued unabated – being 'very near taken up and put into prison at Boulogne', he promptly scuttled back to Scotland.[61] 'Jack is at Aberdeen with no other Company than Kate,' disclosed his sister Augusta, before adding impishly, 'I hope he understands taming a *Shrew*, & then he can never, at least, want Employment.'[62] His failed marriage seemed just another example of Jack's bad luck where his younger brother landed on his feet – despite their whirlwind beginnings, George Anson and Henrietta seemed rapturously happy. 'My Boy thrives apace and will I think be very like his Father,' Henrietta wrote of their new son, George Anson junior, 'my first wish is, that he may resemble him in every thing'.[63] However jaded he was about Catherine, Jack was affectionate about his children, or certainly made a good show of seeming so. He had raved about little George to Augusta: 'He says his Child is a very fine Boy & he seems remarkable fond of him', she told their brother, continuing, 'Dear little Augusta is in Yorkshire & vastly well. It must be a very great satisfaction to Jack that she is so well provided for.'[64]

Determined to find useful employment, the young Newstead heir had decided to join the army – an unusual career path for a future baron and peer, but then he never *had* enjoyed the usual privileges of his rank. He had rattled between his aunts and uncles – Sophy, Jack, Fanny. The latter's continued misdemeanours are perhaps implied by the fact that when she turned up with an infant called Aylmer, her nephew immediately smelled scandal: 'who he is I can't make out very well, but she is as fond of him as if it was her own child'. 'I can't help suspecting certain things', he hinted.[65] It was his uncle George Anson who answered his pleas for financial support. 'I have been writing to Lord Byron to beg that he would do something for me', William John fretted in August, 'for I have not had a farthing from him since you left England nor will he settle any thing for me nor will he ever answer any letters.'[66]

William had, in fact, been busy appealing against the Newstead river verdict, pathetically begging for further delay because 'the Attorney was gone to London, and had taken the defendant's briefs in his pocket'.[67] The excuse was insufficient – the case was lost again. Still smarting, he felt compelled to discuss matters with his young heir and 'sent for him to Newstead' from Sophy's on Christmas Day.[68] They perhaps knew he would be dispatched abroad in the spring – it was William's last chance to impress upon him the importance of resettling the estates as soon as he came of age. Two years and five months to wait. In February 1790, William John was presented at a royal levee as an ensign in the 18th (or Royal Irish) infantry regiment, and braced himself for a new adventure.

As William planned how to most efficiently bleed his ancestral estates dry, Isabella took heart from the prospect of *adding* to her own legacy: she was now a published author. After at least a decade of compiling her manuscript, it was published in November 1789: *Thoughts in the Form of Maxims, Addressed to Young Ladies, on their First Establishment in the World, By the Countess Dowager of Carlisle* sold at two shillings and sixpence. Providing a comfortable taste of genteel femininity in turbulent times, it quickly ran into a second edition. The reputation of the author doubtless had some hand in its popularity – her old friend Horace Walpole was intrigued to learn of its existence from Lady Ossory. 'Of the new noble authoress–dowager I had not heard a word', he wrote, asking for its title and hinting that he did not suppose it was a particularly 'severe' treatise.[69] (Though he did manage to acquire a copy, any critique is sadly lost.)

Likely as oblivious as ever to the smirks of her peers, Isabella must have been delighted by the reviews. The *Analytical Review* concluded that her maxims 'shew the discernment of the writer, and still more clearly evince her goodness of heart'.[70] (Her benevolent advice about servants received particular praise.) 'We have seldom seen so much good sense, and so many useful remarks, comprized in so narrow a compass,' the *Monthly Review* proclaimed; 'there is not a young woman of fashion in the kingdom, who might not reap advantage by making this manual a part of the *useful* furniture of her *toilette*'.[71] But her reputation preceded her, and braver reviewers couldn't resist alluding to the discrepancy between her advice and her history. 'The Dowager Lady Carlisle has written, and with great good sense, on female education', declared one. 'The theory is with her Ladyship; and if any one wishes to know where the best practice of the science is to be found – we are happy to direct the amiable curiosity to the family of the Duchess of Gordon.'[72]

The life into which Isabella settled – dictated by necessity and starved of diversion – was exactly what she had once hoped to avoid. Her literary success had clearly not solved her money troubles. Desperate creditors began to dispatch court orders to Sir William Musgrave, who provided proof of their separation and returned to his library. (Her published thoughts on the need for a wife to bend to the habits and wishes of her husband would have baffled him, had he felt inclined to read them.) The exhilarating pleasures of younger years bowed to lonely evenings of reflection (her recommended topics were the 'beauties of nature, a healthful walk, a rising and setting sun, the prosperity and perfections of your descendants').[73] How she was reduced since those golden summers at Castle Howard – the evenings singing before fashionable assemblies, the applause – the midnight dances in the meadows of Beaucaire.

In August Lady Anne visited, looking rather too thin; the following month 'Miss Byron' – probably her niece Sophy; Julia, increasingly decked in jewels and rouge, preferred to visit in the spring; Frederick tended to drop by as winter set in, and Frances wrote with news of 'the Matches'. Betty was widowed, sending a tide of black cascading across the family. Despite his transgressions, Sophia politely observed the death of her niece's husband in her correspondence: 'the Black wax on your Letter frighted me less because you have so many Relations', Hester wrote, 'I had forgotten Mr Delme'.[74] Isabella felt a wave of nostalgia on hearing that Frederick and Caroline had taken a summer trip to Naworth Castle. 'I think yr La[dyshi]p may be more at leisure to read a dull Letter than any where else, especially if it Rains as often there, as I remember it to do,' she wrote to her daughter-in-law; 'I sincerely wish Ld Carlisle and my Grandson much Diversion in shooting[.] I am very fond of that old Castle, and its Environs.'[75] More tidings came in November, shortly before her seventy-first birthday – Frederick had become a grandfather; and she a *great-grandmother*.

As she sank further from society, *Thoughts in the Form of Maxims* offered a tangible and lasting chance to vindicate herself – to demonstrate her reformation and promote her charitable vision of the world. Be kind, she advised, for one cannot always know the sufferings of others: 'imperfection did, and will exist, as long as this world shall last'.[76] *She* had always been ready to forgive, especially where affairs of the heart were concerned – her downfall had been that she expected the same favour from others.

Sophia, on the other hand, had learned to expect nothing – even from her own children. George Anson, ever his father's son, was always at sea, and her daughters struggled to forgive her history of criticism and interference. In private she poured out her heart to Hester. 'Oh pray send for that kind & skilful Friend Mr Farquahar,' her friend responded, '& make him tye that too active Soul tight in its thin Wire Cage, lest it should bear the house down with fluttering so.'[77] In public she held out magnificently, being carried about Bath supported by pillows, decked in white furs, and still determined to hold court. In the spring of 1790 she held great assemblies and began to delight in music, to the bemusement of her daughters. (Augusta joked that until now her mother 'never could, with all her endeavours, discover the difference between Martini's Minuet & "oh the days when I was young"'.[78] It must, she uncharitably suggested, be an attempt to alleviate the 'stings of Conscience' over 'past sins'.) Her efforts to get to know her daughter's children fell similarly flat. Augusta entertained her brother with a faux pas committed by her eldest boy Peter in April: 'He went to my Mother's, who express'd a wish to see him, & on her desiring him to kiss her he drew back, saying he never kiss'd <u>Old</u> Women.' 'After this unlucky speech', she continued, 'I fear he has very little Chance of the <u>Bible and Diamond</u> Earrings, or of the honour of Ranging at her Watch Chain.'[79] (She was quite right – George Anson's two girls stood to inherit Sophia's diamonds, as well as the cherished Bible and prayer book she had been given by her parents.)

By the summer of 1790, Sophia could maintain the masquerade no longer. In Hester's diary, buried amongst the news of 17 June, trembled a melancholy line: 'I think poor Mrs Byron is dying.'[80] In August Sophy received a report that her mother was 'very low spirit'd & crying continually because she was so unwell' (but was not sufficiently moved to pay her a visit).[81] Fanny had taken a house at Valenciennes, in northern France, to which Jack was planning another debt-escaping sojourn. He left Aberdeen in September with casual promises of returning soon. His wife and son would never see him again. As her errant son left England for the final time, Sophia retired to Bath and wept over kindly notes from Hester, who was on holiday with her husband: 'Bath will restore yr Health I am *sure* it will, it always *did*: and we shall meet at old Greenway's Cold Bath I hope . . . I will come Morning, Noon, & Night to see how your sweet spirits mend.'[82] At sixty years old, Sophia worried about her pains, about being buried alive, about the servant who gleefully awaited her demise. In October, 'expecting my dissolution daily', she asked that all of the letters she had kept should be burned, and left new bequests for those who had helped her during a 'long and painful' illness: a Mr Grant, who had 'taken so much care of me', her friend Lady Aston and her once scorned daughter-in-law.[83] '*And now Lord Jesus receive my soul in peace.*'

Before the end she managed to scribble a quick, pained note to Hester, with instructions for comforting Henrietta, and a final farewell:

> don't be *overcome* with the *little cant* of grief of my Daughter Mrs GB when I am no more – tell her black becomes Her and she will forget it all – once more – adieu – think I have not many more Hours to live thank and beg you never to forget your SB.[84]

'Its a hard struggle', she scrawled, 'and Mr Grant will tell you my suffering.' The Honourable Sophia Byron died at Bath on 6 November 1790 – in tears and anguish – leaving her friends to mourn and her five children to squabble over their inheritance.

In the absence of affection from her children she had been generous to her friends: a fur muff for her god-daughter Mrs Bunbury, a white fur shawl to fellow military widow Mrs Lambart. Of her friend Walter Farquhar, who also attended John in his final days, she lamented, 'I wish I had a Pitt or a Hastings Diamond to leave him as he merits for his friendship and attention towards me at all times and on all occasions the wealth of a Nabob.' For Hester, a sentimental token: 'my little Gold pencil to my much loved friend Mrs Piozzi for with pen or pencil who writes so well'. 'Poor dear dead Mrs Byron!' her friend grieved. 'Nobleness, Elegance, Animated Beauty – Promptitude of Wit, Capacity for Thought – could no longer avail her it seems; no longer keep Soul & Body together, tho against the general Foe few ever made more vigorous Resistance . . . Poor, dear, dead Mrs Byron! Farewell & take my Prayers.'[85] She even composed a long epitaph, intending to erect a memorial at the Abbey:

> . . . You then, that idly range, and thoughtless tread
> These melancholy Mansions of the Dead;
> You that in Wit or Birth, or Beauty trust,
> Reflect that lovelier Byron is but Dust . . .[86]

After six days – and, presumably, Dr Farquhar's promised medical checks – Sophia was interred at Bath Abbey. She might have been gratified that the obituaries made due acknowledgement of her suffering: 'Saturday se'nnight died at Bath, after a long and severe illness, the Hon. Mrs. Byron, relict of the late Admiral Byron.'[87] The surviving shreds of her children's reactions are financial. With George Anson abroad, Fanny took charge of the business and the fragments of John and Sophia's life together were examined and assigned a monetary value. The twisted gold ring he brought from Africa in 1752. Her diamond mourning ring with a curl of his hair. Jack wrote angrily about Henrietta's interference: 'She is a d[amne]d Bitch', he spat to Fanny; 'do not give up a thing'.[88] Though they had never met, Catherine hoped her sister-in-law might spare thirty pounds, as 'me nor my child have not at present a farthing nor know where to get one'. She added bluntly, 'I would not ask you if your mother had not been dead.'[89] Fanny travelled to Newstead to meet her uncle William, whose signature was required for some documents – he hinted at getting cash compensation for the favour. He managed to seek the spoils of every family tragedy.

'There is some Misfortune cast on our family'

Orphanhood did not take an emotional toll on thirty-three-year-old Jack. From his hideout at Valenciennes, he bombarded Fanny with requests for money and lurid, boastful updates of his sexual conquests:

'the <u>Birons</u> are irresistable [*sic*], you know that Fanny, as for La Henry, she told me that I did it so well that she always *spent* twice every time. I know this will make you laugh but she is the best piece I ever /—/.'[90] (Meanwhile, his oblivious wife struggled to settle their son's medical bills.) The letters, in which his affection persistently spilled into something decidedly unbrotherly, imply that even as Sophia lay dying their relationship descended into incest: 'my Dear Fanny you are the only person I sincerely love' – 'do not make yourself too handsome, as I am too mad already that you are my sister' – 'I declare I can find no Woman so handsome as you, I have tried several, but when I do any thing *extraordinary*, I always think of you.'[91]

He gave little thought to the revolution, apparently viewing the simmering unrest as something of a game. While his cousin the caricaturist travelled France gleaning material for new satirical prints, Jack passed his days with petty concerns and in varying states of intoxication. He reported that a married woman 'told me when drunk that she liked me, & I really do not know what to do'; at one dinner he was amused by an inebriated acquaintance who ate too much salad and '*farted* to such a degree . . . that he was beastly'.[92] Meanwhile, pockets of royalist resistance sprang up and were quashed across the country. Swept up in the mood during one trip to the theatre, Jack embraced his aristocratic French ancestry and caused a stir by drunkenly bellowing *Vive le Roi! Vive la Nation!* He sparked a riot at another play after a disagreement with the manager. 'In short there is the most violent fermentation in this Town,' he wrote after hearing that the mob were eager to get hold of him, 'but I am not in the least afraid.'[93] All the while, he proclaimed in awkward French, '*je m'ennui a la mort*' – 'I am bored to death'. He relieved his boredom with sex and indulging a violent temper – the servants bearing the brunt of the latter. When the footman Louis displeased him, Jack threatened to 'break every bone he has', and he had no compunction about striking the maid, Josephine – when she drank too much at Christmas he literally kicked her down the stairs.

He began to feel ill. He had been successfully drowning a cold with wine, but by the end of December he complained that he had been 'spitting Blood for these three days'.[94] But he was not overly concerned. In February he took up swordsmanship lessons, had his picture drawn and talked of joining the local militia. His thoughts strayed to his eight-year-old daughter – Lady Holderness no longer contacted him – and of little George, of whom he was fond but entertained little hopes: 'for my son I am happy to hear he is well, but for his walking tis impossible, as he is club footed'.[95] About Catherine, he was less enthused: 'she is very amiable at a Distance, but I defy you and all the Apostles to live with her two months – for if any body cou'd live with her, it was me'. Even from this distance their disputes raged in correspondence. 'I only answer this to inform you I will have nothing to do with it,' she fumed in one letter,

> if you had taken my advice in place of those that know nothing of your affairs you would not have been in the situation you are . . . and give me leave to say it does not shoe [show] either sense or feeling to behave in the manner you do but expect nothing from me I woud [sic] pity you if it had not been brought on you by your own folly.[96]

(The extent of the misery elicited by this missive is suggested by the presence of a note in French on the envelope, in a neat and decidedly feminine-looking hand, 'I hope you don't go today to St Amand if you go I hope that before you leave you will come to see me'.)[97] While her husband ignored her, Catherine tried to cultivate a friendly correspondence with Fanny. 'Lord Byron would need to have been a very agreeable companion to make your time pass pleasantly,' she chirped, on hearing that her sister-in-law was making another trip to Newstead, 'if not you must have been very dull as he sees so few People.'[98]

In the spring of 1791 an elderly, decrepit-looking gentleman with a powdered wig took up residence in Piccadilly, a few streets away from the glittering family townhouse of his younger days. Like himself, the city wore a very different face to the one he had known then. Green spaces were filling in with ever more houses, and everything seemed louder – more offensive – to his aged ears. Even the women were a different shape: towering wigs tumbled into more natural curls; padded hips replaced by padded rumps. The coffee-house talk was not of the threat from Scotland or of 'giants' abroad but of *révolution* and *liberté* – one recent book actually suggested that *all* men should be allowed to vote! But it is unlikely that Lord Byron troubled himself with national affairs – as ever, his world was focused solely on himself. He had a list of people to see.

First, the Plymouth set's legal representatives. 'One of his motives for coming is to insist on our giving him one hundred Pounds,' Sophy grumbled, 'for signing his name to some paper about Money which unluckily he is Trustee for: and which we cannot receive without his doing so.'[99] Second, he dropped in unannounced on Sir Charles Gould, who thought he looked 'extremely ill'.[100] William performed what he had rehearsed, expressing 'the utmost anxiety' for his grandson in Gibraltar and claiming to be 'afraid he was not happy or contented there'. As Gould struggled to understand this fit of tenderness for his grandson – 'the first he had ever given symptoms of' – his true motives were revealed: if his heir was in England, it would be far easier to resettle the estates when he turned twenty-one. (There were two more years to wait – the old man was getting impatient.) It was 'suggest'd intirely for the honour & happiness' of his grandson, William insisted. Hearing the story, Sophy remarked that she 'cou'd not help calling my Right Honble Uncle the very great Rogue I thought him'. What next? Who else owed him?

He arrived at Downing Street to petition Prime Minister Pitt – still only thirty-two, after seven years in office. He also happened to be the son of one of his old racing rivals. This Pitt was thin and serious, but seemed inclined to help. Sophy's report that her uncle was angling for the pension of £800 available to '*indigent* Peers' was only the start – William had made a list of the petty privileges unclaimed throughout his fifty-year career, planning to invoke them now. On turning twenty-one, his hereditary office of 'Bow Bearer to Sherwood Forest' had entitled him to three trees and three deer per year, which he had never collected. When Master of the Staghounds, he alleged, he was never paid the £300 due to him for upkeep of the liveries. The pension itself would be essential to 'enable him to sustain the dignity of a Lord of Parliament derived to him from his Ancestors'.[101] According to the prime minister's recommendation he submitted a formal written petition, replete with 'respectful Compliments'. (There is no record of success.) William's commissions continued.

The motivation for his fourth call lay entirely elsewhere: with (the now widowed) Mrs Scrimshire. The gossips were amused to see these two antiquated specimens apparently reviving their youthful attachment. 'He still pays his devoirs to *la belle jeune, et tous aimable* Scrimshire,' his niece wrote, 'who goes out and is admired as *much as ever*'.[102] With stories of his old gallantries resurrected by Mrs Bellamy's memoirs, the press speculated cheekily about his roguish intentions, even in his late sixties. 'The attachment of Lord Byron to Mrs S—e is, it seems, only the rekindling of an ancient flame', revealed the *Public Advertiser*. 'Thirty years ago, we are credibly informed, they *burned* for each other.'[103] Just over a week later another paper announced their imminent marriage: 'The ages of Lord Byron and Mrs Skrimshire, who are about to sacrifice at the Altar of Hymen, make together the juvenile number of one hundred and forty.'[104] Much like his old racing friend Lord March – now the Duke of Queensberry, and so notoriously lecherous that he was known as 'the Old Goat of Piccadilly' – William was nothing but a ridiculous old rake. They always found some reason to mock him.

No matter how much of a 'great Rogue' Sophy thought her uncle for his churlish financial demands, if there was one thread that wound itself into all strands of the Byron dynasty it was a perennial and divisive shortness of cash. ('That disease is epidemic in our family,' the poet sighed to his half-sister many years later.)[105] The result was a tangle of favours asked, money owed and mounting resentments. Isabella relied solely on Frederick, who continued to meet a roll of pleas from his Byron aunts, cousins and their offspring: his uncle George's widow Frances couldn't pay for her son's militia uniforms; his uncle Richard wanted help advancing his son's navy career. William continued to bleed his estates, tenants and now his bereaved relatives dry, with no intention of keeping old promises. 'Lord Byron has not made me any allowance and I am afraid he never will although he has said he would do often', protested William John, who had been taking out 'rash and imprudent' drafts on Sykes and stood accused of consorting with lowly surgeon's mates in Gibraltar.[106] '[I]f he will act so unthinkingly he must submit to the disgrace he brings on himself', declared his aunt Sophy, who was struggling herself after unwisely lending significant sums to her brother-in-law Charles Leigh.[107] She quickly killed Sykes's hopes that William might intervene: 'If you was to give yourself that [trouble] of writing to Lord Byron to inform him of the circumstance and request him to extricate his Grand Son from the disgrace it would be of no kind of use.'

The fallout from Sophia's death had only deepened the rifts between the Plymouth set. Sophy wrote to George Anson to vent her frustration about Fanny and Jack, writing that she daren't visit her sister at Brompton Row – 'all her actions are rash and ill judged' – and that 'I now never hear from *notre frère aîné* [our elder brother] for which good luck I am not unthankful'.[108] 'I like Sophy's spirit, & you know mony is her *God*,' Jack jeered to his eldest sister; 'I believe she wou'd sell herself if possible'.[109] Fanny bore the burden of both her impecunious brother and his abandoned wife. Jack – supposedly reduced to one ragged coat and shoes full of holes, but somehow managing to entertain women or attend the theatre every night – dismissed his wife's requests for support with a bald lie: 'she has quite enough & never would give me a farthing'.[110] Catherine's attempts to encourage a sisterly bond were falling flat. 'George is very well and really a charming Boy', she offered, 'I wish you was to see him I am sure you would be very fond of him'.[111] 'George's foot turns inward', she explained in another letter, 'and it is the right foot; he walks quite on the side of his foot'.[112] She had ever kept up the hopes that her infatuation with Jack would eventually be reciprocated, and her outlander son welcomed into the Byron family – they did not survive the summer looming before them.

'There is some Misfortune cast on our family', Jack ruminated at the dawn of his final year, unwittingly echoing his aunt Isabella.[113] Fanny's dark suspicions about their nephew William John, which were certainly relayed to Catherine, might have heartened him – the thought must have occurred that he was next in line to the family inheritance. Catherine's interest was piqued: '[P]ray where is your Nephew William', she asked, 'what makes you think that he will not live long . . . is he in bad health'?[114] Whatever hope was kindled, Jack would see no benefit. His body was wasting away, and by the spring of 1791 he complained that he was 'so alter'd that you will hardly know me – & from being fat & now the reverse – & continually so full of the Bile that I am never well'.[115] He swigged brandy and hoped for the best. In May he complained of enjoying 'neither health nor Comfort', but still spoke of his intentions to return to military service.[116]

Having spent years spinning tales of illness to avoid his responsibilities, Jack's griping fell on deaf ears. Hearing that he spent all of his money on women, Fanny stopped sending any, and his debts reached such a pitch that the town magistrates closed the gates to him. 'I dare not go out as every body points at me.'[117] He grew desperate and his temper flared. He caught Josephine gossiping and boasted of having 'knocked her down & beat her so that she has kept her bed for these two days'.[118] His resentment grew when he heard that Fanny had taken up with a marquis in London – 'Your letter has made me too unhappy to say much', he wrote miserably on 8 June; 'I must try to shift for myself'.[119] A week later he was turfed out of her lodge and bedridden at the house of his only remaining friend, a Mr Chawin. There, early on the morning of 21 June, a frowning huddle of men arrived to take down his will. It was something of a formality. Local officials declared him 'of sound Mind Memory and Understanding (altho' confined to his Bed by sickness) as he appeared to Us by his Conversation'.[120] Fanny, who hurried to him despite their tiffs, was bequeathed the shares he continued to claim from their parents' estate. The only other relative mentioned was three-year-old George, though it was hardly cause for celebration: 'I appoint my son Mr George Biron Heir of My real and personal Estate, and charge him to pay my Debts, Legacies and Funeral Expences.' It was reread, he agreed, and signed: *Biron*.

The notorious Jack Byron died on 2 August, in his mid thirties, probably of consumption. Sykes heard the news from Sophy:

> Being very sensible of the interest you take in every event that concerns our family I lose no time in acquainting you of the melancholy one which has lately happen'd and informing you of the death of my unfortunate eldest Brother. He died at Valenciennes ye 2d of August after a long & suffering illness. He was perfectly resign'd and sensible to the last Moment.[121]

The scattering of newspaper notices merely defined him by his more distinguished relatives: 'Deaths. John Byron, esq; son of the late hon. admiral John Byron, and husband of the late Amelia baroness Coniers.'[122]

It was not until *after* the public announcements that a black-bordered letter arrived at Catherine's door. The news was not gently relayed. 'You wrong me very much when you suppose I do not lament Mr Byron's death,' she grieved to Fanny, who had implied that she would rejoice at the news; 'Necessity, not inclination, parted us, at least on my part, and I flatter myself it was the same with him; and notwithstanding all his foibles for they deserve no worse name I most sincerely loved him.'[123] In a long letter laden with grief (and unencumbered by punctuation) she continued:

> it is a great comfort to me that he was with so kind a friend at the time of his death you say he was sensible to the last did he ever mention me was he long ill and where was he buryed be so good as [to] write all these particulars and also send me some of his hair . . . George is my only comfort and the only thing that makes me wish to live . . .[124]

Little George would never know his father. Ignorant of the rumours that her husband had 'had all the women in Valenciennes', Catherine had always nursed a flicker of hope that he would mend his ways and return to them.[125]

Elsewhere, the legal disputes dragged on as the Wodehouses and Lord Byron made spurious claims on John's estates. Fanny visited Newstead and wrote furious letters about 'being kept so *scandalously* out of the property my poor Father was so good as to leave me', angrily stamping the Byron seal into hot black wax.[126] George Anson advised that their uncle should not be contacted unless absolutely necessary, as he would only demand more money. The captain's benevolent influence was sorely missed at home – 'May the Almighty grant us good news of and from my dear Bro.,' Sophy prayed, 'and then I will not complain of fate.'[127] Mirroring the previous generation, George Anson was the noble officer to his elder brother's dissipated rake. His mother's friends had always praised his 'good Fortune and admirable Behaviour public and private' as 'a Cordial you much wanted'.[128] Where Jack had been a 'wretched father' and a 'scapegrace', he was 'esteemed and respected by all who have had the pleasure of being any way connected with him'.[129] While Jack narrowly avoided prison in Valenciennes, George was dispatched to the East Indies to serve in the new war with the kingdom of Mysore. The British newspapers were flooded with tales of his '*gallant* conduct' abroad: 'I look & feel as proud', Sophy gushed, 'as if I had gaind the honour instead of having been quietly seat'd on my chair all the time.'[130] To everyone's alarm, his run of success was suddenly, painfully interrupted: his boat was overset by a wave, throwing him overboard and striking him twice violently on the chest. 'When he was taken up', his brother-in-law Robert Dallas wrote, 'it was not supposed that he could survive the shock.'[131] The severity of the injury sent George back to England – arriving in Bath in March 1792, he demonstrated his inheritance of another of John's traits by promptly getting his wife pregnant (he was, clearly, not entirely debilitated).

George Anson returned from a distant war to be met with the prospect of another much closer to home. In France, the call for *liberté* was leading it down an increasingly violent path: the royal family was imprisoned, a new Republic declared and the guillotine hung over the aristocrats branded enemies of the state. The Byrons were drawn in to the unfolding drama, along with the rest of Britain.

Catherine was not yet disillusioned with the French cause, though she preferred to follow events from afar. 'I should not like to go abroad at present, in the state they are in', she reasoned after Fanny's invitation to Valenciennes; 'I am very much interested about the French, but I fancy that you and I are on different sides, for I am quite a Democrat and I do not think the King after his treachery and perjury, deserves to be restored.'[132]

Isabella found names she recognised in reports of the dead and mourned the loss of the sparkling Parisian world she had known. Her namesake niece Miss Isabella Byron, daughter of her late brother George, married a Swiss nobleman who fled to England after being the only officer of his regiment to survive a massacre at the Tuileries Palace. Her nephew Frederick George produced a set of prints caricaturing French scenes: in Calais, an officer promenading with a well-dressed woman, urinating as she walks; at Clermont, scrawny revolutionaries in ill-fitting boots; at Breteuil, a nervous-looking fat man beneath a painting of the Bastille, with a barber's blade at his throat. (These prints were among his last – within a year he had fallen ill and died at Bristol aged just twenty-seven.)

Just before Christmas 1792, George Anson wrote to Sykes mingling personal with national news. Henrietta had just given birth to another son – 'by last account they were tolerably well' – and all signs had begun to point to war with France. 'I trust (in that case)', he scribbled optimistically, 'My Health will permit me to go afloat – for I shou'd be sorry to be left behind'.[133] Less than a month later the French king was beheaded and by February 1793 the revolutionary government declared formal hostilities with Britain. Frederick, whose understandable antipathy to the anti-aristocratic proceedings abroad had prompted him to ally with his customary opponents, declared in parliament that he entertained no doubt 'of the necessity and justice of the war' and was astonished that anyone could oppose an issue on which 'there could be but one voice, one heart, and one mind, throughout the nation at large'.[134]

The drudging, dreadful reality of war was hardly a novelty to the older generation. The last seven decades had seen an almost continuous round of conflicts with rival European powers, with colonies proclaiming independence, with Indian kingdoms and peoples across the globe. (Hester's flippant remark to Sophia that, 'Well! The English are always hated somehow by every other Nation, go where one will', was not entirely unjustified.)[135] John had been the family's military champion – now the sword fell to their sons, sons-in-law and grandsons: Richard's eldest and namesake, who had served for years under his cousin's command; Augusta's husband Captain Parker; young William John, already at his post in Gibraltar; John Byron, of the Nottinghamshire set, having overcome 'family misfortunes too complex to enumerate', finally found a new commission in the army.[136] But the family's most promising leader – George Anson – was prevented from joining them.

On 26 February 1793 twenty-nine-year-old Henrietta Byron died in Bath, two months after giving birth, and was swiftly followed by her baby boy. Struggling with his chest injury and now 'the misery of witnessing the dissolution of a beautiful, amiable, and beloved wife', George Anson retreated to Devon to contemplate the changed landscape of his life.[137] His health slumped, and lawyers were called.

His thoughts were all for his family. 'Save me Good God', he begged in his will, 'for the sake of my poor Children Let me live to see them settled in the World[,] to see them virtuous and happy'. He gave grateful tokens to his servants, a small telescope and navy charts to his cousin Richard and the family portraits to his sisters (except one of Sophia, which he saved for his daughters). For Sykes, to whom he owed significant sums, he set aside silver sugar casters bearing the Byron coat of arms and three small blue bottles that were 'my Poor fathers when first he went to Sea', entreating that 'your good heart will never distress my Children'.[138]

Surviving his wife by just three months, the heartbroken George Anson died on 11 June at the age of thirty-four, to an outpouring of grief. 'If the professional character of Captain Byron rated him high in the estimation of his country,' cried the *Bath Chronicle*, 'he was no less distinguished in private life for his benevolent heart and amiable virtues.'[139] His brother-in-law remembered a man 'devout without ostentation, fond of his family, constant in friendship, generous and humane'.[140] The family rallied around his three surviving children – Georgiana, Julia and George Anson junior – who had lost both parents and a baby brother within a matter of weeks. Their worried aunt Sophy and grandfather's old friend Admiral Barrington petitioned both Lord Carlisle and the Admiralty for assistance. 'I should be happy to know if there is any hope, if not, I must take care of them myself,' Barrington valiantly declared. 'Miss Byron is not able to maintain them.'[141] His tireless friendship with John would not allow him, in good conscience, to desert his poor grandchildren. The news flew across the Continent as Sykes wrote to George's nephew in Gibraltar: 'You will receive with great Regret the Death of your Relation & my much valued Friend Capt. Byron.'[142] But the Newstead heir did not have long to mourn.

The weary William John had recently turned twenty-one, but his grandfather's pleas to recall him had led nowhere – he wanted to be useful. 'I wish with all my heart that I was to go to Canada with the Prince or to any other part of the World', he had lamented in his first year abroad. 'I would not mind where for there is no good Done at Gibraltar I am sure.'[143] He wrote to Sophy about family affairs – hinting that Lord Byron's obsessive, fruitless dispute over the Newstead lakes would be dropped as soon as he inherited – and the hardships of army life. 'I have not had my health so well lately as I had owing to the hard duty that we have', he informed her, 'for we have only four Subalterns so that I don't go to bed for 3 & 4 nights in a week.'[144] He frustrated his guardians with continued spending, but wrote apologetically that supplies were twice as expensive abroad. Months drudged on, the war finally reached them and his wish was granted: his regiment was dispatched to the south of France and embroiled in a disastrous siege at Toulon. It was the first notable wartime victory of a junior general named Napoleon Bonaparte. William John – by now a lieutenant – awaited new orders.

From Toulon he was hauled to Corsica, which the combined forces of General Stuart on land and Captain Horatio Nelson at sea intended to liberate from the French. Setting up camp on a ridge of mountains bearing down on the final French-held fortress at Calvi, they prepared for a siege. It was suffocatingly hot – the official report of soldiers dragging cannons up the mountains 'with cheerfulness' masked the true picture of men collapsing under the heat, exhaustion and malaria. With the batteries in place the bombardment began – the fire was vigorously returned (with one shot depriving Captain Nelson of the sight in his right eye) – and the crucial Fort Mozello was taken. Victory! But it was here on the evening of 30 July 1794, weeks into the siege, that William John Byron lived his final moments – a French cannon was fired and the promise of his young life was reduced to rubble and blood. As his body lay somewhere in the mountains above Calvi, the night glowed with British shells firing 'incessantly the whole night' and Nelson recorded the day's deaths in his journal: 'Lieut. Byron 18th Regt., Ensign Boogus 51st Regt., killed.'[145]

'It is with sincere concern I have to inform you of the death of our Friend Mr Byron announced to me by a Letter from the Major of the Regiment,' Charles Gould notified Sophy when the news reached England. 'It is some little satisfaction to learn, that he died honorably in the discharge of his duty, and that he did not suffer much, having been killed by a Cannon Ball.'[146] It was a minor engagement in a vast war, but with a single shot the future of the

Byron dynasty was driven violently onto a new path. William's family line was extinguished.

The consequences of the young man's death cut across the family. In the absence of a will his '*Papa*' laid claim to his stepson's shares, annuities and properties, 'ready Money & Wearing Apparel & personal Articles' and 'Arrears of Pay and Prize money' on behalf of his young son, Robert John Wilmot.[147] (There *was* a sum of prize money – a little under two pounds.) Whether or not his grandfather felt any regret over the countless unanswered letters, he quickly consoled himself with the idea of how he would benefit from the tragedy. With William's direct line of heirs eliminated, surely the power of rights over his estates would revert back to him? As absolute owner rather than 'life tenant' of his estates, he would be free to remortgage or sell them – the Abbey would surely raise a considerable sum – pay his debts, and retire to his Hampstead villa in tolerable comfort. His legal advisor seems to have agreed (perhaps in part because he was amassing a considerable bill for his own services – William had initiated yet another lawsuit). Even the extinction of his family line could be weighed against its potential monetary benefit. Entirely uninterested, William did not trouble himself to trace the line of inheritance, which would now fall to the admiral's male heir.

Reports of varying accuracy crept up to Scotland, but no one felt obliged to actually inform Catherine. 'I should have supposed you would have wrote before now to have enquired after your Newphew [sic]', she hinted to Fanny in November, 'he is a fine Boy and very well and walks and runs as well as any other child'.[148] 'Pray write', she urged, 'I hear Mrs Parker is dead and that your Newphew [sic] Ld Byron's grandson is dead but I have not been informed of it from any of the family.'[149] Confirmation eventually came: her boy was now heir to the Byron barony.

Illustrious title aside, the extent of the inheritance remained to be seen. Fanny suspected that William would 'dispose of the estates that are left, if he can'.[150] By early December Catherine's anger subsided as a new idea dawned – surely his lordship would take an interest in them? 'You know Lord Byron', she wrote with pitiable optimism to her sister-in-law, 'Do you think he will do anything for George, or be at any expense to give him a proper education; or, if he wish to do it, is his present fortune such a one that he could spare anything out of it?'[151] Her hopes were quickly quashed.

'the Youngest, Handsomest & Wittiest Widow in England'

There was, pottering about a genteel house in the shadows of Bath's most fashionable quarter, a reclusive Dowager Countess who might have been inclined to help them – she had nurtured a soft spot for Jack, after all. Isabella had taken a house in Marlborough Buildings, on a gentle slope adjacent to the illustrious Royal Crescent and surrounded by parks. It was serene: a slim, pale stone building with a stream bubbling at the end of the garden. Her society had dwindled to corresponding with her children and occasional visits from old friends who would not lose too much from the association.

New faces hovered before her as old ones gradually disappeared. Her long-serving maid Jane – who had trailed obediently after her during the Weinheim years – was dead. Her brothers John and George were long gone, along with her sisters-in-law Elizabeth and Sophia. Her nieces and nephews were wasted by illness and war. Her dear friend Mrs Howard of Corby, who had kept her spirits afloat in Europe, died in Bath in the spring of 1794. Death followed on death. In France, thousands had been executed, including both king and despised queen. Another familiar name in the long roll of the revolution's victims – John's old nemesis the Comte d'Estaing, condemned for defending his queen. (His reported final words were, 'After my head falls off, send it to the British, they will pay a good deal for it!') Isabella's own days drew on with a relentless, incurable stillness.

She dressed neatly and without ornament, busying herself in pastimes suitable for a lady in her seventies. Hours tending the small garden, nursing flowers, ferns and shrubs – a faltering echo of her mastery of the grounds at Castle Howard. She tried to make little excursions, but struggled with increasingly troublesome swellings in her ankles and eventually required a special step to clamber into carriages. She may have taken her own advice about atoning for youthful vanities by spending one's latter years sewing clothes for the poor – certainly she embarked on continual needlework projects, 'for which my Eyes with too little help from spectacles, hold out surprisingly,' she told her daughter-in-law, 'tho I cannot say so much for my writing, as y[ou]r La[dyshi]p may see by my Lines'.[152] (She was being hard on herself – her handwriting was as hurried and illegible as it ever was.)

Her distinction as a modest light of the female literary world persisted, as her book was swiftly republished in Dublin, excerpted in American anthologies and translated into German. Her reply to Mrs Greville's ode to indifference continued to appear in poetry collections, and had she picked up the *Gentleman's Magazine* in early 1794 she would have been gratified to find her name alongside renowned bluestockings as a rumoured contributor to a new edition of Shakespeare undertaken 'entirely by ladies'.[153] If she ever heard from Weinheim, no evidence of it survives.

A letter from Julia. A call from Frederick. Looking at her children she felt the familiar pangs of lost youth. Even *they* were greying – their chins sagging, their eyes creasing – as they approached their fifties. Forty-six-year-old Betty showed some of her mother's spirit by taking as her second husband twenty-three-year-old navy captain Charles Garnier, her daughter-in-law's brother. 'The late Mr Delme's son married Miss Garnier,' joked the newspapers, 'and young Mr Garnier, to return the compliment paid to his sister, has now married the young gentleman's mother.'[154]

The flowers in Isabella's garden bloomed and died. Her thoughts turned to the end of her own long journey, and she folded into the bleak embrace of the inevitability she found there. 'By beginning early to permit the intrusion of the subject of mortality, some few moments in each day,' she had observed in her *Maxims*, 'you will meet death with more serenity.' Her little brothers, her nieces and nephews, her dearest friends – gone. One of her old poems, 'Melancholy and Pity', meditated on her fall from grace:

> . . . *Fairest and happiest of my Race I liv'd*
> *Guiltless myself suspecting none of Guile*
> *And surest when I was the most deceiv'd*
> *I fear'd no Frowns whene'er I saw a smile*

While thus my stealing Hours did sweetly run
Foul Calumny aproach'd in Friendships guise
I nurs'd the Traitor till I was undone
At once was wretched and at once was wise

What tho condemn'd the Author of the deed
Still is the arrow rankling in my heart
The wounds of Calumny will ever bleed
And each new Object will fresh pain impart

Then let me skreened be from mortal View
Wear out that life of which I'm weary grown
Go gentle Pity to the happy few
Go tell my fate, and warn them of their own.[155]

The winter of 1794 was severe, blanketing the north with snow and driving the populace to their firesides or stores of liquor. '*Let your conduct be such to all around you, as shall lead them to the same path without affright.*' All year news had rolled in of French victories, and it was reported that guillotines were being set up as the enemy army marched through the Netherlands. 'So great a gloom never prevailed over the city as at this time', cried the London newspapers.[156]

It was of this world – gripped with a cold, nervous quiet – that seventy-three-year-old Isabella took her leave. Though her life had been motivated above all else by the pursuit of passion, she had never been able to hold on to the enduring, unshakable love she desperately craved. No matter now: '*A continued and humble resignation will secure your peace in that most aweful of moments – that of your dissolution.*' She had once written of Shakespeare's fairy king, whom mortals implored 'to light some flames, and some revive, to keep some others just alive' – on 22 January 1795, in her home on the edges of respectability, her own flickered and died.

Her demise elicited no fanfare, going unreported for two weeks and then inspiring just one line: 'Lately died at her house in Marlborough-buildings, the Right Hon. Countess Dowager of Carlisle.'[157] She had not made a will – perhaps she saw little point, having nothing to dispose. There is no record of whether her children attended the funeral at All Saints' church, overlooking the

pretty village of Weston near Bath, on Saturday, 31 January. (The
fact that Frederick and his wife were distributing donations to the
poor around Castle Howard in the same week suggests that they
did not.) She might have lamented that the simple inscription on
her grave added to her age by a year: ISABELLA COUNTESS
DOWAGER OF CARLISLE WHO WAS BORN 1720 DIED AT BATH
JANUARY 1795.

On hearing of the death of the woman he once loved, Sir William
Musgrave made a note at the end of his meticulously preserved
correspondence with the Howards, adding, 'I relinquished all claim
to the administration of her effects in favour of her family'.[158] Five
years later she featured in his immense collection of biographies –
eventually published as *Obituary prior to 1800* – reducing her spirited
existence to a name and a cluster of dates. He would outlive her
by just five years.

Isabella's death reduced the Byron siblings to the two whose lives
were most at odds: seventy-two-year-old William, desperate and
dissolute, and the pious seventy-year-old Richard, who boasted both
a family and a devoted flock. Their needy sister-in-law Frances in
Nottingham lost another son (and they a nephew) in nineteen-
year-old Francis – 'an amiable young man, very clever in painting',
one neighbour grieved in her diary.[159] In the spring of 1795 Richard
was appointed rector at Haughton-le-Skerne, near Darlington – he
and his wife Mary would settle here for his remaining sixteen years.
From here they kept an eye on news of the war: their eldest, Richard,
was securely settled in the navy thanks to the patronage of his relatives. A recent report from the rear admiral aboard the *Impregnable*
gave ample cause for pride: 'he is an extraordinary fine young man:
in the late action he was on the Quarter deck with me, when I
observed he was cool and clear, much the Officer, knowing well
what he was about.'[160] '[H]e has ever approv'd himself to me a most
dutiful Son, to his Commanders a brave & diligent Officer,' Richard
wrote fondly, revealing a paternal affection never observed in his
brother William, '& has conducted himself so in private life as to
gain ye general esteem of his acquaintance.'[161] His two younger sons
had been respectably dispatched to Cambridge.

As ever, William was too wrapped up in his own petty business to pay heed to national or family events. As Fanny suspected, he was eager to totally dismantle and dispose of the Byron estates, and began selling off parcels of the Rochdale lands. His rush of optimism did not last long. In June 1796 a letter arrived from his lawyers with news about Newstead: 'Sorry to inform you that Mr Houson is of opinion that Lord Byron has only an Estate for Life in him in Consequence of the Recovery he suffered with his son who had the Reversion in him and on the Sons Death the Reversion went to his right Heir.'[162] According to the resettlement of 1773, he did not have the right to sell. Seeking a second opinion, he descended on the London office of solicitor John Hanson and pleaded that surely this negligence – the fault of his former lawyers, naturally – would not be binding. He was no longer ruled by anger, but desperation; one of Hanson's assistants observed this '*eccentric* fifth Lord Byron' returning day after day, 'under the most painful and pitiable load of distress'.[163] 'I must confess that I felt for him exceedingly', he recalled, 'but his case was past remedy, and, after some daily attendance, pouring forth his lamentations, he appears to have returned home to subside into the reckless operations reported of him.' The law was clear. Defeated, William retreated to Nottinghamshire with little to do but await the end.

With these two elderly brothers confined to their rural outposts by duty and despair respectively, the younger generation awaited news of their military men. The Plymouth sisters were 'very anxious for the return' of Augusta's husband, now Admiral Parker, and worried about the ill luck of the Byron name extending to their cousin Richard.[164] Betty was widowed a second time when her young Captain Garnier was drowned in an accident while attempting to board his ship. Feeling 'much affect'd' on her cousin's behalf, Sophy wrote that she 'thought him very amiable and he was universally liked'.

The children were being raised in a fearful world. Sophy, who had recently turned forty, was immersed in the business of bringing up her orphaned nieces and nephew. (It always puzzled Augusta that she – 'so much better than I am, and so handsome, and so good, and so clever' – was the only sister who remained unmarried.)[165] She sent for sugar and mustard, and tea from Sykes's neighbour Mr Twining. She fretted over a speck she noticed on George Anson junior's eye, and the expenses piled up: a 'Boys Fine Hatt', haircuts, night caps, new shoes every few months, suits that were altered as the boy grew.[166] Prayer books, a writing master and a copy of *Gay's Fables*. His two sisters wanted gingham gowns, handkerchiefs, dancing masters, harp repairs and carriages to school. Her affection for them, and the memory of their father, sustained her through difficult times: 'My heart sinks at the prospect of parting from these precious Children but it must be done', she sighed, as they were comfortably settled with more affluent guardians.[167] 'I imagine George is the happiest and the *naughtiest* boy in London', she smiled in the summer of 1795, 'I fear one of the most *spoilt* tho not quite so much as he was last year . . . I really miss him very much.'[168]

But while George Anson junior was showered with affection and support, his namesake cousin from Aberdeen was not. George Byron Gordon (as he was called before his paternal inheritance outranked that of his mother) remained an outsider, thanks partly to the geographical distance, but also because his aunts had simply not warmed to his mother. Life went on. He was enrolled at Aberdeen Grammar School, chastised neighbours for mentioning his limp and was branded 'that little deevil, Geordie Byron'. Catherine impatiently awaited news of the old man at Newstead, increasingly convinced that Fanny hadn't been truthful about Jack's will. Their relationship, forged and forfeited through correspondence, had broken down entirely. 'I am very much surprized she can say my poor Brother's Debts were triffling, when she knows he was obliged to leave her in consequence of them,' Fanny scoffed, '& I have now Letters of her's to him by me in which she says he may die in a Prison for she will never help him, my Brother in *Debt* several thousand Pounds.'[169] Fortunately, despite Fanny's indifference, Catherine and little George's lives were about to be transformed.

'A sad charicter in everything'

At Newstead, the old lord confined himself to the few furnished rooms and barked orders at his small band of remaining servants. His long career of scheming had left him almost friendless – those who did visit were obliged either by blood ties or by the money they were owed. His nephew John came 'over to dine with Lord Byron every Sunday, when in the Country', and niece Fanny Leigh occasionally arrived on legal business.[170] His solicitor Robert Aisley continued to advise on his string of petulant legal battles. William kept agitating disputes about people supposedly stealing the coal from his lands in Lancashire, and as late as summer 1797 he informed his legal representatives to expect his presence in London, still unwilling to accept the verdict about Newstead.

He clung stubbornly to the wreckage of his former life. The tatty, powdered wig for which he continued to pay his taxes. The lingering rituals of the fine dining he could no longer afford. 'His Lordship always dined quite alone', ran one of Joe Murray's stories,

> & for some years one & the same Bottle of Claret was kept by me by his Lordship's order the cork drawn whenever the Cloth was removed. His Lordship cried aloud – "Joe" ["]Joe put the Claret on the Table[".] His orders were always given in the same Tone of command and always obeyed[.] The Claret was daily removed and re-ordered and reappeared on each successive Day but was never touched.[171]

Unlike his father, who had worked tirelessly to consolidate the Byron legacy in his final years, William betrayed no hint of concern for its future. Unable to benefit from the estate himself, he made no effort to discover where it would fall after his death. According to Catherine's agents, he 'seemed ignorant' of the relationship between himself and his heir. He simply did not care.

A veil of myth was already settling over this picture of an entitled, selfish and isolated man. An account based on Joe's stories later described William 'shutting himself up' at the Abbey, 'where he studiously avoided seeing or being seen by every one for some years'.[172] It was whispered that he had intentionally laid waste to his estate in revenge for his son's elopement. Other legends would follow: that he dined with a pair of loaded pistols on the table; that the dilapidated Abbey hummed with a swarm of crickets, and that William took pleasure from allowing them to crawl and 'race' all over his skin. In the gardens, his two grimacing 'devils' invited fear and suspicion. As William retreated from the public eye, the popular imagination transformed him into an unhinged old aristocrat, hell-bent on destruction. *Why do you slight me?*

At the dawn of another year – 1798 – William lay weakly in the eye of a storm of administration. He did not go swiftly – his final weeks were long and arduous. A network of spies was poised at the gates of the Abbey – in the surrounding neighbourhood – in the city – ready to rush news to Scotland and to John Hanson, who was enlisted to represent Catherine's interests in England. In Nottingham, William's sister-in-law Frances, who had always considered the Abbey her 'favourite' and a 'sweet place', was approached for information.[173] By the end of March, William was 'in a state nearly approaching his dissolution' but had not called on his apothecary – perhaps temporarily content to drift into oblivion or simply refusing to face the reality of it.[174] 'I understand that he had not any medical attendance as he was not now taking any medicine', wrote one of Catherine's informants.[175]

By mid April locals babbled at anyone who enquired that 'Ld. B. was so ill that they did not expect him to survive a single day' and a physician was finally called over from Mansfield.[176] The Reverend Richard hastened down from the north to the Hut tavern, overlooking the estate, and sent for a servant from the Abbey. He was not looking to offer any spiritual guidance or fraternal forgiveness. Having only returned to his childhood home 'in consequence of having heard of his bro.rs death', he left as soon as he was informed that William was still alive. '[H]e never went to the Abbey nor sent to know if it wou'd be agreeable to his Lordship to see him,' came one report, as 'they had a misunderstanding some years since & had never spoken to each other since'.[177] Even now he could not overcome his aversion to his only surviving sibling.

If William called for his chaplain or took any consolation from his faith, as John and Isabella had in their most hopeless moments, it passed by unrecorded. Neither could a man with his history have found much solace in his sister's *Maxims*, in which she counselled that when facing death 'the recollection of having contributed to mitigate the sufferings of others, will soften your own'. He had driven so many people away. Finally, at around one o'clock in the morning of Monday, 21 May 1798 he took his last breath – in the same mansion where he had drawn his first seventy-five years earlier – and was enveloped in the darkness of Newstead.

The news was flying across the country by breakfast. Hearing there were 'only a Housekeeper & servants there', Catherine's legal team swooped in to seal everything up.[178] There were few to mourn the old lord, though a subsequent legend attested that at his death the resident swarm of crickets took flight and left the Abbey in a black cloud, never to return. With no hint of the encomiums lavished upon his brother John, the obituaries reduced William's life to two things: the death of Mr Chaworth in a dimly lit tavern duel, and the wasting of the once beautiful Abbey. The *Gentleman's Magazine* lamented only that he had 'completely dismantled his noble mansion at Newsted, and sold the family pictures' on 'some family difference with his son, since dead'.[179] Others simply stated that he would be succeeded by 'his great nephew, (Grandson of the Admiral Byron,) now George Lord Byron, a minor'.[180] In Aberdeen, the ten-year-old boy was called into his schoolmaster's room, offered some cake and wine and informed that he was a peer of the realm.

Inevitably, the title was not – alas – attended with a ready fortune. William's effects – the debris of a dissipated life – were valued at under £599. 'I am apprehensive we shall have to bury the poor Lord ourselves after all', Hanson worried, expecting the sum to fall short of legal expenses and the funeral.[181] While Newstead and Hampstead were emptied of possessions, Catherine requested that all servants – 'except a man called James [*sic*] Murray' – be dismissed as soon after the burial as decency permitted.[182] (Perhaps Hanson had put in a good word for Joe, knowing his familiarity with Newstead affairs.) In the end, Catherine may not have funded William's funeral, but she did foot the bill for his servants' mourning clothes and the journey from Scotland. With the executor Aisley holding up the proceeds – anxious to secure his own fees, he gave Hanson a 'woeful time' – William, 5th Lord Byron was not buried until 16 June, almost a month after his death. It is unlikely that his final journey to the Byron family vault in Hucknall church attracted much notice, though Hanson did remark that the service 'went off very well'.[183] He brought Mrs Hanson to Newstead and awaited the arrival of the boy from Aberdeen.

*Engraving of the West Front and courtyard of
Newstead Abbey by John Coney, c.1823.*

On a day in August the coach rattled into the courtyard, wound around a curious-looking stone fountain and came to a stop before a sweeping stone staircase. The three travellers – Catherine, little George and nursemaid May – stretched their limbs as they stepped out to survey the building looming over them. They were met by Mr Hanson and introduced to Joe Murray, the only remaining servant, and took a tour of the house and grounds. The glittering lake. The Great Dining Hall. The woodland shrouding two statues with cloven hooves. A forlorn chapel shedding its dull, peeling paint. Newstead's ghosts gathered around them.

The newcomers made their best efforts to integrate into Nottinghamshire society, though their habits and manners were decidedly 'northern'. They took tea and sandwiches with local families and joined George's great-aunt Frances on an excursion to a bowling alley. The marketplace fluttered with flags and blue ribbons to celebrate a recent victory of Captain Horatio Nelson.

They grew close to the Hansons – the solicitor's son noticed that the pain of George's foot threw him into reading, and regularly found him 'quite lost in his Books' until the early hours.[184] 'There could not be a nicer looking Lad than Lord B was at this Time', he later recalled. Surely his father's family would not ignore him now?

Here, suddenly – cocooned in black – were cousins, second cousins, and a triumvirate of aunts in Mrs Leigh, Mrs Parker and Miss Byron. Sophy's affection for her nieces and nephews swiftly extended to George, who later dubbed her 'our aunt the amiable antiquated Sophia' and appreciated her share of the Byrons' 'turn for ridicule'.[185] His aunt Augusta, apparently in the area, had the honour of receiving George's first letter, written at Newstead on 8 November 1798: 'Dear Madam,—My Mamma being unable to write herself desires I will let you know that the potatoes are now ready and you are welcome to them whenever you please.' He concluded this noble missive with 'I am, Dear Aunt, yours sincerely, Byron', and the postscript: 'I hope you will excuse all blunders as it is the first letter I ever wrote'.[186] Fanny made no attempt to overcome her well-established aversion to Catherine and disappeared to Kent.

Fifty-year-old Frederick, on whose charity old Mrs Frances Byron and Jack's daughter Augusta had long depended, was soon petitioned for further assistance: he duly supported a pension of £300 for Catherine, agreed to stand as a legal guardian to George and suggested a London physician to treat his foot. Fifteen-year-old Augusta herself had been endlessly passed between the Osborne and Howard families, and though seeming amiable and happy her half-sister Mary Osborne called her 'shy to a degree beyond all shyness I ever saw before'.[187] She had however grown very pretty – perhaps unsurprising considering her famously attractive parents – and resembled Lady Betty: 'not so regularly handsome, but with much expression and a better figure'.

As the new generation prepared to make their mark on the world, their predecessors felt the spasms of advancing age. The elder generation had been all but swept away. Since those distant November days that had brought Isabella, William and John into the world, the face of the country had been transformed. The Hanoverian royal house had surmounted the Jacobite threat, and a popular king boasted the prospect of seven sons to continue his dynasty. The march of science had supposedly driven superstition out of the world (though Hester was unconvinced: 'no such Thing, 'tis only driven out of Books & Talk').[188] Britain's colonial grasp had been expanded by treaty, by exploration and by force – in the West Indies, in India, in the Pacific – but the great prize of America had been lost; Britain had begun transporting its convicts to a new penal colony in Australia instead. Some within the government questioned the brutal reality that propped up the budding enterprise of empire – a gentle clamour opposing the slave trade was beginning to make itself heard. Elsewhere, a sweeping revolutionary spirit had brought new upheaval and war to Europe, and in literature a new collection of 'experimental' poems, *Lyrical Ballads*, would usher in a new – 'Romantic' – era.

Over the course of a generation the Byrons' fall from grace had been steep and irredeemable. The siblings had weathered some of the most turbulent moments of British history and – in the end – sank under their weight. The comforts they had once enjoyed were gone – melodies drifting from their mother's harpsichord, the smell of sumptuous dinners, the sight of ships preparing for mock battle. This man a champion, this man a rogue. The doomed romantic, the childless mother, the suffering navy wife. Their legacies and their voices lingered in print – a passion-stirring poem, a sensational court case, an incredible tale of survival – and a glimmer of hope for the future of the dynasty rested in John's two grandsons, the 'crockit deevil' George and the ever-cheerful George Anson junior. But there had been no lasting blaze of glory, and the feeling of being hounded by a malevolent force bled down the generations.

'There is a Planet overrules some Familys & blasts every Prospect,' Isabella had lamented, viewing her world through lightning and thunder. 'There is some Misfortune cast on our family,' Jack had groaned as he hid from his creditors at Valenciennes two decades later.

Another generation on and the poet would sit at Newstead – distraught, bereaved – and scrawl, 'Some curse hangs over me and mine'.[189] He embraced the aesthetic of decline; to him, the place was all the livelier for its crowding ghosts and gothics. Following decades of scandal, sorrow and triumph, the fall of the House of Byron had given rise to its most notorious figure: George would be a hero and a villain, at once the privileged elite and an outrageous radical. His inheritance was a picture of perfect desolation, and he was 'the wreck of the line that have held it in sway'. 'Newstead', he will declare, 'has always suited me better than any other.'[190]

Epilogue: The Cloisters

> Shades of heroes, farewell! your descendant departing
> From the seat of his ancestors, bids you adieu!
> Abroad, or at home, your remembrance imparting
> New courage, he'll think upon glory and you.
>
> *On Leaving Newstead Abbey*

March 1816

It is late morning on a Sunday and Joe Murray is pottering about his rooms at the Abbey. Winter is loosening its grip, but today has been cold and it looks likely to rain. Now in his eighties, his health has begun to deteriorate. Two autumns ago, his lordship's publisher Mr Murray had described him as a 'good-looking and respectable old man of about sixty-five years', but now he seems an almost ancient being.[1] When the cheerful young Captain G. A. Byron visited six months since, he left believing that 'Old Joe's days are *nearly* over'.[2] He is, admittedly, not as nimble as he used to be. He wears a medical truss to relieve abdominal pain and is beginning to feel, as he puts it, 'very Poorley'. His advancing age – and his tendency to alleviate his array of ailments with swigs of port from the wine cellar – is leaving him increasingly unsteady on his feet. But now – something else.

Suddenly, just after midday, a deep rumbling sound stirs beneath him and – to his horror – the ground itself undulates almost like water for a few moments. As the whole fabric of the building is sent into a 'Shake and a Totter' he shuffles in a panic from his room, hearing a tremendous crashing sound as if 'all the Roof and the

Ceiling of the long Dining Room' was threatening to give way. He looks about him fearfully as the bones of the Abbey's other remaining residents are rattled in their stone chambers. 'The shock so Terrified me', he writes in the account he immediately sends to his lordship, 'that I thought the next moment of being Buried alive in the Ruins of my poor Old Newstead.'[3]

Since the death of the old lord in 1798 he has been well looked after by the family. Thanks to Miss Augusta he was dispatched first into the service of her half-brother the Duke of Leeds, and then brought back to Newstead at the head of the young lord's household when he took up residence in 1808. 'Old Joe' has proved his worth, answering Hanson's endless questions about the family's history. Did the 4th Lord leave issue by his former wives? Who are the children in the picture hanging in the Dining Room? Did they marry, and where are they buried? He has dealt with servants found cavorting in brothels and overseen another search of the cloisters (which turned up nothing but decayed skeletons). When his lordship's funds were low and a short-lived notice of sale was tacked onto the Abbey door, though Joe was too law-abiding to tear it down he was sufficiently moved by his devotion to 'the ancient honour of the Byrons' to defiantly paste a piece of brown paper over it.

He still gives enthusiastic tours to curious visitors, who have dubbed him an 'aged Cicerone' and the house itself 'literally a mansion for the dead'. He fills his letters to his master with gratitude and prayers, signing off, 'Your Lordships Most faithfull and Obedient Servt at Command till Death Joseph Murray'.[4] The poet reciprocates the old man's fondness, describing him as 'a Rock' who 'will probably outlast some six Lords Byron'.[5] 'Joe has been getting well of a disease that would have killed a troop of horse', he had marvelled to his sister in 1811.[6] The poet has even requested to be buried with the old man and his beloved dog Boatswain at the Abbey, when the time comes. (When confronted with the idea, Joe reportedly mused, 'if I was sure his Lordship would come here, I should like it well enough, but I should not like to lie alone with the dog'.)

In London, the poet picks up Joe's latest letter and reads his 'earthquake epistle' with amusement:

It happened during divine service, and the shock was so great at Mansfield that the Parson left his Pulpit as fast as he could, the Congregation all frighten'd to allmost Death Expecting the Church Every Moment Tumbling about their Ears and Burying them alive, some got out of the Windows as fast as they Could, a many slitely hurt by trying to get out of Church first.[7]

There is some consolation in the idea that if it was an act of divine vengeance it was not directed at his ancestral seat alone. He has not been to Newstead for eighteen months, when he wrote those insincere lines of love to Miss Milbanke and carved his name with his sister's into a tree in Devil's Wood. He will never see the Abbey or Joe Murray again; escaping the wrath of both his wife and the unforgiving public, he is preparing to leave the country. On 25 April 1816, just a few weeks after the earthquake, he leaves England for the final time. His past trails inescapably behind him.

Following his first tour of Newstead in the summer of 1798, George took up his ancient family name with relish. His future had seemed bright. 'There is no young Nobleman in England of greater promise than Lord BYRON,' declared the *Morning Post* when he was just twelve, 'who is now prosecuting his studies with a private tutor, preparatory to his going to a public school.'[8] Lively careers at Harrow School and Cambridge University awaited, but he soon exhibited his ancestors' talent for turbulent living. Unfortunately, as Catherine finally gave up her long struggle to be accepted by her in-laws, the disputes between mother and son became increasingly spectacular. She saw Byron blood in him, and resented it. 'My whole family from the conquest are upbraided,' he complained to his half-sister, who was then staying at Castle Howard, 'myself abused, and I told that what little accomplishments I possess either in mind or body are derived from her and *her alone*.'[9] Catherine had grown bitter. Jack's daughter Augusta had been welcomed into the Carlisle family, and George Anson's three orphans secured a pension and raised under Sophy's care. Why was *her* son any different? 'That Boy will be the death of me & drive me mad,' she complained to Hanson.[10]

Of the elder generation of Byrons – raised amid talk of Jacobites and highwayman Dick Turpin, and the solemn music of Henry Purcell – only two remained. First, the Reverend Richard in his rectory at distant Haughton, who despite having had some friendly contact with Jack remained a total stranger to his great-nephew. (He long outlived his siblings, dying at the grand age of eighty-seven on Gunpowder Treason Day 1811, and was honoured at his church with a memorial stone and hatchment displaying the Byron coat of arms.) Second, and infinitely more helpful, was his sister-in-law Mrs Frances Byron – the widow of his youngest brother George – who still lived in pinched circumstances in Nottingham. To Catherine and young George she offered friendship, a place to stay, the occasional loan and much unsolicited advice, but the little lord was not overly impressed. His nurse May Gray later claimed that this ancient great-aunt inspired one of his earliest (and most decidedly uncomplimentary) verses:

> *In Nottingham county there lives at Swine Green,*
> *As curst an old Lady as ever was seen;*
> *And when she does die, which I hope will be soon,*
> *She firmly believes she will go to the Moon!*

Despite his half-sister's reassurances, his father's illustrious Carlisle cousins were an intimidatingly distant, dusty old brood. Though Frederick had agreed to stand as George's nominal guardian and their relationship began on a friendly footing, it faltered when he declined to assist his young charge in proving his noble lineage in order to take his seat in the House of Lords in 1808. Thankfully, a special inquiry, during which Hanson dispatched a man to hunt around graveyards and parish registers, and interrogate employees and neighbours, eventually turned up sufficient evidence. An elderly Cornish woman who had cooked for John and Sophia's wedding at Caerhays testified that she had seen them coming from the church. The court was presented with an old windowpane from Newstead Abbey, on which had been painstakingly etched the names and dates of the five siblings born there almost a century earlier. ISABELLA, WILLIAM, JOHN, RICHARD, CHARLES. 'Lord Carlisle has used me so infamously & refused to state any particular of my family to the Chancellor,' the poet complained to his mother. 'I have *lashed* him in my *rhymes*, and perhaps his Lordship may regret not being more conciliatory.'[11] Critics of Frederick – who now glitteringly presided over silent dinners – certainly thought he had grown haughty in his old age. (His rouge- and gem-covered youngest sister Julia was, at least, credited with rejecting 'a languid yellow old age' for one 'active, smart, burnished and braced'.[12] Having never married, she lived to the remarkable age of ninety-nine.)

He did form more affectionate ties with the vestiges of the Plymouth set, keeping up some correspondence with his aunt Sophy and befriending a number of his cousins. He later declared that it was an infatuation with his cousin Margaret Parker – a daughter of his aunt Augusta – that inspired his 'first dash into poetry', and struck up an early friendship with his nautical younger cousin (and eventual heir), George Anson junior. 'I think the name of *Byron* is not unknown to the World,' this young ally wrote to George in January 1812, hoping to replicate the glory achieved by his father and grandfather in the navy.[13] Just weeks later, the poet awoke to find himself famous after the publication of his third book, *Childe Harold's Pilgrimage*.

It was his relationship with his half-sister, Augusta Mary, that would be the defining attachment of his life. First meeting in 1803 and becoming close a decade later, they bonded over their shared ancestry, their tendency to social awkwardness, and their ability to make each other laugh. They were protective of their ancestors and especially of their father – in their dealings with the dead it was easier to invent, to confuse, to forgive. 'Augusta and I have always loved the memory of our father', the poet wrote, 'as much as we have loved each other.'[14] 'I think we are *very* degenerate!' she gleefully declared to a friend, reflecting on the history of the Byrons, '& I have a passion for my Ancestors'.[15] Unknowingly mirroring their father's forbidden passion for his own sister, Fanny, they slipped into an incestuous affair. It would be their undoing. '*And loved each other as we should not love . . .*'[16]

His actual residence at the Abbey spanned just six years from 1808 to 1814, during which time his mother was frequently left holding the fort as he whisked himself off on extended trips abroad. But, drawing strength and character from its history, his attachment to the place was undimmed. 'Come what may, *Newstead* and I *stand* or fall together,' he wrote to his mother in March 1809, 'I have now lived on the spot, I have fixed my heart upon it, and no pressure present or future, shall induce me to barter the last vestige of our inheritance.' He finished, definitively, 'I feel like a man of honour, and I will not sell Newstead.'[17] It was a promise he would not be able to keep. Nonetheless, it was there that Catherine Gordon Byron died, still only in her forties, in 1811.

Once again a wolf dog prowled its time-worn rooms – George named his Lyon – and debauched revelries echoed through the halls (though his ancestors' grand soirees and replica battles were reduced to a few inebriated gentlemen clattering about dressed as monks, fencing and telling bawdy stories). He traced the ways in which his family's chequered history continued to impact on his fortunes. Finally relenting to the idea of finding a wife, he wrote flippantly to Augusta, 'Well, I must marry to repair the ravages of myself & my prodigal ancestry.'[18]

Just months after making this begrudging declaration, in March 1812, he met the mathematical Annabella Milbanke. Their marriage also united two families long tied in friendship – her grandmother was Isabella's beloved 'Lady M' from Halnaby and her father was an old friend of his aunt Sophy. On their engagement the latter wrote effusively to George that 'no one can wish you and Miss M: more real permanent felicity in your walk thru life than my stupid self'.[19] In 1815 came the birth of his only legitimate daughter, Ada – a name he claimed to have unearthed after 'hunting it out on hand & knees' from the Byron pedigree in the time of King John.[20]

Neither was he inclined to take full credit for his own personality, encouraging the idea that in his tempers he merely 'shewed some of the blood of my ancestors'. 'It is ridiculous to say' he continued, 'that we do not inherit our passions, as well as the gout, or any other disorder.'[21] He perpetually found ways to pay tribute to their memory. They repeatedly bled into his poetry and when he was swept up in the struggle for Greek independence – the campaign that eventually saw him contract and die of fever at the age of thirty-six – his plumed cavalry helmet carried the family crest and by now woefully doubtful motto *Crede Byron*. 'Trust in Byron'.

Though the poet took undeniable pleasure from the notorious

misdeeds of his family, he furiously objected when their ashes were unceremoniously raked up to provide evidence of the wickedness running through his own veins. In 1811, one journalist branded him 'the illegitimate descendant of a murderer' as well as 'the only son of a profligate father, and a mother whose days and nights are spent in the delirium of drunkenness'.[22] A French biographer of 1823 presented eccentricity as a family disease, portraying his great-uncle as a violent recluse and blaming Amelia's early death on Jack's 'vices' and 'brutality'.[23] George was incensed. 'He may say of me whatever of good or evil pleases him,' the poet wrote in a long letter critiquing the work point by point, 'but I desire that he should speak of my relations only as they deserve.'[24] His father was, he insisted, 'an extremely amiable and joyous character, but careless and dissipated.' 'I cannot bear to have him unjustly spoken of', he seethed, gesturing to Jack's service in America as proof of his military talents and pointing out that he could hardly have *forced* two heiresses into marriage. (Augusta struggled with accusations of the 'Hereditary Insanity' of the Byrons, and Jack's debaucheries in particular, long after the poet's death: 'I am *greatly* vexed at *all* the details of my Father', she complained about one new biography in 1830; 'I think to have said he was a wild & Extravagant gaming Man would have been *quite* sufficient as he died too early to have any influence on my Brother's Character'.)[25]

It was a losing battle. By the time the poet left Newstead for good the whole family was shrouded in legend. 'Collect together each virtue of the dead', Isabella had suggested in one of her less cheerful *Maxims*, 'and, when the remembrance of their faults will arise, think of your own.' But she and the rest of the Byrons, William especially, were afforded no such favours.

Isabella, whose life was ruled by a quest for passion and beauty, was swiftly reduced to a 'very extraordinary' eccentric with 'a fine taste for poetry' who – after shining for years at the heart of the beau monde – suddenly turned her back on society and lived in total solitude.[26] She might have felt a little vindicated had she known that she would be remembered as 'the author of some poetical perform-ances' and 'a lady of some celebrity' – her elegant writing finally rising above the voices of her critics.[27] But such dainty tributes hardly capture the headstrong and romantic spirit that propelled her through life, and she soon fell from popular memory entirely. In practical terms, her eighteenth-century purpose as wife and mother was not only fulfilled but flourishes to this day. Isabella's descendants retain the earldom of Carlisle, and though she could not pass on the Byron name her blood flows through the veins of much of the modern aristocracy – thanks largely to the impressive broods of both her son Frederick and her grandson George, the 6th Earl, whose daughters married into a network of noble houses including the Rutlands of Belvoir Castle, the Sutherlands of Dunrobin Castle and the Devonshires of Chatsworth House. Despite the years of waiting for a son, in the end her dynastic duty was performed to perfection.

William was maligned as a violent and desperate villain long before his own death – the notoriety of his eventual heir saw him posthumously immortalised in print as an irredeemable (and probably insane) murderer. Self-serving, entitled and embittered he certainly was – but the accusations that circulated in his lifetime had spawned an irresistible and enduring caricature. He terrorised his tenants; he tried to drown his wife; he shot a coachman and threw the corpse onto the terrified Lady Byron's lap; he punished his disobedient son by intentionally laying waste to his inheritance. Faring no better in death, he was branded 'a stern and desperate character, who is never mentioned by the neighbouring peasants without a significant shake of the head' and who had slipped into madness and self-imposed isolation at Newstead after the duel of 1765. His grand-nephew's brooding poetical hero was even said to have been inspired by his own 'dark haughty impetuous spirit and mad deeds'.[28] (He certainly featured in two poems of love to George's Nottinghamshire favourite Mary Chaworth, a great-niece of the man William killed at the Star and Garter: 'Oh let not our bosoms inherit their hate . . .')

It was claimed that the Byrons' loss of the Abbey had been written in the stars – that the sixteenth-century soothsayer Mother Shipton had prophesied its fall from the family if a ship laden with heather crossed over Sherwood Forest. (Rumour held that William's discontented tenants had spitefully run alongside his arriving Newstead flagship as it rattled overland on its wheels, 'heaping it with heather all the way'.)[29] By the 1830s William had become the 'Wicked Lord Byron' and subsequent publications named him the 'Mad Lord Byron' or 'Devil Byron', a dark and dangerous figure riding out wild-eyed into the night as an invented, disgraced sister pleaded with him for mercy.

Offering an appealing antithesis to William's villain was John's gallant but ill-starred hero — in British lore at least. His first post-humous biography, published in 1797, credited him with 'the universal and justly acquired reputation of a brave and excellent officer, but of a man extremely unfortunate'.[30] Having already earned the epithet 'Foul-Weather Jack' during his lifetime, he was immortalised in a poem of 1799 as 'Hardy Byron', who — even in the face of blood-thirsty hyenas and treacherous mermaids — never abandoned his faith and his hope: 'Pale, but intrepid, sad, but unsubdued'.[31] In the year his grandson rose to fame, the preface to a new edition of John's *Narrative* praised his lifelong modesty and described him as a man of 'the best talents, and the worthiest qualities' who was cruelly deprived of his deserved success. On his literary legacy — admittedly with some cause for bias — it declared, 'surely there never was an interesting tale more simply or more impressively told'.[32]

Elsewhere, his memory was not so revered. In particular, his wartime campaign at Chaleur Bay in the summer of 1760 — during which his men had burned the village of Acadian refugees seeking assistance from the French — saw him maligned in French-Canadian tradition as a callous destroyer, tearing even women and children from their homes. Eventually he found his own place in local legend: in retribution for this violent act, the 'great navigator' Byron was condemned to sail the seas on a ghost ship 'loaded with the bones of the destroyers of Petite-Rochelle', returning every seven years amid raging storms to the spot where his crimes were committed.[33]

The stark opposition between the two brothers was neatly mirrored in the next generation, with Jack as the cruel, wasteful heir and George Anson as the dashing navy hero. It was the poet's father who attracted the most venom of all, being allowed no redeeming qualities apart from the statement that he was 'one of the handsomest men of his time'.[34] He had certainly been labelled 'Mad Jack' Byron by the time of his son's death in 1824 — with the claim that he had earned it during his army days – and was the following year accused of settling his gambling debts by receiving payments for sex: 'he pursued his amours for the two-fold purpose of satisfying his passions and supplying his purse.'[35] In general he was described as 'one of whom everything that is evil is related'.[36] The trend persisted a generation on, with the poet's reputation for immorality contrasted by his cousin and heir George Anson junior's good-natured character and impressive career. 'He possesses that gay happy disposition, which will make him loved as soon as seen', gushed their aunt Sophy; 'May the Almighty preserve him thro' all the gales of life'.[37]

Old Joe's long service and lively tales had given rise to his status as 'ever a walking & living Legend of Newstead'.[38] He was happy to relive the deeds and misdeeds of the Byrons, perhaps feeling that in some small way he kept their glory days alive. He spoke of William as his 'dear late Lord' and could recount the histories of the generation that came before. Shuffling through empty rooms and gazing through grimy windows, he painted a picture of corridors guarded by gleaming suits of armour, deer bounding through woodlands and rooms filled with paintings of battle-scarred, weather-beaten Byrons. The poet had even commissioned local artist Thomas Barber to immortalise his favourite servant in oils: plump and rosy-cheeked, holding a pipe filled with tobacco. (It now hangs once again in what was the Great Gallery, watching over the Abbey more than two centuries later.) He showed off the poet's former study and his macabre skull cup, which had been fashioned from the remains of a monk unearthed by one of the gardeners.

Some visitors left exhilarated, others heartbroken. When the poet's estranged wife Annabella visited in May 1818, she made a passing mention of 'Old Murray' but was escorted around by a female servant. She felt an immediate affinity with the place, of which she should by rights have been mistress, and wrote in her diary of 'the sunshine – the blue lakes, the reappearing foliage of the remaining woods – the yellow gorse over the wild wastes'. 'In becoming familiarized with the scene I seemed to contemplate this portrait of a friend.'[39] She traced his footsteps and found herself rooted to the floor when she stepped into her husband's bedchamber. Her guide spoke with sorrow of his departure, and the fact that his Lady had never seen it. 'She, poor thing!' she lamented obliviously, 'is not likely to come there now'.

The indefatigable Old Joe remained a fixture of the Abbey even after the departure of the Byrons. When it was finally sold to Colonel Thomas Wildman – one of the poet's schoolmates from Harrow – in the autumn of 1817, the new owner generously offered to retain his place in the household. It was over sixty years since his dear old lord had hired him as a 'sailor boy' and set him to work on the lake. *Fire!*

Since then, each passing year had seen the house and the grounds transformed – for better, and then for worse – and his colourful stories and reminiscences had already provided the foundations for lasting myths about the family. *Joe! Joe, put the claret on the table!* But despite the poet's playful prediction that he would 'probably outlast some six Lords Byron', his shuffling eventually slowed and the air no longer filled with his bawdy songs – who was there to listen? He finally died in the autumn of 1820, well into his eighties, and was laid to rest in Papplewick churchyard on 5 September, reunited with his wife Anne and the infants they had lost some forty years earlier. The poet heard the news from his half-sister and considered it the end of an era for whatever family he had left.

'So – Joe Murray is gathered to his Masters', he replied from Ravenna, 'as you say, the very Ghosts have died with him. Newstead and he went almost together, and now the B's must carve them out another inheritance.'[40]

'Newstead Abbey'

George, 6th Lord Byron (1811)

In the dome of my Sires as the clear moonbeam falls
Through Silence and Shade o'er its desolate walls,
It shines from afar like the glories of old;
It gilds, but it warms not—'tis dazzling, but cold.

Let the Sunbeam be bright for the younger of days:
'Tis the light that should shine on a race that decays,
When the Stars are on high and the dews on the ground,
And the long shadow lingers the ruin around.

And the step that o'erechoes the gray floor of stone
Falls sullenly now, for 'tis only my own;
And sunk are the voices that sounded in mirth,
And empty the goblet, and dreary the hearth.

And vain was each effort to raise and recall
The brightness of old to illumine our Hall;
And vain was the hope to avert our decline,
And the fate of my fathers had faded to mine.

And theirs was the wealth and the fulness of Fame,
And mine to inherit too haughty a name;
And theirs were the times and the triumphs of yore,
And mine to regret, but renew them no more.

And Ruin is fixed on my tower and my wall,
Too hoary to fade, and too massy to fall;
It tells not of Time's or the tempest's decay,
But the wreck of the line that have held it in sway.

Acknowledgements

The seed of the idea for this book was planted late one night when I first stumbled across Thomas Gainsborough's beguiling portrait of Isabella, Lady Carlisle. Since then, tracing the story of the Byrons has taken me down a path I couldn't have navigated without the help of a quite frankly offensively large group of people. My thanks first to Donald Winchester for his help in shaping my enthusiasm into something coherent, and to Mark Richards at John Murray for seeing the potential in it. I am hugely grateful to Joe Zigmond and Caroline Westmore for guiding this labour of love into production and print; to the copy-editor Hilary Hammond and proofreader Morag Lyall for their constructive criticism and their keen eyes; to the rest of the team at John Murray for their help at every step; and to Kirsty McLachlan and the team at David Godwin Associates for helping to bring the book into the world.

My research would have been impossible without years of work by archivists and curators, and my thanks are due especially to those at Castle Howard, the John Murray Archive, the Bodleian Library, Alnwick Castle, the Pforzheimer Collection and Newstead Abbey, as well as to Peter Harrington Rare Books for allowing me access to their manuscript material for John Byron's early career. To Hugh Belsey, Matthew Brenckle, Simon Brown, Mike Chantler, Robin Eagles, Neil Jeffares, Charlotte May, Pete Smith and Kim Sloan, my grateful thanks for lending their expertise on art, poetry, politics, architecture and all things Byronic, and to Natalie Shaw for the wonderful new photography. I am tremendously envious of those connected to the people whose stories unravel in these pages, and my sincerest thanks go to the Earl of Lytton, to Philip Howard and to Robin, 13th Lord Byron for generously allowing access to their personal collections of papers and artworks. Quotations from the Lovelace Byron Papers on deposit at the Bodleian Library, University of Oxford, are reproduced by kind permission of Paper Lion Ltd and the Earl of Lytton. Quotations from the Castle Howard Collection are reproduced by kind permission of the Howard Family, and those from the Thrale-Piozzi papers at the John Rylands Library are reproduced courtesy of the University of Manchester.

I owe much to the wonderful community of historians and friends who have enjoyed and/or endured my company during the research and writing of this book. I am especially grateful for the unwavering patience and support of Tom Power, who has (involuntarily) learned more than he could ever have wished to know about the sex lives of people who died two hundred years ago. This is a book about family, and there are not words to express how much I owe to my own. To Derek and Gill Lynn, and to Bill, Sally and Tom Brand – my endless love and gratitude for years of encouragement, and for managing to avoid the sort of drama so effortlessly kicked up by the eighteenth-century Byrons.

Picture Credits

Images within the text

Chapter 1: *View of a Park with Deer* by William, 4th Lord Byron (Yale Center for British Art, Paul Mellon Collection/B2001.2.697).

Chapter 2: George Anne Bellamy (Alamy Stock Photo).

Chapter 3: *A Patagonian Woman and Boy in Company with Commodore Byron* (Author's collection).

Chapter 4: *Rest on the Flight into Egypt* by Isabella Howard, Countess of Carlisle (Courtesy of the Lewis Walpole Library, Yale University).

Chapter 5: Jack Byron and Lady Carmarthen, *Town and County Magazine*, February 1779 (Courtesy of the Lewis Walpole Library, Yale University).

Chapter 6: North Parade, Bath, *c.*1785 (Courtesy of the Lewis Walpole Library, Yale University).

Chapter 7: West Front and courtyard of Newstead Abbey, engraving by John Coney, *c.*1823 (Author's collection).

Inset

Page 1: William, 4th Lord Byron by Godfrey Kneller, *c.*1695 (Private collection). Frances, Lady Byron, hand-coloured engraving after William Hogarth, *c.*1736 (Author's collection). Richard Byron, self-portrait, *c.*1740 (Private collection).

Page 2: Elizabeth, Lady Byron, miniature attributed to Richard Cosway (By permission of Nottingham City Museums & Galleries). Newstead Abbey, attributed to John Wootton, *c.*1760 (Private collection). *Lord Byron's Household* by Peter Tillemans, 1726 (Private collection).

Page 3: Ticket for the trial of Lord Byron, 1765 (© The Trustees of the British Museum). 'Devil Byron' by William Harvey, printed in the *People's Journal*, January 1847 (Author's collection).

Page 4: Frontispiece to the second edition of John Byron's *Narrative*, 1768 (Wellcome Collection). Sophia Byron by William Hoare, likely around the time of her marriage in 1748 (Private collection).

Page 5: Captain John Byron, unknown artist after Joshua Reynolds, *c*.1759 (Private collection).

Page 6: Coloured engraving of Castle Howard, early nineteenth century (Author's collection). Isabella, Dowager Countess of Carlisle, by Thomas Gainsborough, 1760/1 (From the Castle Howard Collection, reproduced by kind permission of the Howard family).

Page 7: Sir William Musgrave, 6th Bt, mezzotint by John Raphael Smith, *c*.1763 (© National Portrait Gallery, London). Frederick, 5th Earl of Carlisle, by George Romney, *c*.1780 (Collection of the Museum of the Shenandoah Valley, Julian Wood Glass Jr Collection. Photo by Ron Blunt.). *Plan du Combat naval de la Grenade gagné par Mr le C[om]te D'Estaing . . .'*, *c*.1779 (Library of Congress Prints and Photographs Division, Washington, DC).

Page 8: Catherine Gordon Byron by Thomas Stewardson, early nineteenth century (By permission of Nottingham City Museums & Galleries). Joseph Murray by Thomas Barber, early nineteenth century (By permission of Nottingham City Museums & Galleries). Newstead Abbey by William West, mid nineteenth century (Alamy Stock Photo).

Notes

Abbreviations

BL	British Library
Byron collection	Byron family papers, Newstead Abbey
Byron papers	George Gordon Byron Collection, Harry Ransom Center, University of Texas
CH	Castle Howard Archives, Castle Howard, Yorkshire
Gloucester	Gloucestershire Archives, Gloucester
HMC	Historical Manuscripts Commission
John Murray	John Murray Archive, National Library of Scotland
L&J	Marchand, Leslie A. (ed.), *Byron's Letters and Journals* (13 volumes) (John Murray, 1973–94)
Lovelace Byron	Papers of the Noel, Byron and Lovelace families, Bodleian Library, University of Oxford
Morgan	Collection of autograph signed letters by Lord Byron, Lady Byron, family members and friends, The Morgan Library & Museum, New York
NA	Byron family, Barons Byron: Newstead, miscellaneous estate records, Nottinghamshire Archives
NMM	National Maritime Museum, Greenwich, London
Nottingham	Portland papers and Molyneux papers, University of Nottingham, Special Collections
Thrale-Piozzi	Thrale-Piozzi Manuscripts, John Rylands Library, University of Manchester Special Collections
TNA	The National Archives, London
Walpole	Lewis, W. S. (ed.), *The Yale Edition of Horace Walpole's Correspondence* (48 volumes) (Yale University Press, 1937–83)

Introduction

1 Hanson narrative, John Murray, MS.43537.

2 Joe Murray to George, 6th Lord Byron, March 1816, John Murray, MS.43513.

3 Catherine Gordon Byron to John Hanson, October 1803, quoted in Leslie A. Marchand, *Byron: A Portrait* (Futura, 1976), p. 27.

4 George, 6th Lord Byron to Lady Melbourne, 10 October 1813, L&J, vol. 3, p. 136.

5 Hanson narrative, John Murray, MS.43537.

6 John Hanson to James Farquhar, 30 August 1798, Byron papers, Box 7, folder 2.

7 Lucy Hutchinson, *Memoirs of the Life of Colonel Hutchinson* (1806; Cambridge University Press, 2010), p. 27.

8 Charles Skinner Matthews, 1809, quoted in R. Coope and P. Smith, *Newstead Abbey: A Nottinghamshire Country House: Its Owners and Architectural History, 1540–1931* (Thoroton Society Record Series, 2014), p. 95.

9 Charles Skinner Matthews, 1809, quoted in W. Irving, *Abbotsford, and Newstead Abbey* (1835), p. 118.

10 Catherine Gordon Byron to John Hanson, 1803, John Murray, MS.43410.

11 George, 6th Lord Byron [epigram of an old lady who had some curious notions respecting the soul] (1798).

12 George, 6th Lord Byron to Francis Hodgson, 14 November 1810, L&J, vol. 2, p. 27; George, 6th Lord Byron to Augusta Byron, 11 November 1804, ibid., vol. 1, p. 56.

13 Hanson narrative, John Murray, MS.43537.

14 Diary of Samuel Pepys, 26 April 1667, in R. Latham and W. Matthews (eds), *The Diary of Samuel Pepys* (University of California Press, 2000), vol. 8, p. 182.

15 The Earl of Shrewsbury to Sir John Byron, quoted in J. V. Beckett, *Byron and Newstead: The Aristocrat and the Abbey* (University of Delaware Press, 2001), p. 26.

16 Thomas Shipman to William, 3rd Lord Byron, 1677, in V. Walker and M. J. Howell, *The House of Byron: A History of the Family Since the Norman Conquest, 1066–1988* (Quiller Press, 1988), p. 113; *Town and Country Magazine . . . for the year 1773* (1774), p. 625.

17 Quoted in W. S. Lewis (ed.), *Notes by Lady Louisa Stuart on George*

Selwyn and His Contemporaries by John Heneage Jesse (Oxford University Press, 1928), p. 46.

18 George, 6th Lord Byron, 'Journal of Detached Thoughts, 1821–22', L&J, vol. 9, p. 40.

19 George, 6th Lord Byron to Catherine Byron, 6 March 1809, ibid., vol. 1, p. 195.

20 George, 6th Lord Byron, 'Lines Inscribed Upon a Cup Formed from a Skull' (1808).

21 *The Mirror of Literature, Amusement and Instruction*, no. 85, vol. 3 (1824), p. 340.

Chapter 1: The Courtyard

1 George, 6th Lord Byron to Augusta Leigh, 6 August 1805, L&J, vol. 1, p. 72.

2 *The Literary Life of the Rev. William Harness* (1871), pp. 32–3.

3 Deposition of Thomas France regarding Newstead Abbey window, 27 January 1819, John Murray, MS.43558.

4 William, 4th Lord Berkeley of Stratton to Lord Strafford, quoted in *The Wentworth Papers, 1705–1739: selected from the private and family correspondence of Thomas Wentworth, Lord Raby . . . with a memoir and notes by James J. Cartwright* (London: H.M. Public Record Office, 1883), p. 450.

5 Correspondence of Charles, 3rd Earl Sunderland [1715], BL, Add. MS. 38507 ff. 187–8.

6 Lady Strafford to Lord Strafford, 8 April 1712, quoted in *Wentworth Papers*, p. 284.

7 William, 4th Lord Byron to Henry, Duke of Portland, 31 January 1722, NA, DD/NW/4/2/2.

8 William, 4th Lord Byron to Thomas Pelham-Holles, Duke of Newcastle, 16 November 1723, BL, Add. MS 32686.

9 William, 4th Lord Byron to the Duke of Newcastle, 24 November 1723, ibid.

10 Sydney Evelyn to John Evelyn, 30 September 1738, quoted in Coope and Smith, *Newstead Abbey*, p. 48.

11 *Mist's Weekly Journal*, 3 December 1726.

12 J. Mackey, *A Journey Through England* (1714), vol. 1.

13 William, 4th Lord Berkeley to Lord Strafford, 26 January 1734, quoted in *Wentworth Papers*, p. 501.

14 *Recueil des Nouvelles Ordinaires et Extraordinaires . . . pendant 1730* (1731), p. 198.

15 John Locke, *Some Thoughts Concerning Education* (1693), quoted in Anthony Fletcher, *Growing Up in England: The Experience of Childhood 1600–1914* (Yale University Press, 2010), p. 7.

16 *The Ladies Dictionary* (1694), p. 314.

17 M. Fenelon, *Instructions for the Education of Daughters* (R. & A. Foulis, 1750), p. 38.

18 Isabella, Lady Carlisle, *Thoughts in the Form of Maxims Addressed to Young Ladies, on their First Establishment in the World* (T. Cornell, 1789), p. 22.

19 Frances, Lady Byron to unknown, 10 June 1740, TNA, SP 41/12/98.

20 Marchioness de Lambert, *The Works of the Marchioness de Lambert* (1781), vol. 1, pp. 137, 139.

21 Adam Smith, *An Inquiry into the Nature and Causes of the Wealth of Nations* (1776), quoted in B. Hill, *Eighteenth-Century Women: An Anthology* (Routledge, 2013), p. 53.

22 Isabella, Lady Carlisle, *Thoughts in the Form of Maxims*, p. 101.

23 Mrs Delany to Ann Dewes, 7 April 1754, quoted in M. Hilton and J. Shefrin (eds), *Educating the Child in Enlightenment Britain* (Wiley, 2012), p. 101.

24 *Daily Advertiser*, 20 May 1731.

25 Ibid., 23–30 May 1731.

26 Philip Dormer Stanhope, Earl of Chesterfield, to Philip Stanhope, [1740], *Letters written by the . . . Earl of Chesterfield to his son* (1775), vol. 1, p. 97.

27 William Pitt the Elder, quoted in Lord E. Fitzmaurice, *Life of William, Earl of Shelburne* (1875), vol. 1, p. 72.

28 Frederick Reynolds to his mother, 1750, quoted in J. D. Carleton, *Westminster School* (Hart-Davis, 1965), p. 30.

29 William Cowper to Lady Hesketh, 1786, quoted in S. Woodley, "'Oh Miserable and Most Ruinous Measure": The Debate between Private and Public Education in Britain, 1760–1800', in Hilton and Shefrin (eds), *Educating the Child*, p. 21.

30 Lord Chesterfield to Philip Stanhope, 19 March 1750, *Letters written by the . . . Earl of Chesterfield*, vol. 1, p. 518.

31 Quoted in B. Dobrée (ed.), *The Letters of Philip Dormer Stanhope, 4th Earl of Chesterfield* (1932), vol. 6, p. 2646; Lord Chesterfield to Philip Stanhope, 18 January 1750, *Letters written by the . . . Earl of Chesterfield*, vol. 1, p. 499.

32 *Town and Country Magazine . . . for the year 1773* (1774), p. 625.

33 Isabella, Lady Carlisle, *Thoughts in the Form of Maxims*, p. 34.

34 William, Lord Berkeley of Stratton to Lord Strafford, 3 February 1733, *Wentworth Papers*, p. 479.

35 Memorial to William Berkeley, erected by his brother John Berkeley at St Mary's church, Bruton in 1749.

36 *Daily Advertiser*, 11 March 1735.

37 William, 4th Lord Byron to [the Duke of Newcastle], 14 July 1735, TNA, SP 36/35/132, fo. 132.

38 Will of William, 4th Lord Byron, 19 October 1736, TNA, PROB 11/679/302.

39 Isabella, Lady Carlisle, *Thoughts in the Form of Maxims*, p. 98.

40 Duke of Newcastle to Horace Walpole, 16–27 July 1736, quoted in W. Coxe, *Memoirs of the Life and Administration of Sir Robert Walpole* (1798), vol. 3, p. 346.

41 Lady North to Lady Kaye, July [1739], Staffordshire Record Office, D(W)1778/III/178; Nathaniel Buck, 1726, quoted in Coope and Smith, *Newstead Abbey*, p. 39; Sidney Evelyn to J. Evelyn, 30 September 1738, quoted in Beckett, *Byron and Newstead*, p. 31 n16; William Melmoth the Younger to Robert Dodsley, 28 July 1759, quoted in *Select Letters between the late Duchess of Somerset, Lady Luxborough, . . . and others; by Mr. Hull* (1778), vol. 1, p. 262.

42 Lord Byron v Berkeley, TNA, C 11/139/4.

43 *London Evening Post*, 12 August 1736.

44 T. Bennett to the Duke of Newcastle, 18 October 1736, TNA, SP 36/39/197.

45 Lady North to Lady Kaye, July [1739], Staffordshire Record Office, D(W)1778/III/178.

46 J. Plumptre to the Duke of Newcastle, 18 October 1736, TNA, SP 36/39/199.

Chapter 2: Devil's Wood

1 *A Circumstantial and Authentic Account of a Late Unhappy Affair which happened at the Star and Garter Tavern* (1765), p. 14.

2 *The Mirror of Literature, Amusement, and Instruction*, supplementary edition, no. 67, 24 January 1824.

3 Robert Peel, quoted in W. S. Dowden (ed.), *The Journal of Thomas Moore* (University of Delaware Press, 1983), vol. 3, p. 1193.

4   T. Bennett to the Duke of Newcastle, 18 October 1736, TNA, SP 36/39/197.

5   J. Plumptre to the Duke of Newcastle, 18 October 1736, ibid., SP 36/39/199.

6   Frances, Lady Byron to the Duke of Newcastle, 27 June 1737, ibid., SP 36/41/100.

7   Frances, Lady Byron to unknown, 10 June 1740, ibid., SP 41/12/98.

8   Lieutenant's logbook of Lord Byron for the *Victory*, NMM, ADM/L/V/130.

9   G. A. Bellamy, *An Apology for the Life of George Anne Bellamy . . . in five volumes* (Logographic Press, 1785), vol. 1, p. 67.

10 Testimony of Luke Adams, quoted in R. E. Prothero, 'The Childhood and School Days of Byron', *The Nineteenth Century*, 43 (1898), p. 70.

11 William Combe, *The Devil upon Two Sticks in England* (1790), vol. 4, p. 242.

12 Bellamy, *Apology*, vol. 1, p. 68.

13 A. Chaworth to Mr & Mrs Molyneux, 24 November 1755, Molyneux papers, Nottingham, Mol 119.

14 Gertrude Savile, 18 October 1744, in Alan Savile (ed.), *Secret Comment: The Diaries of Gertrude Savile 1721–1757* (Kingsbridge History Society, 1997), p. 255.

15 Robert Ord to Lord Carlisle, 1 August 1745, quoted in Historical Manuscripts Commission, *The Manuscripts of the Earl of Carlisle, preserved at Castle Howard*, Fifteenth Report, Appendix, Part VI (1897) (hereafter *Carlisle Manuscripts*), p. 199.

16 *London Gazette*, 1 October 1745.

17 Quoted in T. Whitehead, *Original Anecdotes of the late Duke of Kingston and Miss Chudleigh* (1792), p. 145.

18 Quoted in Jacqueline Riding, *Jacobites: A New History of the '45 Rebellion* (Bloomsbury, 2016), p. 328.

19 *Derby Mercury*, 28 March 1746.

20 Resignation letter of Lord Byron, 20 March 1746, TNA, SP 54/30/2H.

21 Godfrey Bosville to John Spencer, 28 January 1765, Hull History Centre, U DDBM/32/9.

22 A. Chaworth to A. Molyneux, [*c.*1747], Molyneux papers, Nottingham, Mol 100.

23 Vizer C. Bridge to Timothy Bridge, 24 December 1743 (private collection, courtesy of the Bridge family).

24 *General Advertiser*, 14 July 1746.

25   Bellamy, *Apology*, vol. 1, p. 214.

26   *Caledonian Mercury*, 22 March 1736.

27   A. Chaworth to Mrs Molyneux, 14 December 1746, Molyneux papers, Nottingham, Mol 111.

28   Bellamy, *Apology*, vol. 1, p. 67.

29   Ibid., pp. 70–1.

30   A. Chaworth to Mrs Molyneux, 6 May [?1747], Molyneux papers, Nottingham, Mol 123.

31   Ibid.

32   Gertrude Savile, 19 March 1747, quoted in Savile (ed.), *Secret Comment*, p. 280.

33   Westminster Sessions Papers: Justices' Working Documents, April 1747, *London Lives, 1690–1800*, ref. ID: LMWJPS654410047 (www.londonlives. org).

34   Bellamy, *Apology*, vol. 2, pp. 9–10.

35   *London Evening Post*, 31 October 1749.

36   A. Chaworth to A. Molyneux, 5 July 1749, Molyneux papers, Nottingham, Mol 115.

37   Hanson narrative, John Murray, MS.43537.

38   Elizabeth, Lady Northumberland, [1760], quoted in Coope and Smith, *Newstead Abbey*, pp. 199–200.

39   Quoted in ibid., p. 69.

40   Viscount Grimston, 1768, quoted in Beckett, *Byron and Newstead*, p. 44.

41   *Payne's Universal Chronicle*, 6 May 1758.

42   Elizabeth, Lady Northumberland, [1760], quoted in Coope and Smith, *Newstead Abbey*, p. 200.

43   Arthur Young, *The Farmer's Tour through the East of England* (1771), vol. 1, p. 148n.

44   William Musgrave, 'Catalogue of the Pictures at Newstede', 1762, BL, Add. MS 5726 F(3), fos. 1–3.

45   Diary of Miss Molyneux, 17–18 August 1753, Molyneux papers, Nottingham, Mol 177.

46   Ibid.

47   Newstead estate accounts, 18 January 1757, NA, M 2567–2568.

48   Quoted in Beckett, *Byron and Newstead*, p. 46.

49   A. Chaworth to A. Molyneux, 5 July 1749, Molyneux papers, Nottingham, Mol 115.

50   William, 5th Lord Byron to the Duke of Newcastle, 15 June 1754, BL, Add. MS 32735.

51 William, 5th Lord Byron to [the Duke of Newcastle], 17 June 1761, Byron papers, Box 5, folder 8.

52 A. Chaworth to A. Molyneux, *c.*1748, Molyneux papers, Nottingham, Mol 125.

53 A. Chaworth to A. Molyneux, 24 November 1755, ibid., Mol 119.

54 J. Entinck, *The Constitutions of the Antient and Honourable Fraternity of Free and Accepted Masons* (1755), p. 253.

55 Diary of Miss Molyneux, 28–29 September 1753, Molyneux papers, Nottingham, Mol 177.

56 A. Chaworth to A. Molyneux, 4 November [n.y.], ibid., Mol 118.

57 Quoted in Coope and Smith, *Newstead Abbey*, p. 200.

58 Newstead accounts for 1755, quoted in Beckett, *Byron and Newstead*, p. 44.

59 Will of Frances Shaw, 6 December 1762, TNA, PROB 11/882/120.

60 Isabella, Lady Carlisle to William Musgrave, [July] 1765, Gloucester, D2383/C3.

61 Hanson narrative, John Murray, MS.43537.

62 Newstead accounts, 1757, quoted in Walker and Howell, *House of Byron*, p. 128.

63 Isabella, Lady Carlisle to Jemima Yorke, Lady Grey, 30 July [1752], Bedfordshire Archives, L30/9/58/1.

64 *Public Advertiser*, 31 May 1791.

65 A. Chaworth to A. Molyneux, n.d., Molyneux papers, Nottingham, Mol 121.

66 *Oxford Journal*, 7 June 1760.

67 Horace Walpole to George Montagu, 1 September 1760, Walpole, vol. 9, p. 293.

68 *Gazetteer and London Daily Advertiser*, 26 October 1762.

69 Will of Frances Shaw, 6 December 1762, TNA, PROB 11/882/120.

70 Isabella, Lady Carlisle to William Musgrave, 5 September 1763, Gloucester, D2383/C3.

71 *Oxford Journal*, 14 April 1764.

72 *Leeds Intelligencer*, 11 December 1764.

73 Whitehead, *Anecdotes*, pp. 103–4.

74 Horace Walpole to Horace Mann, 11 February 1765, Walpole, vol. 22, p. 284; Horace Walpole to Horace Mann, 14 May 1765, ibid., p. 293.

75 *The Complete Free-Mason; or Multa Paucis for Lovers of Secrets* (London, 1764), p. 105.

76 *The Tryal of William Lord Byron . . . for the Murder of William Chaworth, Esq* (Dublin, 1765), p. 90.

77 Ibid., p. 93.

78 Ibid., p. 53.

79 Godfrey Bosville to John Spencer, 28 January 1765, Hull History Centre, U DDBM/32/9.

80 Statement concerning duel between William Chaworth and Lord Byron, 27 January 1765, Gloucester, D1833 F7/12.

81 *The Tryal of William Lord Byron*, p. 94.

82 Ibid., p. 93.

83 Miss Mary Townshend to George Selwyn, 8 February 1765, quoted in John Heneage Jesse, *George Selwyn and his Contemporaries* (Richard Bentley, 1843), vol. 1, p. 358.

84 Geoffrey Bosville to John Spencer, 28 January 1765, Hull History Centre, U DDBM/32/9.

85 Horace Walpole to Lord Hertford, 18 April 1765, Walpole, vol. 38, p. 533.

86 *St James Chronicle*, 5–7 February 1765.

87 G. J. Williams to George Selwyn, 22 February 1765, quoted in Jesse, *Selwyn*, vol. 1, p. 359.

88 *Dublin Public Register*, 9 March 1765.

89 *Oxford Journal*, 2 March 1765.

90 *Manchester Mercury*, 12 March 1765.

91 *Derby Mercury*, 1 March 1765.

92 G. J. Williams to George Selwyn, 19 March 1765, quoted in Jesse, *Selwyn*, vol. 1, p. 371.

93 Lord Byron's list of witnesses, Parliamentary Archives, HL/PO/JO/10/7/185.

94 G. J. Williams to George Selwyn, 19 March 1765, quoted in Jesse, *Selwyn*, vol. 1, p. 371.

95 Ibid.

96 *London Lloyd's Evening Post*, 27 February 1765.

97 *Circumstantial and Authentic Account*, p. 14.

98 *Derby Mercury*, 19 April 1765.

99 Horace Walpole to Lord Hertford, 18 April 1765, Walpole, vol. 38, p. 535.

100 *The Tryal of William Lord Byron*, p. 54.

101 Ibid., p. 86.

102 *Boston Evening Post*, 17 June 1765; Horace Walpole to Lord Hertford, 18 April 1765, Walpole, vol. 38, p. 535.

103 *The Tryal of William Lord Byron*, p. 89.

104 *Ipswich Journal*, 20 April 1765.

105 *Derby Mercury*, 26 April 1765.

106 *Public Advertiser*, 4 June 1765.

107 Mr Spratt to William Daws, 1765, NA, M/2569, vol. 1, item 7.

108 *The Tryal of William Lord Byron*, p. 19.

109 Horace Walpole to Horace Mann, 14 May 1765, Walpole, vol. 22, p. 293.

110 Isabella, Lady Carlisle to William Musgrave, 16/17 July 1765, Gloucester, D2383/C3.

111 Isabella, Lady Carlisle to William Musgrave, 7 August 1765, ibid.

112 Isabella, Lady Carlisle to William Musgrave, [July] 1765, ibid.

113 *Lord Byron* v. *Durrant* 1767, TNA, PROB 18/78/9.

114 G. J. Williams to George Selwyn, 2 December 1766, quoted in Jesse, *Selwyn*, vol. 2, p. 91.

115 Letter to William Daws, 19 September 1769, NA M/2570/182.

116 Richard Pearson to William Daws, October 1771, quoted in Beckett, *Byron and Newstead*, p. 76.

117 Diary of Lady Mary Coke, 11 April 1768, quoted in James Home (ed.), *The Letters and Journals of Lady Mary Coke* (David Douglas, 1889–96), vol. 2, p. 236; *Ipswich Journal*, 17 February 1770.

118 Hanson narrative, John Murray, MS.43537.

119 Horace Walpole to Lord Strafford, 4 September 1760, Walpole, vol. 35, p. 305.

120 Arthur Young, *The Farmer's Tour* (1771), p. 141n.

Chapter 3: The Upper Lake

1 John Byron, *The Narrative of the Honourable John Byron* (S. Baker and G. Leigh, 1768), p. 14. The subsequent quotations about the *Wager* disaster that remain without a note are taken from this edition, unless otherwise stated.

2 George, 6th Lord Byron, 'Epistle to Augusta' (1816).

3 J. Bulkeley and J. Cummins, *A Voyage to the South Seas, in the Years 1740–1741* (Jacob Robinson, 1743), p. 1.

4 Commodore Anson, *A Voyage to the South Seas* (R. Walker, 1745), p. 25.

5 L. Millechamp, 'A Narrative of Commodore Anson's voyage', NMM, MSS JOD/36.

6 Ibid.

7 Bulkeley and Cummins, *Voyage to the South Seas*, p. 6.

8   J. Ross, *Memoirs and Correspondence of Admiral Lord de Saumarez . . .* (R. Bentley, 1838), vol. 2, p. 354.

9   R. Walter, *A Voyage Around the World . . . by George Anson* (7th edition, 1748), p. 87.

10 Anson, *Voyage to the South Seas*, pp. vi–vii.

11 R. Walter, *A Voyage Around the World*, p. 66.

12 Ibid.

13 Byron, *Narrative*, pp. 13–14.

14 Bulkeley and Cummins, *Voyage to the South Seas*, p. 13.

15 David Cheap to Richard Lindsey, 26 February 1744, quoted in C. H. Layman, *The Wager Disaster: Mayhem, Mutiny and Murder in the South Seas* (Uniform Press, 2015), p. 20.

16 Bulkeley and Cummins, *Voyage to the South Seas*, p. 17.

17 Byron, *Narrative*, p. 17.

18 Bulkeley and Cummins, *Voyage to the South Seas*, p. 19.

19 Byron, *Narrative*, p. vi.

20 Ibid., p. 36.

21 Bulkeley and Cummins, *Voyage to the South Seas*, p. 80.

22 Ibid., p. 111.

23 Byron, *Narrative*, p. 88.

24 Ibid., p. 109.

25 Ibid., p. 145.

26 Ibid., p. 198.

27 Ibid., p. 225.

28 John Byron to William, 5th Lord Byron, 26 March 1744, BL, Add MS 31037, f. 1.

29 Quoted in P. Shankland, *Byron of the Wager* (Collins, 1975), p. 252.

30 Byron, *Narrative*, p. 192.

31 Bulkeley and Cummins, *Voyage to the South Seas*, p. 110.

32 Quoted in Layman, *Wager Disaster*, p. 246.

33 Admiralty to John Byron, 24 June 1746, in John Byron, Order Book 1746–56 (private collection).

34 George Anson to the Duke of Bedford, 4 November 1746, quoted in John Russell, *Correspondence of John, 4th Duke of Bedford . . .* (Longman Co., 1842–6), vol. 1, p. 175.

35 Hester Thrale-Piozzi, 11 March 1789, in Katherine Balderston (ed.), *Thraliana: The Diary of Mrs Hester Lynch Thrale* (Clarendon Press, 1942), vol. 2, p. 733.

36 Hester Thrale-Piozzi to Harriet Willoughby, 25 August 1820, in E. A. Bloom and L. D. Bloom (eds), *The Piozzi Letters: Correspondence*

of Hester Lynch Piozzi, 1784–1821 (University of Delaware Press, 1989), vol. 6, p. 431; Frances Burney, 29 April 1780, in B. Rizzo (ed.), *The Early Journals and Letters of Fanny Burney, volume 4: The Streatham Years*, Part II (Oxford University Press, 2003), p. 79.

37 Mrs Eliot to Edward Eliot, 8 August 1748, Cornwall Record Office, EL/B/3/1/4.

38 Ibid.

39 Thomas Campbell, *Pleasures of Hope* (1799).

40 Isabella, Lady Carlisle to William Musgrave, [1760], Gloucester, D2383/C3.

41 John Byron, Order Book 1746–56 (private collection).

42 Will of Sophia Byron, 3 February 1791, TNA, PROB 11/1201/63.

43 Letter printed in the *London Gazette*, 7 January 1758.

44 John Byron to the Admiralty, 4 May 1759, TNA, ADM 1/1490.

45 Letter printed in the *Oxford Journal*, 25 October 1760.

46 Lord Colville to William Pitt, in the *Oxford Journal*, 7 October 1760.

47 Isabella, Lady Carlisle to William Musgrave, [1760], Gloucester, D2383/C3.

48 Ibid.

49 *The Monthly Review, or, Literary Journal*, June 1773–January 1774 (1774), vol. 49, p. 137.

50 John Byron to Lord Egmont, 24 February 1765, in Robert E. Gallagher (ed.), *Byron's Journal of his Circumnavigation 1764–6* (Hakluyt Society, 1964), p. 159. All subsequent quotations of John Byron during the *Dolphin* voyage, but without a note, are taken from this edition.

51 John Byron to Philip Carteret, 12 March 1764, NMM, CAR/5.

52 John Hawkesworth, *An Account of Voyages undertaken by order of His Present Majesty for making discoveries in the southern hemisphere . . .* (1773), vol. 1, p. 6.

53 *Byron's Journal of his Circumnavigation*, p. 25.

54 Lord Clive to Richard Grenville, October 1764, quoted in William James Smith, *The Grenville Papers: Being the Correspondence of Rich. Grenville Earl Temple . . .* (John Murray, 1852), vol. 2, p. 445.

55 *Byron's Journal of his Circumnavigation*, p. 26.

56 Ibid., p. 27.

57 Ibid., p. 37.

58 Ibid.

59 Ibid., p. 33.

60 John Byron to Lord Egmont, 24 February 1765, quoted in *Byron's Journal of his Circumnavigation*, p. 155.

61 Anon., *A Journal of a Voyage round the World, in His Majesty's Ship The Dolphin* (M. Cooper, 1767), p. 32.

62 John Byron to Lord Egmont, 24 February 1765, quoted in *Byron's Journal of his Circumnavigation*, p. 153.

63 Journal of Captain Mouat, quoted ibid., p. 60n.

64 John Byron to Lord Egmont, 24 February 1765, quoted ibid., p. 159.

65 Journal entry, 22 March 1765, ibid., p. 76.

66 Journal entry, 7 April 1765, ibid., p. 81.

67 Journal entry, 10 June 1765, ibid., p. 98.

68 Anon., *A Journal of a Voyage round the World*, p. 87.

69 Journal entry, 28/29 November 1765, quoted in *Byron's Journal of his Circumnavigation*, p. 136.

70 John Byron to Lord Egmont, 24 February 1765, quoted ibid., p. 160.

71 Lord Egmont to the Duke of Grafton, 20 July 1765, quoted ibid., p. 161.

72 *London Evening Post*, 5 June 1766.

73 Isabella, Lady Carlisle to William Musgrave, [August] 1765, Gloucester, D2383/C3.

74 *Manchester Mercury*, 3 June 1766.

75 *Boston Newsletter*, 18 September 1766.

76 Horace Walpole, *An Account of Giants Lately Discovered: in a letter to a friend in the country* (1766).

77 *Bath Chronicle*, 20 October 1768.

78 *Scots Magazine*, 4 July 1768.

79 *Kentish Gazette*, 4 June 1768.

80 John Wesley, Journal, 30 April 1769, quoted in Walker and Howell, *House of Byron*, p. 155.

81 *Lloyd's Evening Post*, 25 March 1768.

82 *Gentleman's Magazine*, 1 June 1769.

83 Log of John Byron, 3 June–25 November 1769, TNA, ADM 50/2.

84 Proclamation of John Byron, 8 July 1769, ibid., ADM 80/121/56.

85 *New York Gazette*, 21 August 1769.

86 *Morning Chronicle*, 9 August 1815.

87 Mrs Harris to Lord Malmesbury, 31 October 1770, quoted in Colonel C. A. T. Halliday, *Hallidays* (Portia Press, 1980), p. 16.

88 'Admiral the Honble John Byron Out Shooting' (1770) and 'Admiral the Honble John Byron Hunting His Own Hounds' (1770) by 'Sartorious' (private collection).

89 Mrs Harris to Lord Malmesbury, 31 October 1770, quoted in Colonel C. A. T. Halliday, *Hallidays* (Portia Press, 1980), p. 16.

90 John Delap Halliday to Wilbraham Tollemache, [11 December] 1770, Tollemache Archives, Helmingham Estate, T/Hel/1/844/6.

91 Samuel Johnson to Hester Thrale-Piozzi, 12 November 1781, quoted in B. Redford (ed.), *The Letters of Samuel Johnson* (Princeton University Press, 2014), vol. 3, p. 372.

92 *Bath Chronicle*, 1 June 1769; *Public Advertiser*, 26 December 1768.

93 *Town and Country Magazine . . . for the year 1773* (1774), p. 625.

94 *Critical Review*, vol. 25 (January–June 1768), p. 345.

Chapter 4: The Great Dining Hall

1 Isabella, Lady Carlisle to William Musgrave, [3 September 1759], Gloucester, D2383/C3.

2 George, 6th Lord Byron to Lady Melbourne, 7 January 1815, L&J, vol. 4, pp. 251–2.

3 Quoted in Miranda Seymour, *In Byron's Wake* (Simon & Schuster, 2018), p. 74.

4 George, 6th Lord Byron to Thomas Moore, 2 February 1815, L&J, vol. 4, p. 263.

5 Jonathan Swift, *The Furniture of a Woman's Mind* (1727).

6 Isabella, Lady Carlisle, *Thoughts in the Form of Maxims*, p. 89.

7 Attributed to C. J. Fox in John Galt, *The Life of Byron* (H. Chapman, 1831), p. 42.

8 Mary Wortley Montagu, 1758, quoted in Christopher Ridgeway, 'Isabella, Fourth Countess of Carlisle: No Life by Halves', in Ruth M. Larsen (ed.), *Maids and Mistresses: Celebrating 300 Years of Women and the Yorkshire Country House* (Yorkshire Country House Partnership, 2004), p. 37.

9 Hester Chapone to Samuel Richardson, January 1751, in Hester Chapone, *The Posthumous Works of Mrs Chapone* (John Murray, 1807), vol. 1, p. 122.

10 Marriage settlement, Henry Earl of Carlisle and Isabella Byron, 6 June 1743, CH, A5.63.

11 Frances, Lady Byron to Henry, 4th Lord Carlisle, 14 June 1743, ibid., J12/1/128.

12 Mary Wortley Montagu to Edward Wortley Montagu, 18 October 1743, in R. Halsband (ed.), *The Complete Letters of Lady Mary Wortley Montagu* (Oxford University Press, 1965–7), vol. 2, p. 312.

13 Unknown sender to Henry, 4th Lord Carlisle, 21 March 1744, CH, J12/1/130.

14 Lord Andover to Henry, 4th Lord Carlisle, 4 June 1744, ibid., J12/1/136.

15 *The Ladies Dictionary* (John Dunton, 1694), p. 143.

16 Julia Howard to Anne Molyneux, 1 March [1776], Molyneux papers, Nottingham, Mol 176.

17 Book of receipts of Isabella, Lady Carlisle, CH, J13/1/4.

18 Lord Bath to Henry, 4th Lord Carlisle, 13 September 1744, ibid., J12/1/136.

19 Isabella, Lady Carlisle to Caroline, Lady Carlisle, 18 August 1790, ibid., J15/1/34.

20 Lord Winchilsea to Henry, 4th Lord Carlisle, 6 August 1745, ibid., J12/1/141.

21 Henry, 4th Lord Carlisle to John Waugh, 30 November 1745, quoted in George Mounsey and John Waugh, *Carlisle in 1745* (Longman and Co., 1846), p. 113.

22 Charles Howard to Henry, 4th Lord Carlisle, 7 June 1746, *Carlisle Manuscripts*, p. 201.

23 Lady Irwin to Lord Carlisle, 28 July [n.y.], CH, J12/1/54.

24 *Newcastle Courant*, 28 May 1748.

25 Bernard Mandeville, *The Virgin Unmask'd* (1709), quoted in Hill, *Eighteenth-Century Women*, p. 101.

26 Isabella, Lady Carlisle, *Thoughts in the Form of Maxims*, pp. 1–2.

27 Elizabeth Smithson (later Duchess of Northumberland) to the Countess of Hertford, 31 August [?1745/6], Archives of the Duke of Northumberland at Alnwick Castle, DNP: MS 24 pp. 139–40.

28 *Whitehall Evening Post*, 12 April 1759.

29 Isabella, Lady Carlisle to Juliana Howard, 6 March 1772, CH, J13/1/3.

30 Thomas Harris to James Harris, 22 February 1755, quoted in D. Burrows et al. (eds), *Music and Theatre in Handel's World: The Family Papers of James Harris, 1732–1780* (Oxford University Press, 2002), p. 302.

31 Isabella, Lady Carlisle, *Thoughts in the Form of Maxims*, p. 91.

32 Isabella, Lady Carlisle to Juliana Howard, 25 October 1771, CH, J13/1/3.

33 Draft will of Prince Frederick of Wales, 1747–9, Royal Archives, Geo/Main/54070.

34 John Raphael Smith, note accompanying Isabella's sketch 'The First Oriental Head', BM Prints and Drawings, item ref. 1857,0520.228.

35 Lewis (ed.), *Notes by Lady Louisa Stuart*, p. 46; Isabella, Lady Carlisle to William Musgrave, [November 1759], D2383/C3.

36 *London Magazine*, vol. 40 (1771), p. 167.

37 'Lady Carlisle's Answer', *Gentleman's Magazine . . . for the year 1800*, vol. 70, part 1 (1800), p. 162.

38 Lady Caroline Fox to the Countess of Kildare, 19 August 1758, quoted in B. Fitzgerald (ed.), *Correspondence of Emily, Duchess of Leinster (1731–1814)* (Irish Manuscripts Commission, 1949–57), vol. 1, p. 176.

39 Book of receipts of Isabella, Lady Carlisle, CH, J13/1/4.

40 Isabella, Lady Carlisle to Juliana Howard, ibid., J13/1/3.

41 Isabella, Lady Carlisle, *Thoughts in the Form of Maxims*, p. 26.

42 Thomas Percy to Richard Farmer, 27 August 1768, quoted in D. N. Smith (ed.), *The Percy Letters* (Louisiana State University Press, 1991), vol. 2, p. 149.

43 Isabella, Lady Carlisle, *Thoughts in the Form of Maxims*, p. 21.

44 T. Robinson, Lord Grantham to F. Robinson, 30 March 1779, Bedfordshire Archives, L 30/15/54/128.

45 Mary Wortley Montagu to the Countess of Bute, 31 October 1758, quoted in Halsband (ed.), *The Complete Letters of Lady Mary Wortley Montagu*, vol. 3, p. 184.

46 Isabella, Lady Carlisle to William Musgrave, [November 1759], Gloucester, D2383/C3.

47 Mary Howard to Henry, Lord Carlisle, 22 September [1757], CH, J12/1/40.

48 *London Evening Post*, 31 August 1758; H. S. Conway to Horace Walpole, 27 August 1758, Walpole, vol. 37, pp. 561–2.

49 *Newcastle Courant*, 9 September 1758.

50 Isabella to William Musgrave, [c. November 1759], Gloucester, D2383/C3.

51 Thomas Gray to Thomas Wharton, 2 December 1758, quoted in P. J. Toynbee and L. Whibley (eds), *Correspondence of Thomas Gray* (Oxford University Press, 1971), vol. 2, p. 602.

52 Isabella Ingram, Viscountess Irwin to Mrs Charles Ingram, 26 November [1758], University of Leeds, Special Collections, Yorkshire Archaeological and Historical Society, TN/C/23/55.

53 Mary Wortley Montagu to the Countess of Bute, 31 October 1758, quoted in Halsband (ed.), *The Complete Letters of Lady Mary Wortley Montagu*, vol. 3, p. 184.

54 Katherine Southwell to Edward Southwell, 22 September 1758, Bristol Archives, 45317/2/5/2/38.

55 H. S. Conway to Horace Walpole, 27 August 1758, Walpole, vol. 37, p. 561.

56 H. S. Conway to Horace Walpole, 17 September 1758, ibid., p. 564.

57 Horace Walpole to George Montagu, 14 January 1760, ibid., vol. 9, p. 271.

58 Thomas Gray to Thomas Wharton, 2 December 1758, quoted in Toynbee and Whibley, *Correspondence of Thomas Gray*, vol. 2, p. 602.

59 Countess of Carlisle vs. Earl of Carlisle, 26 February 1759, TNA, C 12/6/10.

60 *Notes by Lady Louisa Stuart*, p. 47.

61 Lady Caroline Fox to the Countess of Kildare, 17 April 1759, quoted in Fitzgerald, *Correspondence of Emily, Duchess of Leinster*, vol. 1, p. 212.

62 Lady Caroline Fox to Countess of Kildare, 15 June 1759, ibid., p. 227.

63 Isabella, Lady Carlisle to William Musgrave, [16 October 1759], Gloucester, D2383/C3.

64 Isabella, Lady Carlisle to William Musgrave, 21 [October 1759], ibid.

65 Isabella, Lady Carlisle to William Musgrave, 22/23 [October 1759], ibid.

66 Isabella, Lady Carlisle to William Musgrave, [November 1759], ibid.

67 Isabella, Lady Carlisle to William Musgrave, [November 1759], ibid.

68 Horace Walpole to George Montagu, 17 November 1759, Walpole, vol. 9, p. 260.

69 *Notes by Lady Louisa Stuart*, pp. 47–8.

70 Isabella, Lady Carlisle to William Musgrave, [November 1759], Gloucester, D2383/C3.

71 Katherine Southwell to Edward Southwell, 21 December 1759, Bristol Archives, 45317/2/5/4/33.

72 Thomas Gray to John Clerke, 12 August 1760, in Toynbee and Whibley, *Correspondence of Thomas Gray*, vol. 2, p. 693.

73 Notes of William Musgrave, Gloucester, D2383/C3.

74 Isabella, Lady Carlisle to William Musgrave, [1760], ibid.

75 Ibid.

76 Ibid.; Isabella, Lady Carlisle to William Musgrave, [November 1760], ibid.

77 Isabella, Lady Carlisle to William Musgrave, [1760], ibid.

78 Horace Walpole to George Montagu, 24 September 1761, Walpole, vol. 9, p. 386.

79 Isabella, Lady Carlisle to William Musgrave, [September 1761], Gloucester, D2383/C3.

80 Isabella, Lady Carlisle to William Musgrave, [November 1760], ibid.

81 Ibid.; Isabella to Julia, 29 June 1772, CH, J13/1/3.

82 Isabella, Lady Carlisle to William Musgrave, 21 August 1763, Gloucester, D2383/C3.

83 Isabella, Lady Carlisle to William Musgrave, 5 September 1763, ibid.

84 Isabella, Lady Carlisle, *Thoughts in the Form of Maxims*, p. 80.

85 Frederick Howard, 5th Earl of Carlisle, quoted in Ridgeway, 'No Life by Halves', p. 38.

86 Horace Walpole to Lord Hertford, 27 January 1765, Walpole, vol. 38, p. 503.

87 Isabella, Lady Carlisle to William Musgrave, [April 1765], Gloucester, D2383/C3.

88 Mary Delany to Viscountess Andover, 27 April 1765, quoted in A. Hall (ed.), *Autobiography and Correspondence of Mary Granville, Mrs Delany* (Cambridge University Press, 2011), vol. 4, p. 46.

89 Isabella, Lady Carlisle to William Musgrave, [April 1765], Gloucester, D2383/C3.

90 Isabella, Lady Carlisle to William Musgrave, [August] 1765, ibid.

91 Isabella, Lady Carlisle to William Musgrave, 7 August 1765, ibid.

92 Isabella, Lady Carlisle to William Musgrave, 3 August 1765, ibid.

93 Frederick, 5th Earl of Carlisle, 'Reminiscences', CH, J14.64–5.

94 Lord Holland to George Selwyn, 17 March 1767, quoted in Jesse, *Selwyn*, vol. 2, p. 154.

95 Lord Kildare to the Duchess of Leinster, 15 June 1768, quoted in A. I. M. Duncan, 'A Study of the Life and Public Career of Frederick Howard, 5th Earl of Carlisle, 1748–1825', D.Phil. thesis (University of Oxford, 1981), p. 4.

96 Frederick, 5th Earl of Carlisle to George Selwyn, 9 January 1768, quoted in Jesse, *Selwyn*, vol. 2, p. 238.

97 Diary of Lady Mary Coke, 12 April 1767, quoted in Home (ed.), *Letters and Journals of Lady Mary Coke*, vol. 1, p. 210.

98 George Selwyn to Frederick, 5th Earl of Carlisle, 15 January 1768, quoted in *Carlisle Manuscripts*, p. 229.

99 William Musgrave to Frederick, 5th Earl of Carlisle, 16 October 1767, quoted in ibid., p. 219.

100 Frederick, 5th Earl of Carlisle to George Selwyn, 10 February 1768, quoted in Jesse, *Selwyn*, vol. 2, p. 252.

101 William Musgrave to Frederick, 5th Earl of Carlisle, 1 December 1767, quoted in *Carlisle Manuscripts*, p. 222.

102 William Musgrave to Frederick, 5th Earl of Carlisle, 12 February 1768, quoted in ibid., p. 241.

103 Diary of Lady Mary Coke, 14 June 1768, quoted in Home (ed.), *Letters and Journals of Lady Mary Coke*, vol. 2, p. 286.

104 Diary of the Duchess of Northumberland, 10 April 1770, quoted in

James Greig (ed.), *The Diaries of a Duchess: Extracts from the Diaries of the First Duchess of Northumberland* (Hodder & Stoughton, 1926), p. 102.

105 William Musgrave to Frederick, 5th Earl of Carlisle, 12 February 1768, quoted in *Carlisle Manuscripts*, p. 241.

106 Isabella, Lady Carlisle to William Musgrave, 20 August 1768, Gloucester, D2383/C3.

107 W. Milbourne to William, 3rd Duke of Portland, [July] 1768, Portland papers, Nottingham, Pw F 6769.

108 William Musgrave draft letter to Isabella, Lady Carlisle, 19 July 1768, Gloucester, D2383/C3.

109 Isabella, Lady Carlisle to William Musgrave, 31 July 1768, ibid.

110 Isabella, Lady Carlisle to William Musgrave, 20 August 1768, ibid.

111 William Musgrave draft letter to Isabella, Lady Carlisle, 12 November 1768, ibid.

112 Isabella, Lady Carlisle to Sir William Musgrave, 7 December 1768, ibid.

113 Isabella, Lady Carlisle, *Thoughts in the Form of Maxims*, p. 87.

114 Draft deed of separation by William Musgrave, Howard papers, Gloucester, D2383/C3; Mem[oran]dum of furniture, ibid.

115 Frederick, 5th Earl of Carlisle to George Selwyn, 1 February 1769, quoted in Jesse, *Selwyn*, vol. 2, p. 362.

116 Elizabeth Harris to James Harris, 10 March 1769, quoted in Burrows (ed.), *Music and Theatre in Handel's World*, p. 539.

117 Lord Kildare to the Duchess of Leinster, 15 June 1768, quoted in Duncan, 'A Study of the Life and Public Career of Frederick Howard', p. 4.

118 Diary of Elizabeth, Lady Northumberland, 26 February 1770, Archives of the Duke of Northumberland at Alnwick Castle, DNP: MS 121/31a, pp. 81–3.

119 Lord Holland to George Selwyn, 2 May 1770, quoted in Jesse, *Selwyn*, vol. 2, p. 394.

120 Isabella, Lady Carlisle to Juliana Howard, 6 December 1771, CH, J13/1/3.

121 Diary of the Duchess of Northumberland, 10 April 1770, quoted in Greig (ed.), *The Diaries of a Duchess*, pp. 101–2.

122 Isabella, Lady Carlisle, *Thoughts in the Form of Maxims*, p. 43.

123 Diary of Lady Mary Coke, 26 September 1770, quoted in Home (ed.), *Letters and Journals of Lady Mary Coke*, vol. 3, p. 292.

Chapter 5: Folly Castle

1 Isabella, Lady Carlisle to Juliana Howard, [July 1772], CH, J13/1/3.
2 Isabella, Lady Carlisle to Juliana Howard, 6 March 1772, ibid.
3 Diary of Lady Mary Coke, 27 September 1771, quoted in Home (ed.), *Letters and Journals of Lady Coke*, vol. 4, p. 457.
4 Mary Godwin, quoted in Ridgeway, 'No Life by Halves', p. 48.
5 George, 6th Lord Byron to John Murray, 22 July 1816, L&J, vol. 5, p. 85.
6 George, 6th Lord Byron to Augusta Leigh, 8 September 1816, ibid, p. 91; George, 6th Lord Byron to Augusta Leigh, 28 September 1816, ibid., p. 105.
7 Diary of Lady Mary Coke, 15 January 1771, quoted in Home (ed.), *Letters and Journals of Lady Coke*, vol. 3, p. 355.
8 Thomas Percy to Richard Farmer, 27 August 1768, in Smith (ed.), *Percy Letters*, vol. 2, p. 150.
9 Richard Byron to Frederick, 5th Earl of Carlisle, 5 December 1775, CH, J14/1/548.
10 Thomas Percy to Richard Farmer, 27 August 1768, in Smith (ed.), *Percy Letters*, vol. 2, p. 150.
11 Frederick, 5th Earl of Carlisle, 'Reminiscences', quoted in Venetia Murray, *Castle Howard* (Viking, 1994), p. 86.
12 Isabella, Lady Carlisle to Juliana Howard, 6 July 1772, CH, J13/1/3.
13 Hanson narrative, John Murray, MS.43537.
14 Marriage settlement of William Byron and Juliana Elizabeth Byron, 18 October 1771, Lovelace Byron 161, fol. 1.
15 Isabella, Lady Carlisle to Juliana Howard, 17 November 1771, CH, J13/1/3.
16 Mr Brown to William Daws, September 1771, quoted in Beckett, *Byron and Newstead*, p. 67; Charles Gould to William Daws, October 1771, quoted ibid.; Ann Mason to William Daws, November 1771, quoted ibid., p. 59.
17 Quoted ibid., p. 68.
18 Mr. Christie, *A catalogue of all that grand and noble collection of . . . pictures, of a nobleman Brought from his Lordships Seat in Nottinghamshire* (1772).
19 Charles Gould to unknown recipient, 9 June [1772], BL, Add. MS 43688.
20 Isabella, Lady Carlisle to Juliana Howard, c.14 January 1772, CH, J13/1/3.
21 Diary of Lady Mary Coke, 17 December 1770, quoted in Home (ed.), *Letters and Journals of Lady Mary Coke*, vol. 3, p. 338.
22 Isabella, Lady Carlisle to Juliana Howard, [July] 1772, CH, J13/1/3.

23 Isabella, Lady Carlisle to George Selwyn, 8 May 1771, quoted in Jesse, *Selwyn*, vol. 4, p. 124.

24 Isabella, Lady Carlisle to George Selwyn, 29 July [1771], quoted in ibid., p. 220.

25 Diary of Lady Mary Coke, September 1771, quoted in Home (ed.), *Letters and Journals of Lady Mary Coke*, vol. 3, p. 479.

26 Ibid.

27 Thomas Robinson to Anne Robinson, 2 December 1771, Bedfordshire Archives, L30/17/4/13.

28 Isabella, Lady Carlisle to Juliana Howard, 29 November 1771, CH, J13/1/3.

29 Ibid.

30 John Warner to George Selwyn, 10 January 1779, quoted in Jesse, *Selwyn*, vol. 3, p. 392.

31 Lady Mary Coke, September 1771, quoted in Home (ed.), *Letters and Journals of Lady Mary Coke*, vol. 3, p. 457.

32 Diary of the Duchess of Northumberland, n.d. May 1771, quoted in Greig (ed.), *The Diaries of a Duchess*, p. 153.

33 Isabella, Lady Carlisle to Juliana Howard, 29 March 1772, CH, J13/1/3.

34 Isabella, Lady Carlisle to Juliana Howard, 13 July 1772, ibid.

35 Horace Mann to Horace Walpole, 24 November 1772, Walpole, vol. 23, p. 447.

36 Diary of Lady Mary Coke, 14 October 1772, quoted in Home (ed.), *Letters and Journals of Lady Coke*, vol. 4, p. 129.

37 *Gazetta Toscana*, no. 46, vol. 7 (November 1772), p. 181; Journal of Sir Philip Francis in Italy, 5 November 1772, BL, Add. MS 40759.

38 Horace Mann to Horace Walpole, 24 November 1772, Walpole, vol. 23, p. 447.

39 John Thorpe to Henry Arundell, 8th Lord Arundell of Wardour, 21 December 1774, Wiltshire Archives, WSA 2667/20/22/8.

40 Diary of Lady Mary Coke, 10 April 1774, quoted in Home (ed.), *Letters and Journals of Lady Coke*, vol. 4, p. 329.

41 Frederick, 5th Earl of Carlisle, 'Reminiscences', quoted in Murray, *Castle Howard*, p. 85.

42 W. Alexander, *The History of Women* (1779), quoted in Hill, *Eighteenth-Century Women*, p. 111.

43 Sophia Byron to Hester Thrale-Piozzi, 16 October 1779, Houghton Library, MS Hyde 3 (16).

44 Anne Sophia Egerton to Jemima Yorke, 2 December [1770], Bedfordshire Archive, L30/9/32/10.

45 Isabella, Lady Carlisle to Juliana Howard, 6 March 1772, CH, J/13/1/3.

46 *Town and Country Magazine . . . for the year 1773* (1774), pp. 624–7.

47 John Warner to George Selwyn, 10 January 1779, quoted in Jesse, *Selwyn*, vol. 3, p. 392.

48 *London Chronicle*, 23 August 1774.

49 Sophia Byron to James Sykes, 2 January 1775, Morgan, MA 1294.10.

50 *Westminster Magazine*, vol. 1 (1773), p. 561.

51 Sophia Byron to James Sykes, 2 January 1775, Morgan, MA 1294.10.

52 John Byron to Lord Sandwich, 14 September 1775, quoted in G. R. Barnes and J. H. Owen (eds), *The Private Papers of John, Earl of Sandwich* (Navy Records Society, 1932–8), vol. 1, p. 75n.

53 King George III to Lord Sandwich, 18 September 1775, quoted in ibid., p. 74.

54 John Byron to James Sykes, 2 December 1775, Morgan, MA 1294.11.

55 *Bath Chronicle*, 16 May 1776.

56 *Edinburgh Advertiser*, 8 August 1775.

57 Mrs Julia Howard to Anne Molyneux, 25 June 1776, Molyneux papers, Nottingham, Mol 167.

58 *Oxford Journal*, 1 June 1776.

59 Quoted in [W. Cobbett], *The Parliamentary History of England* (1813), vol. 18, column 1368.

60 Account of Captain John Byron with James Sykes, Lovelace Byron 160, fo. 246.

61 William Combe, *The First of April, or, The Triumphs of Folly* (1777).

62 John Byron to the Admiralty, 27 January 1778, quoted in Barnes and Owen (eds), *Sandwich Papers*, vol. 2, p. 43n.

63 John Byron to Lord Sandwich, 1 May 1778, quoted ibid.

64 Philip Stephens to Lord Sandwich, 1 May 1778, quoted ibid., p. 43.

65 William, 5th Lord Byron to the Duke of Devonshire, 28 March 1778, NA, M/164.

66 Richard Kaye to the Duke of Portland, 12 December 1775, Portland papers, Nottingham, Pw F 6042.

67 Catalogue of sale, transcribed in Coope and Smith, *Newstead Abbey*, p. 194.

68 William, 5th Lord Byron to William Daws, 6 April 1779, John Murray, MS.43513.

69 Madame du Deffand to Horace Walpole, 17 June 1778, Walpole, vol. 7, pp. 50–1.

70 Isabella, Lady Carlisle to Juliana Howard, [summer 1772], CH, J13/1/3.

71 Isabella, Lady Carlisle, *Thoughts in the Form of Maxims*, p. 129.

72 John Warner to George Selwyn, n.d. January 1779, quoted in Jesse, *Selwyn*, vol. 4, p. 11.

73 Ibid.

74 Anne Robinson to Frederick Robinson, 6 January 1779, Plymouth and West Devon Record Office, 1259/1/1.

75 John Warner to George Selwyn, 13 December 1778, quoted in Jesse, *Selwyn*, vol. 3, p. 362.

76 John Warner to George Selwyn, 3 January 1779, quoted in ibid., p. 382.

77 John Warner to George Selwyn, 13 December 1778, quoted in ibid., p. 360.

78 Ibid., p. 365.

79 John Warner to George Selwyn, 13 December 1779, quoted in ibid., p. 364.

80 Madame du Deffand to George Selwyn, January 1779, in ibid, p. 389.

81 John Warner to George Selwyn, [January 1779], in ibid., p. 392.

82 John Warner to George Selwyn, 3 January 1779, in ibid., p. 384.

83 John Warner to George Selwyn (quoting Madame du Deffand), 4 March 1779, quoted in ibid., vol. 4, p. 47.

84 *Derby Mercury*, 15 September 1830.

85 John Warner to George Selwyn, 14 February 1779, quoted in Jesse, *Selwyn*, vol. 4, p. 57.

86 John Warner to George Selwyn, 13 April 1779, in ibid., p. 67.

87 Frederick Robinson to Thomas Robinson, 20 April 1779, Bedfordshire Archives, L30/14/333/199.

88 John Warner to George Selwyn, 3 January 1779, quoted in Jesse, *Selwyn*, vol. 3, p. 387.

89 *Town and Country Magazine . . . Vol. XI, for the year 1779* (1779), pp. 9–11.

90 Anon., *Trials for Adultery, or, The History of Divorces, Vol. II* (1779), Carmarthen case, p. 4.

91 Ibid., p. 21.

92 *Journals of the House of Lords*, vol. 35, p. 699.

93 Elizabeth Montagu to her sister, [December] 1778, quoted in R. Blunt (ed.), *Mrs Montagu, 'Queen of the Blues': Her Letters and Friendships from 1762 to 1800* (Constable, 1928), vol. 2, p. 64.

94 Frederick Robinson to Thomas Robinson, Bedfordshire Archives, L30/14/333/154.

95 Francis Osborne, Lord Carmarthen to Amelia, Lady Carmarthen, 15 December 1778, quoted in M. and M. Bakewell, *Augusta Leigh: Byron's Half-Sister* (Pimlico, 2002), p. 11.

96 Horace Walpole to Lady Browne, 18 December 1778, Walpole, vol. 31, p. 194.

97 Francis Osborne, Lord Carmarthen to Amelia, Lady Carmarthen, 21 December 1778, Lewis Walpole Library, LWL Mss File 87; Francis Osborne, Lord Carmarthen to Amelia, Lady Carmarthen, 22 December 1778, ibid.

98 Francis Osborne, Lord Carmarthen to Amelia, Lady Carmarthen, 23 December 1778, ibid.

99 Enforcement order for payment of £500 against John Byron for assault, 23 January 1779, Special Collections, University of Leeds, DD5/13/58.

100 Amelia, Lady Carmarthen, to Francis Osborne, Lord Carmarthen, n.d., quoted in M. and M. Bakewell, *Augusta Leigh*, p. 12.

101 Frederick Robinson to Thomas Robinson, 15 January 1779, Bedfordshire Archive, L30/14/333/170.

102 *Town and Country Magazine* (1779), pp. 9–11.

103 *The Westminster magazine, or, The Pantheon of Taste . . . volume 6* (T. Wright, 1778), p. 624.

104 *The Westminster magazine, or, The Pantheon of Taste . . . volume 7* (T. Wright, 1779), p. 5.

105 *Journals of the House of Lords*, vol. 35, p. 698.

106 *Trials for Adultery*, Carmarthen case, p. 45.

107 J. G. Loten to G. J. van Hardenbroek, quoted in A. J. P. Raat, *The Life of Governor Joan Gideon Loten* (Hilversum Verloren, 2010), p. 453.

108 Frederick Robinson to Thomas Robinson, 23 February 1779, Bedfordshire Archives, L30/14/333/181.

109 J. G. Loten to G. J. van Hardenbroek, quoted in Raat, *Life of Governor Joan Gideon Loten*, p. 453.

110 Admiral Gambier to Lord Sandwich, 31 July 1778, quoted in *The Sandwich Papers*, vol. 2, p. 307.

111 Frederick, 5th Earl of Carlisle to Caroline, Lady Carlisle, 15 September 1778, quoted in *Carlisle Manuscripts*, p. 365.

112 Lady Louisa Conolly to the Duchess of Leinster, 18 October 1778, quoted in *Correspondence of Emily, Duchess of Leinster*, vol. 3, p. 321.

113 George Washington to J. A. Washington, 26 October 1778, quoted in *The Papers of George Washington Digital Edition* (University of Virginia Press, Rotunda, 2008), http://rotunda.upress.virginia.edu/founders/GEWN-03-17-02-0613 [accessed 18 September 2019].

114 Frederick, 5th Earl of Carlisle to Lafayette, 11 October 1778, quoted in *The Annual Register . . . for the year 1779* (4th edition, 1802), p. 318.

115 John Byron to Frederick, 5th Earl of Carlisle, 9 November 1778, quoted in *Carlisle Manuscripts*, pp. 388–9.

116 Ibid., p. 389.

117 Frederick, 5th Earl of Carlisle to John Byron, 13 November 1778, quoted ibid., p. 390.

118 John Byron to Philip Stephens, 7 January 1779, TNA, ADM 1/312.

119 John Byron to Philip Stephens, 3 April 1779, ibid.; Jonathan Williams to Benjamin Franklin, 4 February 1779, *Founders Online*, National Archives [US], https://founders.archives.gov/documents/Franklin/01-28-02-0399 [accessed 18 September 2019].

120 Samuel Cooper to John Adams, 4 January 1779, *Founders Online*, National Archives [US], https://founders.archives.gov/documents/Adams/06-07-02-0215 [accessed 18 September 2019].

121 *General Advertiser and Morning Intelligencer*, 14 June 1779.

122 John Byron to Philip Stephens, 5 February 1779, TNA, ADM 1/312.

123 Unknown to Conrad-Alexandre-Gerard, 27 January 1779, enclosed in a letter from John Jay to George Washington, quoted in *The Papers of George Washington Digital Edition*, http://rotunda.upress.virginia.edu/founders/GEWN-03-19-02-0256 [accessed 18 September 2019].

124 Thomas Campbell to unknown recipient, 10 January 1779, quoted in *Carlisle Manuscripts*, p. 411.

125 Unknown to Conrad-Alexandre-Gerard, 27 January 1779, enclosed in a letter from John Jay to George Washington, quoted in *The Papers of George Washington*, http://rotunda.upress.virginia.edu/founders/GEWN-03-19-02-0256 [accessed 18 September 2019].

126 Frederick, 5th Earl of Carlisle to George Selwyn, 29 April 1779, quoted in Jesse, *Selwyn*, vol. 4, p. 110.

127 *Westminster Magazine*, vol. 7 (1779), p. 333.

128 John Byron to Philip Stephens, 3 April 1779, TNA, ADM 1/312.

129 George Macartney to John Byron, 18 June 1779, Bodleian Library, GB 0162 MSS.W.Ind.s.9, fo. 75.

130 John Byron to Philip Stephens, 8 July 1779, TNA, ADM 1/312.

131 Ibid.

132 James Grant to Lord George Germain, 8 July 1779, in *Westminster Magazine*, vol. 7 (1779), p. 481.

133 John Byron to Philip Stephens, 8 July 1779, TNA, ADM 1/312.

134 James Grant to Lord George Germain, 8 July 1779, in *Westminster Magazine*, vol. 7 (1779), p. 481.

135 Thomas Digges to Benjamin Franklin, 10 August 1779, *Founders Online*, National Archives [US], https://founders.archives.gov/documents/Franklin/01-30-02-0156 [accessed 18 September 2019].

136 *Pennsylvania Packet*, 12 August 1779; *Martinique Gazette*, 22 July 1779.

137 Robert Troup to Alexander Hamilton, 11 August 1779, *Founders*

Online, National Archives [US], https://founders.archives.gov/documents/Hamilton/01-02-02-0389 [accessed 18 September 2019].

138 John Byron to Philip Stephens, 4 August 1779, TNA, ADM 1/312.

139 Captain Johnstone to Lord Sandwich, 19 October [n.y.], quoted in *Sandwich Papers*, vol. 3, p. 182.

140 Sophia Byron to Hester Thrale-Piozzi, 21 August 1779, Thrale-Piozzi GB 133, Eng. MS 546.

141 Horace Walpole to H. S. Conway, 5 June 1779, Walpole, vol. 39, p. 323.

142 Beaumont Hotham to the Duke of Portland, 16 September 1779, Portland papers, Nottingham, Pw F 5464.

143 Madame du Deffand to Horace Walpole, 1 October 1779, Walpole, vol. 7, p. 179.

144 *London Courant*, 8 January 1780.

145 Diary of Hester Thrale-Piozzi, 1 September 1779, quoted in Balderston (ed.), *Thraliana*, vol. 1, p. 407.

146 Philip Stephens to Sophia Byron, 9 September 1779, quoted in *Morning Post and Daily Advertiser*, 18 September 1779; Beaumont Hotham to the Duke of Portland, 16 September 1779, Portland papers, Nottingham, Pw F 5464.

147 Lord F. Cavendish to the Duke of Portland, 10 September 1779, Portland papers, Nottingham, Pw F 2591; Beaumont Hotham to the Duke of Portland, 16 September 1779, ibid., Pw F 5464; *Public Advertiser*, 25 July 1780.

148 Samuel Johnson to Hester Thrale, 16 November 1779, quoted in Redford (ed.), *Letters of Samuel Johnson*, vol. 3, p. 216.

149 William, 5th Lord Byron to William Daws, 25 January 1779, NA, M/5603.

150 Newstead accounts, NA, M/2568.

Chapter 6: The Great Gallery

1 Isabella, Lady Carlisle, *Thoughts in the Form of Maxims*, p. 121.

2 John Byron to Sophia Maria Byron, 15 June 1784, Lovelace Byron 161, fos. 103–4.

3 *Morning Post and Daily Advertiser*, 27 August 1785.

4 Lord Fife, quoted in A. and H. Tayler (eds), *Lord Fife and his Factor; being the correspondence of James, second Lord Fife* (W. Heinemann, 1925), p. 173.

5 *Blackwood's Edinburgh Magazine*, no. XXIV (August 1819).

6 'Some Observations upon an Article in Blackwood's Edinburgh Magazine no. XXIV, August 1819', quoted in T. Moore, *The Works of Lord Byron Complete in One Volume with Notes* (John Murray, 1837), p. 802.

7 Hester Thrale-Piozzi to Robert Gray, 27 November 1814, quoted in Bloom and Bloom (eds), *The Piozzi Letters*, vol. 5, p. 309.

8 Hester Thrale-Piozzi to Frances Burney, 18 January 1821, quoted in ibid., vol. 6, p. 486.

9 Sophia Byron to Hester Thrale-Piozzi, 16 October 1779, Houghton Library, MS Hyde 3 (16).

10 Ibid.

11 Frederick, 5th Lord Carlisle to George Selwyn, 18 June [1779], quoted in Jesse, *Selwyn*, vol. 4, p. 198.

12 Correspondence of John Hewett, 3 December 1779, NA, DD/FJ/11/1/4/270-1.

13 William Mason to Horace Walpole, 12 November 1779, Walpole, vol. 28, p. 472.

14 Diary of Frances Burney, 29 April 1780, quoted in Rizzo (ed.), *Early Journals and Letters*, vol. 4, part 2, p. 79; Diary of Frances Burney, 24 May 1780, quoted in ibid., p. 113.

15 Frances Burney to Hester Thrale-Piozzi, 9 June 1781, quoted in ibid., p. 361.

16 Anne Sophia Egerton to Jemima Yorke, 2 December [1770], Bedfordshire Archives, L30/9/32/10.

17 Sophia Byron to Hester Thrale-Piozzi, [December] 1779, Thrale-Piozzi, GB 133 Eng MS 546, fo. 26.

18 Frances Burney to Hester Thrale-Piozzi, 16 December 1781, quoted in Rizzo (ed.), *Early Journals and Letters*, vol. 4, part 2, p. 533.

19 Hester Thrale-Piozzi to Sophia Byron, 1 September 1789, Thrale-Piozzi, GB 133 Eng MS 546, fo. 22.

20 Sophia Byron to Hester Thrale-Piozzi, 19 December [n.y.], ibid., fo. 29.

21 Diary of Frances Burney, c.27 May 1780, quoted in Rizzo (ed.), *Early Journals and Letters*, vol. 4, part 2, p. 120.

22 Hester Thrale-Piozzi to Harriet Willoughby, 25 August 1820, Bloom and Bloom (eds), *The Piozzi Letters*, vol. 6, p. 431.

23 Diary of Hester Thrale-Piozzi, July 1778, quoted in Balderston (ed.), *Thraliana*, vol. 1, p. 329.

24 Samuel Johnson to Hester Thrale-Piozzi, 15 April 1780, quoted in Chapman (ed.), *Letters of Samuel Johnson*, vol. 2, pp. 341–2.

25 Diary of Hester Thrale-Piozzi, 24 March 1779, quoted in Balderston (ed.), *Thraliana*, vol. 1, p. 375.

26 Quoted in J. Timbs, *A Century of Anecdote from 1760–1860* (R. Bentley, 1864), vol. 2, p. 51; Diary of Hester Thrale-Piozzi, December 1778, quoted in Balderston (ed.), *Thraliana*, vol. 1, p. 348; Diary of Hester Thrale-Piozzi, 7 December 1779, quoted in ibid., vol. 1, p. 414.

27 Diary of Frances Burney, April 1780, quoted in Rizzo (ed.), *Early Journals and Letters*, vol. 4, part 2, p. 41.

28 Diary of Frances Burney, 29 April 1780, quoted in ibid, p. 79.

29 R. Cumberland, *Memoirs of Richard Cumberland, written by himself* (Boston, 1806), p. 194.

30 Certificate of health, enclosed in Sophia Byron to James Sykes, 9 June 1780, BL, Add. MS 39992.

31 Sophia Byron to James Sykes, 9 June 1780, ibid.

32 Ibid.

33 *Memoirs of Cumberland*, p. 194.

34 Diary of Frances Burney, c.6 December 1780, quoted in C. Barrett (ed.), *Diary and Letters of Madame D'Arblay, edited by her niece* (Henry Colburn, 1842), vol. 1, p. 425.

35 Hester Thrale-Piozzi to Frances Burney, 7 February 1781, quoted in R. Brinsley Johnson (ed.), *The Letters of Mrs Thrale* (Bodley Head, 1926), p. 64.

36 John Byron to Frederick, 5th Earl of Carlisle, 25 February 1781, CH, J14/1/671.

37 Freres Andistres & co. to F. Gregg [in French], 27 June 1781, ibid., J14/13/5.

38 Diary of Lady Mary Coke, July 1781, quoted in W. H. Smith, *Originals Abroad: The Foreign Careers of some Eighteenth-Century Britons* (Yale University Press, 1952), p. 112.

39 Frances Burney to Hester Thrale-Piozzi, 16 December 1781, quoted in Rizzo (ed.), *Early Journals and Letters*, vol. 4, part 2, p. 534.

40 George Selwyn to Frederick, 5th Earl of Carlisle, 13 June 1781, CH, J14/1/276.

41 George Selwyn to Frederick, 5th Earl of Carlisle, 24 June 1781, ibid., J14/1/285.

42 Frances Burney to Hester Thrale-Piozzi, 10 June 1781, quoted in Rizzo (ed.), *Early Journals and Letters*, vol. 4, part 2, p. 363.

43 John Byron to James Sykes, 15 October 1781, Byron collection, NA 2014/(a).

44 John Byron to Juliana and Sophia Maria Byron, 1 November 1782, BL, Add. MS 31037, f. 2.

45 Sophia Byron to Hester Thrale-Piozzi, 19 December [n.y.], Thrale-Piozzi, GB 133 Eng MS 546, fo. 29.

46 Frances Burney to Hester Thrale-Piozzi, 9 June 1781, quoted in Rizzo (ed.), *Early Journals and Letters*, vol. 4, part 2, p. 361.

47 Sophia Byron to Hester Thrale-Piozzi, [December] 1779, Thrale-Piozzi, GB 133 Eng MS 546, fo. 26.

48 Dedication to 'the Hon. Mrs Byron' in Hardwicke Lewis, *An Excursion to Margate* (1787); Sophia Byron to Hester Thrale-Piozzi, Thrale-Piozzi, GB 133 Eng MS 546, fo. 27.

49 Sophia Byron to Hester Thrale-Piozzi, n.d., ibid., fo. 28.

50 Sophia Byron to Hester Thrale-Piozzi, 19 December, ibid., fo. 29.

51 Frances Burney to Hester Thrale-Piozzi, February 1782, quoted in Rizzo (ed.), *Early Journals and Letters*, vol. 5, p. 8.

52 Sophia Byron to James Sykes, 9 May 1782, Byron papers, Box 6, folder 26.

53 John Byron to Juliana Elizabeth Byron, *c.*18 December 1782, quoted in *Wilmot v. Woodhouse 1793*, *Reports of Cases Argued and Determined in the High Court of Chancery*, vol. 4 (1795), p. 229.

54 John Byron to James Sykes, 17 September 1783, Morgan, MA 1294.17.

55 George Anson Byron to Lord Shelburne, 9 December 1782, BL, Add. MS 88906/4/1, fo. 158.

56 Jack Byron to Frances Leigh, 21 March 1788, Lovelace Byron 161, fo. 122.

57 *Morning Herald and Daily Advertiser*, 10 January 1782.

58 *Byron v. Holland*, October 1782, TNA, C 12/2129/4.

59 William, 5th Lord Byron, quoted in Beckett, *Byron and Newstead*, p. 76.

60 *Morning Post and Daily Advertiser*, 19 May 1783. The site of the villa on Hampstead Heath was acquired by Lord Leverhulme in the Edwardian era, and subsequently cleared to make way for his Pergola and Hill Garden.

61 *Whitehall Evening Post*, 20 March 1784.

62 *Morning Herald*, 20 September 1784.

63 *Public Advertiser*, 24 August 1785.

64 *Public Advertiser*, 26 September 1782.

65 C. J. Fox, 'The Meteors, the Comet, and the Sun', in *The European Magazine and Review . . . for 1782* (1782), vol. 1, p. 468.

66 Lady Mary Coke, November 1783, quoted in Smith, *Originals Abroad*, p. 112.

67 Quoted in *Mémoires de l'Académie de Vaucluse, deuxième série, tome XI* (François Seguin, 1911), p. 183.

68 Account of Isabella Dowager Countess of Carlisle, January 1779–July 1783, Carlisle Archive Centre, DHN/EXTRA/1982/21/35.

69 Frederick, 5th Earl of Carlisle to Isabella, Lady Carlisle, [1781], CH, J14/13/3.

70 Isabella, Lady Carlisle to F. Gregg, 17 December 1780, ibid., J14/13/1.

71 Frederick, 5th Earl of Carlisle to Isabella, Lady Carlisle, [1781], ibid., J14/13/3.

72 Isabella, Lady Carlisle to F. Gregg, 25 May 1781, CH, J14/13/4.

73 George Selwyn to Frederick, 5th Earl of Carlisle, 13 June 1781, *Carlisle Manuscripts*, p. 498.

74 Freres Andistres & co. to [F. Gregg], 27 June 1781, CH, J14/13/5.

75 George Selwyn to Frederick, 5th Earl of Carlisle, 13 June 1781, *Carlisle Manuscripts*, p. 755.

76 Frederick, 5th Earl of Carlisle to Isabella, Lady Carlisle, [1781], CH, J14/13/3.

77 George Selwyn to Frederick, 5th Earl of Carlisle, 13 November 1781, *Carlisle Manuscripts*, p. 530.

78 Isabella, Lady Carlisle to F. Gregg, February 1782, CH, J14/13/6.

79 Monsieur de Weinheim to Frederick, 5th Earl of Carlisle, 21 February 1783 [in French], ibid., J14/13/7.

80 George Selwyn to Frederick, 5th Earl of Carlisle, 20 June 1781, *Carlisle Manuscripts*, p. 504n.

81 Isabella, Lady Carlisle, 1771, quoted in Ridgeway, 'No Life by Halves', p. 39.

82 Quoted in Mary Delany, *The Autobiography and Correspondence of Mary Granville, Mrs Delany* (Bentley, 1862), vol. 3, p. 165.

83 Frances Burney, 18 December 1783, quoted in Rizzo (ed.), *Early Journals and Letters*, vol. 5, p. 449.

84 Isabella, Lady Carlisle to George Selwyn, 19 December [n.y.], quoted in Jesse, *Selwyn*, vol. 4, p. 306.

85 Isabella, Lady Carlisle, *Thoughts in the Form of Maxims*, p. 134.

86 Queen Charlotte to General Jacob de Budé, [1783], in A. Aspinall (ed.), *Later Correspondence of George III*, vol. 5, p. 702.

87 Quoted in M. and M. Bakewell, *Augusta Leigh*, p. 15.

88 Diary of Miss Hamilton, 4 December 1783, quoted in Delany, *Autobiography and Correspondence*, vol. 3, p. 153.

89 *Derby Mercury*, 5 February 1784.

90 *Scots Magazine*, January 1784.

91 Richard Byron to Sophia Byron, 1 February 1784 (private collection).

92 John Byron to Augusta Byron, 21 February 1784, Byron papers, Box 6, oversize folder 3.

93 Ibid.

94 John Byron to Sophia Maria Byron, 15 June 1784, Lovelace Byron 161, fos. 103–4.

95 Hester Thrale-Piozzi to Hester Elphinstone, 15 July 1784, quoted in Bloom and Bloom, *Piozzi Letters*, vol. 1, p. 90.

96 Settlement of Isabella's debts, 21 April 1784, Carlisle Archive Centre, HNP/N/79/32.

97 Isabella, Lady Carlisle, 'Melancholy and Pity', transcribed in the papers of Elizabeth Simpson, Lady Bridgeman, Staffordshire Record Office, D1287/19/6/19.

98 Elizabeth, Lady Byron to George Stubbs, n.d. [1784], Morgan, MA 1294.50.

99 Will of Caroline Byron, 19 November 1784, TNA, PROB 11/1123/334.

100 G. A. Bellamy, *Apology*, vol. 2, p. 16.

101 Lord Fife to William Rose, 30 April 1785, quoted in Tayler and Tayler (eds), *Lord Fife and His Factor*, pp. 172–3.

102 *Creswell and Burbage's Nottingham Journal*, 14 May 1785.

103 Ibid.

104 Will of William, Lord Byron, 6 July 1798, Borthwick Archives, University of York, Prog. July 1798, V142, F150.

105 Lady Anne Howard to William, 3rd Duke of Portland, 31 December 1795, Portland papers, Nottingham, Pw F 5490.

106 Frederick Robinson to Thomas Robinson, 20 April 1779, Bedfordshire Archives, L30/14/333/199.

107 John Byron to Monsieur Perigand, [September] 1784, New York Public Library Pforzheimer Collection, MS B'ANA 0530.

108 Isabella, Lady Carlisle to Francis [*sic*] Sykes, 16 January 1785, ibid., MS B'ANA 0767.

109 Jack Byron to Frances Leigh, 12 December 1790, Lovelace Byron 161, fo. 133.

110 Pryse L. Gordon, *Personal Memoirs, or, Reminiscences of Men and Manners* (Colburn and Bentley, 1830), vol. 2, p. 330.

111 Dr Glennie, quoted in the *Southern Review*, vol. 5, February & May 1830 (A. E. Miller, 1830) p. 480.

112 Catherine Byron to John Hanson, 12 March 1804, John Murray, Box 13a.

113 Charlotte Lewis to Hester Thrale-Piozzi, quoted in Megan Boyes, *My Amiable Mama: A Biography of Mrs Catherine Gordon Byron* (J. M. Tatler, 1991), p. 15.

114 Abigail Adams to John Quincy Adams, 4 July–11 August 1785, *Founders Online*, National Archives [US], https://founders.archives.gov/documents/Adams/04-06-02-0072 [accessed 18 September 2019].

115 William John Byron to [Sophia Maria] Byron, 19 April 1791, Byron papers, Box 6, folder 28.

116 Sophia Byron to James Sykes, 19 December 1785, Morgan, MA 1294.19.

117 JY' to Mary Young, 12 July 1785, Northamptonshire Archive, Y(O) 1575.

118 Richard Byron to Frederick, 5th Earl of Carlisle, 5 December 1775, CH, J14/1/548.

119 William, 5th Lord Byron to William Pitt, 19 May 1791, TNA, PRO 30/8/118.

120 C. J. Fox, 'The Meteors, the Comet, and the Sun' (1782); *Étrennes du Parnasse; choix de poésies* (1780), pp. 84–5.

121 Newstead Abbey accounts, quoted in Beckett, *Byron and Newstead*, p. 79.

Chapter 7: The Chapel

1 Will of Sophia Byron, 3 February 1791, John Murray, PROB 11/1201/63.

2 John Murray to George, 6th Lord Byron, 24 October 1814, TNA, MS.43494.

3 John Murray to Anne Murray, 5 October 1814, quoted in Samuel Smiles (ed.), *A Publisher and His Friends: Memoir and Correspondence of John Murray* (John Murray, 1891), vol. 1, p. 234.

4 John Murray to George, 6th Lord Byron, 24 October 1814, John Murray, MS.43494.

5 Alexander Duthie to Alexander Russell, 15 July 1785, quoted in Boyes, *My Amiable Mama*, p. 16.

6 Quoted in Tayler and Tayler (eds), *Fife and His Factor*, p. 177.

7 John Leslie to James Watson, 7 February 1788, quoted in Boyes, *My Amiable Mama*, pp. 28–9.

8 Colonel Frank S. Russell, letter printed in the *Aberdeen Press and Journal*, 27 October 1896.

9 'Miss Gordon of Gight', in Isaac Cooper, *Thirty New Strathspey Reels* (1783), BL, Music Collections e.41.m.

10 'Miss Gordon of Gight', in Peter Buchan, *Ancient Ballads and Songs of the North of Scotland* (1828), vol. 1, p. 258.

11 *Derby Mercury*, 23 March 1786; diary of William Gould, 18 March 1785, quoted in M. Hanson (ed.), *Ducal Estate Management in Georgian Nottinghamshire and Derbyshire* (Thoroton Society, 2006), p. 102.

12 Sophia Byron to James Sykes, 26 April 1786, Lovelace Byron 161,

fo. 48; George Anson Byron to Frances Leigh, 24 January 1787, ibid., fo. 105.

13 Ibid.

14 Ibid.

15 Quoted in Layman, *Wager Disaster*, pp. 258, 264.

16 Isabella, Lady Carlisle to William Musgrave, [1760], Gloucester, D2383/C3.

17 Sophia Byron to James Sykes, Friday, 9 April [1786], Byron collection, RB A62.

18 Sophia Byron to James Sykes, 20 April 1786, Lovelace Byron 161, fo. 44.

19 Sophia Byron to James Sykes, 22 April 1786, ibid., fos. 46–7.

20 Lord Fife to W. Rose, 22 April 1786, quoted in Tayler and Tayler (eds), *Fife and His Factor*, p. 182; Lord Fife to W. Rose, 24 April 1786, quoted in ibid.

21 Charlotte Lewis to Hester Thrale-Piozzi, 8 May 1786, quoted in Balderston (ed.), *Thraliana*, vol. 2, p. 739.

22 Jack Byron to James Sykes, 5 May 1786, Morgan, MA 1294.22.

23 George Anson Byron to Frances Leigh, 24 January 1787, Lovelace Byron 161, fo. 105.

24 Catherine Byron to Miss Urquhart, 13 November 1786, quoted in Boyes, *My Amiable Mama*, p. 20.

25 William Abercrombie to Mrs Rose, 9 September 1787, quoted ibid., p. 23.

26 John Warner to George Selwyn, [1779], quoted in Jesse, *Selwyn*, vol. 4, p. 56.

27 Isabella, Lady Carlisle to Frederick, 5th Earl of Carlisle, 8 November 1786, CH, J14/13/12.

28 *Bath Chronicle*, 8 May 1788.

29 *Notes by Lady Louisa Stuart*, p. 49.

30 Isabella, Lady Carlisle, *Thoughts in the Form of Maxims*, p. 119.

31 *Hereford Journal*, 27 December 1787.

32 Jack Byron to James Watson, 26 January 1788, John Murray, MS.43413.

33 Mr Farquharson to James Watson, 24 January 1788, Byron papers, 'Letters Regarding the Birth of Lord Byron', Box 7, folder 14.

34 Catherine Byron to Hugh Watson, 22 February 1788, John Murray, MS.43410.

35 Miscellaneous note in the Watson papers, [?1786], ibid., MS.43547.

36 Jack Byron to Frances Leigh, 21 March 1788, Lovelace Byron 161, fo. 122.

37 Diary of Hester Thrale-Piozzi, 8 May 1789, quoted in Balderston (ed.), *Thraliana,* vol. 2, p. 746.

38 Jack Byron to Frances Leigh, 21 March 1788, Lovelace Byron 161, fo. 122.

39 *London Annual Register*, 1788.

40 Hester Thrale-Piozzi, 1 April 1789, in *Thraliana*, vol. 2, p. 739.

41 Will of Elizabeth, Lady Byron, 15 July 1788, TNA, PROB 11/1167/311.

42 Sophia Byron to Hester Thrale-Piozzi, 16 October 1779, Houghton Library, MS Hyde 3 (16).

43 Samuel Johnson to Hester Thrale-Piozzi, 18 April 1780, quoted in Redford (ed.), *Letters of Samuel Johnson*, vol. 3, p. 241.

44 Sophia Byron to Hester Thrale-Piozzi, [December] 1779, Thrale-Piozzi, GB 133 Eng MS 546, fo. 26.

45 Hester Thrale-Piozzi to Sophia Byron, 1 September 1789, ibid., fo. 22.

46 Diary of Hester Thrale-Piozzi, 11 March 1789, quoted in Balderston (ed.), *Thraliana*, vol. 2, pp. 733–4.

47 Diary of Hester Thrale-Piozzi, 8 May 1789, quoted ibid., p. 746.

48 Hester Thrale-Piozzi to Sophia Byron, 25 September [1788], Thrale-Piozzi, GB 133 Eng MS 546, fo. 14.

49 Isabella, Lady Carlisle to F. Gregg, 17 December 1780, CH, J14/13/1.

50 Isabella, Lady Carlisle, 'Melancholy and Pity', papers of Elizabeth Simpson, Lady Bridgeman, Staffordshire Record Office, D1287/19/6/19.

51 Hanson narrative, John Murray, MS.43537.

52 Diary of Hester Thrale-Piozzi, 1 April 1789, quoted in Balderston (ed.), *Thraliana*, vol. 2, p. 739.

53 *Kentish Gazette*, 15 May 1789.

54 *Derby Mercury*, 26 November 1789.

55 Hester Thrale-Piozzi to Sophia Byron, 11 July 1789, Thrale-Piozzi, GB 133 Eng MS 546, fo. 19.

56 Hester Thrale-Piozzi to Sophia Byron, 3 August 1789, ibid., fo. 20.

57 Catherine Byron to Frances Leigh, 31 May 1791, John Murray, MS.43410.

58 William Mason to Lord Harcourt, 10 June 1789, quoted in E. W. Harcourt (ed.), *The Harcourt Papers* (James Parker and Co., 1880), vol. 7, p. 161.

59 William John Byron to George Anson Byron, 4 August 1789, Morgan, MA 1294.24.

60 *Morning Post*, 1 August 1789.

61 William John Byron to George Anson Byron, 4 August 1789, Morgan, MA 1294.24.

62 Augusta Parker to George Anson Byron, 19 April 1790, ibid., MA 4728.11.

63 Henrietta Byron to James Sykes, 5 January 1790, BL, Add. MS 39992, fo. 353.

64 Augusta Parker to George Anson Byron, 19 April 1790, Morgan, MA 4728.11.

65 William John Byron to George Anson Byron, 4 August 1789, ibid., MA 1294.24.

66 Ibid.

67 *London Oracle*, 12 August 1789.

68 Sophia Maria Byron to James Sykes, 18 January 1790, BL, Add. MS 39992.

69 Horace Walpole to Lady Ossory, 26 December 1789, Walpole, vol. 34, p. 89.

70 *Analytical Review*, vol. 6 (January–April 1790), p. 103.

71 *Monthly Review*, vol. 2 (May–August 1790), p. 361.

72 *London Star*, 11 January 1791.

73 Isabella, Lady Carlisle, *Thoughts in the Form of Maxims*, p. 130.

74 Hester Thrale-Piozzi to Sophia Byron, 1 September 1789, Thrale-Piozzi, GB 133 Eng MS 546, fo. 22.

75 Isabella, Lady Carlisle to Caroline, Lady Carlisle, 18 August 1790, CH, J15/1/34.

76 Isabella, Lady Carlisle, *Thoughts in the Form of Maxims*, p. 125.

77 Hester Thrale-Piozzi to Sophia Byron, 11 September 1789, Thrale-Piozzi, GB 133 Eng MS 546, fo. 23.

78 Augusta Parker to George Anson Byron, 19 April 1790, Morgan, MA 4728.11.

79 Ibid.

80 Diary of Hester Thrale-Piozzi, 17 June 1790, quoted in Balderston (ed.), *Thraliana*, vol. 2, p. 770.

81 Sophia Maria Byron to James Sykes, 10 August 1790, Lovelace Byron 159, fo. 1.

82 Hester Thrale-Piozzi to Sophia Byron, 19 September 1789, Thrale-Piozzi, GB 133 Eng MS 546, fo. 24.

83 Will of Sophia Byron, 3 February 1791, TNA, PROB 11/1201/63.

84 Sophia Byron to Hester Thrale-Piozzi, [1790], Thrale-Piozzi, GB 133 Eng MS 546, fo. 30.

85 Diary of Hester Thrale-Piozzi, [November 1790], quoted in Balderston (ed.), *Thraliana*, vol. 2, p. 787.

86 Hester Thrale-Piozzi, 'For the Abbey Church, Bath', [1790], Thrale-Piozzi, GB 133 Eng MS 546, fo. 31.

87 *Leeds Intelligencer*, 23 November 1790.

88 Jack Byron to Frances Leigh, 12 December 1790, Lovelace Byron 161, fo. 133.

89 Catherine Byron to Frances Leigh, 21 January 1791, quoted in Boyes, *My Amiable Mama*, p. 35.

90 Jack Byron to Frances Leigh, 12 December 1790, Lovelace Byron 161, fo. 133.

91 Jack Byron to Frances Leigh, 1 December 1790, ibid., fo. 128; Jack Byron to Frances Leigh, 16 February 1791, ibid., fo. 159; Jack Byron to Frances Leigh, 15 October 1790, ibid., fo. 124.

92 Jack Byron to Frances Leigh, 1 December 1790, ibid., fo. 128.

93 Jack Byron to Frances Leigh, 2 January 1791, ibid., fo. 144.

94 Jack Byron to Frances Leigh, 29 December 1790, ibid., fo. 142.

95 Jack Byron to Frances Leigh, 16 February 1791, ibid., fo. 159.

96 Catherine Byron to Jack Byron, n.d., Byron papers, Box 6, folder 22.

97 Ibid.

98 Catherine Byron to Frances Leigh, 27 March 1791, Pforzheimer Collection, MS B'ANA 0081.

99 Sophia Maria Byron to George Anson Byron, 18 May 1791, Morgan, MA 4728.4.

100 Ibid.

101 William, 5th Lord Byron to William Pitt, 19 May 1791, TNA, PRO 30/8/118.

102 Sophia Maria Byron to George Anson Byron, 18 May 1791, Morgan, MA 4728.4.

103 *Public Advertiser*, 31 May 1791.

104 *The Star*, 9 June 1791.

105 George, 6th Lord Byron to Augusta Leigh, 30 August 1822, Lovelace Byron 154, fo. 25.

106 William John Byron to James Sykes, 27 April 1790, Lovelace Byron 161, fo. 62.

107 Sophia Maria Byron to James Sykes, 10 August 1790, Lovelace Byron 159, fo. 1.

108 Sophia Maria Byron to George Anson Byron, 18 May 1791, Morgan, MA 4728.4.

109 Jack Byron to Frances Leigh, 29 December 1790, Lovelace Byron 161, fo. 142.

110 Jack Byron to Frances Leigh, 4 February 1791, ibid., fo. 155.

111 Catherine Byron to Frances Leigh, 27 March 1791, Pforzheimer Collection, MS B'ANA 0081.

112   Catherine Byron to Frances Leigh, 31 May 1791, John Murray, MS.43410.

113   Jack Byron to Frances Leigh, 2 January 1791, Lovelace Byron 161, fo. 144.

114   Catherine Byron to Frances Leigh, 31 May 1791, John Murray, MS.43410.

115   Jack Byron to Frances Leigh, 10 April 1791, Lovelace Byron 161, fo. 169.

116   Jack Byron to Frances Leigh, 15 May 1791, ibid., fo. 179.

117   Jack Byron to Frances Leigh, 13 April 1791, ibid., fo. 171.

118   Jack Byron to Frances Leigh, 4 May 1791, ibid., fo. 177.

119   Jack Byron to Frances Leigh, 8 June 1791, ibid., fo. 187.

120   Will of John Biron (translation), 21 June 1791, John Murray, MS.43547.

121   Sophia Maria Byron to James Sykes, 9 August 1791 (private collection).

122   *Universal Magazine*, vol. 89 (1791), pp. 157–8.

123   Catherine Byron to Frances Leigh, 23 August 1791, John Murray, MS.43410.

124   Ibid.

125   Jack Byron to Frances Leigh, 2 February 1791, Lovelace Byron 161, fo. 153.

126   Frances Leigh to James Sykes, 29 December 1791, Morgan, MA 4728.9.

127   Sophia Maria Byron to James Sykes, 25 December 1791, Lovelace Byron 159, fo. 11.

128   Hester Thrale-Piozzi to Sophia Byron, 31 October 1788, Thrale-Piozzi, GB 133 Eng MS 546, fo. 17.

129   *Daily Advertiser*, issue 222, 16 September 1790.

130   Sophia Maria Byron to George Anson Byron, 18 May 1791, Morgan, MA 4728.4.

131   Robert Dallas, *Miscellaneous Writings* (T. N. Longman, 1797), p. 231.

132   Catherine Byron to Frances Leigh, 29 November 1792, BL Add. MS. 31037, fo. 9.

133   George Anson Byron to James Sykes, 23 December 1792 (private collection).

134   Frederick, 5th Earl of Carlisle, 1 February 1793, quoted in H. J. Rose, *A New General Biographical Dictionary* (1848), vol. 6, p. 50.

135   Hester Thrale-Piozzi to Sophia Byron, 11 July 1789, Thrale-Piozzi, GB 133 Eng MS 546, fo. 19.

136   John Byron, Esq., to William Pitt, 20 August 1794, TNA, PRO 30/8/118.

137   Dallas, *Miscellaneous Writings*, p. 231.

138   Will of George Anson Byron, 27 July 1793, TNA, PROB 11/1234/284.

139   *Bath Chronicle and Weekly Gazette*, 4 July 1793.

140 Dallas, *Miscellaneous Writings*, p. 231.

141 Samuel Barrington to Evan Nepean, 2 January 1793, TNA, HO/42/24.

142 James Sykes to William John Byron, 29 June 1793, Lovelace Byron 161, fo. 73.

143 William John Byron to [Sophia Maria] Byron, 19 April 1791, Byron papers, Box 6, folder 28.

144 Ibid.

145 Horatio Nelson, journal of the siege of Calvi (1794), TNA, ADM 1/2224 (N15).

146 Charles Morgan to [Sophia Maria Byron], n.d., John Murray, MS.43483.

147 Probate inventory of William John Byron, August 1798, TNA, PROB 31/898/590.

148 Catherine Byron to Frances Leigh, 23 November 1794, BL, Add. MS 31037, fo. 11.

149 Ibid.

150 Catherine Byron to Frances Leigh (quoting her sister-in-law), 8 December 1794, John Murray, MS.43410.

151 Ibid.

152 Isabella, Lady Carlisle to Caroline, Lady Carlisle, 18 August 1790, CH, J15/1/34.

153 *Gentleman's Magazine*, vol. 75 (January–June 1794), p. 327.

154 *Norfolk Chronicle*, 11 January 1794.

155 Isabella, Lady Carlisle, 'Melancholy and Pity', papers of Elizabeth Simpson, Lady Bridgeman, Staffordshire Record Office, D1287/19/6/19.

156 *Bath Chronicle and Weekly Gazette*, 29 January 1795.

157 Ibid., 5 February 1795.

158 Sir William Musgrave, obituary note for Isabella Howard, Gloucester, D2383/C3.

159 Diary of Abigail Cawthorne, February 1796, quoted in Adrian Henstock (ed.), *The Diary of Abigail Cawthorne 1751–1810* (Thoroton Society, 1980), p. 66.

160 Rear Admiral Benjamin Caldwell to Richard Byron, 12 June 1794, TNA, Chatham Papers, PRO 30/8/118.

161 Richard Byron to Richard Farmer, 15 November 1794, TNA, Chatham Papers, PRO 30/8/118.

162 William Browne to Robert Toplis, enclosed in Robert Toplis to William, Lord Byron, 4 June 1796, BL, Egerton MS 2612 vol. I, fo. 244.

163 Letter from W. S. Hasledon, *Notes & Queries*, no. 192, July–December 1853 (1853), p. 2.

164 Sophia Maria Byron to James Sykes, 26 December 1796, Lovelace Byron 159, fo. 87.

165 Diary of Frances Burney, 29 April 1780, quoted in Rizzo (ed.), *Early Journals and Letters*, vol. 4, part 2, p. 80.

166 James Sykes, account of Sophia Maria Byron, 1793–6, Lovelace Byron 160, fos. 30–52.

167 Sophia Maria Byron to James Sykes, 22 December [1794], Lovelace Byron 159, fo. 14.

168 Sophia Maria Byron to James Sykes, 17 June 1795, ibid., fo. 17.

169 Frances Leigh to James Farquhar, 5 June 1795, Byron papers, Box 7, folder 4.

170 Samuel Bolton to James Farquhar, 2 April 1798, ibid., Box 6, folder 16.

171 Hanson narrative, John Murray, MS.43537.

172 Ibid.

173 Frances Byron to George, 6th Lord Byron, 25 October 1812, John Murray, MS.43412.

174 Unknown to Samuel Bolton, 31 March 1798, Byron papers, Box 6, folder 16.

175 Samuel Bolton to James Farquhar, 2 April 1798, ibid.

176 Samuel Bolton to James Farquhar, 12 April 1798, ibid.

177 Samuel Bolton to James Farquhar, 14 April 1798, ibid.

178 Samuel Bolton to James Farquhar, 12 April 1798, ibid.

179 *Gentleman's Magazine*, vol. 68, part 1 (1798).

180 *Derby Mercury*, 31 May 1798.

181 John Hanson to James Farquhar, 4 June 1798, Byron papers, Box 6, folder 31.

182 Alexander Crombie to James Farquhar, 8 June 1798, ibid., folder 30.

183 John Hanson to James Farquhar, 22 June 1798, ibid., folder 31.

184 Hanson narrative, John Murray, MS.43537.

185 George, 6th Lord Byron to Augusta Byron, 25 October 1804, L&J, vol. 1, p. 53; George, 6th Lord Byron to Augusta Leigh, 5 October 1821, ibid., vol. 8, p. 235.

186 George, 6th Lord Byron to Augusta Parker, 8 November 1798, ibid., vol. 1, p. 39.

187 Extract of a letter from Lady Mary Osborne, 16 August 1798, John Murray, MS.43483.

188 Diary of Hester Thrale-Piozzi, [October] 1790, quoted in Balderston (ed.), *Thraliana*, vol. 2, p. 786.

189 George, 6th Lord Byron to Scrope B. Davies, 7 August 1811, L&J, vol. 2, p. 68.

190 George, 6th Lord Byron to Lady Melbourne, 29 January 1814, ibid., vol. 4, p. 40.

Epilogue

1 John Murray to Anne Murray, 3 October 1814, quoted in Smiles (ed.), *A Publisher and His Friends*, vol. 1, p. 253.

2 George Anson Byron (later 7th Lord Byron) to George, 6th Lord Byron, 17 October 1815, John Murray, MS.43412.

3 Joe Murray to George, 6th Lord Byron [18–20] March 1816, ibid., MS.43513.

4 Joe Murray to George, 6th Lord Byron 15 July 1813, ibid.

5 George, 6th Lord Byron to Augusta Leigh, 21 August 1811, L&J, vol. 2, p. 74.

6 George, 6th Lord Byron to Augusta Leigh, 30 August 1811, ibid., p. 85.

7 Joe Murray to George, 6th Lord Byron, [18–20] March 1816, John Murray, MS.43513.

8 *Morning Post and Gazetteer*, 24 October 1800.

9 George, 6th Lord Byron to Augusta Leigh, 17 November 1804, L&J, vol. 1, p. 58.

10 Catherine Byron to John Hanson, 4 March 1806 (copy), John Murray, MS.43537.

11 George, 6th Lord Byron to Catherine Byron, 6 March 1809, L&J, vol. 1, p. 196.

12 Harriet, Lady Granville to Georgiana, Lady Carlisle, 1822, quoted in Murray, *Castle Howard*, p. 124.

13 George Anson Byron to George, 6th Lord Byron, 8 January 1812, John Murray, MS.43412.

14 George, 6th Lord Byron to J. J. Coulmann, July 1823, L&J, vol. 10, p. 208.

15 Augusta Leigh to M. A. Cursham, 1832, quoted in Walker and Howell, *The House of Byron*, p. 1.

16 George, 6th Lord Byron, 'Manfred', Act II, Scene I, in *The Works of Lord Byron* (John Murray, 1837), p. 180.

17 George, 6th Lord Byron to Catherine Byron, 6 March 1809, L&J, vol. 1, pp. 195–6.

18 George, 6th Lord Byron to Augusta Leigh, 30 August 1811, ibid., vol. 2, p. 85.

19 Sophia Maria Byron to George, 6th Lord Byron, 9 December 1814, John Murray, MS.43413.

20 John Murray to George, 6th Lord Byron, *The Letters of John Murray to Lord Byron* (ed. A. Nicholson) (Liverpool University Press, 2005), p. 355.

21 Quoted in T. Medwin, *Journal of the Conversations of Lord Byron noted during a residence with his Lordship at Pisa* (A. and W. Galignani, 1824), vol. 1, p. 51.

22 'Lord Byron', in *The Scourge* (March 1811), vol. 1, p. 191.

23 A. Pichot (1823), *Essai sur le génie et le caractère de lord Byron* (1824), p. 27.

24 George, 6th Lord Byron to J. J. Coulmann, July 1823, L&J, vol. 10, p. 209.

25 Augusta Leigh to the editor of the *Quarterly Review*, 2 February 1831, John Murray, MS.43482; Augusta Leigh to John Hanson, 25 January 1830, ibid., MS.43480.

26 *Notes by Lady Louisa Stuart*, p. 47; *Stamford Mercury*, 4 June 1819.

27 *The European Magazine, and London Review . . . for 1785* (1785), vol. 8, p. 327; *Court Magazine and Belle Assemblee* (July–December 1837), p. 151.

28 *The Mirror of Literature, Amusement, and Instruction*, no. 67, 24 January 1824.

29 T. Moore, *Letters and Journals of Lord Byron, with Notices of his Life* (John Murray, 1830), vol. 1, p. 22.

30 J. Charnock, *Biographia Navalis; or, Impartial Memoirs of the Lives and Characters of Officers of the Navy of Great Britain* (R. Faulder, 1797), vol. 5, p. 439.

31 Thomas Campbell, *Pleasures of Hope* (1799).

32 'Memoir of the Life of the Honourable John Byron', in *Narrative of the Hon. John Byron* (J. Ballantyne & Co, 1812), p. xv.

33 A. Galibois, *La Gaspésie pittoresque et légendaire* (1928), pp. 64–5.

34 Cosmo Gordon, *The Life and Genius of Lord Byron* (Baudry, 1824), p. 38.

35 George Clinton, *Memoirs of the Life and Writings of Lord Byron* (1825), p. 33.

36 *Edinburgh Annual Register* (1824), p. 252.

37 Sophia Maria Byron to James Sykes, 27 December 1803, Lovelace Byron 159, fo. 109.

38 Hanson narrative, John Murray, MS.43537.

39 Lady Byron's notebook, Lovelace Byron 118, fos. 74–5.

40 George, 6th Lord Byron to Augusta Leigh, [?18] October 1820, L&J, vol. 7, p. 208.

Select Bibliography

Primary Sources

Bodleian Library, Oxford: Papers of the Noel, Byron and Lovelace families

British Library, London: Egerton MSS; Additional MSS; Burney Newspapers Collection

British Newspaper Archive: online database, https://www.britishnewspaperarchive.co.uk

Castle Howard Archives, Castle Howard, Yorkshire: papers and correspondence of the Howard family

Gloucestershire Archives, Gloucester: Sir William Musgrave correspondence with the Howard family

Harry Ransom Center, University of Texas at Austin: George Gordon Byron papers

John Murray Archive, National Library of Scotland, Edinburgh: Byron family papers, correspondence and legal documents

John Rylands Library, University of Manchester: Thrale-Piozzi manuscripts

University of Leeds, Special Collections: Duke of Leeds manuscripts

Lewis Walpole Library, Yale University, Farmington, Connecticut: Horace Walpole correspondence

The Morgan Library & Museum, New York: Byron family papers. Collection of autograph signed letters by Lord Byron, Lady Byron, family members and friends

The National Archives: legal papers relating to the Byron family and the Newstead estate; Admiralty paybooks, musters and correspondence; Army paybooks, musters and correspondence; Tower of London order books

National Maritime Museum, Greenwich, London: manuscript material relating to Admiral John Byron

Newstead Abbey, Nottinghamshire: Byron collection and Byron family papers

University of Nottingham, Special Collections: Molyneux papers and Portland (London) papers

Nottinghamshire Archives, Nottingham: Byron family, Barons Byron: Newstead, misc. estate records (Newstead Abbey)

Parliamentary Archives, UK Parliament: manuscript material relating to the trial of William, 5th Lord Byron

Pforzheimer Collection, New York Public Library: Byron family papers

Printed Primary Sources

A Circumstantial and Authentic Account of a Late Unhappy Affair which happened at the Star and Garter Tavern (1765)

Balderston, Katherine (ed.), *Thraliana: The Diary of Mrs Hester Lynch Thrale* (2 volumes) (Clarendon Press, 1942)

Bellamy, G. A., *An Apology for the Life of George Anne Bellamy . . . in five volumes* (Logographic Press, 1785)

Byron, John, *The Narrative of the Honourable John Byron* (S. Baker and G. Leigh, 1768, 1812)

—— (ed. Robert E. Gallagher), *Byron's Journal of his Circumnavigation 1764–6* (Hakluyt Society, 1964)

Historical Manuscripts Commission, *The Manuscripts of the Earl of Carlisle, preserved at Castle Howard*, Fifteenth Report, Appendix, Part VI (1897)

Home, James (ed.), *The Letters and Journals of Lady Mary Coke* (4 volumes) (David Douglas, 1889–96)

Jesse, John Heneage (ed.), *George Selwyn and His Contemporaries, With Memoirs and Notes* (4 volumes) (Richard Bentley, 1843)

Lewis, W. S. (ed.), *The Yale Edition of Horace Walpole's Correspondence* (48 volumes) (Yale University Press, 1937–83)

Marchand, Leslie A. (ed.), *Byron's Letters and Journals* (13 volumes) (John Murray, 1973–94)

Moore, Thomas, *Letters and Journals of Lord Byron* (John Murray, 1830)

—— *The Works of Lord Byron Complete in One Volume with Notes* (John Murray, 1837)

Rizzo, B., Troide, Lars E., et al. (eds), *The Early Journals and Letters of Fanny Burney* (4 volumes) (Oxford University Press, 1988–2003)

The Tryal of William Lord Byron . . . for the Murder of William Chaworth, Esq (Dublin, 1765)

Secondary Sources

Bakewell, Michael, and Bakewell, Melissa, *Augusta Leigh: Byron's Half-Sister* (Chatto & Windus, 2000)

Beckett, J. V., *Byron and Newstead: The Aristocrat and the Abbey* (University of Delaware Press, 2001)

Boyes, Megan, *My Amiable Mama: A Biography of Mrs Catherine Gordon Byron* (J. M. Tatler & Son Ltd, 1991)

Coope, R., and Smith, P., *Newstead Abbey: A Nottinghamshire Country House: Its Owners and Architectural History, 1540–1931* (Thoroton Society Record Series, 2014)

Langley Moore, D., *Lord Byron: Accounts Rendered* (John Murray, 1974)

Layman, C. H., *The Wager Disaster: Mayhem, Mutiny and Murder in the South Seas* (Uniform Press, 2015)

MacCarthy, Fiona, *Lord Byron: Life and Legend* (John Murray, rev. edn 2014)

Marchand, Leslie A., *Byron: A Biography* (3 volumes) (John Murray, 1957)

Murray, Venetia, *Castle Howard* (Viking, 1994)

Ridgeway, Christopher, 'Isabella, Fourth Countess of Carlisle: No Life by Halves', in Ruth M. Larsen (ed.), *Maids and Mistresses: Celebrating 300 Years of Women and the Yorkshire Country House* (Yorkshire Country House Partnership, 2004), pp. 35–52

Rowse, A. L., *The Byrons and Trevanions* (Weidenfeld & Nicolson, 1978)

Shankland, P., *Byron of the Wager* (Collins, 1975)

Walker, V., and Howell, M. J., *The House of Byron: A History of the Family Since the Norman Conquest, 1066–1988* (Quiller Press, 1988)

Index

Index